PERGAMON INTERNATIONAL LIBRARY
of Science, Technology, Engineering and Social Studies

*The 1000-volume original paperback library in aid of education,
industrial training and the enjoyment of leisure*

Publisher: Robert Maxwell, M.C.

Changing Priorities
on the International Agenda:
The New International Economic Order

THE PERGAMON TEXTBOOK
INSPECTION COPY SERVICE

An inspection copy of any book published in the Pergamon International Library will gladly
be sent to academic staff without obligation for their consideration for course adoption or
recommendation. Copies may be retained for a period of 60 days from receipt and returned
if not suitable. When a particular title is adopted or recommended for adoption for class use
and the recommendation results in a sale of 12 or more copies, the inspection copy may be retained with our compliments. The Publisher will be pleased to receive suggestions for revised
editions and new titles to be published in this important International Library.

SYSTEMS SCIENCE AND WORLD ORDER LIBRARY

General Editor: Ervin Laszlo

Explorations of World Order

GIARINI, O. & LOUBERGÉ, H.
The Diminishing Returns of Technology

LASZLO, E. & BIERMAN, J.
Goals in a Global Community
    Volume I: Studies in the Conceptual Foundations
    Volume II: The International Values and Goal Studies

LASZLO, E.
The Inner Limits of Mankind:
Heretical Reflections on Todays Values, Culture and Politics

TÉVOÉDJRÈ, A.
Poverty: Wealth of Mankind

Innovations in Systems Science

COOK, N. D
Stability and Flexibility:
An Analysis of Natural Systems

GEYER, F. R.
Alienation & General Systems Theory

JANTSCH, E.
The Self Organizing Universe:
Scientific and Human Implications of the Emerging Paradigm of Evolution

Changing Priorities on the International Agenda: The New International Economic Order

Edited by

Karl P. Sauvant

PERGAMON PRESS

OXFORD • NEW YORK • TORONTO • SYDNEY • PARIS • FRANKFURT

189961

337.09
C 454

U.K.	Pergamon Press Ltd., Headington Hill Hall, Oxford OX3 0BW, England
U.S.A.	Pergamon Press Inc., Maxwell House, Fairview Park, Elmsford, New York 10523, U.S.A.
CANADA	Pergamon of Canada, Suite 104, 150 Consumers Road, Willowdale, Ontario M2J 1P9, Canada
AUSTRALIA	Pergamon Press (Aust.) Pty. Ltd., P.O. Box 544, Potts Point, N.S.W. 2011, Australia
FRANCE	Pergamon Press SARL, 24 rue des Ecoles, 75240 Paris, Cedex 05, France
FEDERAL REPUBLIC OF GERMANY	Pergamon Press GmbH, 6242 Kronberg-Taunus, Pferdstrasse 1, Federal Republic of Germany

Copyright © 1981 Karl P. Sauvant

All Rights Reserved. No part of this publication may be reproduced, stored in a retrieval system or transmitted in any form or by any means; electronic, electrostatic, magnetic tape, mechanical, photocoyping, recording or otherwise, without permission in writing from the publishers.

First edition 1981

British Library Cataloguing in Publication Data

Changing priorities on the international
agenda. - (Pergamon international library)
1. Economic development - International
cooperation
2. Economic assistance
I. Sauvant, Karl P.
382.1   HD82   80-40440

ISBN 0-08-023117-9 (Hardcover)
ISBN 0-08-026806-4 (Flexicover)

Printed in the United States of America

To Erich, Heidemarie, Jochen, Vishwas, and Wolfgang

Contents

Detailed Table of Contents

List of Figures

List of Tables

List of Tables in Appendix C

Foreword

In the welter of political pressures and maneuvers, and the sensationalistic events of everyday politics, the issues of the international economic order tend to take second place. News media relegate them to the back pages of business news, and academics guard them jealously within the confines of their own specialties. The public knows next to nothing about them and, what is of even more immediate concern, national decision makers are also poorly informed.

But the problems of the world economy are not merely of "academic" interest. Upon their resolution depends the well-being of all people, and the very survival of a growing majority of the global population. No issue could be of more importance and relevance for every man, woman, and child today than the issue of how to guide the thrust of the economic relationships that weave the nations and peoples of the world into an ever closer fabric of interdependence. The simplistic assumption that the world economy is a free economy, unguided by anyone, no longer has force. Today's economy is strongly oriented by vast and powerful interests constituted by major industrial powers, by transnational corporations, and by the producers and exporters of vital commodities and energy resources. The question is only how the world economy is to be oriented, and by whom. And this, precisely, is the crux of the new phenomenon on the international scene, known as the North-South debate or, more exactly, the global negotiations concerned with the fate of the New International Economic Order.

The New International Economic Order is a sleeping giant that is now awakening. It originated with the Non-Aligned Countries, came to be a chief platform of the Group of 77 developing countries, and graduated to the status of an internationally approved program in the framework of the United Nations. It has occasionally moved out of the U.N. to other forums, but it has returned now, with greater force than ever, to the General Assembly. Its presence there does not make it an issue of mainly diplomatic interest, something that is a fit subject for long speeches and formal but ineffective declarations and resolutions. It is at the U.N. because that organization is the only universal forum mankind possesses, and the New International Economic Order is an issue of truly universal scope and concern.

Delegates from all countries of the world can try their best to come to reasoned agreements, but they cannot succeed in producing binding and effective measures unless their national capitals understand what is at stake, and bring up the will to participate in the debates with sufficient commitment to act on their outcome. In turn, national capitals are sensitive to popular feelings and to the pressure of special interest groups, and devote adequate attention to global and long-term economic issues only if their constituencies are aware of them and demand action.

Ultimately, success in the present endeavors to create a new and more satifactory set of economic relationships depends crucially on an awareness of problems and the insight into the possibilities of surmounting them. The interconnected issues that make up the substance of the program of the New International Economic Order must move from the back to the front pages of newspapers, from the confines of specialized academic departments to the front lines of public debate, and from the sphere of economics to that of practical politics.

Odette Jankowitsch, Donald O. Mills, Karl P. Sauvant, and Rüdiger von Wechmar have made a major contribution toward the achievement of this mutation. In the present book they have brought together the principal features of the new order and made it accessible to the general reader. But they have provided more than a popularization of the issues; they also offer here new and important perspectives on them. Sauvant and Jankowitsch illuminate the nature of the issues themselves, within their requisite historical and political context. Mills presents a broad perspective which reflects the interests and rationale of the developing countries, while von Wechmar clarifies the response of the developed world. There is no other single volume, to the best of this writer's knowledge, that would do as much, and do it in such an important matter. It is only to be hoped that it will find a wide readership, and, thus, that it will prove to be not only a description and elucidation of the issues and problems of the world economy, but also a modest but intellectually potent instrument toward generating that critical modicum of understanding which is the sine qua non of their successful resolution.

Ervin Laszlo
November 1979

Preface

Thirty years ago, the Third World was under colonial or hegemonial domination. It was an object of world politics, not a participant in it.

Thirty years hence, the Third World will be a full partner in political, military, economic, and socio-cultural international relations. It will participate in world affairs on an equal and independent basis.

Today, we are in a process of transition. It is a process of adapting the colonial structures of the past to the realities of tomorrow. The task is to manage this transformation as rationally, smoothly, and speedily as possible. Three billion of the world's four billion inhabitants are striving for their rights.

The transformation began with the achievement of political independence. Political decolonization was largely completed by the end of the 1960s. The emergence of the movement of the Non-Aligned Countries during the 1960s signaled the successful organization of the Third World as an independent international political force.

With the consolidation of political independence, it became increasingly apparent that it had to be complemented by economic decolonization if a real change in the dependency relationships of the developing countries was to occur. The result of this realization was the politicization of the development issue. In the 1950s and 1960s, development issues were "low politics," dealt with by the ministers of economics, finance, planning, etc., i.e., by technical ministries. Beginning with the 1970s, however, development issues became "high politics," and were elevated from the ministerial level to the level of heads of state or government.

The Fourth Summit Conference of the Non-Aligned Countries in Algiers in September 1973 marked the formal recognition of this change. About half a year later, in April/May 1974, the Sixth Special Session of the United Nations General Assembly made the development issue a priority item on the international agenda.

At that session, the "Declaration on the Establishment of a New International Economic Order" and the "Programme of Action on the Establishment of a New International Economic Order" were formulated. Together with the "Charter of Economic Rights and Duties of States," passed later that year by the Twenty-ninth Regular Session of the General Assembly, and the resolution on "Development and International Economic Co-operation," adopted in September 1975 by the Seventh Special Session, these documents contain the programmatic foundations of the New International Economic Order (NIEO). For easy reference, these documents, along with the reservations expressed by some delegations, are reprinted in Appendix A of this volume.

The purpose of these resolutions is to make development a main objective of the international economic system, a system constructed without the active participation of the developing countries and designed primarily to serve the needs of the developed countries. The NIEO program is an effort to outline the changes required in the main areas of North-South interaction to make the international economic system maximally conducive to the development of the Third World.

The international economic system is the external dimension of the development effort. According to a strategy pursued by almost all developing countries and fully endorsed by the industrialized countries, development is to occur in a framework of close relations between North and South. International exchanges, and especially trade, are to trigger and then to maintain the development process. Hence, the framework within which international transactions take place, the purposes that they serve, the mechanisms that regulate them, and the structures that they create are of crucial interest to the developing countries. This concern for the external framework is not meant to deny the importance of the internal dimension of development. It merely reflects the recognition that, in the prevailing development model, international exchanges strongly influence whether or not domestic development is encouraged and what direction it takes. (Of course, the restriction of the program to external measures also reflects the attitude of most states that domestic policies of individual countries are not subject to international negotiations.) The NIEO program—and, hence, this volume—focuses, therefore, almost exclusively on the external requirements for development. But a comprehensive development program, to be successful, must provide for fundamental changes in both international and domestic structures. The recent course of international discussions seems to indicate that this interrelationship is being increasingly appreciated.

The specific requirements and negotiating priorities of each individual Third World country are, of course, different. But the developing countries all share one common characteristic and they were reminded of it by Mwalimu Julius K. Nyerere in his speech before the 1979 Fourth Ministerial Meeting of the Group of 77 in Arusha:

> . . . our diversity exists in the context of one common and overriding experience. What we have in common is that we are all, in relation to the developed world, dependent—not interdependent—nations. Each of our economies has developed as a by-product and a subsidiary of development in the industrialized North, and is externally oriented. We are not the prime movers of our own destiny.

It was in view of the common Third World dependency on the North and the common experience that each developing country is too weak by itself to bring about the desired changes, that the NIEO program was formulated. With the exception of particularly disadvantaged countries—e.g., those most seriously affected by economic crises as well as the least developed, land-locked, and island developing countries—the program speaks, therefore, only of the requirements of the Third World as a whole. The following chapters reflect this approach.

Given the nature of the Third World's development strategy, the emphasis of the NIEO program is on North-South and not South-South interactions. Greater cooperation among developing countries receives, therefore, only limited attention in the program. This latter approach, which is captured in the concept of individual and collective self-reliance and which may well represent an alternative development strategy to the prevailing integrative approach has, however, been elaborated in the context of the non-aligned movement. While no effort is made here to outline a self-reliance program in any detail, some of its elements are mentioned where appropriate.

With these parameters in mind, the purpose of this book is to provide a clear, concise, and comprehensive overview of the main issues related to the NIEO program: the origin of the program, the need for it, the key proposals of the developing countries, and the chief criticisms of the industrialized countries.

The introduction places the discussions in an historical context and points out the need to change existing structures so as to create a more equitable international system, a system that can be accepted by all its members.

Chapter 1 examines the origins of these discussions and identifies the main factors responsible for making the development issue a priority item on the international agenda.

One of these factors is the transformation of the movement of Non-Aligned Countries into an international pressure group for the reorganization of the international economic system. The emergence of this movement, its organization, its transformation, and the crucial role it played in changing the priorities of the international agenda are the topic of chapter 2. A tabular presentation of the developing countries' participation in various international organizations and economic gatherings supplements this chapter in Appendix B.

In chapter 3, the principal proposals of the NIEO program in each of its main subject areas are presented and progress toward their implementation since 1974 is noted. In order to clarify the significance of these proposals and to underline the need for change, they are related to the existing situation in each of the main areas of North-South relations. Extensive statistical material, contained in Appendix C, provides the necessary empirical documentation. (The term "billion" signifies one thousand million.)

The proposals of the Third World have met with a number of criticisms from the developed countries. These are surveyed and explained in chapter 4.

As indicated, the aim of this volume is to give an overview of the NIEO discussion. No effort is made to examine whether the proposals of the developing countries are in fact sufficiently far-reaching to bring about, if implemented, the structural changes that are being sought. I doubt that they are. But then, the NIEO program is constantly being developed further as the understanding of the problems and the pressures to resolve them increase. There is no doubt, however, that the NIEO program as it is now formulated addresses itself to the most pressing immediate difficulties of the Third World. Furthermore, it reflects the Third World's recognition that the structures of the international economic system have to be changed if there are to be fundamental improvements. And, finally, the discussions surrounding the NIEO program have succeeded in giving the development task the proper international attention and priority.

If this volume succeeds in making a broader audience privy to these discussions, if it succeeds in increasing the understanding of the positions taken in them, and, particularly, if it succeeds in creating a sense of urgency about the development task, it will have served its purpose.

There remains the pleasant task of acknowledging the help of all those who have made this volume possible. Donald O. Mills and Baron Rüdiger von Wechmar were kind enough to take the time to prepare contributions to this volume. I have profited greatly from the advice of Odette Jankowitsch. The criticisms of Ann H. Rogers have been invaluable. The arduous labors of preparing the manuscript were shared with me by Ruth Beier, Marion Kämper, and Francisca F. Martinez. Finally, the Zentrum für interdisziplinäre Forschung of the Universität Bielefeld, under the direction of Norbert Horn, provided the support to complete the largest part of this volume during my leave of absence from the United Nations in 1978/79. To all of them: thank you very much.

Needless to say, the views expressed in this book do not necessarily reflect those of the institutions with which the editor is currently affiliated.

Karl P. Sauvant
Bielefeld, August 1979

Introduction

Donald O. Mills

In recent times, a number of issues and ideas have emerged which have been directed at the creation of the concept of a global community with a common destiny, capable of sharing in the world's bounty, or of destroying the very basis of human existence. Among these are the movement toward the preservation of the environment, the concept of the abundant resources of the oceans as a common heritage, and the concern over the massive accumulation and sale of armaments.

The establishment of the United Nations system 35 years ago has done much to bring the notion of the world as essentially a single community more and more into focus, and has provided the institutional framework through which such ideas and issues could be promoted or discussed.

One of the most far-reaching transformations of global relationships took place over the past 20 years as the international community came to accept the principle that the system of colonization was unacceptable, and that all countries should have the right to self-determination and independence and to participate as equals in the community of nations, while preserving the right to establish their own forms of government and to maintain their own social and cultural identity.

The world now faces a new concept, a new movement, and one which has gathered force in the past five years, becoming more and more the centerpiece of international concerns and discussions. It is the concept of the New International Economic Order. The words themselves have become the subject of dispute, but the basic idea of a consciously articulated set of changes in the framework of international economic activities and relationships has seized the imagination of countries across the world. All have been drawn into the issue—whether to advance the proposition and to press for its realization, or to resist it in order to defend what they perceive to be their interests.

The concept of the New International Economic Order emerged as a demand by developing countries for the creation of a new set of economic relationships which would place these countries, most of whom achieved their political independence in the era of decolonization, in a position to participate fully in international economic affairs. They called for the restructuring of the international economic system, which was created to satisfy the requirements of a few countries, mostly in the North, and had its origins in those periods in which they conquered and ruled over vast territories across the world.

1

But the discussions and negotiations on this matter have broadened and deepened. Gradually, it has become clear that what started as a movement essentially concerned with global economic justice contains considerable social and political implications, particularly in terms of the conditions within countries, both rich and poor. This development was inevitable. It started as some interests in industrialized countries sought to establish what they saw as a logical connection between global equity and internal social and economic conditions. In some of those countries there has been what appears to developing countries to be a move to change the focus toward conditions inside their communities—and, in some instances, to make action toward global change conditional on internal improvements.

Particularly in light of the lack of progress in achieving concrete advance toward establishing an equitable global economic system, developing countries have resisted these attempts to change the direction of the dialogue. But the connection between the two levels of concern has emerged more clearly, as the dialogue between and within countries has deepened. This must have the most far-reaching implications for the future.

But it is not only the conditions in developing countries that have been drawn into the issue. One of the primary concerns in recent years—brought to world attention by such organizations as the Club of Rome—has been the rate at which the earth's nonrenewable resources are being used up, and the fact that a small number of countries, the industrialized countries in fact, use the overwhelming proportion of these. The fact that a very large share of these natural resources are located in developing countries and in the past have been exploited mainly by transnational corporations and other interests from industrialized countries has added other dimensions to this issue.

More specifically, the life styles in industrialized countries have gradually come under scrutiny, particularly by persons within those countries. What might have been regarded as a marginal concern for some time, more recently has assumed greater significance as the realization has grown that the global economy and the economies of many industrialized countries face long-term problems—it is no longer possible to anticipate a return in the near future to the vigorous growth which was so beneficial in the 1960s. This situation has resulted in internal political pressures and elements of political instability in a number of industrialized countries, and the view has been expressed by more than one political leader that the very basis of their political systems is threatened.

Events in a number of countries involving terrorist activities have been linked by some analysts to the disaffection among young people in the face of what they regard as a way of life devoted mainly to material things in their communities. In any event, in light of the changing economic circumstances, developed countries are facing more and more the need for major structural changes in their economies, and this realization has caused them to look at their relationships with developing countries from a new perspective.

It is now six years since the call for the New International Economic Order at the 1974 Sixth Special Session of the United Nations, and there is little to show by way of concrete progress toward its establishment. But a great deal has happened insofar as the consciousness that there must and will be major changes in economic structures and in relationships is concerned. Those industrialized countries which see the proposals as a threat to their positions and influence still remain very much on the defensive. Yet they have been forced to accept the fact that change will come. It is now to be seen whether they move from a defensive position to a constructive one, in which they attempt to participate actively in the design of a new system and a new set of relationships, or to an openly aggressive stance in which they try to counter by explicit economic and political action the movement initiated by developing countries.

Particularly under the pressure of present economic problems, industrialized countries are developing an awareness of the existence of a global economy in which developing countries occupy a position of some significance. There are some interests in these countries which see the need for encouraging, and even contributing, through trade and investment for example, to the promotion of economic development and growth in developing countries as a means of providing long-term stimulus to their own economies. Others are more inclined to look toward protectionist measures in the face of the actual and potential export growth of developing countries; or to foster the trilateral relationship, which embraces the economic interests of North America, Western Europe, and Japan.

There may well have emerged in industrialized countries a conflict between political concerns in the sense of immediate or short-term considerations, and the requirements of "statesmanship," that is, the consideration of their longer-term interests. Certainly, the issue of the New International Economic Order and the economic situation which now faces the global community have significant political implications for all countries. Even if the major industrialized countries continue to resist the movement toward fundamental change along the lines proposed by developing countries, they face the necessity of making painful structural and perhaps social adjustments internally, and these will call for political courage and foresight.

Developing countries face enormous problems. They must, if they are to have significant success in bringing about global change, persist in their efforts and fashion more effective political and institutional means for carrying out the task. They face increasing internal economic, political, and social problems and pressures and will be called upon to make major adjustments and improvements in the coming years.

The roots of the present economic system and the relationships surrounding it go far back into the past. Attempts to draw attention to this fact are often met with the response that the call for global economic equity today is, in fact, a demand for reparation for exploitation of the developing countries in the past, and that there is no justification for such a demand. Be that as it may, the fact is that it is not possible to arrive at a real understanding of today's attitudes and of the call for fundamental change in the global economic system without reference to the past.

It is arguable that there is more than sufficient justification in the circumstances of today for fundamental changes in international economic relationships and, particularly, those between industrialized and developing countries. Past relationships, and especially those going back over the centuries, help to explain present circumstances and relationships, and must certainly be seen as reinforcing fully the demand and need for such changes.

The story of past relationships is, in large part, the history of the expansion of European economic, political, and cultural influence across the globe, a story which could be said to have begun some five centuries ago.

The story is summarized in the words of Douglas Johnson, in his introduction to *The World of Empires:*

> Well before the industrial age in Europe had begun Europeans had been crossing the Atlantic and were settling in different parts of the New World, expanding eastwards towards the Pacific, moving towards the Delhi of the Moghuls in India, travelling northwards from Cape Colony in South Africa. Even when there had been set-backs

and when European states lost power, as when the United States became independent from Britain, independence was won by Spanish America, and Brazil broke away from Portugal, still European civilization or European influences persisted. And after 1800 the process of European expansion received a great acceleration. It could be said that prior to this date European civilization could not always force itself, or did not always wish to force itself on non-European cultures. But once the European traders realized that they had more to sell than to buy, once it appeared that the non-European societies could not move into the same machine age or organize great commercial firms, once it was feared that they could not create the political and legal conditions which the new commerce had to have if it was to prosper then the real European expansion began. Competition between European powers was sometimes real, sometimes imaginary. At all events all the conditions made annexation, or colonialism, a popular form of European expansion.

Thus the expansion of Europe was political and administrative and can be seen in the coloration of the world map. It was also commercial and financial and can be seen in the investments which Europeans made in non-European territories and in terms of certain commodities (vegetable oil, rubber, cotton, sugar, ivory, coffee, diamonds, gold, crude oil, etc.). This expansion was also human. Because of plantation requirements in the Americas millions of Africans were transported there as slaves. Because of bad conditions in Europe or opportunities beyond Europe, many millions of Europeans emigrated and by 1939 it was said that one-quarter of the people of European origin lived outside Europe. It was an expansion which was also ideological and cultural, associated with Christianity, with a money economy, with the various forms of administration and government which had grown up in Europe. It was an expansion which was individualistic, since governments were often preceded by adventurers, buccanneers, traders, or by scientists of one sort or another.[1]

At one time or another, virtually all of North and South America and the Caribbean, almost all of the African continent, the Middle East, large parts of Asia, and Oceania were under the sovereignty or economic dominance of European countries. At one time or another, most West European countries were involved in this process.

The colonial system has had the most profound effects on the countries wielding the power and control as well as on the communities which they held in their power. The extent of this influence, in economic, political, and cultural terms, can be judged from the vast amount of territory and the large populations that were involved.

In 1800 Europe and its possessions (including excolonies) covered about 55 per cent of the land surface of the world; in 1878, 67 per cent; and in 1914, 84.4 per cent. Expansion continued: by 1939 the only significant countries which had never been under European rule were Turkey, parts of Arabia, Persia, China, Tibet, Mongolia and Siam.[2]

With all this came the development of a system of investment and trade and a world market in which the countries of the North wielded the power and the influence, while the South provided the land, the labor, and the minerals which formed the basic economic factors upon which the system came to depend.

Much of this system survived through to the end of World War II. The years since then have seen the establishment of the United Nations organization, along with a complex of international institutions designed to bring some order to the economic and political relationships in the world. But perhaps the most far-reaching development in the postwar period has been the movement which has resulted in the freeing of over 100 communities which once formed part of the colonial empires and their emergence as independent sovereign states and members of the United Nations. Today, these countries are engaged in a struggle to bring fundamental changes in the global economic system. But the time may well come when it will be recognized that even more fundamental than the vast differences in economic conditions between different countries, and mainly between industrialized and developing countries, is the value system and the attitudes that influence the relationships between countries. In particular, there still exist feelings and beliefs related to political as well as cultural differences, race and other factors which are rooted in past relationships and experiences, in which one group of countries—mainly European and white—dominated vast numbers of communities across the world.

Again, caught as we now are in a struggle in which one sector of the world is demanding the right to full participation in global affairs, we also need to try to see the possibilities which the future might hold, in order that we may avoid some of the real dangers facing the world, or that, by the actions that are taken today, we may help to fashion the future.

In the long run, the establishment of a peaceful world community based on the principles of equality and interdependence will require fundamental changes in existing attitudes in political and cultural matters.

The continued existence of white minority racist regimes in Southern Africa and the reluctance on the part of interests in North Atlantic countries to remove material support to these regimes which they give, especially by their involvement in the economies of the area, is a measure of the persistence of past notions and forms of domination.

Not unrelated to these factors are the fears which seem to lurk in the minds of some, fears centered around the three concerns of population, poverty, and proliferation. Indeed, the prospect of a world in which the balance of population continues to shift toward an overwhelming predominance in numbers in the South living in absolute or relative poverty is already a disparate one. Add to that the possibility or probability that, gradually at least, a few countries of the South will acquire nuclear weapons—and the picture becomes even more stark.

The Western world has already taken a considerable interest in the population factor and has increased its efforts to persuade developing countries to establish population control programs, and to provide assistance toward this aim. It is also becoming more and more concerned about poverty in the Third World; its response to the demand for the New International Economic Order is being expressed mainly in the direction of the eradication of poverty, as opposed to the specific issue of restructuring of global economic relationships.

The failure of the international community to deal effectively with the continued build-up of production of armaments is a sad and discouraging fact, and it is to be seen whether efforts to correct this through the proposed World Conference on Disarmament will bring positive results.

The prospect of establishing a peaceful and truly equitable global community will depend also on the manner in which the relationship between East and West evolves. Up to the present time, it has not been possible to establish a dialogue on economic issues which rises above the ideological and other differences between these two sectors of the world.

In addition, most of the socialist countries of Eastern Europe, as well as China, are not members of two major international economic institutions—the International Monetary Fund and the World Bank—in spite of the fact that they are participating more and more in global economic activity. One may wonder whether this situation will change with the establishment of universal membership of what would have to be refashioned institutions in this field.

There are many other questions and issues which will have a strong influence on the future. The manner and content of the response of industrialized countries to the call for global economic equity will be a major factor. This could take the direction of continued pressure for the elimination of poverty in the Third World, with significantly increased transfer of resources, tied to conditions including the performance of developing countries in respect of human rights and the provision of basic human needs for their people, and to the flow of goods from the industrialized countries.

There are those who now feel that, in the face of present serious economic difficulties, there will be an increase in protectionism in industrialized countries and a movement in the direction of autarchy. On the other hand, there will certainly be attempts by some to strengthen the trilateral relationship between North America, Europe, and Japan.

The outcome will depend, among other things, on the extent to which the current realization—a new phenomenon—of the material benefits which industrialized countries can obtain from improving economic conditions in developing countries persists and is reinforced by active research and concrete action. It will also depend on the maintenance of the unity of the developing countries in their pursuit of the goals of the New International Economic Order.

Developing countries are seeing more and more clearly the need to move vigorously toward implementing the principles of economic cooperation among themselves, in a move toward collective self-reliance. Success in this will no doubt have a significant impact on the dialogue on the New International Economic Order.

Finally, it is necessary that the issues which are now the subject of discussion and negotiation between governments should become the subject of wide public discussion and understanding. The awareness of the need for such an extension of the dialogue is becoming more evident. But a great deal remains to be done in order to create a truly global consciousness on this vital matter of the future economic, social, and cultural relationships among the people of this planet.

Notes

1. Douglas Johnson, ed., *The Making of the Modern World,* vol. 2, *The World of Empires* (London: Benn Ltd., 1973), pp. 7–9.

2. D. K. Fieldhouse, *The Colonial Empires: A Comparative Survey from the Eighteenth Century* (London: Weidenfeld and Nicolson, 1966), p. 178.

1

The Origins of the NIEO Discussions

Karl P. Sauvant

When one examines the historical context in which the discussions of the New International Order (NIEO) arose, six factors of particular importance emerge:

1. the consolidation of the political independence of the developing countries and the stabilization of the global political-military situation;
2. the full recognition of the importance of economic development and disenchantment with the development efforts of the 1960s;
3. doubts about the prevailing development model;
4. the emergence of the movement of Non-Aligned Countries as an international pressure group for the reorganization of the international economic system;
5. the politicization of the development task;
6. the growing assertiveness of the developing countries.

National Political Consolidation and International Political-Military Stabilization

Most developing countries (DCs) had become independent by the beginning of the 1960s or liberated themselves from the political domination of their former hegemonic powers (see table 1.1). The highest priority of these countries was, naturally, to consolidate their independence. This was all the more important since, during the period of the Cold War, pressures to affiliate with one of the two rival superpowers were particularly intense. The 1955 Afro-Asian Conference of Bandung was the first major attempt of those DCs that desired to resist these pressures to secure political independence through international cooperation. The foundation of the movement of the Non-Aligned Countries during its first summit in Belgrade in September 1961 gave this cooperation a stronger and continuing basis.[1] The main objectives of the Non-Aligned Countries were at that time principally of a political nature and reflected the militarily weak and politically threatened position of the individual members of the movement: decolonization, national self-determination, opposition to apartheid, dissolution of the political and military alliances and blocs, peaceful coexistence, dissolution of military bases on foreign territories, disarmament, recognition of the territorial integrity of all states, noninterference in the internal affairs of states, and the strengthening of the United Nations.

Table 1.1. Membership of Developing Countries[a]
in the United Nations: Year of Entry[b]

Year	Cumulative number	Developing country
1945	31	Argentina, Bolivia, Brazil, Chile, Colombia, Costa Rica, Cuba, Dominican Republic, Ecuador, Egypt, El Salvador, Ethiopia, Guatemala, Haiti, Honduras, India, Iraq, Iran, Lebanon, Liberia, Mexico, Nicaragua, Panama, Paraguay, Peru, Philippines, Saudi Arabia, Syrian Arab Republic, Uruguay, Venezuela, Yugoslavia[c]
1946	33	Afghanistan, Thailand
1947	35	Pakistan, Yemen
1948	36	Burma
1950	37	Indonesia
1955	44	Democratic Kampuchea, Jordan, Lao People's Democratic Republic, Libyan Arab Republic, Nepal, Romania, Sri Lanka
1956	47	Morocco, Sudan, Tunisia
1957	49	Ghana, Malaysia
1958	50	Guinea
1960	67	Benin, Central African Empire, Chad, Congo, Cyprus, Gabon, Ivory Coast, Madagascar, Mali, Niger, Nigeria, Senegal, Somalia, Togo, United Republic of Cameroon, Upper Volta, Zaïre
1961	70	Mauritania, Sierra Leone, United Republic of Tanzania
1962	76	Algeria, Burundi, Jamaica, Rwanda, Trinidad and Tobago, Uganda
1963	78	Kenya, Kuwait
1964	81	Malawi, Malta, Zambia
1965	84	Gambia, Maldives, Singapore
1966	88	Barbados, Botswana, Guyana, Lesotho
1967	89	Democratic Yemen
1968	92	Equatorial Guinea, Mauritius, Swaziland
1970	93	Fiji
1971	98	Bahrain, Bhutan, Oman, Qatar, United Arab Emirates
1973	99	Bahamas
1974	102	Bangladesh, Grenada, Guinea-Bissau
1975	108	Cape Verde, Comoros, Mozambique, Papua New Guinea, Sao Tomé and Príncipe, Suriname
1976	111	Angola, Samoa, Seychelles
1977	113	Djibouti, Viet Nam
1978	115	Dominica, Solomon Islands
1979	116	Saint Lucia

[a] Determined on the basis of simultaneous membership in the Group of 77. Some members of the Group of 77 do not belong to the United Nations.

[b] In addition, 11 centrally-planned economies and 25 developed market economies are members of the United Nations.

[c] The developing countries among the United Nations founding members.

By the beginning of the 1970s, many of these objectives had either been achieved or lost their urgency. Most colonies had become independent and most of the new countries had consolidated their sovereignty in its formal political aspects. The global rivalry of the superpowers — and the resulting pressure on the countries of the Third World — had receded, and competition seemed to have been channeled into the acceptance of strategic balance and peaceful coexistence. A certain global political-military stability had been achieved through the confirmation of the respective spheres of influence (Czechoslovakia 1968); the world political deescalation of the Vietnam war; the beginning of détente (including Ostpolitik); and the (ultimately successful) negotiation of the nonproliferation treaty, the limitation of strategic weapons (SALT), European security, and Berlin. Although these developments did not resolve the fundamental problems of the East-West conflict, they stabilized the political-military situation sufficiently to allow greater attention to other international problems.

Disappointing Development Results

For the DCs, this meant that questions of economic development began to receive greater attention. After independence, it was widely believed that many of the problems of the DCs had been largely a function of their political status. Once independence had been achieved, they would become full and equal members of the international community. Participation in international economic interactions — the benefits of which were expected to trickle down quickly to them — supported by a number of regional and international development efforts, would soon result, it was hoped, in a considerable improvement in their economic situation.

By the end of the 1960s, these hopes had been shattered. The First United Nations Development Decade, launched with high hopes in 1961, fell short of its objectives; its extension in 1970 was viewed with dampened expectations. The Alliance for Progress, also launched in 1961 with similar hopes, quietly faltered. Another regional effort, the First Yaoundé Convention of 1963, was replaced by the Second Yaoundé Convention and the Arusha Convention (1969), but the expectations associated with them were not fulfilled (in spite of the improved conditions negotiated in the latter two agreements). The United Nations Conference on Trade and Development (UNCTAD) had a promising start with its first meeting in 1964, but did not make considerable progress during its second (1968) and third (1972) meetings, thus only increasing the sense of frustration in the developing countries. The same can be said for the Group of 77, which had been established in 1964 during UNCTAD I, and whose main purpose is to represent the economic interests of the DCs in the day-to-day work of UNCTAD and the United Nations General Assembly and its committees.[2]

By the end of the decade it became apparent that the economic situation of the DCs, aggravated further by unchecked population growth, had remained desperate. For many of them, in fact, it had worsened in comparison to that of the developed market economies (DMEs). Although per capita income (at 1970 prices) in the DMEs increased from about $2,000 to $3,000 during the period 1960 to 1975, in the DCs it rose by a mere $91 — from $169 to $260 (see table 1.2).

Not only do these figures highlight the absolute poverty in the Third World, but they also show that the relative gap between North and South, if anything, has widened: income per capita in the DCs amounted to 8.5 percent of that in the DMEs in 1960 and to 8.3 percent of that in the DMEs in 1975. A ratio of 12 : 1 continues to characterize the average income difference between the two groups of countries. (It should be noted, however, that these figures reflect the different population increases in the country groups concerned.) The situation is even worse since these overall figures conceal considerable disparities among DCs (see table 1.3) and an extremely skewed income distribution within countries. If the per capita income in the DMEs is put in relation to that in the non-petroleum-exporting, lower-income developing countries, the ratio widens to 21 : 1 in 1960 and 28 : 1 in 1976.[3] In other words, a population of over 1 billion had to subsist, in 1975, on $112 (constant 1970 dollars) per capita per year — hardly more than the weekly gross income of an industrial worker in the Federal Republic of Germany during the same year.

Table 1.2 GDP per Capita in Developed and Developing Countries, 1960–1975
(Constant 1970 dollars and percent)

Country group	Year			
	1960	1965	1970	1975
Developed market economies	1988	2403	2846	3123
Developing countries	169	190	222	260
Developing countries as percentage of developed countries	8.5	7.9	7.8	8.3

Source: United Nations, "Development Trends since 1960 and Their Implications for a New International Development Strategy: Paper Prepared by the Secretariat" E/AC.54/L.98, February 13, 1978.

Table 1.3 Population and GDP per Capita by Income Group of
Developing Countries, 1960–1975
(Constant 1970 dollars and percent)

Country group and sub-group	Population (1970) (Millions)	GDP per capita (Year)			
		1960	1965	1970	1975
Developed market economies	739	1988	2403	2846	3123
Developing countries	1638				
Lower-income developing countries[a]	1151				
Petroleum exporters	175	82	85	98	121
as percent of DMEs		4.1	4.3	3.4	3.9
Other countries	976	93	100	110	112
as percent of DMEs		4.7	4.2	3.9	3.6
Middle-income developing countries[b]	222				
Petroleum exporters	30	278	291	331	404
as percent of DMEs		14.0	12.1	11.6	13.0
Other countries	192	207	237	274	318
as percent of DMEs		10.4	9.9	9.6	10.2
Higher-income developing countries[c]	266				
Petroleum exporters	51	408	522	681	994
as percent of DMEs		20.5	21.7	23.9	31.8
Other countries	215	487	554	658	789
as percent of DMEs		24.5	23.1	23.1	25.2

Source: Same as Table 1.2.

[a]Countries with per capita GDP in 1970 of less than $200. The countries are: *petroleum-exporting countries:* Indonesia and Nigeria; *other countries:* Afghanistan, Bangladesh, Benin, Botswana, Burma, Burundi, Cape Verde, Central African Empire, Chad, Comoros, Ethiopia, Gambia, Guinea, Guinea-Bissau, Haiti, India, Kenya, Lesotho, Madagascar, Malawi, Mali, Mauritania, Nepal, Niger, Pakistan, Philippines, Rwanda, Sierra Leone, Somalia, Sri Lanka, Sudan, Thailand, Togo, Uganda, United Republic of Cameroon, United Republic of Tanzania, Upper Volta, and Zaïre.

[b]Countries with per capita GDP in 1970 of $200 or more but less than $400. The countries are: *petroleum-exporting countries:* Algeria, Ecuador, and Iraq; *other countries:* Angola, Bolivia, Colombia, Congo, Dominican Republic, Egypt, El Salvador, Equatorial Guinea, Ghana, Guatemala, Guyana, Honduras, Ivory Coast, Jordan, Liberia, Malaysia, Mauritius, Morocco, Mozambique, Nicaragua, Paraguay, Republic of Korea, Senegal, Southern Rhodesia, Swaziland, Syrian Arab Republic, and Tunisia.

[c]Countries with per capita GDP in 1970 of $400 or more. The countries are: *petroleum-exporting countries:* Gabon, Iran, Kuwait, Libyan Arab Jamahiriya, Saudi Arabia, Trinidad and Tobago, and Venezuela; *other countries:* Argentina, Barbados, Brazil, Chile, Costa Rica, Fiji, Hong Kong, Israel, Jamaica, Mexico, Namibia, Panama, Peru, Réunion, Singapore, Suriname, Uruguay, and Zambia.

Absolute poverty in all its dimensions was not contained, let alone eliminated. The figures are staggering.[4]

Out of a total 1975 population of nearly 2.1 billion in developing market economies, an estimated 770 million lived in absolute poverty in 1975; in the low-income countries, over half of the population belongs to this category (see table 1.4). Assuming the continuation of current trends, the number of absolute poor will not have fallen below 600 million by the year 2000. Conservatively estimated, more than 400 million — over one-fifth of the total population — remained undernourished (see table 1.5) (as compared to 360 million during 1969/1971) and more than twice as many lived in inadequate housing.

The very poor state of health care, especially in the low-income countries (which alone have a population of 1.2 billion with an average per capita income in 1977 of less than $300), further aggravates this situation. In these countries, one physician and one nurse were available (in 1976) per 10,000 persons — as compared, at the other end of the spectrum, with ratios of 1 : 400 for physicians, and 1 : 240 for nurses in the centrally-planned economies. (It has to be stressed that these data — as well as the other figures reported here — do not take into account the distribution within countries. Thus, for instance, physicians and nurses tend to be concentrated in the urban areas resulting in even

Table 1.4 Dimensions of Poverty in Developing Market Economies,
by Income Group of Countries, 1975, 2000

| | | 1975 | | Estimate for 2000[a] | |
Country group	Total population 1975 (Billions)	Number of absolute poor[b] (Millions)	Percentage of population	Number of absolute poor[b] (Millions)	Percentage of population
Low-income countries[c]	1.2	630	52	540	27
Middle-income countries[d]	0.9	140	16	60	4
All developing countries	2.1	770	37	600	17

Source: World Bank, *World Development Report 1978* (Washington: World Bank, 1978).

[a]Based on the assumption that the GNP growth rates projected for the period 1975-85 hold to the end of this century; and that the inequality of incomes is likely to increase in the early stages of development and decrease in the later stages, implying that the incomes of the poorer population segments will grow more slowly than average income per person over the period projected.

[b]Absolute poverty is defined (conservatively) in terms of income levels that are insufficient to provide adequate nutrition (2,250 calories per caput), using essentially South Asian standards.

[c]Bhutan, Cambodia, Lao People's Democratic Republic, Ethiopia, Mali, Bangladesh, Rwanda, Somalia, Upper Volta, Burma, Burundi, Chad, Nepal, Benin, Malawi, Zaire, Guinea, India, Viet Nam, Afghanistan, Niger, Lesotho, Mozambique, Pakistan, Tanzania, Haiti, Madagascar, Sierra Leone, Sri Lanka, Central African Empire, Indonesia, Kenya, Uganda, Yemen Arab Republic.

[d]Togo, Egypt, Yemen (People's Democratic Republic of), Cameroon, Sudan, Angola, Mauritania, Nigeria, Thailand, Bolivia, Honduras, Senegal, Philippines, Zambia, Liberia, El Salvador, Papua New Guinea, Congo (People's Republic of), Morocco, Rhodesia, Ghana, Ivory Coast, Jordan, Colombia, Guatemala, Ecuador, Paraguay, Korea (Republic of), Nicaragua, Dominican Republic, Syrian Arab Republic, Peru, Tunisia, Malaysia, Algeria, Turkey, Costa Rica, Chile, China (Republic of), Jamaica, Lebanon, Mexico, Brazil, Panama, Iraq, Uruguay, Romania, Argentina, Yugoslavia, Portugal, Iran, Hong Kong, Trinidad and Tobago, Venezuela, Greece, Singapore, Spain, Israel.

Table 1.5. Dimensions of Poverty in Developing Market Economies:
Undernourishment,[a] by Region, 1969/71 and 1974/76
(Average numbers and percentage)

Region	Total number (Millions)		Percentage of total population	
	1969/71	1974/76	1969/71	1974/76
Africa	70	68	25	22
Far East	256	286	25	27
Latin America	44	41	16	13
Near East	31	19	18	11
TOTAL	401	414	24	22

Source: Food and Agriculture Organization, *The Fourth World Food Survey* (Rome: FAO, 1977) and *Agriculture: Toward 2000* (Rome: FAO, 1979).

[a]Persons with a calorie intake below the critical minimum level of 1.2 times the basal metabolic rate. This rate represents the energy needed under resting and fasting conditions; it varies between individuals depending on weight and sex.

worse health services in the rural areas than is indicated by these averages.) Furthermore, three-quarters of the population in the low-income countries have no access to safe water. Not surprisingly, then, the mortality rate per thousand reaches 122 and life expectancy at birth is a mere 50 years — as compared with, respectively, 15 per thousand and 74 years in industrialized countries (see table 1.6).

Conditions are similarly unfavorable in education. In the low-income countries, less than three-quarters of all children of primary-school age were enrolled in 1976 (compared with all children in the developed countries); less than one-quarter entered into secondary schools (over four-fifths in the DMEs); and only 5 percent were enrolled in higher education (34 percent in the DMEs). As a result, the literacy rate in the low income countries was only 36 percent in 1975 (99 percent in the DMEs) (see table 1.6).

Naturally, the combination of undernourishment, poor health, and illiteracy severely impairs income-earning possibilities: out of a total labor force of approximately 770 million, 330 million are unemployed (5 percent) or are underemployed (40 percent), i.e., do not have sufficient income to meet their basic needs (see table 1.7).

These are the dimensions of poverty in the developing countries. It appeared, thus, that the international and regional development efforts (or, more generally, the mechanisms of the international economic system) had failed to contain, let alone eliminate, absolute poverty. This was all the more disappointing since the DMEs had experienced unparalleled growth during the 1960s. In the words of the UNCTAD Secretariat:

> The fact that the developing countries did not share adequately in the prosperity of the developed countries when the latter were experiencing remarkably rapid expansion indicates the existence of basic weaknesses in the mechanisms which link the economies of the two groups of countries. . . . The weakness of this structure, the inadequacy of the mechanisms by which growth in the developed centres is transmitted to the third world, are manifested in each of the major areas of economic relations between developed and developing countries — in the trade in commodities and in manufactures, in the transfer of technology and in the provision of financial resources through the international monetary and financial system.[5]

Table 1.6. Dimensions of Poverty in Developing Market Economies: Health and Education, by Income Group of Countries, Various Years (Weighted average)

Indicator	Year	Low-income countries[a]	Middle-income countries[b]	Capital-surplus oil exporters[c]	Centrally-planned economies[d]	Industrialized countries[e]
Population (millions)	1976	1 193	936	12	1 276	661
Health						
Health care[f]						
Population per physician	1976	10 300	4 470	1 140[g]	400	630
Population per nurse	1976	9 720	1 930	340[g]	240	210
Population with access to safe water (percentage)	1975	28	59	87[h]	...	...
Daily per caput calorie supply as percentage of requirements	1974	91	107	...	110	130
Life expectancy at birth (years)	1977	50	60	53[h]	66	74
Mortality rates per thousand[f,i]	1975	122[j]	46[k]	...	...	15[l]
Education						
School enrollment[f]						
Primary school (as percentage of age group)	1976					
Total		73	92	90[h]	100	102
Female		59	86	84[h]	99	104
Secondary school (as percentage of age group)	1976	24	36	45[h]	69	82
Higher education (as percentage of population aged 20–24)	1975	5	10	7[h]	20	34
Adult literacy rate[f]	1975	36	69	...	...	99

Source: World Bank, *World Developoment Report, 1978* (Washington: The World Bank, 1978) and *World Development Report, 1979* (Washington: The World Bank, 1979).

[a]Developing countries with income per person of $300 and below in 1977: Bhutan, Cambodia, Bangladesh, Lao People's Democratic Republic, Ethiopia, Mali, Nepal, Somalia, Burundi, Chad, Rwanda, Upper Volta, Zaire, Burma, Malawi, India, Mozambique, Niger, Viet Nam, Afghanistan, Pakistan, Sierra Leone, United Republic of Tanzania, Benin, Sri Lanka, Guinea, Haiti, Lesotho, Madagascar, Central African Empire, Kenya, Mauritania, Uganda, Sudan, Angola, Indonesia, Togo.

[b]Developing countries with 1977 income per person of above $300: Egypt, Cameroon, Yemen People's Democratic Republic, Ghana, Honduras, Liberia, Nigeria, Thailand, Senegal, Yemen Arab Republic, Philippines, Zambia, Congo (People's Republic of), Papua New Guinea, Rhodesia, El Salvador, Morocco, Bolivia, Ivory Coast, Jordan, Colombia, Paraguay, Ecuador, Guatemala, Korea (Republic of), Nicaragua, Dominican Republic, Peru, Tunisia, Syrian

Table 1.6. Dimensions of Poverty in Developing Market Economies. (cont.)

Arab Republic, Malaysia, Algeria, Turkey, Mexico, Jamaica, Lebanon, Chile, China, Republic of, Panama, Costa Rica, South Africa, Brazil, Uruguay, Iraq, Argentina, Portugal, Yugoslavia, Iran, Trinidad and Tobago, Hong Kong, Venezuela, Greece, Israel, Singapore, Spain.

[c] Kuwait, Libyan Arab Jamahiriya, Oman, Qatar, Saudi Arabia, and United Arab Emirates.

[d] Albania, Bulgaria, Cuba, People's Republic of China, Czechoslovakia, German Democratic Republic, Hungary, Democratic People's Republic of Korea, Mongolia, Poland, USSR.

[e] Australia, Austria, Belgium, Canada, Denmark, Finland, France, Federal Republic of Germany, Iceland, Ireland, Italy, Japan, Netherlands, New Zealand, Norway, Sweden, South Africa, Switzerland, United Kingdom, United States.

[f] For a number of countries, data are for years other than specified.

[g] 1974, median value.

[h] 1975, median value.

[i] Infants aged 0–1.

[j] Countries with income per person of $250 and below in 1976, median value.

[k] Countries with income per person of above $250 in 1976, median value.

[l] Median value.

Table 1.7. Dimensions of Poverty in Developing Market Economies: Unemployment and Underemployment, by Region, 1977 (Millions and percent)

Region	Total labor force	Unemployment[a]		Underemployment[b]		Total	
		Number	Percent	Number	Percent	Number	Percent
Africa	149	12	8.1	60	43.8	72	48.3
Asia[c]	508	22	4.3	200	41.2	222	43.7
Latin America	108	6	5.6	30	29.4	36	33.3
Oceania	2	—	—	1	50.0	1	50.0
TOTAL	767	40	5.2	291	40	331	43.2

Source: ILO, Follow-up of the World Employment Conference: Basic Needs (Geneva: ILO, 1979).

[a] Defined as "persons without a job and looking for work."

[b] Defined as "persons who are in employment of less than normal duration and who are seeking or would accept additional work" and "persons with a job yielding inadequate income."

[c] Excluding socialist countries of Asia.

Importantly, the disappointments with the functioning of the international economic system came at a time when political-military developments allowed the full realization of the implications of its failures. It became increasingly apparent that political independence would be a mere chimera unless complemented by a minimum of economic independence, unless genuine development were to transform the hierarchical structures of economic dependence that characterize the relationships between developing and developed countries into horizontal structures of interdependence. Economic development came to be sought with greater urgency.

Doubts About the Prevailing Development Model

The question arose, therefore, of whether the continuing difficulties of the DCs might not be, at least partially, a function of the nature of the international economic system and especially the mechanisms and structures through which the DCs were linked with the DMEs. Doubt was even cast on the development model of the overwhelming majority of the Third World nations. Two of the main characteristics of the prevailing model were questioned in particular: its world-market orientation and its emphasis on GNP growth rates.

Doubts About the World-Market Orientation of the Development Strategy

The key characteristic of the development model of virtually all countries of the Third World — and one strongly supported by the DMEs — is that its frame of reference is the world economy and the world market. The close integration of the Third World countries into the world economy and their orientation toward the world market are expected to trigger and then maintain the development process. Although this integration involves a whole range of transactions (e.g., technology, consumption patterns, skills, capital), trade has traditionally been regarded as the most important among them. Aid-by-trade, then, is the key mechanism of the prevailing model, and trade is the "engine" of development. The operative assumptions are that the industrial states continue to grow, that this growth translates itself into increased demand for imports from the developing countries, and that this in turn stimulates the industrial development of the latter. Conversely, if the economic growth of the industrial countries slows down (e.g., through a recession or a deliberate zero-growth policy), or if this growth does not translate itself into equally increased demand for goods and services from the Third World (e.g., because of changing demand patterns or the production of substitutes), then the export-led industrialization process of the South also slows down or comes to a halt. In this model, free access to the markets of the North is, therefore, of crucial importance.

The linkage between developed and developing countries can be characterized further. Although, in principle, interactions with all countries are expected to generate the desired stimulating effect, the historically determined reality for the developing countries is that the lion's share of their interactions is with the developed countries (and, among them, especially the former colonial or hegemonic powers). (Trade among developing countries accounts for only one-fifth of their total trade.) This in turn has immediate implications for the contents of trade: if trade is geared to the world market, and if this world market is largely identical with that of the industrial states, then the goods and services to be provided by the DCs are those that respond to the consumption patterns of the developed countries. Under this model, the growth of production capacities in the Third World is designed to serve the market of the developed countries as well as its extension into the developing economies, i.e., the domestic upper and upper-middle classes (whose income allows them to replicate the consumption patterns of the developed countries). Raw material enclaves and export platforms on the one hand and import substitution of luxury-consumption goods on the other are the two logical extremes of this model. For a policy that places a premium on this type of industrialization and considers the modern sector as the most dynamic component of the economy, it is only natural to measure performance by GNP growth rates. The program for the First United Nations Development Decade epitomizes this orientation in that one of its two quantitative targets specified a minimum annual rate of growth of aggregate national income (of 5 percent).

The implications of an integrative approach also extend to the nature of the production capacities to be established. Since the products of the developing countries must compete in the world market, they must meet its standards. As a rule, this requires the most advanced technology — which has to be imported. Ease of access to this technology, therefore, becomes crucial.

The creation of production capacities, furthermore, has to take into account the existing global distribution of the factors of production and the conditions under which they can be utilized (e.g., availability of capital, skills, and governmental support for R and D; large and sophisticated markets; various external economies; perceived investment climate and political risk). In the North-South context, this means that production in the Third World (apart from raw materials) tends to be labor-intensive and low–technology oriented. Industrial processes and industries exhibiting these characteristics, therefore, are encouraged to expand in, or be redeployed to, the Third World.

The international division of labor resulting from these processes is not a horizontal one, i.e., a division where one group of countries specializes on one set of industries and another group on a set of comparable industries. Rather, the division is vertical, i.e., it cuts across industrial processes (typified by assembly operations in DCs) and industries according to their degree of standardization, allocating the more sophisticated ones (including R and D) to the developed countries. The main directionality of the linkages in this division of labor — and the international economic system of which it is a part — is, therefore, such that the developed countries tend to provide consumption patterns, technology, skills, capital, and so on to the developing countries, which establish production facilities to service the markets of the North. The openness of the system and the dominant role of private (corporate, Northern) actors in it ensure the reproduction of the existing structures and their associated inequalities. The lack of autonomous development inherent in these circumstances, and particularly the resultant uneven distribution of benefits (including spin-off effects), are aptly described by one of the key concepts of the present system: the "trickle-down effect." This concept succinctly captures the hierarchical character of the system, the (indirect) mechanisms through which it is supposed to benefit the Third World, and the magnitude of the benefits involved.

Although trade is designed to play a central role in advancing economic development, it is acknowledged that trade alone cannot generate all the resources needed for industrialization. A supplementary transfer of resources is therefore required and is in fact recognized as the second pillar of the traditional development model. This is reflected in the program for the first United Nations Development Decade, whose only other quantitative target in addition to that for growth was a target for the aggregate net transfers of financial resources to developing countries in terms of a proportion (of 1 percent) of the GNP of the developed countries.[6]

The experiences of the 1960s had made suspect a number of the elements of this approach. Trade was not as dynamic as was expected and, in fact, the share of the developing countries in world trade decreased continuously. At the same time, financial transfers in the form of development assistance stagnated in real terms and decreased in terms of percentage of the GNP of the industrial countries. Growth and prosperity had not trickled down to the extent desired and, when it occurred, were often perceived as mainly benefiting transnational enterprises. Furthermore, in the 1970s, the recession in the DMEs highlighted the dependence of the DCs on the vagaries of the world market, and the increased protectionism raised questions as to the absorption capacity of the DMEs for industrial products originating in the DCs. (See chap. 3 for data on trade, financial transfers, dependence on DMEs, and protectionism.) The latter development, in particular, threatened to undermine the entire rationale of a world-market oriented, export-led development strategy. In fact, since the growing protectionism also affected the developed countries; since, even more importantly, the disintegration of the Bretton Woods arrangements had left the international monetary system in disarray; since it appeared to be impossible to control world inflation; and since the insecurity over the supply of primary products continued, the old order appeared no longer to serve even the interests of the developed countries.

For the Third World nations, an additional consideration must be mentioned. In many countries, the prevailing development strategy tended to accentuate structural underdevelopment. In other words, even if the mechanisms of the export-led development model would work, the "best" that could be achieved would be dependent development. The structural nature of underdevelopment[7] is mainly a function of the malformation of the DC economies and their economic dependence on the industrialized countries.

Structural malformation is based on the absence of key production sectors (especially the capital-goods sector) and, partially as a result, on the absence of integrated production circuits (from the production of technology to the production of sophisticated consumption goods). The production circuits that do exist (complete or incomplete, and particularly those linking agriculture) tend to be isolated from each other. The result is a low degree of coherence of the economies of the Third World and a low capacity to reproduce themselves. The consequences also include the emergence of parallel modes of production. For instance, the modern world-market oriented sector (or, more precisely, fragments of various modern production circuits located in the developing countries) and the geographic and societal spaces in which it is located remain distinct from the traditional sector and its geographic and societal spaces, with few linkages between the two.[8] The emphasis placed on the modern sector also leads to the marginalization of a large part of domestic economic activity and of the majority of the population.

Malformations of this kind in and of themselves create external economic dependence. It is dependence of a structural nature, due to the special characteristics of the existing malformations and especially the impossibility of autonomous reproduction. The production apparatus of the developing countries are formed by the demands (e.g., for raw materials, cheap labor) of the industrialized countries. Hence, they are geared toward the developed countries, specializing in parts of certain production circuits. If the demand changes, so does the production apparatus. The impulse for this change, it should be noted, is generated by the industrial countries. The explicit world-market orientation of the industrialization strategies of most developing countries further aggravates this economic dependence and malformation.

At the beginning of the 1970s, the recognition of these processes and implications had barely begun. In fact, even the NIEO program is still based on the prevailing development model. However, the perception of the causes of underdevelopment clearly shifted, and systemic and structural factors began to attract greater attention. The realization spread that economic emancipation may not be possible in the framework of the traditional development model.

These doubts found their expression in the emergence and rise of the concept of individual and collective self-reliance. Instead of looking toward external impulses for growth, the self-reliance approach looks toward internal impulses, particularly the creation and expansion of a domestic market; transactions (especially trade) with the DMEs are no longer the engine of development but rather have a supplementary function.

The concept of self-reliance had been introduced into the development debate by the President of Tanzania, Mwalima Julius K. Nyerere, in a speech before the 1970 Dar-es-Salaam Preparatory Conference of the Non-Aligned Countries. In the subsequent Third Conference of Heads of State or Government of Non-Aligned Countries at Lusaka in September 1970, the concept became the main plank of the economic program of the Non-Aligned Countries. During later conferences, and through concrete efforts among nonaligned and other developing countries, the concept of individual and collective self-reliance was elaborated further and became the main substantive contribution of the Non-Aligned Countries to the international development debate.

The logic of the concept also required a common approach to foreign direct investment and transnational enterprises. This was recognized at the Dar-es-Salaam Preparatory Conference and also found its way into the 1970 Lusaka Summit "Declaration on Non-Alignment and Economic Progress." There, the Non-Aligned Countries pledged themselves "to ensure that external components of the developmental process further national objectives and conform to national needs; and in particular to adopt so far as practicable a common approach to problems and possibilities of investment of private capital in developing countries."[9]

Although the concept of self-reliance was not to inspire the main documents laying down the foundations of the New International Economic Order — in fact, most measures suggested in these documents were derived from the prevailing development strategy — it has steadily gained support in the Third World. This is borne out most impressively by the declaration adopted by the Group of 77 at their Fourth Ministerial Meeting in Arusha in February 1979, during which the DCs formulated their positions for the May/June 1979 UNCTAD V session in Manila. For the first time in its history, the Group of 77, as the principal organization of the DCs for matters of collective economic interest within the United Nations system,[10] shifted away from its exclusive dependence on the integrative, world-market oriented development strategy and embraced the concept of self-reliance. The document adopted in Arusha — the "Arusha Programme for Collective Self-Reliance and Framework for Negotiations" — signaled this shift in its very title.[11]

The self-reliance approach has not become the prevailing development model. This remains an export-led strategy. Still, fundamental economic elements of the approach — mostly under the title "co-operation among developing countries" — have entered into all important international development programs, including the resolutions adopted at the Sixth and Seventh Special Sessions. There they are, because of their domestic- (and Third World-) market orientation, out of harmony with the overwhelming thrust of the respective programs, which remain world-market oriented. This applies as much for the programs of the United Nations as it does for those of the Group of 77 and the Non-Aligned Countries.

Nevertheless, the self-reliance model has clear and important functions. It remains an alternative development strategy that — even if it is very difficult to implement in its extreme form of "de-linking" the South from the North[12] — can at least provide guidance for the kinds of change that are required to eliminate underdevelopment. As an ideal-type, it can provide direction for partial strategies. Naturally, the attractiveness of this alternative increases as the limitations of the export-led approach become more evident and/or the negotiations about the implementation of the NIEO program remain deadlocked. The Arusha Programme is a case in point.

The most important contribution of the self-reliance discussions to the movement toward the NIEO, however, was that it led the DCs to recognize the political dimensions of development and to examine seriously the international framework of the development effort. This led to a questioning of the purposes of the international economic system and channeled the development discussion into more fundamental directions. (See chap. 2 for a more comprehensive discussion.)

Doubts about the Quantitative Growth Emphasis of the Development Strategy

Apart from the world-market orientation of the prevailing development strategy, it was particularly its quantitative growth emphasis that drew criticism and contributed to the rising doubts about the model itself. As indicated, the First United Nations Development Decade had two quantitative targets: a net transfer of (official plus private) financial resources from developed to developing countries in the amount of 1 percent of the former's GNP, and the attainment by the DCs of a minimum annual growth rate of 5 percent in aggregate national income by 1970. These targets were later used for performance evaluation.

Criticisms were particularly voiced against the prevalent practice of measuring development by — and equating it with — the growth of GNP. It was pointed out that the growth rate specified for the First Development Decade was a group target, whose attainment might disguise the fact that many countries are growing at a slower pace. More importantly, however, such a GNP growth target may well be achieved although some sectors (e.g., agriculture) perform very poorly, whole regions (e.g., rural areas) remain untouched by growth, and certain groups of the population (especially the poor) actually experience declining incomes.[13] Growth alone does not eliminate poverty and general growth rates do not provide information about the quality and the distribution of growth. If development is understood to involve the qualitative improvement of the standard of living of the entire population, growth and development cannot be equated.[14] The basic question was raised again: what kinds of improvement are sought for whom? In other words, what is the objective of development?

In response, the concept of basic needs rose to prominence. Accordingly, development meant first of all that the needs of the entire population for primary consumption goods (food, clothing, shelter), services (water, health, education, transport), and employment had to be satisfied and that development policy had to address itself squarely to this objective. Such a goal orientation also requires growth, but growth that is qualitatively different from that of the past and, most notably, that is directly geared toward the 40 percent of the population that has so far been neglected. This model no longer subscribes to an internal trickling-down effect but focuses instead on domestic production and consumption patterns.

As far as the international discussion is concerned, the return to the basic objective of development had already taken place in the 1970 Preparatory Conference of the Non-Aligned Countries referred to above. In the "Document on Economic Development and Co-operation" adopted at that meeting, it is noted that:

> The participants also recognise that economic development is a complex and many sided process and that no single target such as a rate of growth of Gross Product could represent an adequate index of development. Any national plan which conveys no targets for reducing poverty, unemployment, inequality, ignorance, and disease can scarcely be considered a development plan; and this is as true for an international strategy of development. The Non-aligned Countries recognise that the ultimate purpose of development is to provide opportunities for a better life to all sections of their population by *inter alia* removing glaring inequalities in the distribution of income and wealth, eliminating mass poverty and social injustice, creating new employment opportunities and providing better education and health facilities. Such measures are both the end products and instruments of economic and social change. Recognising that a sustained increase in *per capita* Gross Product is a necessary condition for strengthening the process of social change, there is equally need for international agreement on minimum targets in each of these areas of social development as part of the strategy of the Second Development Decade. Development plans incorporating such minima should find external, financial and technical support from international institutions.[15]

Since self-reliance had been one of the main themes of this conference, the simultaneous discussion of basic needs is not surprising: the substantive content of a self-reliant development strategy is easily compatible with the satisfaction of basic needs (and perhaps even requires it) because both approaches are oriented toward the domestic market and that of the Third World.

The observations of the Preparatory Conference were not stated with this clarity in the final documents of the 1970 Lusaka Summit. Possibly, a discussion of the purposes of development was regarded as interference into internal affairs. Later documents did, however, address themselves to this question. The "Economic Declaration" adopted at the 1973 Algiers Summit stated, for instance:

> Clearly, however, only a proper conception of development which is based on the requisite internal structural changes particular to each country, and which encompasses growth in all the key sectors, will enable our countries to achieve their development targets. This process is inseparable from another process, social in nature, which calls for the highest possible employment levels, income redistribution and the over-all solution of problems such as health, nutrition, housing and education. It is equally obvious that these aims can be achieved only with the conscious and democratic participation of the masses, which are the determining factors in any national endeavour to achieve dynamic, effective and independent development.[16]

The basic-needs theme immediately found its way into the discussions of the United Nations, where the Committee for Development Planning[17] decided at its 1971 session to make poverty and unemployment the focal point of its next meeting. The report of the 1972 session — programmatically entitled "Attack on Mass Poverty and Unemployment'' — started out with the following observation: "Mass poverty continues to be a dominating feature in the developing countries, and unemployment has assumed serious proportions in many of them. Even countries that have achieved high rates of growth of output have not escaped these problems. In many countries the situation has deteriorated in recent years."[18]

It is not the objective of this chapter to examine and elaborate on the basic-needs concept. Suffice it to say that the concept was strongly supported in the following years by nongovernmental institutions,[19] and was discussed in some of its aspects during specialized United Nations world conferences;[20] received strong endorsement by the members of the OECD Development Assistance Committee;[21] and was made the basis of the concrete policy of several important organizations of the United Nations system.[22] The ILO "Tripartite World Conference on Employment, Income Distribution and Social Progress, and the International Division of Labour" (held in Geneva during June 1976), in particular, played an important role in stimulating and broadening the discussions.[23] The ILO and World Bank also included basic-needs considerations among the guidelines of their development projects.

Although the basic-needs discussion had been under way before the Sixth Special Session, it did not become one of the main focuses until after the adoption of NIEO documents. The criticisms of the basic-needs approach predate the NIEO debates as well. They include the fear that the satisfaction of basic needs is only a pretext for interference in internal affairs and the concern that the question of basic needs could be used as an excuse to digress from the fundamental task of restructuring the international economic order.

It is certainly correct that the discussion about basic needs has drawn considerable attention to the internal dimension of the development process; but it is equally true that the proponents of this approach accept that the individual countries determine for themselves what they define as basic needs and when they consider them as being fulfilled. The rationale of the basic-needs orientation is to draw attention to the *objective* of development, shifting attention from the *means* of development to its *ends*. It forces policymakers (in particular, those for whom growth seemed to have become an end in itself) to examine whether the means that have been applied actually do serve the desired ends. The merit of the basic-needs concept is, therefore, its tendency to force decision makers to set certain priorities. Seen from this perspective, the basic-needs concern is not a strategy but rather an objective and, as such, hardly disputed. And it leaves open the question: through which concrete set of measures can it best be accomplished?

Although a discussion of the elements of a strategy[24] aimed at the satisfaction of basic needs is beyond the scope of this chapter, some general observations are in order concerning the compatibility of the internal and external dimensions of a comprehensive development strategy. The basic-needs orientation focuses attention primarily on the internal dimension. However, since the development of any particular country takes place in the framework of the international economic system and its structures, this framework requires attention as well. A comprehensive development strategy, therefore, has to deal with both internal and external measures. Moreover, the direction of both the internal and external strategies has to be consistent: a certain type of domestic strategy requires a certain type of international strategy, and vice versa; otherwise, conflicts are bound to arise in their implementation. To be more specific: if domestic priority is given to the satisfaction of basic needs and, hence, production and consumption patterns are oriented toward the domestic (and Third World) market, then an external strategy that aims at the satisfaction of the needs of the world market obviously presents problems — and vice versa. In such a situation, planners and policy makers in developing countries are constantly confronted with the dilemma of deciding which concrete projects should receive the scarce resources, what role should be played by foreign direct investment, and so on. The satisfaction of basic needs and the satisfaction of world-market needs are opposed to one another because of the different production and consumption patterns dictated by each.[25] A combination of both ideal types is certainly possible, at least in principle. But this requires a very clear and effective development plan in order to avoid the de facto predominance of one approach over the other in day-to-day decision-making processes.

The Role of the Non-Aligned Countries

Thus, a number of developments converged at the beginning of the 1970s: most developing countries had obtained and consolidated their political independence; the global political-military situation had stabilized; the countries of the Third World began to pay greater attention to development questions; the regional and international development programs had shown disappointing results; and doubts were raised about the propriety of the prevailing development model. By drawing the political consequences from the combination of these processes, the Non-Aligned Countries came to play a crucial role in the promotion of the development issue. Only the non-aligned movement could do this because it was the only organization of the Third World that could draw political conclusions and lend them the weight necessary in the arena of international discussions.

The role of the Non-Aligned Countries in the events leading to the adoption of the NIEO program is examined in detail in chapter 2. Only some brief observations are, therefore, required here.

First, the non-aligned movement established itself as the principal political coalition of the developing countries. From 25 members at the first summit in Belgrade in 1961, membership increased to 85 members at the fifth summit in Colombo in 1976. In addition, a number of observer and guest countries participated in the movement. In 1976, 75 percent of the members of the Group of 77 were also members of the non-aligned movement. If observers are added, the percentage increased to 90. Thus, the non-aligned movement had succeeded in mobilizing most of the nations of the Third World.

Second, the movement had set up a highly structured organization. Before the 1970 Lusaka summit, the movement's organizational structure consisted of only the summit conferences (held at irregular intervals) and the preparatory conferences of foreign ministers. Since 1970, several organizational layers emerged which reached down to the level of seminars and symposia. The importance of these increased institutionalized contacts lay in the fact that they created horizontal lines of communication (i.e., lines of communication that are independent from the former colonial powers), led to intensified contacts, and allowed the Non-Aligned Countries to exchange information, define their interests, and coordinate their policies — all in a framework that is characterised by stronger political awareness than that of the Group of 77.[26] The non-aligned movement provides, therefore, the organizational infrastructure for effective cooperation.

Third, the non-aligned movement embraced the development issue and included it among its principal objectives. Before the 1970 Lusaka summit, the Non-Aligned Countries had mainly a political perspective. At the Lusaka summit, development questions received considerable attention for the first time. This shift developed further at the 1972 Georgetown foreign ministers conference and was ratified during the 1973 Algiers summit. The economic program adopted at Algiers called for fundamental reforms of the international economic system; it was, in fact, the basis of the resolutions adopted several months later during the Sixth Special Session.[27]

After the Algiers summit, the overwhelming share of the organized activities of the Non-Aligned Countries (and, in fact, the dynamics of the movement) shifted toward economic matters. The non-aligned movement had become a pressure group for the reorganization of the international economic system.

Politicization

This transformation of the non-aligned movement had a crucial effect on the way in which development matters were perceived, presented, and pursued. During the 1960s — and as late as UNCTAD III (1972) — questions of economic development were regarded as "low politics": they were left to the ministers of economics, finance, and planning. Therefore, attempts to politicize these issues (for example, the Group of 77's Charter of Algiers [1967] which had been adopted in preparation for UNCTAD II) failed. With the beginning of the 1970s, however, this attitude changed and development questions became "high politics": they were elevated from the level of heads of departments to the level of heads of state or government. The development issue had become politicized.

It is not important that many of the concrete suggestions had already been presented earlier in other forums in one form or another. It is, perhaps, not even important that basic changes were desired. What is important, however, is that the movement of the Non-Aligned Countries, as the political association of the Third World, embraced these suggestions and supported them with its entire political weight. The decisive factor was not the novelty of the ideas but their political relevance and the political support that was given to them.

The Algiers summit represents the formal recognition by the decision makers of the DCs that their problems were not a function of their political status alone but also of their economic status. Consequently, new efforts, particularly relating to producers' associations, were undertaken to increase economic cooperation among developing countries. (See chap. 2.) Consequently, the Non-Aligned Countries desired to bring the development issue before the United Nations, but not, as in the past, in the context of a committee of the General Assembly but, rather, "at a high political level" in a special session "devoted exclusively to the problems of development."[28] This request was supported by the United Nations General Assembly, which decided, on December 17, 1973, "to hold a special session of the General Assembly at a high political level"[29] about development questions. This decision led to the 1975 Seventh Special Session which was meant to be the first United Nations special session on development.

The Algiers summit had made the development task a priority item on the agenda of the Non-Aligned Countries; with the Seventh Special Session it was scheduled to become a priority item on the international agenda. These were the political consequences drawn by the Third World countries from the experiences of the 1960s, and they were consequences that could only be drawn and implemented by a political and not a technical body. But the timetable of the Non-Aligned Countries (which also included the "Conference of Developing Countries on Raw Materials" that was held in Dakar February 4–8, 1975) was compressed when, one month after the end of the summit, war broke out between Israel and the Arab states, petroleum was used to put pressure on the developed countries, and the price of oil quadrupled.

The Growing Assertiveness of the Third World

With their growing appreciation of the importance of economic matters, the DCs became increasingly aware of their bargaining power. Limited as this bargaining power is, it lies in the economic sphere and depends on the ability of the Third World to maintain a minimum of solidarity. Primary products play a key role.

This role has two aspects. The first concerns the generation of financial resources for development and the full integration of the production of raw materials into the domestic economy. Since primary commodities are essential for the development process of most developing countries, they have to be fully utilized for this purpose. The greatest efforts are needed, therefore, to ensure that the largest possible share of the value created through their production accrues to the developing countries. Prices, royalties, and the like are the means through which this objective can be achieved. In addition, efforts have to be made to capture the indirect (multiplier) effects created through the processing of raw materials in order to utilize them for the stimulation of domestic development. Consequently, a larger share of processing has to be located in the producing countries. But since, for historical reasons, raw materials are frequently controlled by transnational enterprises — whose normal preference is to favor transnational vertical linkages over national horizontal ones (i.e., backward and forward linkages in the host economy) — the DCs reserve their right to nationalize these natural resources and the production facilities associated with them if this should become necessary in the interest of national economic development.

The discussions surrounding the question of nationalization on the basis of the principle of permanent sovereignty over natural resources, and the increased application of this principle, reflect the growing assertiveness of the developing countries. During the 1960s, the assertion of the principle of permanent sovereignty over natural resources was always accompanied by references to international law in case conflicts should occur in its implementation.[30] Disputes, usually concerning the question of what constitutes "prompt, adequate, and effective" compensation in the case of nationalization, therefore, would not be settled under domestic law. During the 1970s, the developing countries discontinued this reference to international law (among other reasons, because they had not participated in its formulation) and insisted, instead, that any disputes that might arise should be settled in accordance with the national legislation of each state.[31]

Incidents of nationalization became, indeed, more frequent during the 1970s, increasing from an annual average of 46 nationalizations during the 1960s to 131 in each of the first seven years of the 1970s. The total number of cases for the entire period, 1960 to 1976, amounted to 1,369 (see table 1.8). This figure, however, has to be put into perspective. It is very small compared to the total number of some 80,000 existing foreign affiliates of transnational enterprises,[32] and about half of all cases are concen-

Table 1.8. Takeover of Foreign Enterprises, by Major Industrial Sector and Region, 1960–1976
(Number of takeovers)

Region and period	Total	Sector							
		Mining	Petroleum	Agriculture	Manufacturing	Trade	Public utilities	Banking and insurance	Other
Africa, south of Sahara									
1960–1969	138	19	2	40	35	15	12	15	—
1970–1976	467	19	62	68	85	17	13	130	73
1960–1976	605	38	64	108	120	32	25	145	73
West Asia and North Africa									
1960–1969	152	2	19	—	35	5	2	73	16
1970–1976	123	—	71	—	6	2	—	19	25
1960–1976	275	2	90	—	41	7	2	92	41
South and East Asia									
1960–1969	130	4	8	57	5	8	4	44	—
1970–1976	161	—	16	87	5	—	—	53	—
1960–1976	291	4	24	144	10	8	4	97	—
Western hemisphere									
1960–1969	35	7	11	1	1	—	13	1	1
1970–1976	163	29	31	19	49	1	14	14	6
1960–1976	198	36	42	20	50	1	27	15	7
All developing regions									
1960–1969	455	32	40	98	76	28	31	133	17
1970–1976	914	48	180	174	145	20	27	216	104
1960–1976	1,369	80	220	272	221	48	58	349	121

Source: United Nations, *Transnational Corporations in World Development: A Re-examination* (New York: United Nations, 1978).

trated on nine countries that, mainly for basic sociopolitical considerations, have undertaken large-scale nationalization programs (see table 1.9). Not surprisingly, over 40 percent of all incidents involved foreign affiliates in primary commodities. The change in ownership patterns is particularly impressive in the petroleum industry. Although in 1970 hardly any crude oil production facilities in OPEC countries had been domestically controlled, foreign majority ownership was the exception rather than the rule by the end of 1974. Similar developments, even if not quite as far-reaching, took place in the bauxite, copper, and iron ore industries.[33] However, compensation payments, at times very substantial, were made in most cases.

The second aspect of the role of primary products concerns their function as a bargaining instrument in North-South relations. The developed countries together obtain nearly half of their primary-commodity imports from the DCs (see table 1.10). For some important products — minerals, fuels, and related materials as a group — this dependence ranges between 70 percent for the European Community to over 80 percent for Japan and the United States. For some specific products (see fig. 1.1) — like uranium or petroleum in the case of the European Community — it can reach nearly 100 percent.

Naturally, this dependence provides the DCs with a certain bargaining leverage — and not only for the purpose of maximizing the economic returns on raw materials. But the sine qua non for the exercise of this leverage is cooperation among the producing countries. Producers' associations offer the framework for such cooperation. They facilitate, for instance, the exchange of relevant information (e.g., about new production technologies), strengthen the bargaining position of each member vis-à-vis consumer countries and transnational enterprises, allow efforts to contain price and income fluctuations, and, finally, facilitate the formulation and implementation of common policies.[34]

Given the potential utility of producers' associations, it is not surprising that developing countries wished to see them officially legitimized and that they place great expectations on them. Partially, these hopes were the result of a *faute de mieux* effect: since at least the middle of the 1950s, the DCs have consistently advocated the establishment of consumer-producers' agreements for a number of raw materials without, however, obtaining the cooperation of the DMEs.[35] It became, therefore, unavoidable that the Third World would make every effort to exhaust its own possibilities. Among these efforts were an agreement to create a "Fund for the Financing of Buffer Stocks of Raw Materials and Primary Products Exported by Developing Countries" and to form a "Council of Associations of Developing Countries Producers-Exporters of Raw Materials," the establishment of which was recommended by the 1975 Dakar Conference of Developing Countries on Raw Materials. The statutes of both organizations were adopted in 1978 and will enter into force upon ratification. That of the Council will become effective 180 days after five producers' associations have notified the depository state, Sri Lanka, of their decision to join the Council (for the potential membership of the Council, see table 1.11).[36]

The prototype of a producers' association is, of course, OPEC. OPEC also demonstrates how increased awareness of the importance of economic factors has influenced the actions of the Third World. Although established in 1960, OPEC spent the entire decade of the 1960s negotiating minor improvements in the division of revenues which, in the end, resulted in additional governmental income of $25 million. Between

Table 1.9. Takeover of Foreign Enterprises by Host Country, 1960–1976

	Number of cases							
	1–5	6–10	11–15	16–20	21–25	26–30	31–50	over 50
	Afghanistan Bolivia Brazil Chad Costa Rica Dominican Republic Ecuador El Salvador Gabon Gambia Guatemala Guinea Haiti Honduras Iran Kenya Democratic Kampuchea Kuwait Lebanon Liberia Mauritania Nepal Pakistan Panama Philippines Qatar Senegal Suriname Saudi Arabia Swaziland Syrian Arab Republic Togo Trinidad and Tobago Yemen	Bangladesh Central African Empire Colombia Guyana Jamaica Malaysia Malawi Mexico Mozambique Sierra Leone United Arab Emirates	Benin Iraq Somalia	Argentina Ghana Zaire	Burma Congo Morocco Venezuela	Madagascar	Chile India Libyan Arab Jamahiriya Nigeria Peru Zambia	Algeria Angola Egypt Ethiopia Indonesia Sri Lanka Sudan United Republic of Tanzania Uganda
Countries								
Total	71	11	3	3	4	1	6	9
Percentage	100	15	4	4	6	1	8	13
Cases								
Total	93	80	37	56	91	26	236	750
Percentage	7	6	3	4	7	2	17	55

Source: Same as table 1.8.

27

Fig. 1.1. Import dependence of the European Community, by product and developing country, 1977.[a]

Product	Percent and country				Percent of all DCs
	0	50	100		
Beef	43.6	15.1		Argentina, Botswana	70.4
Processed meat	29.9	18.1	4.2	Argentina, Brazil, Kenya	59.1
Tuna	23.3	22.1	13.7	Ivory Coast, Senegal, Taiwan	72.6
Pineapples fresh	78.8			Ivory Coast	96.3
Pineapples processed	27.1	17.5	12.5	Ivory Coast, Kenya, Malaysia	84.6
Tea	34.5	19.8		India, Kenya	95.3
Groundnut oil	59.4			Senegal	97.2
Groundnut cake	37.4	31.4		India, Senegal	99.2
Copra	81.7			Philippines	99.8
Copra oil	84.6			Philippines	99.9
Copra cake	57.1			Philippines	99.7
Palm oil	63.1			Malaysia	63.1
Palm nuts	81.0			Malaysia	100.0
Palm cake	53.5			Malaysia	96.9
Cocoa beans	21.0	20.8	19.2	Nigeria Ivory Coast, Ghana	96.4
Cocoa paste, nondefatted	38.1	34.8		Ivory Coast, Ecuador	99.6
Cocoa paste, defatted	34.6	24.4		Ivory Coast, Ghana	98.5
Cocoa butter	30.4	16.5	16.4	Ghana, Brazil, Nigeria	87.7
Sugar	26.6	15.4	10.6	Mauritius Réunion, Fiji	96.0
Rum	27.8	20.0	12.6	Bahamas, Martinique, Guyana	96.5
Natural rubber	68.1			Malaysia	99.2
Sisal fibers	48.8	20.6		Brazil, Tanzania	99.2
Gum arabic	74.1			Sudan	98.9
Wood, nonconif.	34.2	11.9	7.8	Ivory Coast, Gabon, Cameroon	82.9
Calcium phosphates	39.6	13.4		Morocco, Togo	67.2
Copper ore	45.3	12.8		Papua N.G., Chile	72.8
Copper for refining	41.5	15.5		Zaire, Chile	63.3
Refined copper	23.7	17.4	15.8	Zambia, Chile, Zaire	61.6

Product	Percent and country				Percent of all DCs
	0	50	100		
Aluminum ore	39.7	9.9	4.3	Guinea, Guyana, S. Léone	59.3
Aluminum oxide	25.1	19.9	6.2	Jamaica, Suriname, Guinea	53.2
Tin ore	43.5	19.0		Bolivia, Zaire	82.2
Cobalt	42.5	26.4		Zaire, Zambia	70.0
Petroleum oils	29.8	16.5	9.6	Saudi Arabia, Iran, Iraq	95.2

Source: The Courier, No. 52 (Nov.–Dec. 1978).
[a]Products for which three or fewer developing countries account for 50 percent or more of imports.

1970 and 1974, on the other hand, the income of OPEC member countries increased by about $80 billion. Moreover, as already pointed out, most oil production facilities passed into domestic ownership. It is not surprising that OPEC's success led to the expansion of old and the creation of new producers' associations (see table 1.12). OPEC itself gained new members after 1973, as did the Intergovernmental Council of Copper Exporting Countries, the Asian and Pacific Coconut Community, the Cocoa Producers' Alliance, the Association of Natural Rubber Producing Countries, and the Inter-African Coffee Organization. In 1974, the International Bauxite Association (IBA), the Association of South East Asian Timber Producing Countries, the International Association of Mercury Producing Countries, the Union of Banana Exporting Countries, and the Economic Group of Latin American and Caribbean Sugar Exporting Countries were established. One year later, the iron-exporting countries, the African timber exporting countries, and the primary tungsten producing countries followed suit.

One of the most successful new organizations was the IBA. The establishment of such an organization had already been proposed several years earlier by Guyana in order to obtain the solidarity of other countries for Guyana's nationalization negotiations with Alcan. Guyana was not supported until the end of 1972 when Jamaica, for similar reasons, renewed the initiative. At that time, Jamaica announced that it wanted to renegotiate its contracts with the transnational bauxite/aluminum enterprises operating in that country.[37]

The IBA was founded in March 1974 during a conference in Conakry of the most important bauxite-exporting countries.[38] Shortly thereafter, Jamaica opened negotiations with the transnational bauxite/aluminum enterprises. During the negotiations, the government requested that the formula for the determination of royalty and producer-levy payments for the bauxite sold be linked to the price of the finished product, aluminum[39]; that the lands currently owned by the enterprises revert to the government; that the government reacquire control of the bauxite ore; and that the government par-

Table 1.10. Developed Market Economies: Dependence on
Primary Commodity Imports from Developing Countries, 1974–1976
(Percent)

| Raw materials[a] | All DMEs | of which | | |
		European Community	Japan	United States
All raw materials (0–5)				
1974	48.1	43.0	63.6	63.9
1976	46.3	38.4	62.6	66.6
Food, beverages, tobacco (0-1)				
1974	29.7	21.4	34.8	59.7
1976	29.7	22.2	34.3	59.2
Crude materials, excl. fuels, oils, fats (2,4)				
1974	28.7	24.9	36.7	40.6
1976	27.1	23.2	36.6	33.7
Minerals, fuels and related materials (3)				
1974	78.5	78.5	87.4	79.1
1976	74.9	70.3	85.0	83.6
Chemicals (5)				
1974	4.4	2.4	19.2	13.2
1976	3.7	2.1	15.6	12.0

Source: United Nations, *Yearbook of International Trade Statistics 1977,* vol. 1 (New York: UN, 1978).
[a]SITC, rev., Section Nos. given in parentheses.

ticipate in the ownership of the bauxite and aluminum operations in Jamaica. By the end of 1974, all issues had been resolved to the government's satisfaction (although several years later concessions had to be made again on the level of the bauxite levy). The country's income due to higher payments on bauxite alone increased during this year from $25 million to $160 million.

Although these negotiations were not conducted within the framework of the IBA, other bauxite-producing countries immediately followed Jamaica's example. The Dominican Republic began, in April 1974, to negotiate with Alcoa about, among other things, the introduction of the vertical indexation procedure. Guyana proposed the same measure in July of that year. Suriname concluded a contract with Alcoa in November 1974 that was expected to increase the bauxite revenue of the country from about $7–10 million to $23–35 million in 1974 alone. Through similar negotiations, Haiti increased its annual income from $1.8 million to more than $11 million. In Australia, the state government of Queensland increased royalty levies from A$0.05 to A$0.50 per ton for bauxite processed in the country. The Australian federal government followed this initiative and requested increased royalty payments as well. By the end of the year, Sierra Leone had entered into negotiations with Alusuisse, and Guinea had announced that it would introduce vertical indexation.[40]

The developments in the bauxite industry during 1974 demonstrate the effects of the new consciousness of the developing countries. They also demonstrate which impulses can be generated by the establishment of a producers' association. It should be noted

Table 1.11. Producers' Associations (and Their Members) that are Possible Members of the Council of Producers' Associations, 1978[ab]

Producers' association	Africa	Asia	Middle East	Western hemisphere	Other
African Groundnuts Council	Gambia, Mali, Niger, Nigeria,**** Senegal, Sudan				
Afro-Malagasy Coffee Organization	Benin,* Central African Empire,** Congo,* Gabon,**** Ivory Coast,*** Madagascar,** Togo,** United Rep. of Cameroon***				
Asian and Pacific Coconut Community		India,*** Indonesia,****** Malaysia,*** Papua New Guinea,** Philippines,** Samoa, Singapore,* Solomon Islands, Sri Lanka,* Thailand,*			
Association of Iron Ore Exporting Countries	Algeria,** Mauritania,* Sierra Leone,** Tunisia	India***		Peru,*** Venezuela**	Australia,*** Sweden
Association of Natural Rubber Producing Countries		Indonesia,****** India,*** Malaysia,*** Papua New Guinea,** Singapore,* Sri Lanka,* Thailand,* Viet Nam*			
Cocoa Producers' Alliance	Gabon,**** Ghana,** Ivory Coast,*** Nigeria,**** Togo,** United Rep. of Cameroon***			Brazil,** Ecuador,** Trinidad and Tobago*	

Table 1.11. Producers' Associations (and Their Members) that are Possible Members of the Council of Producers' Associations, 1978[ab] (cont.)

Producers' association	Africa	Asia	Middle East	Western hemisphere	Other
Economic Group of Latin American and Caribbean Sugar Exporting Countries		(Philippines**)		Argentina, Barbados, Brazil,** Colombia,* Costa Rica,* Cuba, Dominican Republic,** Ecuador,** El Salvador, Guatemala,* Guyana,* Honduras,* Jamaica,* Mexico,** Nicaragua, Panama,* Paraguay, Peru,*** Trinidad and Tobago,* Venezuela**	
Inter-African Coffee Organization	Angola, Benin,* Burundi, Central African Empire,** Congo,** Ethiopia, Gabon,**** Ivory Coast,*** Kenya, Liberia,* Madagascar,** Nigeria,**** Rwanda,* Sierra Leone,** Togo,** Uganda, United Rep. of Cameroon,*** United Rep. of Tanzania,* Zaire***				
Inter-African Organization of Timber	Central African Empire,** Congo,** Equatorial Guinea, Gabon,**** Ghana,** Ivory Coast,*** Liberia,*				

32

Organization	Africa	Asia and Pacific	Arab countries	Latin America	Developed countries
Intergovernmental Council of Copper Exporting Countries	(Mauritania*), Zaire,*** Zambia	Indonesia,****** (Papua New Guinea**)		Chile, Peru***	(Australia***), (Yugoslavia*))
International Bauxite Association	Ghana,** Guinea, Sierra Leone**	Indonesia******		Dominican Republic,** Guyana,* Haiti, Jamaica,* Suriname	Australia,*** Yugoslavia*
Organization of Petroleum Exporting Countries	Algeria,** Gabon,**** Libya, Nigeria****	Indonesia******	Iran, Iraq, Kuwait, Qatar, Saudi Arabia, United Arab Emirates	Ecuador,** Venezuela**	
Pepper Community		India,*** Indonesia,****** Malaysia***			
Primary Tungsten Association	Rwanda,* Zaire***	(China), (Rep. of Korea), Thailand*		Bolivia, (Brazil**), Mexico,** Peru***	Australia,*** (Canada), Portugal
Union of Banana Exporting Countries	Madagascar,** Nigeria,**** United Rep. of Cameroon,*** United Rep. of Tanzania,* Zaire***			Colombia,* Costa Rica,* Dominican Republic,** Guatemala,** Honduras,* Panama*	

Source: Gonzalo Martner, *Producers-Exporters Associations of Developing Countries: An Instrument for the Establishment of a New International Economic Order* (Geneva: IFDA, 1978); Helge Hveem, *The Political Economy of Third World Producer Associations* (Oslo: Univeritetsforlaget, 1978), and various other sources.

[a] Only intergovernmental producers' associations can become members of the Council. For this reason, the Council of the Southeast Asian Lumber Producers' Association and the International Association of Mercury Producing Countries are not included here.

[b] Countries in parenthesis have associate or observer status. Countries with double membership (regardless of whether a full member or observer) are starred once, those with triple membership twice, etc.

Table 1.12. Producers' Associations: Enlargements and Establishments
Before and After 1973[a]
(As of 1978)

Name and year of establishment	Members before 1973	Members 1973 and later
Afro-Malagasy Coffee Organization (1960)	Benin, Central African Empire, Congo, Gabon, Ivory Coast, Madagascar, Togo, United Rep. of Cameroon	
Inter-African Coffee Organization (1960)	Benin, Burundi, Central African Empire, Congo, Ethiopia, Gabon, Ivory Coast, Kenya, Liberia, Madagascar, Nigeria, Rwanda, Sierra Leone, Togo, Uganda, United Rep. of Cameroon, United Rep. of Tanzania, Zaire	Angola
Organization of Petroleum Exporting Countries (1960)	Abu Dhabi,[b] Algeria, Indonesia, Iran, Iraq, Kuwait, Libya, Nigeria, Qatar, Saudi Arabia, Venezuela	Ecuador, Gabon, United Arab Emirates[c]
Cocoa Producers' Alliance (1962)	Brazil, Ghana, Ivory Coast, Nigeria, Togo, United Rep. of Cameroon	Ecuador, Gabon, Trinidad and Tobago
African Groundnuts Council (1964)	Gambia, Mali, Niger, Nigeria, Senegal, Sudan	
Intergovernmental Council of Copper Exporting Countries (1967)	Chile, Peru, Zaire, Zambia	Australia,[d] Indonesia, Mauritania,[d] Papua New Guinea,[d] Yugoslavia[d]
Asian and Pacific Coconut Community (1969)	India, Indonesia, Malaysia, Philippines, Singapore, Sri Lanka, Thailand	Papua New Guinea, Samoa, Solomon Islands[d]
Association of Natural Rubber Producing Countries (1970)	Indonesia, Malaysia, Singapore, Sri Lanka, Thailand, Viet Nam	India, Papua New Guinea
Pepper Community (1972)	India, Indonesia, Malaysia	
Council of the Southeast Asian Lumber Producers' Association (1974)		Indonesia, Malaysia, Philippines
Economic Group of Latin American and Caribbean Sugar Exporting Countries (1974)		Argentina, Barbados, Brazil, Colombia, Costa Rica, Cuba, Dominican Republic, Ecuador, El Salvador, Guatemala, Guyana, Honduras, Jamaica, Mexico, Nicaragua, Panama, Paraguay, Peru, Philippines,[d] Trinidad and Tobago, Venezuela
International Association of Mercury Producing Countries (1974)		Algeria, Italy, Mexico, Spain, Turkey
International Bauxite Association (1974)		Australia, Dominican Republic, Ghana, Guinea, Guyana, Haiti, Indonesia, Jamaica, Sierra Leone, Suriname, Yugoslavia

Union of Banana Exporting Countries (1974)	Colombia, Costa Rica, Dominican Republic, Guatemala, Honduras, Panama
Association of Iron Ore Exporting Countries (1975)[e]	Algeria, Australia, India, Mauritania, Peru, Sierra Leone, Sweden, Tunisia, Venezuela
Inter-African Organization of Timber (1975)	Central African Empire, Congo, Equatorial Guinea, Gabon, Ghana, Ivory Coast, Liberia, Madagascar, Nigeria, United Rep. of Cameroon, United Rep. of Tanzania, Zaire
Primary Tungsten Association (1975)	Australia, Bolivia, Brazil,[d] Canada,[d] China,[d] Mexico, Peru, Portugal, Rep. of Korea,[d] Rwanda, Thailand, Zaire

Source: Same as Table 1.11.

[a]In 1978, the establishment of the following producers' associations was under discussion: Association of Phosphate Producers, Association of Oilseed Producing Countries, Asian and Pacific Tropical Timber Community, Association of Fishmeat Producers, and Latin American Meat Producers' Association. An effort to establish a producers' association for jute did not succeed.

[b]Later replaced by the United Arab Emirates.

[c]Replaces Abu Dhabi.

[d]Associate or observer.

[e]Chile withdrew in 1977.

that the IBA qua organization had originally not initiated any concerted or common efforts.[41] Rather, the initiatives were taken on the national level and parallel to each other on the basis of precedents and the demonstration effect associated with them. The function of the IBA was to facilitate the exchange of information; in addition, it served as a kind of safety net, since the formulation of a consensus had reduced the probability that, on the one hand, one producer country could jeopardize the negotiating position of another producer country by offering more favorable conditions and, on the other hand, that the transnational enterprises of the industry could play off the producer countries against each other. Thus, this kind of parallel-action solidarity strengthened the negotiating position of each country.

Most producers' associations will not be as successful as the OPEC or the IBA, even if the Council of Producers' Associations should succeed in improving their effectiveness through coordination, and even if multiple membership of individual countries in several associations should facilitate cooperation. The growing number of these associations and the increased insistence of the DCs on permanent sovereignty over natural resources demonstrate, however, that the nations of the Third World have become considerably more self-confident and assertive and no longer fear conflicts if their development is at stake.

The success of one of these producers' associations, OPEC, was, in fact, responsible for speeding up the schedule agreed upon at the 1973 Algiers summit. Following the oil embargo and the quadrupling of oil prices, the United States invited the major developed oil-consuming countries to a conference in Washington, scheduled to take place February 11-13, 1974. In reaction to this suggestion, the Algerian President, Houari Boumediène, in his capacity as the President-in-Office of the movement of the Non–Aligned Countries, requested the Secretary-General of the United Nations to convene a special session on the problems of raw materials and development. The Sixth Special Session, thus, was called to take place from April 9 to May 2, 1974. It adopted the "Declaration on the Establishment of a New International Economic Order" and the "Programme of Action on the Establishment of a New International Economic Order." The restructuring of the international economic system had become a priority item on the international agenda.

Notes

1. The documents of the Non-Aligned Countries and the "Final Communiqué" of the Bandung Conference are contained in Odette Jankowitsch and Karl P. Sauvant, eds., *The Third World without Superpowers: The Collected Documents of the Non-Aligned Countries* (Dobbs Ferry, N.Y.: Oceana, 1978), 4 vols.

2. Every developing country, regardless of United Nations membership, automatically belongs to the Group of 77. In 1979, its membership was 119. Yugoslavia has been included since the beginning. In addition, the Republic of Korea and Vietnam are members and, since the 1976 Manila ministerial meeting, so are Malta and Romania.
    The most important meetings of the Group take place at the ministerial level in order to prepare the negotiating positions of the developing countries for the UNCTAD conferences. The first ministerial conference took place in Algiers in 1967 and adopted the "Charter of Algiers"; the second was held in Lima in 1971 and adopted the "Lima Declaration and Programme of Action"; the third was the Manila Conference of 1976 and adopted the "Manila Declaration and Programme of Action"; and the fourth took place in Arusha in 1979 and adopted the "Arusha Programme for Collective Self-Reliance and Framework for Negotiations." All documents are contained in Karl P. Sauvant, ed., *The Third World without Superpowers,* 2d ser., *The Collected Documents of the Group of 77* (Dobbs Ferry, N.Y.: Oceana, 1980).

3. It is also this latter group of countries that registered the lowest GDP (and GDP per capita) growth rates in the 1960s and even lower ones in the first half of the 1970s.

4. See also United Nations, "Implementation of the Declaration on Social Progress and Development: Report of the Secretary-General" (E/CN.5/563), December 27, 1978; United Nations, *1978 Report on the World Social Situation* (New York: United Nations, 1979); and United Nations, *Patterns of Government Expenditure on Social Services: Supplement to the 1978 Report on the World Social Situation* (New York: United Nations, 1979).

5. UNCTAD, "New Directions and New Structures for Trade and Development: Report by the Secretary-General of UNCTAD to the Conference" (TD/183), April 14, 1976, pp. 5-6.

6. This target was not formally included in the resolution 1710 (XVI) of December 19, 1961 designating the decade of the 1960s as the Development Decade; however, a target of 1 percent of national income for foreign assistance was adopted by the UN in 1960, and in 1968 was changed by UNCTAD to 1 percent of GNP. This latter target came to be regarded as one of the fundamental objectives of the First Development Decade.

7. The processes involved here have, of course, been discussed extensively and most prominently in the *dependencia* literature. For a bibliography, see, for instance, Dieter Senghaas, ed., *Imperialismus und strukturelle Gewalt: Analysen über abhängige Reproduktion* (Frankfurt: Suhrkamp, 1972). See also the contributions in his *Peripherer Kapitalismus: Analysen über Abhängigkeit und Unterentwicklung* (Frankfurt: Suhrkamp, 1974); and, most importantly, his *Weltwirtschaftsordnung und Entwicklungspolitik: Plädoyer für Dissoziation* (Frankfurt: Suhrkamp, 1977).

8. Modern-sector-led GNP growth rates, then, do not necessarily measure progress toward a coherent economy, but rather tend to measure a worsening of structural heterogeneity.

9. In Jankowitsch and Sauvant, *Documents of the Non-Aligned Countries,* p. 86. Follow-up action on this pledge was taken during the 1972 Georgetown Conference of Ministers of Foreign Affairs of Non-Aligned Countries. See chap. 2.

10. As will be discussed in chap. 2, a major part of the activities of the Non-Aligned Countries takes place outside the United Nations system.

11. Naturally, the Group of 77 had already dealt with questions pertaining to economic cooperation among developing countries. In fact, it had even convened, in Mexico City, in September 1976, a "Conference on Economic Co-operation among Developing Countries" which adopted a number of detailed decisions. However, as the Group of 77 observed in the introduction of its "Arusha Programme," economic cooperation is but one (even if important) aspect of self-reliance: "Mindful . . . that Economic Co-operation among Developing Countries is *a key element* in a collective self-reliant strategy . . ." (emphasis added). The preceding ministerial conference of the Group of 77 in Manila, in January/February 1976 (in preparation of UNCTAD IV), dealt only with economic cooperation among developing countries and did not mention the concept of self-reliance. All documents are contained in Sauvant, *Documents of the Group of 77*.

12. See especially Senghaas, *Plädoyer für Dissoziation*.

13. GNP is also increased by efforts made to maintain or increase internal and external security (i.e., efforts that do not necessarily contribute to an improvement of the standard of living) or which become necessary to deal with undesired side effects of industrialization. The 1972 United Nations Conference on Environment highlighted the latter problem. For a discussion of the growth critique, see United Nations, *The International Development Strategy: First Over-all Review and Appraisal of Issues and Policies. Report of the Secretary-General* (New York: United Nations, 1973).

14. In the DMEs, another set of concerns — the energy and food (including fish) crises of the early 1970s (which raised the spectre of impending raw material scarcity) and the growing concern about the deterioration of the environment — led to doubts about the very desirability of growth-oriented economic policy. The Club of Rome's study by Donella H. Meadows et al., *The Limits to Growth: A Report for the Club of Rome's Project on the Predicament of Mankind* (New York: New American Library, 1972) was particularly influential in drawing attention to these questions. This general growth pessimism was rejected by the policymakers of the DCs as being dangerous for their industrialization plans.

15. In Jankowitsch and Sauvant, *Documents of the Non-Aligned Countries*, p. 178.

16. Ibid., pp. 217–18.

17. The Committee for Development Planning is an advisory body established by the Economic and Social Council to assist the United Nations in its activities concerning aspects of national planning and the work connected with the assessment of progress in the implementation of the International Development Strategy for the Second United Nations Development Decade.

This is not to say that the United Nations development debate had treated poverty as a side issue. The International Development Strategy for the Second United Nations Development Decade, for instance, stated explicitly in its preamble that "the ultimate objective must be to bring about sustained improvement in the well-being of the individual and bestow benefits on all." Furthermore, among its "goals and objectives," the Strategy specified:

> As the ultimate purpose of development is to provide increasing opportunities to all people for a better life, it is essential to bring about a more equitable distribution of income and wealth for promoting both social justice and efficiency of production, to raise substantially the level of employment, to achieve a greater degree of income security, to expand and improve facilities for education, health, nutrition, housing and social welfare, and to safeguard the environment. Thus, qualitative and structural changes in the society must go hand in hand with rapid economic growth, and existing disparities — regional, sectoral and social — should be substantially reduced. These objectives are both determining factors and end-results of development; they should therefore be viewed as integrated parts of the same process . . . [United Nations, *International Development Strategy* (New York: United Nations, 1970), pp. 2, 4.]

The criticism was, however, that the link between these objectives and the continuing growth emphasis had not been adequately constructed but had rather been left to an internal trickle-down effect.

18. United Nations, *Attack on Mass Poverty and Unemployment: Views and Recommendations of the Committee for Development Planning* (New York: United Nations, 1972), p.1.

19. Particularly important was the July 1975 issue of *Development Dialogue* (a journal published by the Swedish Dag Hammarksjöld Foundation) which was entitled "What Now: Another Development." See also William H. Matthews, ed., *Outer Limits and Human Needs: Resources and Environmental Issues of Development Strategies* (Uppsala: Dag Hammarskjöld Foundation, 1976); and Marc Nerfin, ed., *Another Development: Approaches and Strategies* (Uppsala: Dag Hammarskjöld Foundation, 1977).

20. In particular the 1972 Stockholm Conference on the Human Environment, the 1974 Rome World Food Conference, the 1974 Bucharest World Population Conference, the 1975 Mexico World Conference of the International Women's Year, the 1976 World Employment Conference, the 1976 Vancouver Conference on Human Settlements, the 1977 Mar del Plata Water Conference, and the 1978 Alma Ata International Conference on Primary Health Care.

21. See OECD, *Development Co-operation: 1977 Review* (Paris: OECD, 1977), pp. 149–51. A further discussion of this topic is contained in OECD, *Development Co-operation: 1978 Review* (Paris: OECD, 1978), especially pp. 27–36.

22. See, especially, the preparatory report for the World Employment Conference: ILO, *Employment, Growth and Basic Needs: A One-World Problem. Report of the Director-General of the International Labour Office* (Geneva: ILO, 1976) and the results of that conference: ILO, *Meeting Basic Needs: Strategies for Eradicating Mass Poverty and Unemployment. Conclusions of the World Employment Conference 1976* (Geneva: ILO, 1977).

The influence of the United Nations Environmental Programme was mainly based on studies and activities funded and supported by it. See, especially, the above-mentioned project of the Dag Hammarskjöld Foundation; a study by John McHale and Magda Cordell McHale, *Basic Human Needs: A Framework for Action. A Report to the U.N. Environment Programme* (New Brunswick, N.J.: Transaction Books, 1978); and an international symposium on "Patterns of Resource Use, Environment and Development Strategies," organized in cooperation with UNCTAD and held in Cocoyoco, Mexico, October 8–12, 1974. This symposium adopted the influential "Cocoyoco Declaration" which stated, inter alia:

> Our first concern is to redefine the whole purpose of development. This should not be to develop things but to develop man. Human beings have basic needs: food, shelter, clothing, health, education. Any process of growth that does not lead to their fulfillment — or, even worse, disrupts them — is a travesty of the idea of development. We are still in a stage where the most important concern of development is the level of satisfaction of basic needs for the poorest sections in each society which can be as high as 40 per cent of the population. The primary purpose of economic growth should be to ensure the improvement of conditions for these groups. A growth process that benefits only the wealthiest minority and maintains or even increases the disparities between and within countries is not development. It is exploitation. And the time for starting the type of true economic growth that leads to better distributions and to the satisfaction of the basic needs for all is today. We believe that 30 years of experience with the hope that rapid economic growth benefiting the few will "trickle down" to the mass of the people has proved to be illusory. We therefore reject the idea of "growth first, justice in the distribution of benefits later" [A/C.2/292 of November 1, 1974, p. 4].

23. Compare the literature cited in the preceding footnote. For an exposé of the basic-needs approach, see Paul P. Streeten, "Basic Needs: Premises and Promises," *Journal of Policy Modeling* 1 (January 1979): 136–46.

24. See especially Streeten, ibid., and Senghaas, *Weltwirtschaftsordnung*.

25. The emphasis, as far as the external dimension is concerned, is on "world market." A conflict does not necessarily arise in the case of an orientation toward other developing countries, precisely because at least parts of their consumption patterns are similar. In fact, the small domestic market size makes cooperation with other DCs (collective self-reliance) imperative for many DCs.

26. In fact, the Non-Aligned Countries perceive themselves as playing a "catalyst role" in the Group of 77; see chap. 2. For the broader theme of South-South co-operation, see Volker Matthies, "Süd/Süd-Beziehungen and Kollektive 'Self-Reliance'," *Verfassung und Recht in Übersee* 11 (1978): 59–87.

27. The concrete contents of the economic program of the Non-Aligned Countries — as far as world-market orientation is concerned — derive from the developmental concepts elaborated under Raúl Prebisch in the Economic Commission for Latin America in the early 1950s. Through the establishment in 1964 of UNCTAD — whose first Secretary-General was Prebisch — these concepts found a broader audience and subsequently became the basis of the work of the Group of 77 and the formulation of the strategies for the United Nations Development Decades. (See chap. 2 for a detailed discussion of the Non-Aligned Countries' economic program.)

28. Fourth Conference of Heads of State or Government, "Action Programme for Economic Co-operation," in Jankowitsch and Sauvant, *Documents of the Non-Aligned Countries*, p. 237.

29. Resolution 3172 (XXVIII).

30. The 1961 Belgrade "Declaration" of the Non-Aligned Countries, for instance, stated: "All people may, for their own ends, freely dispose of their natural wealth and resources without prejudice to any obligations arising out of international economic co-operation, based upon the principle of mutual benefit, and international law." In Jankowitsch and Sauvant, *Documents of the Non-Aligned Countries*, p. 5.

31. See, for instance, Chapter II, art. 2,2 (c) of the Charter of Economic Rights and Duties of States, quoted in chap. 3.

32. Although many of the nationalized affiliates have a very low book value (e.g., nationalizations in the banking and insurance sector account for one-quarter of all cases), a number of others, especially those in primary-products sectors, have a very high book value. A calculation based on book value may, therefore, suggest that nationalizations have been more important than indicated by numbers of cases alone. On the

other hand, it has to be taken into account that perhaps 10 percent of all nationalized affiliates were eventually returned to their former parent enterprises. Indonesia and Chile are particularly important examples for such reversals of policy.

33. See the data reported in United Nations, "Permanent Sovereignty over Natural Resources" (A/9716) and Corr. 1 of September 20, 1974, and (E/C/7/53), January 31, 1975.

34. Compare, in this context, the objectives of the International Bauxite Association and those of the Council of Producers' Associations cited below.

35. With a few exceptions; this proposal dates back at least to the 1955 Bandung Conference and is also contained, with details, in the "Final Act" adopted by UNCTAD I.

36. The relevant resolutions, the reports of the two expert groups charged with the establishment of these institutions, as well as the draft statutes, can be found in Jankowitsch and Sauvant, *Documents of the Non-Aligned Countries.* One of the functions of the Fund was to prepare for the possible failure of the Common Fund negotiations within UNCTAD. With the agreement reached in early 1979 on the Common Fund (see chap. 3), however, this facility may be quietly abandoned.

The Statute of the Council, as adopted by the Plenipotentiary Conference during an April 1978 meeting in Geneva, is contained in NAC/PC/1 of April 7, 1978. The aims and objectives of the Council are specified as follows (chap. 2, art. 2):

1. Promotion of effective methods of co-operation in order to restructure international trade in commodities, secure just and remunerative prices for the export products of developing countries, and to protect and improve in real terms the purchasing power of their export earnings. In the process the interests of all developing countries should be safeguarded by means of appropriate measures.
2. Mobilization of support for the measures taken by developing countries to recover control of their resources, and of production and marketing structures.
3. Organization of regular exchange of experience and results of scientific and technological research in the relevant fields between the various producer-exporter associations and also making their expertise available to any other group of developing countries producing a primary product and wishing to establish a similar producer-exporter association.
4. Co-ordination of the actions of the various associations and, if necessary, mobilization of common support for any particular association, within the framework of solidarity among developing countries and full exercise of their sovereignty over their natural resources, and the exploitation, processing and marketing thereof.
5. Co-operation and collective action against all coercive policies, practices and measures either direct or indirect against any of its members.
6. Promotion of financial co-operation between the various producer-exporter associations in the financing of such measures as their activities may require in pursuance of the aims and objectives of the Council.
7. Identification of the common measures to be taken by the producer-exporter associations in conformity with the measures and policies adopted by developing countries to control and regulate the activities of transnational corporations, inter alia, with a view to preserving and consolidating the permanent sovereignty of developing countries over their natural resources.
8. Assistance to and strengthening of existing producers' associations including the adherence to the fullest extent possible of non-participant producer developing countries, and encouragement for the establishment of new associations of developing countries' producers-exporters of raw materials.

37. At the time of the negotiations, Jamaica accounted for half of the bauxite imports of the United States and even a higher percentage of the imports of individual transnational bauxite/aluminum enterprises. Each of the four largest transnational enterprises of this industry — Alcan, Alcoa, Kaiser, and Reynolds — has important mines on the island.

38. The Statutes of the IBA, contained in the "Final Act of the International Conference of Bauxite-Producing Countries," specified the following objectives for the organization:

(a) To promote the orderly and rational development of the bauxite industry;
(b) To secure for member countries fair and reasonable returns from the exploitation, processing and marketing of bauxite and its products for the economic and social development of their peoples, bearing in mind the recognized interests of consumers;
(c) Generally to safeguard the interests of member countries in relation to the bauxite industry.

For this purpose, the members agreed to:

(a) Exchange information concerning all aspects of the exploitation, processing, marketing and use of bauxite and its derivatives;
(b) Endeavour to harmonize their decisions and policies relating to the exploration, mining, processing and marketing of bauxite, alumina and aluminium, bearing in mind the need to ensure that:
    (i) Member countries enjoy reasonable returns from their production;
    (ii) The consumers of these commodities are adequately supplied at reasonable prices;

(c) Take action aimed at securing maximum national ownership of and effective national control over the exploitation of this natural resource within their territories and to support as far as possible any such action on the part of member countries;

(d) Endeavour to ensure that operations or projected operations by multinational corporations in the bauxite industry of one member country shall not be used to damage the interests of other member countries;

(e) Conduct jointly such research as may be deemed appropriate in their mutual interest;

(f) Explore the possibilities of joint or group purchasing of materials and equipment and of providing common services to member countries in their mutual interest.

39. No international bauxite market exists since nearly all transactions are intracompany transactions or tied up in long-term purchasing agreements. Bauxite prices are, therefore, not suitable as a basis for the calculation of royalties and taxes (although they have been used for this purpose in the past). This was previously recognized by the U.S. government: "Bauxite is not subject to an *ad valorem* rate of duty and the average values may be arbitrary for accountancy between allied firms, etc." See United States, Department of the Interior, Bureau of Mines, *Minerals Yearbook*, 1972. vol. 1, *Metals, Minerals and Fuels* (Washington, D.C.: Superintendent of Documents, 1974), p. 194.

40. For further details, see United Nations, "Permanent Sovereignty."

41. This does not mean, however, that the organization remained inactive. In November 1974, for instance, a conference was organized to discuss the establishment of processing facilities in IBA countries. Later, the IBA decided to establish a minimum pricing policy for bauxite exports, with a base price of $24 per ton (c.i.f.) for 1978. In December 1978, the IBA agreed on a minimum standard price for bauxite of 2 percent of the North American price for aluminum ingot (it is expected that this minimum will increase to 2.5–3.0 percent). A goal range for the alumina price of 16–19 percent of the aluminum price was adopted as well. See United Nations, "Permanent Sovereignty over Natural Resources: Report of the Secretary-General" (E/C.7/99), March 14, 1979.

2

The Initiating Role of the
Non-Aligned Countries*

Odette Jankowitsch and Karl P. Sauvant

The non-aligned movement was founded in 1961 by a group of developing countries. During the first decade of its existence, the movement's activities focused mainly on the consolidation of the political independence of its members. At the turn of the decade, however, economic issues—and, more precisely, the problems of development— began to command increasing attention. Today, the non-aligned movement has become an international pressure group for the reorganization of the international economic system. In fact, it has played a key role in making the development issue a priority item on the international agenda.

Our objective in this chapter is to trace the transformation of the non-aligned movement from a loosely organized, political club into a highly structured, international pressure group and to examine its role in the discussions leading to the adoption of the program for the New International Economic Order. More specifically, we examine how the developing countries mobilized and organized themselves in the non-aligned movement; realized the importance of economic development as an essential component of political independence; formulated their economic program; submitted this program for action to the international community as a whole; and, finally, implanted their concerns on the international agenda. Since these processes were largely completed at the time of the Sixth and Seventh Special Sessions of the United Nations General Assembly, at which the resolutions pertaining to the New International Economic Order were adopted, this analysis of the non-aligned movement and its role does not extend beyond 1974/75.

In focusing on the set of questions identified in the preceding paragraph, we did not deal with a number of others that are also important. Particularly noteworthy among them is the role of the Group of 77. The Group of 77, together with the United Nations Conference on Trade and Development, was crucial in elaborating many of the individual elements of the program for the New International Economic Order. Another

*An earlier version of this chapter was presented at the Seventeenth Annual Convention of the International Studies Association, Toronto, February 1976. We gratefully acknowledge helpful comments by Ernst–Otto Czempiel, Rashleigh E. Jackson, Donald O. Mills, and Breda Pavlić.

one involves the political program of the Non-Aligned Countries.[1] Although economic matters have become the main source of the dynamics of the movement, political objectives remain high on its agenda; they are also important since some of them are a source of internal tensions and, thereby, may jeopardize the unity maintained so far on international economic matters. However, as far as the broad economic program is concerned, the commonalities are much more important than the differences. Hence, we did not analyze the internal cohesion of the movement. We recognize the importance of these questions, but we think they are sufficiently distinct to allow their exclusion from this chapter whose scope, in any case, is already a very broad one.

Mobilization and Organization

Mobilization

The origin of the non-aligned movement is the bipolar structure of the international system of the 1950s and the competition of both superpowers for allies among the emergent nations of the Third World. In reaction to this situation, a small number of states began to seek possibilities of maintaining their independence from the blocs while, simultaneously, establishing their role in the international political arena. The first major expression of these efforts was the Bandung Conference in 1955 at which a group of 29 Afro-Asian states discussed general socio-political problems and possibilities of cooperation.[2] Although non-alignment as a political concept was not the dominant ideological framework of that conference, the meeting gave important impetus to the formation of the non-aligned movement.

The movement began to crystallize at the end of the 1950s around some of the most prominent leaders of the emerging nations: Gamal Abdel Nasser, Jawaharlal Nehru, Kwame Nkrumah, Ahmed Sukarno, and Josip Broz Tito. On September 1, 1961, the First Conference of Heads of State or Government of Non-Aligned Countries opened in Belgrade.[3] With the exception of Ethiopia and Yugoslavia, all 25 countries attending the conference had achieved independence only after World War II and, taken individually, played only a marginal role in international politics.

During the first Summit of the Non-Aligned Countries and the preparations leading to it, guidelines for membership were defined and the broad philosophy of the movement was spelled out. The criteria of membership, which focused on the fundamental tenet of the group: non-alignment with either of the two superpowers, are:

1. The country should have adopted an independent policy based on the co-existence of States with different political and social systems and on non-alignment or should be showing a trend in favour of such a policy.
2. The country concerned should be consistently supporting the movements for National Independence.
3. The country should not be a member of a multilateral military alliance concluded in the context of Great Power conflicts.
4. If a country has a bilateral military agreement with a Great Power, or is a member of a regional defence pact, the agreement or pact should not be one deliberately concluded in the context of Great Power conflicts.
5. If it has conceded military bases to a foreign Power, the concession should not have been made in the context of Great Power conflicts.[4]

These criteria, however, indicate that non-alignment was not to mean a passive role in world politics. Rather, the states involved aim at formulating their own independent positions. Apart from a natural support for national self determination and opposition to apartheid, the primary objectives and interests of the Non-Aligned Countries were then (and continue to be) nonadherence to multilateral military pacts, disarmament, noninterference in the internal affairs of state, strengthening of the United Nations, democratization of international relations, and socioeconomic development. Added later were individual and collective self-reliance and the restructuring of the international economic system. At each gathering, acute political issues were discussed and resolutions passed on them; but, as a rule, they related directly or indirectly to the general principles of the movement and especially to the question of decolonization.

At the Belgrade Summit, only 25 countries participated as full members. This number expanded considerably with each of the following four summit and six foreign minister conferences, partly reflecting, thereby, the progress of decolonization. At the 1964 Cairo Summit, 47 countries participated as full members. The 1970 Lusaka Summit was attended by 53 countries, the 1973 Algiers Summit by 75, and participation reached 85 countries at the 1976 Colombo Summit (see table 2.1 for individual countries).

Throughout the 1960s, and especially since 1972, the non-aligned movement thus became increasingly attractive to the countries of the Third World and succeeded in mobilizing a growing number of them. While, in 1961, the Non-Aligned Countries represented only 25 percent of the United Nations' membership (28 percent if observer countries are added), this percentage reached 58 in 1976 (67 percent if observer countries are added). In reference to the membership in the Group of 77, this ratio changed from about 60 percent in 1964 to about 75 percent in 1976 (see Appendix B); if observer countries are added, the change is from about 75 percent to about 90 percent. The high stability in participation should be noted; once a country had joined the movement, it continued to attend with great regularity and regardless of changes in government. (Exceptions—like Chile's non-participation after 1973—however, do occur.)

The growing attractiveness of the movement can also be seen from the number of delegations participating in its conferences as observers or guests (see table 2.1 and Appendix B). Depending on the gathering, their rights range from full participation in all meetings (without, however, being part of the decision-making process) to participation in plenary meetings only. A number of countries so represented —and especially national liberation movements—have eventually become full members. Multilateral organizations also participate, although the United Nations did not attend until the 1970 Lusaka Summit. Finally, delegations have been invited to attend as guests. They include the four European neutral states (Austria, Finland, Sweden, and Switzerland); since the 1975 Lima Conference of Foreign Ministers, also Portugal and Romania; since the 1976 Colombo Summit, the Philippines; and since the 1978 Belgrade Conference of Foreign Ministers, Pakistan and San Marino.[5] Membership status is granted—upon application and in the light of the criteria mentioned above—by decision of a summit conference or by the Conference of Ministers of Foreign Affairs of Non-Aligned Countries.

However, the appeal of the movement has not been equally strong to countries in all geographical regions. It has already been noted that the movement has its roots in the Afro-Asian group of countries. This group dominated the movement numerically until the 1972 Georgetown Conference of Foreign Ministers. The location of this conference signaled that the countries of the developing western hemisphere had become both acceptable and interested and had begun to join (or to attend as observers) in greater numbers. (The participation of a growing number of Latin American countries is particularly noteworthy since it indicates that the movement is no longer viewed by them as

Table 2.1. Summit Conferences of the Non-Aligned Countries: Record of Participation, 1961–1976.

Members

Belgrade Summit 1961	Cairo Summit 1964	Lusaka Summit 1970	Algiers Summit 1973	Colombo Summit 1976[a]
Afghanistan	Afghanistan	Afghanistan	Afghanistan	Afghanistan
Algeria	Algeria	Algeria	Algeria	Algeria
Burma	Angola	Botswana	Argentina	Angola
Cambodia	Burma	Burundi	Bahrain	Argentine Republic
Ceylon	Burundi	Cameroon	Bangladesh	Bahrain
Congo	Cambodia	Central African Republic	Bhutan	Bangladesh
Cuba	Cameroon	Ceylon	Botswana	Benin
Cyprus	Central African Republic	Chad	Burma	Bhutan
Ethiopia	Ceylon	Congo (Brazzaville)	Burundi	Botswana
Ghana	Chad	Congo (Kinshasa)	Cambodia	Burma
Guinea	Congo (Brazzaville)	Cuba	Cameroon	Burundi
India	Cuba	Cyprus	Central African Republic	Cameroon (United Republic of)
Indonesia	Cyprus	Equatorial Guinea	Chad	Cape Verde
Iraq	Dahomey	Ethiopia	Chile	Central African Empire
Lebanon	Ethiopia	Ghana	Congo	Chad
Mali	Ghana	Guinea	Cuba	Comoros
Morocco	Guinea	Guyana	Cyprus	Congo
Nepal	India	India	Dahomey	Cuba
Saudi Arabia	Indonesia	Indonesia	Egypt (Arab Republic of)	Cyprus
Somalia	Iraq	Iraq	Equatorial Guinea	Democratic Kampuchea
Sudan	Islamic Republic of Mauritania	Jamaica	Ethiopia	Egypt (Arab Republic of)
Tunisia	Jordan	Jordan	Gabon	Equatorial Guinea
United Arab Republic	Kenya	Kenya	Gambia	Ethiopia
Yemen	Kuwait	Kuwait	Ghana	Gabon
Yugoslavia	Laos	Laos	Guinea	Gambia
	Lebanon	Lebanon	Guyana	Ghana
	Liberia	Lesotho	India	Guinea
	Libya	Liberia	Indonesia	Guinea-Bissau
	Malawi	Libya	Iraq	Guyana
	Mali	Malaysia	Ivory Coast	India
	Morocco	Mali	Jamaica	Indonesia
	Nepal	Mauritania	Jordan	Iraq
	Nigeria	Morocco	Kenya	Ivory Coast
	Saudi Arabia	Nepal	Kuwait	Jamaica
	Senegal	Nigeria	Laos	Jordan
		Rwanda	Lebanon	

Sierra Leone
Somalia
Sudan
Syria
Togo
Tunisia
Uganda
United Arab Republic
United Republic of Tanga-
nyika and Zanzibar
Yemen
Yugoslavia
Zambia

Sengal
Sierra Leone
Singapore
Somalia
South Yemen
Sudan
Swaziland
Syria
Tanzania
Trinidad and Tobago
Togo
Tunisia
Uganda
United Arab Republic
Yemen Arab Republic
Yugoslavia
Zambia

Kenya
Korea (Democratic
People's Republic of)
Kuwait
Lao People's Democratic
Republic
Lebanon
Lesotho
Liberia
Libyan Arab Jamahiriya
Ma;agascar
Malaysia
Maldives
Mali
Malta
Mauritania
Mauritius
Morocco
Mozambique
Nepal
Niger
Nigeria
Oman
Palestine Liberation
Organization
Panama
Peru
Qatar
Rwanda
Sao Tomé and Principe
Saudi Arabia
Senegal
Seychelles
Sierra Leone
Singapore
Somalia
Sri Lanka
Sudan
Swaziland
Syrian Arab Republic
Tanzania (United Republic
of)

Lesotho
Liberia
Libyan Arab Republic
Madagascar
Malaysia
Mali
Malta
Mauritania
Mauritius
Morocco
Nepal
Niger
Nigeria
Oman
Peru
Qatar
Rwanda
Saudi Arabia
Senegal
Sierra Leone
Singapore
Somalia
South Viet-Nam (Pro-
visional Revolutionary
Government of)
Sri Lanka
Sudan
Swaziland
Syrian Arab Republic
Togo
Trinidad & Tobago
Tunisia
Uganda
United Arab Emirates
United Republic of
Tanzania
Upper Volta
Yemen Arab Republic
Yemen (People's Demo-
cratic Republic of)
Yugoslavia
Zaire

Table 2.1. Summit Conferences (cont.)

Belgrade Summit 1961	Cairo Summit 1964	Lusaka Summit 1970	Algiers Summit 1973	Colombo Summit 1976[a]
			Zambia	Togo Trinidad & Tobago Tunisia Uganda United Arab Emirates Upper Volta Viet Nam (Socialist Republic of) Yemen Arab Republic Yemen (People's Democratic Republic of) Yugoslavia Zaire Zambia
TOTAL 25	47	53	75	85

Observers

Belgrade Summit 1961	Cairo Summit 1964	Lusaka Summit 1970	Algiers Summit 1973	Colombo Summit 1976
Bolivia Brazil Ecuador	Argentina Bolivia Brazil Chile Finland Jamaica League of Arab States Mexico Organization of African Unity Trinidad & Tobago Uruguay Venezuela	Argentina Barbados Bolivia Brazil Chile Ecuador Organization of African Unity Peru Republic of South Viet Nam (Provisional Revolutionary Government) United Nations Uruguay Venezuela	Afro-Asian Peoples' Solidarity Organization Angola: MPLA (Angola Popular Liberation Movement) FNLA (Angola National Liberation Movement) Arab League Barbados Bolivia Brazil Comores: MOLINACO (Comores Liberation Movement) Djibouti: MLD (Djibouti Liberation Movement)	Afro-Asian Peoples' Solidarity Organization Arab League Barbados Bolivia Brazil Djibouti: MLD (Djibouti Liberation Movement) FLCS (Somali Coast Liberation Movement) Ecuador El Salvador Grenada Islamic Conference Mexico Namibia: SWAPO (South West Africa People's

Organization)
Organization of African Unity
Puerto Rico: Socialist Party of Puerto Rico
South Africa: ANC (African National Congress) PAC (Pan African Congress of Azania)
United Nations
Uruguay
Venezuela
Zimbabwe: African National Council of Zimbabwe

FLCS (Somali Coast Liberation Front)
Ecuador
Guinea (Bisseau): PAIGC (African Front for the Liberation of Guinea and Cape Verde)
Mexico
Mozambique: FRELIMO (Mozambique Liberation Front)
Namibia: SWAPO (South West Africa Peoples' Organization)
Organization of African Unity
Palestine: PLO (Palestine Liberation Organization)
Panama
Puerto Rico: Socialist Party of Puerto Rico
São Tomé and Príncipe: CLS São Tomé (Liberation Committee for Príncipe and São Tomé)
Seychelles: SPUP (Seychelles People's Union Party)
South Africa: ANC (African National Congress) PAC (Pan African Congress of Azania)
United Nations
Uruguay
Venezuela
Zimbabwe: ZANU (Zimbabwe African National Union) ZAPU (Zimbabwe African People's Union)

| Total | 3 | 12 | 12 | 24 | 19 |

Table 2.1. Summit Conferences (cont.)

Belgrade Summit 1961	Cairo Summit 1964	Lusaka Summit 1970	Algiers Summit 1973	Colombo Summit 1976[a]
Guests				
		Afro-Asian Peoples' Solidarity Organisation	Austria	Austria
		Angola: UNITA (Uniao Nacionale para a Independencia Totale de Angola)	Finland	Finland
		Austria	Sweden	Philippines
		Finland		Portugal
		Mozambique: FRELIMO (Mozambique Liberation Front)		Romania
		South Africa: ANC (African National Congress) PAC (Pan African Congress)		Sweden
				Switzerland
TOTAL		6	3	7

[a]Belize has consultative status.

48

marginal but as an important factor in world politics.) Until then, only Cuba and several other Caribbean countries had taken part as full members; others had attended as observers. Thus, by 1978, the movement encompassed virtually the whole African continent, most of Asia, and about one-fourth of the countries of the developing western hemisphere (adding the observers from the last group, the share is close to three-fifths).

It should be noted that a number of countries of the Third World have *not* been invited to participate because of strong objections by a few countries (as had been the case with Pakistan, although with India's objections waning in recent years and Pakistan's interest increasing, the country was represented for the first time at the 1978 Belgrade Conference of Foreign Ministers), or because of more general opposition (e.g., the case of the Republic of Korea). On the other hand, a number of countries have remained outside the movement because they did not apply for membership due to national policy considerations. The case of Korea, as well as that of several other countries, also demonstrates the increased importance attached to the movement since strong efforts have been made by these countries to obtain invitations. The application of the original criteria for membership has, however, become more flexible over the years with the admission of such countries as Iraq, Saudi Arabia, and—with varying status—all but one of the Latin American countries. This reflects both the changing character of the movement and the hope that membership in the non-aligned group would have a socializing effect (i.e., encourage independent policy), thereby vindicating the criteria *ex post*.[6] Nevertheless, although the non-aligned movement includes most developing countries, it is not identical with the Group of 77 which encompassed 119 developing countries in 1979. The Non-Aligned Countries perceive themselves as having a higher common denominator than the Group of 77 and wish to play a catalyst role within the 77 to give a more political direction to the work of that group.[7]

Organization

The mobilization of Third World countries was accompanied by an intensification of their interaction. During the first decade of the movement, the organizational interaction of Non-Aligned Countries was confined to summits and preparatory foreign minister conferences held at irregular intervals. During that period, the non-aligned group resembled more an informal gathering of like-minded leaders than a movement or even a caucus. Signs of change became apparent at the end of the 1960s and, since then, the movement has developed an increasingly complex organizational structure (see fig. 2.1).

The principal organ of the movement is the Conference of Heads of State or Government. Since 1970, it is convened at three-year intervals. The leader of the country hosting a summit becomes the President-in-Office of the non-aligned group until the next summit[8] and as such is entrusted "with the function of taking all necessary steps to maintain contacts among member states, ensure continuity, and carry into effect the decisions, resolutions and directives of the Conference of Non-Aligned Countries."[9] During this period, the presiding country coordinates all activities of the non-aligned movement (unless otherwise specified; see, for instance, the role of the Co-ordinator Countries discussed below). In the absence of a secretariat, it also fulfills all necessary technical functions.[10]

The declarations, action programs, statements, and resolutions adopted at summit conferences reflect the agreement of the member countries at the highest level.[11]

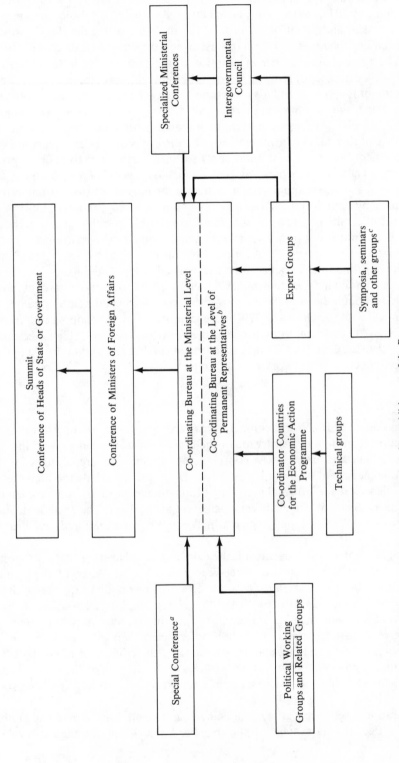

Figure 2.1. The organizational structure of the non-aligned movement.

[a]The first Special Conference, Cairo 1962, took place before the establishment of the Bureau.
[b]The Co-ordinating Bureau at the Level of Permanent Representatives also functions as preparatory committee for summits, foreign minister conferences, and meetings of the Bureau at the ministerial level.
[c]If no competent expert group exists, these meetings may report to any other body of the non-aligned movement.

Decision-making procedures follow the rule of consensus, i.e., no formal votes are taken. If a country disagrees, it can register its reservations, a practice used rather sparingly but increasingly. The decisions, communiqués, reports, and texts of meetings of the Non-Aligned Countries at all other levels are adopted according to the same procedures. (The practice of reservations is limited to high-level meetings.)

Summit conferences are prepared and immediately preceded by conferences of foreign ministers. Such conferences are also convened in the interim to review, coordinate, and stimulate the work of the movement (i.e., the Conferences of Ministers of Foreign Affairs at Georgetown 1972, Lima 1975, and Belgrade 1978) or to deal with special questions (i.e., the Extraordinary Conferences of Ministers of Foreign Affairs at New York in September 1977 and May 1978).

Until 1970, these two institutional layers were the only regular organs of the movement, supported by occasional ad hoc gatherings at various levels, as well as the work of the Preparatory Committee. After the third summit (Lusaka 1970), the Preparatory Committee was entrusted with additional responsibilities for coordinating the activities of the movement. At the next summit (Algiers 1973), a decision was taken to establish formally the Co-ordinating Bureau of Non-Aligned Countries at the Ministerial Level with the tasks of, inter alia,

> Making preparations for the Fifth Summit Conference of the non-aligned countries;
>
> Making preparations on matters of substance, for the next conference of Ministers for Foreign Affairs to be held between the Fourth and Fifth Summit Conferences;
>
> Co-ordinating the activities and the positions of Governments, particularly in the United Nations; . . .
>
> Supervising and facilitating the discharge of the responsibilities incumbent upon the various members with regard to the Action Programme for Economic Co-operation among Non-Aligned Countries.[12]

In the course of the following years, the scope of the Bureau's work increasingly expanded to include all tasks necessary for the functioning of the movement. Consequently, it became necessary to delegate part of the work from the ministerial to the ambassadorial level for implementation by the Co-ordinating Bureau of the Non-Aligned Countries at the Level of Permanent Representatives.[13]

An organizational decision of the fifth summit (Colombo 1976) formalized this division of labor and the expanded functional responsibility of the Bureau.[14] Thus, today the Co-ordinating Bureau of the Non-Aligned Countries, composed of representatives of up to 25 countries (see fig. 2.2), meets at two levels: (1) "at the level of Ministers of Foreign Affairs or special Government representatives once a year or as necessary," and (2) "on a continuing basis, at the level of Permanent Representatives of Non-Aligned Countries at the United Nations Headquarters in New York, once a month as a rule."[15] Summit conferences renew the mandate of the Bureau and decide upon its composition. In fact, the Co-ordinating Bureau, with the presiding country in the chair, has become the executive organ of the movement.

A new organizational entity seems to be emerging in the form of Specialized Ministerial Conferences. Attended by ministers of a given substantive area, they serve to focus attention on themes of particular concern to the developing countries. So far, three such conferences have taken place, one dealing with information and mass media, one with cooperation in fishery questions, and the third one with labor questions.

A distinct time pattern is emerging as far as high-level meetings between summits are concerned (see fig. 2.3): a summit is usually held in August/September, before the

Fig. 2.2. Members of the Co-ordinating Bureau of Non-Aligned Countries, 1976–1979

1. Algeria	14. Niger
2. Angola	15. Nigeria
3. Bangladesh/Afghanistan[a]	16. Palestine Liberation Organization
4. Botswana	17. Peru
5. Chad	18. Sri Lanka[b]
6. Cuba	19. Sudan
7. Guinea	20. Syrian Arab Republic
8. Guyana	21. United Republic of Tanzania
9. India	22. Viet Nam
10. Indonesia	23. Yugoslavia
11. Iraq	24. Zaire
12. Jamaica	25. Zambia
13. Liberia	

[a]Bangladesh occupies the seat for the first half and Afghanistan for the second half of the three-year term of office.
[b]In the chair.

beginning of the United Nations General Assembly. A meeting of the Bureau at the ministerial level during the early months of the next year reviews the results of both the summit and of the General Assembly. It is followed by another meeting of the Bureau at the ministerial level in time for the next General Assembly. A mid-term conference of foreign ministers, prepared by a meeting of the Bureau at the ministerial level (which also reviews the outcome of the preceding General Assembly) deals with the entire agenda of the movement, especially in the light of the impending General Assembly. Finally, the next summit is prepared by a conference of foreign ministers, which is itself preceded and prepared by the Bureau at the ministerial level. Bureau meetings at the level of permanent representatives are held during the entire period and have been held at least once a month since the Colombo Summit.

As determined at the Algiers Summit, the Bureau also supervises the work of the Co-ordinator Countries for the Action Programme for Economic Co-operation Among Non-Aligned Countries. The 1972 Georgetown Conference of Foreign Ministers identified four fields of activity related to this Action Programme; at a later meeting, several countries were appointed for its implementation. Subsequently, new areas were added for a total of 19 by the end of 1978 (see table 2.2). The Co-ordinator Countries have come to carry out a substantial part of the Non-Aligned Countries' economic activities and some of them have become the driving force for extensive interregional projects.[16] In so doing, they have initiated a number of technical groups that lend them the necessary detailed analysis.[17]

In certain areas, the Co-ordinator Countries can also draw on the results of expert groups that have sprung up mostly in the aftermath of the 1973 Algiers Summit.[18] Virtually all of them deal with economic matters, reflecting the increased emphasis placed, since 1973, on development issues. Some of these expert groups were established by the Conference of Developing Countries on Raw Materials (Dakar 1975)[19] and all developing countries are expressly invited to participate in them.[20] Their main focus is UNCTAD. The work of these expert groups is particularly important because it determines, to a large extent, the detailed, substantive content of the policies of the Non-Aligned Countries.

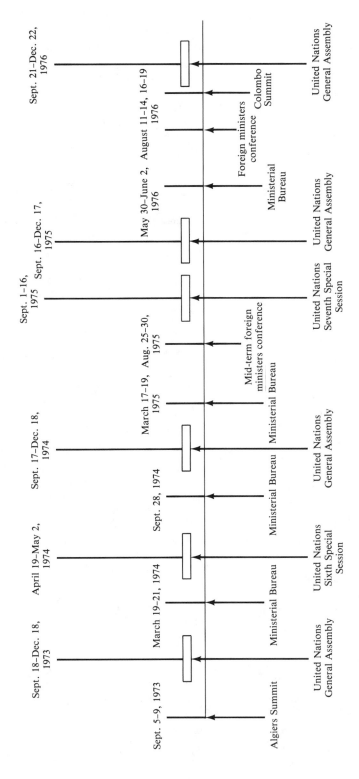

Fig. 2.3. Time pattern of high-level meetings of Non-Aligned Countries between Summits, exemplified for the period between the Algiers and Colombo Summits.

Table 2.2. Action Programme for Economic Co-operation: Fields of Activity
and Co-ordinator Countries, August 1978[a]

Field of activity	Co-ordinator countries[b]
1. International Cooperation for Development*	*Egypt,* Nigeria, Panama
2. Trade, Transport, and Industry*	Afghanistan, *Guyana*
3. Financial and Monetary Cooperation*	Cuba, India, Indonesia, Peru, Sri Lanka, *Yugoslavia*
4. Scientific and Technological Development*	*Algeria,* India, Peru, Somalia, Yugoslavia
5. Technical Cooperation and Consultancy Services	*India,* Panama
6. Food and Agriculture	Democratic Republic of Korea, Ethiopia, Morocco, Somalia, Sri Lanka, *Sudan,* Tanzania, Viet Nam
7. Fisheries	Angola, *Cuba,* Libya, Malta, Morocco, Somalia, Sri Lanka, Viet Nam
8. Telecommunications	Burundi, *Cameroon,* Central African Empire
9. Insurance	[c]
10. Health	Central African Empire, *Cuba,* Yugoslavia
11. Employment and Human Resources Development	Bangladesh, Cuba, Nigeria, Panama, *Sri Lanka,* Tunisia
12. Tourism	Cameroon, Cyprus, Morocco, *Tunisia,* Yemen Arab Republic
13. Transnational Corporations	Algeria, *Cuba*
14. Sports	*Algeria,* Cuba
15. Raw Materials	Afghanistan, Algeria, Cameroon, Cuba, Indonesia, Iraq, Panama, Peru, Senegal[d]
16. Research and Information System	India, Peru, Sri Lanka, Tunisia, *Yugoslavia*
17. Ad Hoc Group for the Solidarity Fund for Economic and Social Development	Bangladesh, Kuwait, *Sri Lanka*
18. Role of Women in Development	Angola, Bangladesh, Cameroon, Central African Empire, Cuba, Democratic Peoples' Republic of Korea, India, *Iraq,* Jamaica, Liberia, Yugoslavia
19. Peaceful Uses of Nuclear Energy	Algeria, Argentina, Central African Empire, Cuba, Egypt, Ethiopia, Gabon, Indonesia, Libya, Morocco, Niger, Nigeria, Tunisia, Yugoslavia[e]

[a]The starred fields of activity are the four original ones decided upon at the 1972 Georgetown Conference of Foreign Ministers.

[b]The countries that are italicized are the principal coordinator countries; as a rule, they take the initiative for calling meetings of the group, etc.

[c]No coordinator country has as yet been designated.

[d]The group meets in Geneva. No principal coordinator country has been designated.

[e]The principal coordinator country has not yet been designated since this field was only designated by the 1978 Belgrade Conference of Foreign Ministers.

In the political area, the substantive preparatory work is usually carried out through Working Groups (see table 2.3) that function primarily in the framework of the main political organs of the United Nations. They evolved in a formal manner only after the Algiers Summit and have the specific purpose of defining "a common position for the Group as a whole and for suggesting an appropriate course of action in the General Assembly."[21] The members of these working groups initiate and sponsor resolutions, organize support for them, coordinate speakers on a given item, and, more generally,

Table 2.3. Composition of the Working and Related Groups of the Non-Aligned Countries
in the United Nations in New York, August 1978[a]

Group	Member
Working Group on Korea	Algeria, Cuba, Somalia, Sri Lanka, Syria
Working Group on Disarmament and International Security	Algeria,[b] Argentina,[b] Bangladesh, Brazil,[b,c] Cyprus, Egypt,[b] Ethiopia, India,[b] Indonesia, Iraq, Malaysia,[b] Mali, Mexico,[b,c] Morocco, Nepal, Nigeria,[b] Peru,[b] Sri Lanka,[b] Yugoslavia[b]
Working Group for the Solidarity Fund for the Reconstruction of Viet Nam and Laos[d]	Algeria,[e] Angola, Cuba,[e] Guyana, India, Iraq, Laos, Libya, Panama, Sri Lanka,[e] Tanzania, Viet Nam, Yugoslavia[e]
Working Group on Southern Africa	Angola, Botswana, Chad, Cuba, Guinea, Guyana, India, Jamaica, Liberia, Nigeria, Palestine Liberation Organization, Sri Lanka, Sudan, Syria, Viet Nam, Yugoslavia
Working Group for the Solidarity Fund for the Liberation of Southern Africa[f]	Algeria, Cuba, Guyana, India, Sri Lanka, Yugoslavia
Working Group on Palestine and the Middle East	Algeria, Chad, Cuba, Guinea, India, Iraq, Jordan, Kuwait, Mali, Niger, Palestine Liberation Organization, Sri Lanka, Sudan, Syria, Viet Nam, Yugoslavia
Working Group on the United Nations	Algeria, Bangladesh, India, Iraq, Jamaica, Libya, Sri Lanka, Yugoslavia, Zambia
Contact Group on Cyprus	Algeria, Guyana, India, Mali, Sri Lanka,[g] Yugoslavia
Drafting Group on Interferences in International Affairs of States	Algeria, Angola, Bangladesh, Botswana, Cuba, Guyana, Liberia, Sri Lanka, Yugoslavia, Zambia

[a]The Working Group on the Admission of Viet Nam to the United Nations ceased to exist upon the admission of Viet Nam to the United Nations in 1977. Its members were Algeria, Angola, Cuba, Guyana, Sri Lanka, and Viet Nam.

[b]Member of the Drafting Group for the Special Session of the General Assembly devoted to disarmament.

[c]Observer in the non-aligned movement.

[d]After the establishment of the Solidarity Fund for the Reconstruction of Viet Nam and Laos, the Working Group converted itself into the Administrative Council for the purpose of operating this fund. Originally, this fund was also planned to be earmarked for Kampuchea; however, that country declined any foreign assistance.

[e]Co-ordinator.

[f]After the establishment of the Solidarity Fund for the Liberation of Southern Africa, the Working Group converted itself into the Administrative Council for the purpose of operating this fund.

[g]Ex-officio.

perform a management function for the non-aligned group and even the developing countries as a whole.

These working groups usually function in an informal manner[22] and form part of a broader and increasingly intricate set of consultations and coordination efforts of the Non-Aligned Countries at all levels. At times, these informal routine meetings—which, since the 1976 Colombo Summit, also include the frequent meetings of the Co-ordinating Bureau at the Level of Permanent Representatives—are concluded by formal statements or communiqués.[23] Most of these on-going activities take place within the United Nations which is still the main focus of the Non-Aligned Countries' attention.[24]

While the institutions described so far constitute the regular organizational layers of the non-aligned movement, a number of meetings have been convened on an ad hoc basis. As a rule, they originate in the initiative of individual countries particularly interested in a given subject matter, and take the form of technical symposia, seminars, and the like.[25] Their conclusions are taken up by competent expert groups; in the absence of such expert groups, results may be taken up by any other part of the organization.

In two instances, however, such ad hoc activities took place at a high political level: the Conference on the Problems of Economic Development (Cairo 1962), and the Conference of Developing Countries on Raw Matierials (Dakar 1975). Moreover, they were explicitly designed to include all developing countries in order to discuss questions of paramount importance to the entire Third World in the broadest possible framework. The Dakar conference, most notably, led to the creation of a number of (non-aligned) expert groups—most important among them were those dealing with raw-material issues—and thus gave great impetus to the economic work of the movement.

The 1970 Lusaka Summit, at which several delegations had stressed the need for increased, regular, and closer cooperation among the developing countries, marked the beginning of a more structured and institutionalized phase of the non-aligned movement. It also marked a certain change of outlook of the movement. While earlier meetings addressed themselves to third countries and especially to the superpowers,[26] later ones chiefly emphasized intragroup communication. This reflects the growing acceptance—and the mechanics—of the principle of self-reliance which had been enunciated at the 1970 Lusaka Summit. The result of these changes was increased coordination and communication among Non-Aligned Countries leading, also, to the involvement of a growing number of representatives at more levels of responsibility who produced increasingly subject-oriented, comprehensive, and detailed documents. For instance, the first two summits expressed their deliberations in short statements. The 1976 Colombo Summit, on the other hand, adopted two declarations, one action program, 33 resolutions, and one decision.

The intensified interaction among Non-Aligned Countries serves an important function in establishing lines of communication that did not exist before. During the colonial period, all lines of communication (including infrastructure) were directed toward the metropolitan areas, and hardly any communication existed among colonies, not to speak of territories belonging to different colonial administrations. These inherited structures constitute a severe handicap for coordination and cooperation among the developing countries. Beyond that, gatherings of the Non-Aligned Countries provide newly independent countries with a medium (in addition to the Group of 77 and the United Nations) through which they are introduced and socialized into international politics and, especially, the overall concerns of the Third World. Consequently, even where gatherings and institutions may not have had the desired follow-up (in relation to their terms of reference), the non-aligned movement has succeeded in mobilizing most developing countries, in setting up a highly structured organization, and in establishing a close network of communication for intensive interaction among its members.

The Emergence of an International Economic Pressure Group

The impetus to the economic work of the movement provided by the 1975 Dakar Conference accelerated a trend that had originated at the 1970 Lusaka Summit, further evolved at the Georgetown Conference of Foreign Ministers, and culminated at the 1973 Algiers Summit: the emergence of development and related economic issues as principal objectives of the non-aligned movement. While political matters did not decline in absolute importance for the movement, they did so in relative importance. The result was a dramatic shift in the substantive orientation of the movement and the beginning of a particularly active phase in its history. Meetings at all levels multiplied, notably those dealing with economic matters.[27] At the same time, the Non-Aligned Countries also pressed their economic objectives in a number of other pertinent international conferences (Appendix B).

The shift began with the 1970 Lusaka Summit. Before that, the heads of state or government as well as the foreign ministers of Non-Aligned Countries concentrated their attention almost exclusively on political matters—witness the list of objectives given above. This reflected directly the preoccupation of the members of the movement to consolidate and ensure their political independence. Not that economic issues did not play a role before Lusaka; only, they were not considered matters of first priority but, rather, as subjects of a technical nature. In fact, the 1955 Bandung Conference had already given considerable attention to development. And much of the work in the late 1950s and the 1960s in the United Nations was related to the First United Nations Development Decade which had received repeated and strong support from the Non-Aligned Countries. Similar support was given to UNCTAD. And the Non-Aligned Countries themselves held (in 1962) a Conference on Problems of Economic Development—the only non-aligned conference of this kind in the 1960s.

By the end of the 1960s, however, the developing countries had become very sceptical. As documented in chap. 1, the economic situation of most developing countries had not improved appreciably. In fact, relative to the developed countries, it had worsened for many of them. Although a number of proposals had been made over the years to create better conditions for development, few of them had found acceptance through international negotiations. As a result, frustration mounted and disappointments accumulated. It seemed clear that a new approach was needed.

Elements of a possible new approach emerged at the 1970 Lusaka Summit with the enunciation of the concept of individual and collective self-reliance whose successful implementation in China had impressed many Third World leaders.[28] As pointed out in chap. 1, the discussions of the concept greatly contributed to the recognition that the structures of the international economic system are important determinants of the development efforts of the developing countries, and that these countries themselves may have to take the initiative for changing the patterns of interaction underlying them. The concept of individual and collective self-reliance was born precisely out of the disappointments resulting from the perceived failure of the regional and international cooperative attempts of the 1960s. Intentionally, it therefore advocated closer cooperation among developing countries as a means of improving their situation. Since such a reorientation would require a conscious and fundamental political decision, the non-aligned movement offered the appropriate framework.

The "Declaration of Non-Alignment and Economic Progress," adopted at the 1970 Lusaka Summit,[29] indicated that such a decision had been taken in principle. For the first time, it gave a detailed and concrete meaning to the call for self-reliance, defined, at that time, primarily in terms of increased economic cooperation among developing countries. Consequently, various forms of such cooperation, its purposes and mechanisms, were outlined. It was realized that any meaningful cooperation had to be based on an adequate exchange of information and on the need for raw material inputs; obviously, it could also benefit greatly from shared experiences in the application of science and technology and the learning of appropriate skills. Special attention, therefore, was given to matters such as the optimal utilization of natural resources, the development of a technological and scientific capacity, trade, industrial production, and infrastructure (including the establishment of direct communication links among developing countries). The 1972 Georgetown Conference of Foreign Ministers further elaborated this program,[30] which led to the designation of Co-ordinator Countries for the Action Programme for Economic Co-operation Among Developing Countries (see table 2.2 above).

The Lusaka Declaration is significant not only for its introduction of self-reliance as a major objective of the non-aligned movement, but also because it represents the first time that the heads of state or government had recognized that economic questions are matters deserving intensive discussion at the highest level. This recognition was facilitated by a number of changes in the international political system as well as in the national situation of individual states (see chap. 1).

Thus, at the end of the 1960s and the beginning of the 1970s, trends in international politics and economic development merged to create a new emphasis in the non-aligned movement and a change in its character. Political issues—especially relating to the remnants of colonialism and to acute political crises such as in Southeast Asia—remained important items on the agenda of the Non-Aligned Countries, but economic issues swiftly gained equal importance.[31] Within a few years, most of the dynamics of their gatherings was generated by economic questions and concrete work related to self-reliance and development. In fact, a very broad and continuous consensus soon emerged on these issues—a consensus seldom achieved for crucial political matters.[32] This changing emphasis is reflected in the amount of attention given to economic matters in the documents of the Non-Aligned Countries as well as in their organizational development.

The first two summits had dealt almost exclusively with political matters. Out of the three chapters and 27 points of the "Declaration" adopted at the 1961 Belgrade Summit, only three and a half points addressed themselves to economic questions.[33] Similarly, out of the 11 chapters of the "Programme" adopted by the 1964 Cairo Summit, only one dealt with economic issues.[34] The other pre-Lusaka gatherings were dedicated virtually completely to political matters.[35] The 1970 Lusaka Summit itself saw, for the first time, the adoption of two declarations: one on political and one on economic subjects. Basically, this format was maintained at subsequent conferences.

After Lusaka, the balance changed swiftly. The 1972 Georgetown Conference of Foreign Ministers was the first for which a special economic committee undertook preparatory work. After the Georgetown Conference, and especially after the 1973 Algiers Summit, specialized economic committees and working groups multiplied rapidly. More importantly, active efforts were made to transform proposals into reality. The 1973 Algiers Summit[36] authorized, for instance, the establishment of an information center on transnational enterprises, the establishment, in principle, of a Solidarity Fund for Economic and Social Development in Non-Aligned Countries, and the holding of a conference on raw materials and development. It also called for a Special Session of the United Nations General Assembly devoted to development (the later Seventh Special Session). By the time of the 1975 Lima Conference of Foreign Ministers, some of these proposals had already been implemented, while others were ready for decision. Thus, the Seventh Special Session of the General Assembly had been scheduled for September 1975, and a Conference of Developing Countries on Raw Materials had been held in Dakar in February 1975 (the Dakar Conference),[37] which itself had a number of institutional spin-offs, and which also decided on the strategy to be pursued concerning participation of developing countries in the North-South Paris Conference. Furthermore, at Lima, it was also decided, inter alia, to locate the Information Center of Non-Aligned Countries on Transnational Corporations in Havana; to establish a Special Fund for the Financing of Buffer Stocks of Raw Materials and Primary Products Exported by the Developing Countries; to set up a Council of Associations of Developing Countries' Producers-Exporters of Raw Materials (for membership, see Appendix B); and to create the Solidarity Fund. Furthermore, a host of other activities were authorized, all aimed at increasing cooperation among, and the self-reliance of, the developing countries.[38]

To be sure, the political apparatus of the movement also expanded. The increased activities of the Co-ordinating Bureau at the Level of Permanent Representatives as well as continuous consultations in the framework of the United Nations are an expression of the political will of the Non-Aligned Countries to intensify cooperation. But at the same time, the meetings increasingly involved economic matters, especially the elaboration of common platforms and the coordination of positions for the United Nations and international economic conferences.

In the light of international political developments, this changing balance in the activities of the Non-Aligned Countries infused new vitality into the movement and increased its attractiveness, as the development of its membership (discussed above) demonstrates. This is particularly true with respect to influential Latin American countries. Countries from this region—the most active members of the (entirely development-oriented) Group of 77—had been particularly frustrated by the lack of success of UNCTAD and, more generally, by the lack of progress in the development efforts (including those undertaken in the framework of their regional arrangement). This frustration contributed to the realization that economic proposals, in order to be considered, required political backing. The new focus of the non-aligned movement, and its emergence as a platform on which the initiative for the solution of international economic problems was being taken, offered such backing. Joining it, therefore—or participating more actively[39]—became very appealing.

Within a few years, the non-aligned movement had transformed itself from an informal gathering of like-minded leaders who discussed global political strategies into a highly structured movement, in fact a caucus, the largest part of whose detailed and concrete activities revolve around economic matters. The developing countries had mobilized and organized themselves to promote development.

Since it was soon realized that the successful implementation of this objective required changes in the purposes, mechanisms, and structures of the international economic system, the achievement of these changes became one of the major aims of the Non-Aligned Countries. Thus, the "Economic Declaration" and the "Action Programme for Economic Co-operation" of the 1973 Algiers Summit,[40] which ratified the new substantive orientation of the movement, refer to "a new type of international economic relations," "a new and more equitable international division of labour," a "new international monetary system."[41] In fact, the Economic Declaration even contained a reference in which it was decided "to use all possible means" to achieve the economic objectives of the Non-Aligned Countries which include "the establishment of a new international economic order."[42] With the 1973 Algiers Summit, the Non-

Aligned Countries had become an international economic pressure group for the reorganization of the international economic system. To quote the President in Office of the non-aligned movement in his report to the 1976 Colombo Summit: "The IVth Summit in Algiers attributed particular importance to economic problems, adopting a Declaration, an Action Programme and a series of Resolutions on the subject. These constitute a decisive turning point in the aims of the Non-Aligned Countries, which determined henceforth to work towards the constitution of a New International Economic Order."[43]

A short excursion may be in order here. Not only did the Algiers Summit ratify the ascendance of economic matters as a priority item on the agenda of the Non-Aligned Countries, but it also may have sown the seed for an additional focus of work: sociocultural emancipation. During the colonial period, the developing countries were subjected to sociocultural as well as to political and economic colonization. In the process, important segments of Third World societies adopted values and behavioral patterns—including consumption preferences—that reflect the relative abundance and the wants of the developed countries rather than the absolute poverty and the needs of the developing ones. Satisfaction of these wants requires, therefore, a certain allocation of domestic production resources as well as continued inputs from abroad. The result is a further confirmation and accentuation of dependent development. Thus, successful economic development may well be, to a certain extent, a function of sociocultural emancipation.[44]

The awareness of some of these processes is not new. The "Final Communiqué" of the 1955 Bandung Conference had already observed that "the existence of colonialism . . . supresses the national cultures of people."[45] But it was not until the 1973 Algiers Summit, and especially the following 1975 Lima Conference of Foreign Ministers, that steps were initiated addressing themselves to this problem area. The first steps have been taken in the area of information where, indeed, the establishment of a New International Information Order is the objective.[46] In pursuit of this objective, a number of organizational measures have been taken, a Press Agencies Pool of the Non-Aligned Countries has been created, and the discussion of the subject matter has been carried into UNESCO.[47]

The Algiers Summit: The Stage Set

The intensified concern of the Non-Aligned Countries with international economic matters naturally led to a broadening and detailed elaboration of their economic program beyond the objective of self-reliance. The first comprehensive program was adopted by the heads of state or government at the 1973 Algiers Summit in the form of an "Economic Declaration" and an "Action Programme for Economic Co-operation." The roots of this program are to be found only partially in previous documents of Non-Aligned Countries because, as observed in the preceding section, not much attention had previously been paid to economic matters.[48] Since all the Non-Aligned Countries are also members of the Group of 77 and participate in the deliberations of UNCTAD, they could draw—and consciously did so—on an ample fund of experience and work. The preparation of the Second United Nations Development Strategy constituted an additional important reservoir of relevant experience.[49]

The Heritage

The economic situation of the developing countries had been perceived by the non-aligned movement since its first two summits as a set of imbalance in international relations resulting from colonial structures and mechanisms and constituting as such a permanent threat to world peace. (See chap. 3 for data.) The concept of economic decolonization as an essential component of national liberation (formulated at the 1964 Cairo Summit) established the link between the agreed priority of general decolonization and the need for development. At the 1973 Algiers Summit, this connection between the political and economic realities (between peace and security on the one hand and economic conditions in the developing countries on the other) was given its clearest expression. By that time, it had evolved into a clear and specific economic program consisting of suggestions addressed mainly to the industrialized countries and of concrete proposals for cooperation among the non-aligned and other developing countries. It evolved by broadening the basis of economic analysis, by adding a steadily increasing number of specific issues, and by concretizing the political will of the countries for cooperation among themselves.

A general call to remove economic imbalances inherited from colonialism and to accelerate agricultural and industrial development in the developing countries summarizes the essence of the economic points included in the Declaration of the 1961 Belgrade Summit. Concrete ideas were few: just terms of trade should be established and efforts should be made to eliminate excessive fluctuations in primary commodity trade and to abolish restrictive measures and practices that adversely affect trade and revenues of developing countries. None of them were elaborated in any detail. The statement that all countries may "freely dispose of their natural wealth and resources" added that this should be done "without prejudice to any obligations arising out of international economic co-operation, based upon the principle of mutual benefit, and international law."[50]

At the 1964 Cairo Summit, the Non-Aligned Countries stated again the right of countries to dispose freely of their natural resources. A few new issues were added to those listed in Belgrade: a new international division of labor to accelerate industrialization (which was a subject of particular concern to the newly independent African countries), the democratization of economic decision making, and access to the developed countries' markets on an equitable basis for primary products and on a preferential basis for manufactured goods. As concerns financial resources for development, the summit asked for an increase of capital transfers under improved terms. Without entering into any specifics, the conference also expressed its support for the "Joint Declaration" passed by a group of developing countries in preparation for the first meeting of UNCTAD, and asked for the implementation of the recommendations of UNCTAD's "Final Act."[51] Thus, in the fields of trade and industry (where the establishment of a specialized agency for industrial development was recommended), the Non-Aligned Countries expressed only general and outside support for action to be undertaken by the United Nations system; they did not specifically incorporate any of these issues into their own program.

The 1970 Lusaka Summit (insofar as it did not deal with self-reliance) further supported the trend of these policies and addressed some specific, but not elaborated, suggestions to the developed countries through the United Nations: action on primary commodities, including fair and equitable returns for producers; free access to consumer markets; the promotion of processing in the developing countries; the implementation of a scheme of nondiscriminatory and nonreciprocal preferences; adjustment of the production structures in the developed countries to increase the trade of developing countries; untied aid; a net flow of financial transfers of a minimum of 1 percent of GNP of each developed country to be reached by 1972; and, by the same target date, the establishment of a link between Special Drawing Rights and development finance. Other sections of the Declaration related to transfer of technology and the need to devise special measures for improving the productive capacities and the infrastructure of the least-developed and the landlocked developing countries.

UNCTAD

The concept of an international integrative development process—one in which the developing countries would develop in close interaction with the developed countries—provided the framework needed to elaborate and articulate an increasingly clear perception of the developing countries' position on international economic relations. The heart of this process, of this interaction, is trade. UNCTAD's name symbolizes this, its program revolves around it. It is not surprising, therefore, that the detailed work carried out by the Group of 77[52] in UNCTAD found its way into the economic substance of the non-aligned movement. Since many aspects of the economic program of the 1973 Algiers Summit reach back to UNCTAD's first session, we shall briefly review the main measures suggested by that session.

The principles and recommendations adopted by UNCTAD I and further elaborated in later UNCTAD sessions,[53] were based on the assumption—fully supported by the industrialized countries—that trade is the engine of development. Since trade with the developed countries was particularly important, access to their markets became a chief concern for the Third World. An entire set of proposals aimed at achieving this objective. With respect to the developed market economies, they included standstill, removal of obstacles to trade, cessation of uneconomic protection, the granting of preferences, and the generalization of preferential arrangements. The socialist countries were encouraged to expand imports from developing countries on favorable terms and to pay attention to the trade needs of their partners in economic planning. All developed countries were asked to accord nonreciprocal benefits to the developing countries and to avoid subsidizing exports.

A distinct set of problems related to trade concerned commodities, an issue that always rated high on UNCTAD's priority list. UNCTAD I saw the solution to commodity problems first of all in terms of arrangements concluded primarily on a commodity-by-commodity basis. Such arrangements, it was expected, would eventually ensure the predictability and growth of real export earnings of the developing countries; and they would prevent excessive fluctuations and facilitate long-term adjustments of production.

However, the commodity resolutions of UNCTAD I were not implemented. A new program, devised in 1968 at UNCTAD II for 19 designated agricultural and mineral products, suffered the same fate, as did attempts at UNCTAD III (1972) to reach agreement on a commitment to a specific action-oriented program concerning access to markets and pricing policy for commodities. An earlier call to the World Bank Group to concentrate on the problems of financing buffer stocks also did not bring entirely satisfactory results. Thus, almost ten years after UNCTAD I, the 1973 Algiers Summit noted the lack of cooperative international commodity agreements and, in their absence, placed strong emphasis on self-help, i.e., the establishment and strengthening of producers' associations for major commodities to halt the deterioration of their terms of trade. A comprehensive scheme for the international financing of buffer stocks for a group of commodities was only elaborated in 1975, again by UNCTAD, in the framework of an Integrated Programme for Commodities and in response to a request by the Sixth Special Session of the United Nations General Assembly.

The financing of trade and, more generally, the financing of development constituted another major area of concern of UNCTAD I. It was felt that financial flows to developing countries should be continuous and that the external resources available to them should be multilateralized as far as possible, thereby allowing the recipients to freely use them in acquiring goods and services. As to their terms and conditions, specific targets were set, e.g., a maximum of 3 percent interest on official loans. A related recommendation of UNCTAD I tentatively spoke of examining possibilities to liberalize the International Monetary Fund's terms of the compensatory credit system and of providing supplementary financial resources to developing countries experiencing shortfalls in export proceeds. In the course of the two following sessions of UNCTAD, other specific proposals were added, including the establishment of a link between Special Drawing Rights and development financing.

In the final analysis, all the measures suggested regarding trade, commodities, and finance were geared toward promoting the industrialization of the Third World. While this objective was not programmatically elaborated as a separate area, several substantive points were, nevertheless, discussed by UNCTAD I. For instance, industrial branch agreements were encouraged to establish a better division of labor between developed and developing countries. In the same vein, a more rational division of labor was later demanded by UNCTAD III from the international community and, to that end, developed countries were requested to adopt suitable adjustment assistance policies to help industries achieve a better allocation of resources. This item became the basis for the (stronger) urging in later years to relocate suitable industries to developing countries. The need for more comprehensive action on industrial development had already been reflected in the call for the establishment of a United Nations specialized agency in this field; the result was the establishment of UNIDO in 1968.

By the beginning of the 1970s, a relatively clear picture had emerged for most developing countries on what measures had to be implemented to achieve the development objectives proclaimed during the past ten years. Against the background of evolving détente and the strong and dynamic economies of the developed countries, it seemed only a question of political will on the part of the industrial world and of political persuasion—or pressure—on the part of the developing countries to implement some of their important reform proposals. In fact, overemployment (with the ensuing problems of imported labor) and the widening public concern about environmental protection from polluting industries led, in Japan and Western Europe, to calls for a redeployment of certain industries.

However, the early 1970s did not produce any major breakthrough in international cooperation; the increased efforts concerning self-reliance date, in fact, from this time. The United Nations Second Development Decade had been launched without any better guarantees than before that it would, indeed, be implemented. The resolutions adopted by UNCTAD lacked political clout, although the "Charter of Algiers," [54] adopted in 1967 by the Group of 77, made a first attempt at politicizing the economic concerns of the developing countries. But the ideas of the Group of 77 had begun to enter non-aligned economic programs; and by 1973, the non-aligned movement was ready to give these ideas its full political backing. This occurred at the 1973 Algiers Summit, to whose economic program in key areas we turn next.

The Algiers Summit Economic Program

The 1973 Algiers Summit of Non-Aligned Countries incorporated the essence of the economic ideas of the Third World into its Political Declaration:[55] not only war, but also poverty and the deterioration of economic conditions were seen to be the opposite to peace. Peace, therefore, meant accelerated development and freedom from economic dependence; or, phrased in more concrete terms, the genuine independence of developing countries was seen to require control over natural resources—without qualifications. Furthermore, the analysis of the problems and the formulation of the solutions began to be infused by the feeling that a radical departure was needed regarding the nature of changes that were required to achieve the economic objectives of the Third World: a reform of the mechanisms alone is not sufficient; the very structure of the international economic system will have to be changed.

In spite of this realization, most of the concrete measures suggested by the Economic Declaration and the Action Programme of the Algiers Summit were based on the traditional concept of aid-by-trade. The developed countries' performance concerning their expansion of imports from the developing countries (as well as the latter's benefit from it) continued to be regarded as a main indicator for evaluating the developed countries' will to support development. The structural inequality of world trade was seen to be augmented by the fact that the developing countries' share was decreasing and their terms of trade deteriorating. Furthermore, the Generalized System of Preferences (GSP) excluded (and still does) the developing countries' main agricultural products and imposed (and still does) strict controls on the import of all products considered sensitive by industrialized countries. Therefore, the GSP had to be expanded. Multilateral trade negotiations offered the appropriate framework in which to achieve the desired changes—provided the developed countries accepted the principles of nonreciprocity, nondiscrimination, and preferential treatment for developing countries—principles that were also sought to be included in any reform of the GATT.

As already stressed repeatedly in UNCTAD, the Non-Aligned Countries felt that a coordinated approach to trade and monetary problems should ensure that fullest account be taken of the special interests of developing countries. But whereas a 1971 Consultative Meeting of Ministers of Foreign Affairs of Non-Aligned Countries only saw the need for consultations with developing countries in the elaboration of effective measures for the maintenance of orderly and equitable exchange rates and for improving the monetary arrangements "that have been carefully worked out since the Bretton Woods Conference,"[56] the Algiers Summit Economic Declaration stated categorically that the financial system devised at Bretton Woods "has served only the interests of some developed countries."[57] Therefore, a new international monetary system had to be established with the participation of the developing countries on an equal footing, guaranteeing the stability of financial flows and taking into account the needs of the developing countries on the basis of preferential treatment. The new monetary system also had to ensure the effective participation of developing countries in all relevant decision-making processes. Clearly, the criticism of the developing countries was becoming more fundamental.

Regarding the need for increased financial resources for development, the Algiers Summit requested, as did other gatherings in the past, the establishment of a link between the distribution of Special Drawing Rights and appropriation of development finance. Furthermore, the developed countries were asked to accept the time-bound program for the implementation of net-flow targets contained in the United Nations Strategy for the Second Development Decade and to increase the official component of their transfers. In references to the burden of external debt contracted on hard terms and to debt-servicing, appropriate alleviating measures, e.g., rescheduling, were stressed.

The objective of individual and collective self-reliance led the Algiers Summit deliberations to pay special attention to raw materials in the broadest sense. As previously discussed, the right to exercise sovereignty over natural resources had always been affirmed in non-aligned economic statements. However, the Algiers Summit went beyond a restatement of this general principle and resolved that nationalizations of foreign-controlled production facilities was a means to safeguard natural resources and that states had the right to determine the amount and mode of possible compensation. In strong opposition to the reigning theory of developed countries, the Summit endorsed the right of every State to settle nationalization disputes in accordance with its own national legislation. This approach was to be included in a somewhat modified form in the 1974 "Declaration on the Establishment of a New International Economic Order"[58] and the 1974 "Charter of Economic Rights and Duties of States."[59] Its lack of reference to international law and more specified modes of compensation constituted one of the major clauses opposed by the developed market economies.

In the context of sovereignty over natural resources, the Algiers Summit Economic Declaration recommended "the establishment of effective solidarity organizations for the defence of the interests of raw material producing countries"[60] for the purpose of ensuring increasingly substantial export earnings and income in real terms. Specific reference was made to the producers' associations of oil and copper-exporting countries, OPEC and CIPEC.

Problems relating to private foreign direct investment and the need to evolve a common approach among Non-Aligned Countries had been discussed at previous non-aligned meetings. ITT's activities in Chile, however—which were later dramatically described by President Salvador Allende in a speech before the United Nations General Assembly[61]—contributed to placing the issue into a new topical context. Thus, the 1972 Georgetown Conference of Foreign Ministers, foreshadowing President Allende's address to the United Nations and his call for international action, requested that a Committee of Experts on Private Foreign Investment be established to draw up a draft statute on foreign direct investment which would include provisions to organize the exchange of information on the operations of transnational enterprises. The Algiers Summit denounced the practices of transnational enterprises and recommended joint action through, among other things, the adoption of common rules, support of nationalizations, and the joint establishment of an information center. The need for the establishment of such a center was confirmed by the 1975 Lima Conference of Foreign Ministers and the decision was taken to locate it in Havana. In the context of technology transfer, monopolistic practices, market-sharing, and price-fixing by transnational enterprises were condemned. This summit further endorsed a number of conclusions reached by the Committee of Experts, e.g., on the need for a system of government control and authorization of investments and the prohibition of foreign takeovers.[62]

Independent of restrictive business practices, transfer of technology was an area of major concern of the Algiers Summit Action Programme. The implementation of the relevant provisions of the Second United Nations Development Strategy was requested, including international cooperation to support the developing countries' research and development efforts with the aim of creating indigenous technology, promotion of the transfer of technology and its adaptation to local circumstances, and facilitation of access to patented and nonpatented technology on favorable terms. In addition, two issues that had been worked out by UNCTAD were put forward: new international legislation in the form of a code of conduct for the transfer of technology, and urgent measures to stop the brain-drain from developing countries.

The issue of environment had been given some attention by the 1972 Georgetown Conference of Foreign Ministers. However, as was clearly stated at the Algiers Summit, environmental control was seen as essentially a preoccupation of the developed countries; the developing countries did not want it to hamper industrialization.

On shipping, a service industry of great importance to developing countries, the Action Programme supported UNCTAD's work on a code of conduct for liner conferences which, as requested by the Group of 77, should be a legally binding international instrument. It was also requested that developing countries be placed in a position to increase their freight and insurance operations and be allowed to participate in any relevant decision influencing the cost of shipping.

The food problem was seen mainly in the context of the Sahelian drought for which the Algiers Summit urged special relief measures, including what later became the United Nations World Food Conference.

Finally, as at the 1970 Lusaka Summit and in the 1972 Georgetown Declaration, great emphasis was placed upon the spirit of self-reliance and the need for economic cooperation among Non-Aligned Countries. Such cooperation was considered necessary for all aspects of their international economic relations, including purchase, sales and joint marketing agreements for industrial raw materials, trade expansion, mutual preferences, encouragement of industrial subcontracting, joint ventures, trade fairs and missions, and the strengthening of transport links. Cooperation would also include financial and monetary matters, e.g., multilateral clearing arrangements, banking relations, and export-guarantee institutions. Concrete steps were also urged for a common approach on foreign direct investment policies. And, of course, the establishment or strengthening of producers' associations was encouraged.

Thus, the 1973 Algiers Summit, attended by the largest number of heads of state or government ever gathered in an international conference, encompassed the widest range of developmental objectives ever formulated at such a high political level. It is not so much the novelty of each individual proposal, but rather the integration of all proposals into one program, the intended orientation of this program toward structural changes and, above all, the level of endorsement which gives the Algiers Declaration and Action Programme its significance. It was recognized that the improvement of the situation of the developing countries is not only a technical matter but that this situation is embedded in an international environment whose mechanisms and structures are important determinants of the development process. The objective, therefore, became to change the international environment in such a way as to make it more responsive to the needs of the developing countries. If the Algiers Summit made changes in the international economic system a priority item on the agenda of the Non-Aligned Countries, the Sixth Special Session of the United Nations General Assembly made the establishment of the New International Economic Order a priority item on the agenda of the international community as a whole.

Changing Priorities on the International Agenda:
The Sixth Special Session

At the 1973 Algiers Summit, the economic course of the non-aligned movement had been chartered and launched. During the next few years, intensive work would be done in a number of issue areas to prepare both the next foreign ministers conference and the requested special session of the United Nations General Assembly—the Seventh Special Session—planned to be the first devoted exclusively to the problems of development. Events on the international scene intervened, however, to alter this course and to accelerate its pace.

One month after the Algiers Summit, on October 6, 1973, war broke out in the Middle East. On October 16, the Gulf States raised the posted price of benchmark crude oil from $3.01 to $5.12 per barrel. One day later, Arab oil ministers agreed to support the Arab cause by cutting oil exports and embargoing unfriendly states. Two days later, several OPEC states proclaimed an embargo on oil exports to the United States. Subsequently, the embargo was extended to other states and oil production cuts were enacted. OPEC's November conference endorsed these decisions and, in December, the OPEC Ministerial Committee of the Gulf States decided to raise the posted price of benchmark crude to $11.65 per barrel, effective January 1, 1974.

The immediate reaction of the developed countries was to take national measures. In early January 1974, however, the United States invited the major oil-consuming developed countries to a conference, scheduled for February 11–13, 1974, in Washington, to elaborate a common approach to the events. Several consumer countries feared this initiative for its potential of confrontation with the oil-exporting countries, especially since the Arab oil-producing states had expressed misgivings about the forthcoming Washington Conference. Notably, the policy of France was strongly directed toward avoiding a confrontation with the oil-exporting countries. Thus, after receiving the invitation to the Washington Conference, the government of France, in a letter to the Secretary-General of the United Nations, dated January 18, 1974, immediately proposed an international conference of oil producing and consuming developed and developing countries, to be held preferably within the framework of the United Nations.[63] This proposal, if accepted, would have discouraged the efforts to create a consumer counterassociation and would have diffused the imminent confrontation. The French initiative did not succeed at that time, and the Washington Conference took place as scheduled.[64]

Also in reaction to the proposed Washington Conference and the major consumer's efforts to organize themselves, President Houari Boumediène of Algeria, in his capacity as President in Office of the Group of Non-Aligned Countries, requested a special session of the United Nations General Assembly to study the problems of raw materials and development.[65] The question of energy, thus, was placed in the broader context of all questions relating to all raw materials. Since this initiative was immediately supported by more than a minimum number of countries necessary, the Sixth Special Session of the United Nations General Assembly was called by the Secretary General for April 9 to May 2, 1974. It was the first Special Session dedicated to questions of development. It adopted, by consensus, the "Declaration on the Establishment of a New International Economic Order" and the "Programme of Action on the Establishment of a New International Economic Order."[66] With these two resolutions, the developing countries, under the leadership of the Non-Aligned Countries, had succeeded in carrying the discussions about the international economic system into the international arena.[67]

The intellectual foundations of these documents and their priorities, however, had largely been laid in the economic program of the 1973 Algiers Summit which, as discussed earlier, had drawn heavily upon the work of the Group of 77, UNCTAD, and the General Assembly. The similarities, in fact, are striking. (The New International Economic Order program will be discussed in detail in chap. 3)

The final instruments adopted at the Algiers Summit and the Sixth Special Session used the same format, i.e., a declaration and a program of action. But while the Algiers Summit declaration contained a review and discussion of the economic conditions of developing countries and, in the process, summarized the key measures to be taken in key economic areas, the declaration of the Sixth Special Session took a more fundamental approach. It states in its preamble that:

> *We, the Members of the United Nations,* . . . *solemnly proclaim* our united determination to work urgently for THE ESTABLISHMENT OF A NEW INTERNATIONAL ECONOMIC ORDER based on equity, sovereign equality, interdependence, common interest and co-operation among all States, irrespective of their economic and social systems which shall correct inequalities and redress existing injustices, make it possible to eliminate the widening gap between the developed and the developing countries and ensure steadily accelerating economic and social development and peace and justice for present and future generations.

This statement was further elaborated by 20 principles which were declared to constitute the foundation of the new economic order. They include a number of basic concepts such as noninterference and "full permanent sovereignty of every State over its natural resources and all economic activities . . . including the right to nationalization,"[68] as well as general objectives such as access to technology, improvements in the terms of trade, and supervision of transnational enterprises. Many of these priniciples and objectives are substantively very similar to key provisions of the Algiers Summit Declaration and are frequently repeated in a more operationalized way in the United Nations' Programme of Action.[69]

The "Programme of Action" of the Sixth Special Session is more elaborate than the "Action Programme" of the Algiers Summit, reflecting, in some cases, additional UNCTAD material, in others, material submitted to the Algiers Summit but not used in its final documents. A direct comparison of respective sections, however, is misleading since the sections used in the two documents are not always identical. Proposals contained in one section of the Algiers Summit Action Programme are frequently shifted to another section in the document of the Sixth Special Session. If this is taken into account, key policies are largely the same.

This is particularly noticeable in the Sixth Special Session's section on "Fundamental Problems of Raw Materials and Primary Commodities as Related to Trade and

Development.'' Given the focus of the session, a section with such a title had to be included, and special attention had to be given to raw materials. The subsection on raw materials grouped together permanent sovereignty over natural resources, the utilization of natural resources for the promotion of self-reliance, the reversal of price declines, and the promotion of producers' associations—all familiar principles. Also added were old UNCTAD ideas on the elaboration of a link between the prices of developing countries' exports and their imports,[70] the promotion of local processing,[71] and the expansion of markets for natural products in relation to synthetics.

Similarly, the subsection on trade contained all the relevant trade measures included in the Algiers Summit document (e.g., commodity agreements, improvement of the GSP, structural adjustments), repeated some measures already mentioned elsewhere (e.g., synthetics), and added a few new ones. Most notable among the last was a request (UNCTAD heritage) to prepare an overall integrated program for a comprehensive range of commodities of export interest to developing countries. This request was, however, not yet linked (as in the later Seventh Special Session) to the other new issue of improved compensatory financing and the setting up of buffer stocks. New—as far as the non-aligned movement is concerned—was also the issue of restitution (by developed countries) of dues levied on imports from developing countries.[72] It is also noteworthy that agreement was reached that the multilateral trade negotiations should be guided by "the principles of non-reciprocity and preferential treatment of developing countries"[73]—principles whose recognition had been sought in the Algiers Summit document.[74]

Another major section in both action programs pertained to the international monetary system and the financing of development. Here, virtually all measures suggested by the Algiers Summit were adopted—frequently verbatim (see table 2.4)—by the Sixth Special Session.[75] Added was the thought that international liquidity should be created only through multilateral mechanisms (i.e., not via national reserve currencies); that financial assistance should be untied;[76] that developing countries should be exempted from developed countries' import and capital-outflow controls; that foreign investment should be promoted; and, finally, that the IMF should review, among other things, its system of compensatory financing and the terms of the financing of commodity buffer stocks.

Raw materials and trade, and monetary and financial matters are two areas that had been the major focus of UNCTAD's work. It is therefore not surprising that the Non-Aligned Countries as well as the United Nations General Assembly dealt with them in great detail. As far as the Non-Aligned Countries were concerned, self-reliance was, of course, equally important.

Cooperation among developing countries—a section contained in both action programs—was, therefore, accorded much more attention in the Algiers Summit document. There, it was the introductory section which, in the tradition of the 1970 Lusaka Summit and the 1972 Georgetown Conference of Foreign Ministers, suggested a number of measures toward individual and collective self-reliance. Collective self-reliance was also the objective of a section in the Sixth Special Session document, but a number of measures that had been spelled out in detail in the earlier document were only summarized in more general formulations.[77] An important principle with implications for the relations between developed and developing countries was, however, contained in both documents in the same formulation: no developing country should grant more

Table 2.4. Selected Provisions of the Action Programmes Adopted at the Algiers Summit and the Sixth Special Session

September 1973 Algiers Summit of Non-Aligned Countries: "Action Programme".	May 1974 Sixth Special Session of the General Assembly of the United Nations: "Programme of Action"
"The international financial institutions should effectively play their role as development financing banks without resorting to political discrimination against countries" (para. 4*).	"International financing institutions should effectively play their role as development financing banks without discrimination on account of the political or economic systems of any member country, assistance being untied" (section II, para. 2b).
"The international financial institutions should increasingly orient their lending policies to suit the emerging needs of developing countries" (para. 8*).	"International financial institutions should take into account the special situation of each developing country in reorienting their lending policies to suit these urgent needs" (section II, para. 2h).
Developing countries should participate fully and on an equal footing in the formulation and application of an equitable and durable international monetary system. . . . The new monetary system should ensure the effective participation by developing countries in the decision-making process . . ." (paras. 1 and 3*).	"Full and effective participation of developing countries in all phases of decision-making for the formulation of an equitable and durable monetary system and adequate participation of developing countries in all bodies entrusted with this reform . . ." (section II, para. 1d).
"A link should be established between special drawing rights (SDRs) and development financing in the interests of developing countries" (para 3*).	"Early establishment of a link between special drawing rights and additional development financing in the interest of developing countries, consistent with the monetary characteristics of special drawing rights" (section II, para. 1f).
"The adverse consequences for the current and future development of developing countries arising from the burden of external debt contracted on hard terms should be neutralized by appropriate international action" (para. 6*).	"Appropriate urgent measures, including international action, should be taken to mitigate adverse consequences for the current and future development of developing countries arising from the burden of external debt contracted on hard terms" (section II, para. 2f).
"Credit relations should be developed on a preferential basis between developing countries" (para. xi).	"To promote . . . the development of credit relations on a preferential basis and on favourable terms" (section VII, para. 1f).
"No developing country should accord to imports from developed countries more favourable treatment than that accorded to imports from developing countries" (para. ii).	"To insure that no developing country accords to imports from developed countries more favourable treatment than that accorded to imports from developing countries" (section VII, para. 1e).
"The developed countries should accept a time-bound programme for the implementation of targets of net flow of financial resources to developing countries. The official components of the net transfer of financial resources to the developing countries should be increased" (para. 5*).	"Implementation at an accelerated pace by the developed countries of the time-bound programme, as already laid down in the International Development Strategy for the Second United Nations Development Decade, for the net amount of financial resource transfers to developing countries; increase in the official component of the net amount of financial resource transfers to developing countries so as to meet and even to exceed the target of the Strategy" (section II, para. 2a).

*Section on "International Monetary and Financial Systems."

favorable treatment to imports from developed countries than to imports from other developing ones. On the other hand, an Algiers Summit's strong encouragement to "establish and strengthen producers' associations"[78] in order, among other things, to halt the deterioration of developing countries' terms of trade was watered down to "All efforts should be made . . . to facilitate the functioning and to further the aims of producers' associations."[79]

The remaining issue areas were less elaborately treated in both action programs. As to transfer of technology, the Sixth Special Session dealt with the same concerns covered directly or indirectly[80] at the Algiers Summit, including a call for a code of conduct and the creation of indigenous technology but excluding a special reference to the brain drain. Regarding food,[81] an area which had not previously been given much attention by the Non-Aligned Countries, the United Nations document focused on food production and the import and export interests of developing countries. In transport and insurance[82] (an area of considerable work by UNCTAD), provisions regarding insurance and re-insurance as well as freight rates were added to those specified earlier by the developing countries. In reference to transnational enterprises, the Sixth Special Session's call for a code of conduct regulating the behavior of these enterprises drew largely on the intensive work done in preparation for the Algiers Summit, work which was reflected in the summit's document, but not as a separate section. Another issue area not singled out in the Algiers Summit document was industrialization. The measures delineated here by the United Nations remained, however, rather sketchy until the 1975 UNIDO Conference elaborated a comprehensive program[83] in time for the 1975 Lima Conference of Ministers of Foreign Affairs of Non-Aligned Countries and the 1975 Seventh Special Session. Finally, the Non-Aligned Countries' concern for the least developed and landlocked developing countries—reflected in the Algiers Summit document in dispersed references to their special situation—resulted in a section outlining a program (including the establishment of a Special Fund) for the developing countries most seriously affected by the economic crisis.[84]

This brief comparison suggests that the economic principles and measures adopted by the Sixth Special Session of the United Nations General Assembly represented an enriched version—although at times qualified—of the economic program of the Algiers Summit, the enrichment originating in UNCTAD's work and the Second Development Strategy, and the qualifications coming from the developed market economies. Many of these principles and measures were codified in December 1974 in the Charter of Economic Rights and Duties of States; and further consolidated, refined—but also weakened—in the formulations of the 1975 resolution on "Development and International Economic Co-operation" adopted on September 15, 1975, by the Seventh Special Session.[85]

The noted similarities between the documents adopted at the Algiers Summit and the Sixth Special Session are not surprising. The Non-Aligned Countries had called the Sixth Special Session. They were primarily responsible for, and interested in, drafting a final document—and in terms that reflected their concerns. At the same time, since the session had been called on very short notice, they did not have (and no other group had) sufficient time to prepare thoroughly. On the other hand, the session took place shortly after the Non-Aligned Countries (and in many cases the same representatives) had extensively dealt with the same subject matter at their September 1973 Algiers Summit and had produced the first comprehensive economic program of the movement, a program carried by a solid consensus. It is not surprising, then, that not only the philosophy of the Algiers Summit documents but also individual formulations found their way into the Programme of Action of the Sixth Special Session.[86] The time pressure explains also why the final resolutions of the Sixth Special Session somewhat resembled an aggregation of principles and measures, and were not as structured as the resolution adopted at the much better prepared Seventh Special Session.

The Sixth Special Session demonstrated that the Non-Aligned Countries' efforts regarding economic issues had begun to pay off, that they had succeeded in building an effective movement. Although the threat that was perceived as originating from the Washington Conference applied only to the OPEC countries, and although the non-OPEC developing countries had also suffered under OPEC's price policy,[87] President Boumediène's request for a special session found the immediate support needed to convene the General Assembly. Certainly, it was fortunate for the non-aligned movement, that it had, with President Houari Boumediène, a President in Office at the time of the crisis who provided strong leadership and who also played an important role in OPEC. The rallying of the Third World countries behind OPEC may have also been influenced by the satisfaction derived from OPEC's successful challenge and defiance of the industrial countries. Above all, the Sixth Special Session showed the high degree of solidarity and cohesion achieved by the non-aligned movement. And, equally important, the Sixth Special Session gave the developing countries a considerable psychological boost in their dealings with the developed countries: it demonstrated that when they stood united, they could make themselves heard and could introduce changes in global economic relations.

The consensus of the Third World to hold the special session (the speed with which approval was obtained is itself a remarkable achievement) was greatly facilitated by the proposed topic. The broadening of the session's agenda to include raw materials in general embedded OPEC's confrontation with the industrial states over oil into a confrontation of the entire Third World with the developed states over raw materials and development and made the session positively desirable to the Third World. This move diffused the perceived threat to OPEC and put the confrontation into an area where the 1973 Algiers Summit had just achieved a solid consensus. Moreover, it had the additional effect of binding more conservative (but important) members of OPEC into the solidarity of the Third World, thereby strengthening the developing countries in general and decreasing possible temptations for these countries to make separate arrangements.

The developments before and after the Sixth Special Session require another important observation. While the events surrounding OPEC's success were instrumental in putting the reorganization of the international economic system on the international agenda, and while the solidarity of OPEC with the other developing countries is very important to maintain its priority, the drive for reorganization draws support from multiple sources. Most important, the non-aligned movement has successfully mobilized and organized the Third World into a pressure group for change in the international economic system. In other words, the emergence of the development issue as an important item on the international agenda and the pressure to establish the New International Economic Order are not merely a by-product of OPEC's success. Independent of OPEC, the urgency of these issues had gathered momentum, and the foundation had been laid to ensure that they obtain the attention they deserve. Thus, whatever OPEC's evolution, and even if other producers' associations are not (or cannot be) mobilized in the pursuit of the developing countries' objective, the issues related to the reorganization of the international economic order are bound to continue to occupy an important place on the international agenda.

Notes

1. On this subject, see, for example, Leo Mates, *Non-Alignment: Theory and Current Policy* (Dobbs Ferry, N.Y.: Oceana, 1972).

2. See, Asian-African Conference, "Final Communiqué," in *The Third World without Superpowers: The Collected Documents of the Non-Aligned Countries*, ed., Odette Jankowitsch and Karl P. Sauvant (Dobbs Ferry, N.Y.: Oceana, 1978), pp. lvii–lxviii.

3. Ibid., for a listing of the meetings of the Non-Aligned Countries since 1961.

4. Preparatory Meeting of Representatives of Non-Aligned Countries, "Communiqué," ibid., p. 41.

5. Guests are invited to attend summit and foreign ministers conferences and, on occasion, also other meetings. They are conference guests, i.e., invitations are extended to them for each occasion separately. At the Lima Conference, Australia was also represented as a guest.

6. Considerations of this kind played a role in the membership case of Malta and the guest-status issues of Pakistan, the Philippines, Portugal, and Romania. In the case of Malta, efforts to terminate a base agreement were recognized and the difficulties of such action understood.

7. See Fourth Conference of Heads of State or Government of Non-Aligned Countries, "Annotated Agenda" in Jankowitsch and Sauvant, *Documents of the Non-Aligned Countries,* p. 323. For a more recent expression of this perception, see the "Final Communiqué" adopted at the 1978 Havana meeting of the Co-ordinating Bureau of Non-Aligned Countries at the Ministerial Level. There, under the heading of "Role of the Non-Aligned Countries," the Bureau "reiterated the need for the Movement to maintain its catalytic role in the Group of 77" (contained in United Nations document A/33/118 of June 7, 1978, p. 29).

8. Since the Lusaka Summit, the Presidents-in-Office were: Kenneth D. Kaunda, (Zambia 1970–1973) Houari Boumèdiene (Algeria, 1973–1976), Sirimavo Bandaraneike/Junius Jayewardene (Sri Lanka, 1976–1979).

9. Third Conference of Heads of State or Government of Non-Aligned Countries, "Resolution on the Strengthening of the Role of the Non-Aligned Countries," in Jankowitsch and Sauvant, *Documents of the Non-Aligned Countries*, p. 106.

10. Repeated efforts have been made to establish a secretariat, but suggestions to this effect never found the necessary consensus mainly because a number of countries opposed this degree of institutionalization and/or feared that it could invite predominance by one or a few countries.

11. The non-aligned movement has no charter, constitution, or formal rules of procedure. Nevertheless, it has developed a body of principles, concepts, and programs that represents a consensus which constitutes an important basis of Third World practice and aspirations, even if not regularly implemented. This consensus is contained in the declarations, action programs, statements, resolutions, decisions, communiqués, messages, reports, and texts of the meetings of the Non-Aligned Countries.

12. Fourth Conference of Heads of State or Government of Non-Aligned Countries, "Decision Regarding the Mandate of the Bureau of the Conference," ibid., p. 270. Originally, the Bureau had been the conference Bureau of the 1973 Algiers Summit. It continues to maintain this function during conferences so that conceivably it could also meet at the level of heads of state or government.

13. As the title indicates, it consists of Permanent Representatives to the United Nations (in New York and Geneva), i.e., representatives with ambassadorial rank.

14. Fifth Conference of Heads of State or Government of Non-Aligned Countries, "Decision Regarding the Composition and the Mandate of the Co-ordinating Bureau," ibid., pp. 917–21.

15. Ibid., p. 918. Since the Colombo Summit, records are being kept by the presiding country of the regular meetings of the Co-ordinating Bureau at the Level of Permanent Representatives; these records are adopted at each following meeting. Seats in the Bureau are apportioned on the basis of the principle of balanced geographical distribution. The present geographical allocation is 12 seats for Africa, 8 for Asia, 4 for Latin America, and 1 for Europe. Bureau meetings at the level of Permanent Representatives also take place on economic matters at the United Nations headquarters in Geneva.

16. For a review of the activities of the Co-ordinator Countries as of April 1977, see the "Report on the Implementation of the Colombo Action Programme for Economic Co-operation and Annexes," ibid., pp. 2132–237.

17. This has been done most notably by Guyana in the field of trade, transport, and industry.

18. They include the Group of Experts on Science and Technology, the Group of Experts on the Information and Research System in the Field of Economic Co-operation, and the Committee of Experts on Private Foreign Investment. The reports of these groups are reprinted in ibid.

19. They include the Intergovernmental Group of Non-Aligned Countries on Raw Materials, the Group of Experts on the Establishment of a Council of Associations of Developing Countries Producers-Exporters of Raw Materials, and the Expert Group on the Establishment of a Fund for the Financing of Buffer Stocks of Raw Materials and Primary Products Exported by Developing Countries. The reports of these groups are reprinted in ibid.

20. Thus, the work of these groups—and that of all others to which all developing countries are invited—increasingly tends to intermesh with that of the Group of 77.

21. Co-ordinating Bureau of Non-Aligned Countries at the Level of Permanent Representatives, "Report of the Activities of the Co-ordinating Bureau of Non-Aligned Countries in New York since the Fifth Conference of Heads of State or Government in Colombo in August 1976," ibid., p. 2240.

22. Consequently, and as a rule, no formal documents are adopted. The main exception is the Working Group on Disarmament and International Security which is the oldest Working Group—thereby reflecting one of the key concerns of the Non-Aligned Countries—and which issued several statements in its preparatory work for the 1978 Special Session of the General Assembly devoted to Disarmament.

In all Working Groups the presiding country chairs the proceedings. The only group in which this is not the case is the Contact Group on Cyprus, where Algeria continues to remain in the chair.

23. See, for instance, the Ministerial Consultative Meeting of Non-Aligned Countries (September 1971) and the communiqués issued by the Co-ordinating Bureau at the Level of Permanent Representatives. As already indicated, the Bureau also prepares summaries of the decisions reached at its meetings, but these are purely of an internal character.

24. Apart from the main organs of the United Nations organization as well as UNCTAD, the Non-Aligned Countries are also beginning to coordinate their activities in some of the specialized agencies of the United Nations, especially the World Health Organization, the International Labour Organisation and the United Nations Educational, Scientific, and Cultural Organization. See, for instance, the "Final Report" of the Meeting of Health Representatives of the Movement of Non-Aligned and Other Developing Countries, ibid., pp. 2351–402.

25. See, for instance, the Symposium of Non-Aligned Countries on Information and the Meeting of Representatives of Governments of Developing Countries for the Establishment of the International Center for Public Enterprises in Developing Countries; for texts see ibid.

26. The Declaration adopted at the 1961 Belgrade Summit had been transmitted by personal letter to President John F. Kennedy and Premier Nikita Krushchev; see ibid., pp. 9–10.

27. For a summary of the activities of the Non-Aligned Countries during the period between the 1976 Colombo Summit and the 1977 New Delhi meeting of the Co-ordinating Bureau at the Ministerial Level, see the "Report on the Activities of the Bureau in New York since the Colombo Summit" and the "Decisions of the Co-ordinating Bureau of Non-Aligned Countries in Geneva"; for their activities between the Algiers and Colombo Summits, see the "Report by the President in Office and Messages sent by the Presiding Country"; and for their activities during the Twenty-ninth United Nations General Assembly (Fall 1974), see the "Report on the Activities of the Group of Non-Aligned Countries during the Twenty-ninth Session of the General Assembly: Report of the Co-ordinating Bureau in New York"; these documents are contained in Jankowitsch and Sauvant, pp. 2239–2252, 2269–2270, 1019–1156, and 1438–1458, respectively. For a summary of the activities of the Non-Aligned Countries between the 1977 New Delhi Bureau meeting and the 1978 Havana Bureau meeting, see Seventh Conference of Ministers of Foreign Affairs of Non-Aligned Countries, "Report of the Activities of the Co-ordinating Bureau of Non-Aligned Countries in New York since the Ministerial Meeting of the Bureau in New Delhi, April 1977" (NAC/CONF.5/FM/WP.2), July 22, 1978.

28. The concept of individual and collective self-reliance was introduced in the movement's discussion at the 1970 Dar-es-Salaam Preparatory Conference of Non-Aligned Countries for the Lusaka Summit, during which President Julius Nyerere addressed himself to this objective; the documents of the Dar-es-Salaam meeting are reprinted in Jankowitsch and Sauvant, *Documents of the Non-Aligned Countries*, pp. 162–79.

29. Reprinted ibid., pp. 85–90.

30. Reprinted ibid., pp. 446–58.

31. The major item on the agenda of the 1972 Georgetown Conference of Foreign Ministers — the general view of the international situation — was subdivided into political issues, economic issues, and cooperation and coordination among Non-Aligned Countries. A Political Committee of the Conference dealt with political issues and an Economic Committee dealt with the other two issues areas. The 1973 Algiers Summit and the 1975 Lima Conference of Foreign Ministers were structured in a similar way.

32. In questions like the representation of Cambodia in, and the admission of the Republic of Korea to, the United Nations, for instance, the Non-Aligned Countries were deeply divided.

33. First Conference of Heads of State or Government of Non-Aligned Countries, "Declaration," ibid., pp. 3–7.

34. Second Conference of Heads of State or Government of Non-Aligned Countries, "Programme for Peace and International Co-operation," ibid., pp. 44–59.

35. Note, however, the exception of the 1962 Conference on the Problems of Economic Development, which adopted the "Cairo Declaration of Developing Countries," ibid., pp. 72–5.

36. Ibid., pp. 189–279 for text.

37. Ibid., pp. 1989–2044 for text.

38. Ibid., pp. 1214–81 for text.

39. Peru as a member, for instance, Mexico as an observer.

40. Fourth Conference of Heads of State or Government of Non-Aligned Countries, "Economic Declaration" and "Action Programme for Economic Co-operation," ibid., pp. 214–26 and 227–37, respectively.

41. See, for instance, ibid., pp. 216, 219.

42. Ibid., p. 222.

43. Fifth Conference of Heads of State or Government of Non-Aligned Countries, "Report by the President in Office and Messages Sent by the Presiding Country," ibid., p. 1039.

44. For an elaboration of this issue area, see Karl P. Sauvant, "His Master's Voice," *CERES* 9 (Sept.–Oct. 1976): 27–32.

45. In Jankowitsch and Sauvant, *Documents of the Non-Aligned Countries*, p. lx.

46. To quote from the "Declaration" of the 1976 Ministerial Conference on the Press Agencies Pool: "Non-aligned countries meeting for the first time at the high political level of Ministers of Information . . . have recognized the need to liberate their information and mass media from the colonial legacy. . . . The Conference noted that: . . . Just as political and economic dependence are legacies of the era of colonialism, so is the case of dependence in the field of information which in turn retards the achievement of political and economic growth. . . . The Conference reaffirmed . . . that the establishment of a New International Order for Information is as necessary as the New International Economic Order." Ibid., pp. 1553–55.

47. The main steps after Algiers and Lima were the March 1976 symposium on information in Tunis which clarified a number of conceptual questions, the July 1976 Ministerial Conference on the Press Agencies Pool in New Delhi, the establishment of a Co-ordination Committee of the Press Agencies Pool of Non-Aligned Countries, and the formation of an Intergovernmental Council for the Co-ordination of Information among Non-Aligned Countries. The documents relating to these activities are contained in ibid. For a brief summary of these developments, see Herbert I. Schiller, "Decolonization of Information: Efforts Toward a New International Economic Order," *Latin American Perspectives* 5 (Winter 1978): 35–48.

48. The 1970 Lusaka Summit Economic Declaration and the 1972 Georgetown Foreign Ministers Declaration focused primarily on self-reliance.

49. United Nations, *International Development Strategy: Action Programme of the General Assembly for the Second United Nations Development Decade* (New York: United Nations, 1970).

50. First Conference of Heads of State or Government of Non-Aligned Countries, "Declaration," in Jankowitsch and Sauvant, *Documents of the Non-Aligned Countries*, p. 5.

51. The "Final Act" is contained in UNCTAD, *Proceedings of the United Nations Conference on Trade and Development, Geneva, 23 March–16 June 1964*, vol. I, *Final Act and Report* (New York: United Nations, 1964), pp. 3–98. This volume also contains the "Joint Declaration" which dealt with the international trade and development policies that a number of developing countries—the later Group of 77—expected to emerge from UNCTAD I.

52. As indicated in chap. 1, the developing countries had formed, during UNCTAD I, an ad hoc voting alliance of their African, Asian, and Latin American groups for the purpose of coordinating and presenting their positions. This voting alliance subsequently became the Group of 77, a permanent but noninstitutionalized body to articulate and pursue the economic interests of the the the developing countries within the United Nations. For an analysis of the origin, organization, and objectives of the Group of 77 and their documents, see Karl P. Sauvant, ed., *The Third World without Superpowers*, 2d Ser., *The Collected Documents of the Group of 77* (Dobbs Ferry, N.Y.: Oceana, 1980).

53. For UNCTAD II, see UNCTAD, *Proceedings of the United Nations Conference on Trade and Development, Second Session, New Delhi, 1 February–29 March 1968*, vol. 1, *Report and Annexes* (New York: United Nations 1968); for UNCTAD III, see UNCTAD, *Proceedings of the United Nations Conference on Trade and Development, Third Session, Santiago de Chile, 13 April to 21 May 1972*, vol. 1, *Report and Annexes* (New York: United Nations, 1973): and for UNCTAD IV, see UNCTAD, *Proceedings of the United Nations Conference on Trade and Development, Fourth Session, Nairobi, 5–31 May 1976, vol. 1, Report and Annexes* (New York: United Nations, 1977). The texts adopted during these conferences, as well as during other UNCTAD conferences, are contained in Sauvant, *The Collected Documents of the Group of 77.*

54. Reprinted ibid.

55. Fourth Conference of Heads of State or Government of Non-Aligned Countries, "Political Declaration," in Jankowitsch and Sauvant, *Documents of the Non-Aligned Countries*, pp. 189–206.

56. "Communiqué, Reservations and Annex," ibid., p. 507.

57. Ibid., p. 219.

58. United Nations General Assembly resolution 3201 (S-VI), adopted May 1, 1974, by the Sixth Special Session of the United Nations General Assembly, reprinted in Appendix A of this volume.

59. United Nations General Assembly resolution 3281 (XXIX), adopted December 12, 1974, by the regular Twenty-ninth Session of the United Nations General Assembly, reprinted in Appendix A of this volume. Negotiations on the elaboration of the Charter had started early in 1973 in a Working Group of 40 countries.

60. In Jankowitsch and Sauvant, *Documents of the Non-Aligned Countries*, p. 222.

61. See, United Nations, General Assembly, Twenty-seventh Session, *Official Records,* United Nations document A/PV.2096, pp. 1–10. This speech set in process a motion that eventually led to the establishment within the United Nations of the Commission on Transnational Corporations and the Centre on Transnational Corporations.

62. The documents relevant to these developments are contained in Jankowitsch and Sauvant, *Documents of the Non-Aligned Countries*.

63. In a letter to the Secretary-General of the United Nations, dated January 18, 1974.

64. Thirteen major developed nations participated. France participated, but dissented in many points of the final communiqué in which the United States initiatives were generally adopted. While no explicit call for an oil price decrease was included in the communiqué, then Secretary of State Henry Kissinger made it clear that a "fair price" for crude petroleum — a price lower than the existing one but considerably higher than that of September 1973 — was a major objective of the United States policy.

Decisions taken at the Washington Conference eventually (November 18, 1974) led to agreement on an International Energy Programme, to be implemented through an International Energy Agency (set up by the Council of the OECD and within the framework of that organization). For further details, see Wolfgang Hager, "Die Internationale Energie-Agentur: Problematische Sicherheitsallianz für Europa," in *Erdöl und Internationale Politik*, ed. Wolfgang Hager (Munich: Piper, 1975).

65. See "Request for the convening of a special session of the General Assembly: Letter dated 30 January 1974, addressed to the Secretary-General by the Permanent Representative of Algeria to the United Nations" A/9541, February 5, 1974.

66. United Nations General Assembly resolutions 3201 (S-VI) and 3202 (S-VI), adopted May 1, 1974, reprinted in Appendix A of this volume.

67. The origin of the Sixth Special Session in the intensifying North-South conflict was probably largely responsible for the rather combative atmosphere during that session.

68. *Declaration*, Paragraph 4(e).

69. It should be noted that several countries expressed their reservations regarding a number of the articles of the "Declaration" as well as the "Programme of Action" after these resolutions had been adopted by consensus; they are contained in United Nations documents A/PV.2229-2231 and are reprinted in Appendix A of this volume.

70. The first of these suggestions is implicitly contained in the Algiers Summit Action Programme's paragraphs calling for expeditious agreements on commodity arrangements and its observation regarding terms of trade.

71. A specific reference to the promotion of the processing of primary products had, however, been included in the "Declaration" adopted at the 1970 Lusaka Summit.

72. While the Sixth Special Session had an explicit reference to access to consuming markets, such a reference is not contained in the Algiers Summit document; however, as observed earlier, both the 1964 Cairo and 1970 Lusaka Summits urged action in this direction.

73. Programme of Action, section I, para. 3b.

74. As mentioned above, the non-aligned formulation also included a quest for "non-discrimination."

75. Not included were a clause on the use for development of funds released by disarmament and a special reference to preferential treatment for developing countries in international monetary arrangements; the latter matter was, however, covered by a blanket provision in the "Declaration."

76. Earlier documents of the non-aligned movement also contained such a request.

77. For instance, "to promote close co-operation in the fields of finance, credit relations and monetary issues" (Programme of Action, section VII, para. 1.f).

78. Action Programme, para. xii.

79. Programme of Action, section I, para. lc; see also elsewhere in the Declaration and the Programme of Action. An even weaker reference is contained in section VII, para. la, of the Programme of Action, but one making an explicit reference to OPEC.

80. The section on technology in the Algiers Summit Action Programme asked for the implementation of the pertinent provisions in the United Nations Second International Development Strategy which spelled out a comprehensive set of measures relating to technology.

81. In the Programme of Action of the Sixth Special Session, food was a sub-section of the section on raw materials and trade.

82. In the Programme of Action of the Sixth Special Session, this item, too, was a sub-section of the section on raw materials and trade.

83. The text of the 1975 UNIDO "Lima Declaration and Plan of Action on Industrial Development and Co-operation" is contained in Sauvant, *The Collected Documents of the Group of 77.* The contents of these documents is largely identical with the documents adopted by the preceding Second Ministerial Meeting of the Group of 77, contained in ibid.

84. The programme of Action of the Sixth Special Session also contained brief separate sections on the Charter of Economic Rights and Duties of States (urging its adoption at the Twenty-ninth session of the General Assembly); assistance in the exercise of permanent sovereignty over natural resources; and the strengthening of the role of the United Nations system in the field of international economic cooperation. These subject matters reflected special concerns of the developing countries, in some cases of very long standing. On the other hand, the areas of environment and cooperation with socialist countries did not enter the United Nations document.

85. Resolution 3362 (S-VII), reprinted in Appendix A of this volume.

86. Given that the non-aligned movement had largely been ignored by the developed countries, it would not be surprising if delegations of these countries were not aware of this fact.

87. OPEC's price-hike did, however, produce internal strain in the movement (which expressed itself especially on regional levels). Suggestions were advanced to give special considerations to non-oil-exporting developing countries through, for instance, the introduction of two price levels and the establishment of a special fund. The strain caused by the oil price change is also reflected in the "Final Document" of the March 1974 meeting of the Co-ordinating Bureau of Non-Aligned Countries at the Ministerial Level. A paragraph noted as one major event in international relations, "the increasingly effective mobilization by the non-aligned and other developing countries of their national resources for the benefit of their economic development. The joint action undertaken in this connexion by the whole group of oil exporting countries represents an initial success and an encouragement to persist in this course," and this was immediately followed by another paragraph pointing to the "paramount need for co-operation among the non-aligned countries in evolving, urgently and in a spirit of solidarity, all possible measures to assist the non-aligned and other developing countries to cope with the immediate problems resulting from this legitimate and perfectly justified action." The Co-ordinating Bureau even recommended that a working group be set up "for discussions with the Organization of Petroleum Exporting Countries designed to explore the possibilities of co-operation between non-aligned countries for resolving the difficulties facing certain non-aligned countries." (In Jankowitsch and Sauvant, *Documents of the Non-Aligned Countries,* pp. 1382, 1385, respectively.) Although selected OPEC members made concessions to selected non-oil-exporting developing countries, OPEC as an organization has so far not adopted relief measures.

3

The NIEO Program: Reasons, Proposals, and Progress

Karl P. Sauvant

In the first two chapters, the origin and evolution of the program for the New International Economic Order (NIEO) were examined. In this chapter, I shall examine the underlying approach of the program as well as its substantive content in the main areas of North-South interaction[1]: trade and commodities, finance and money, science and technology, industrialization and transnational enterprises, and food and agriculture.

The first objective of this chapter, then, is to outline what it is that the developing countries have proposed and that the United Nations has accepted as a whole in principle.[2]

The NIEO program has not, of course, been formulated in a vacuum but, rather, in reference to the concrete situation of the developing countries. To understand the program fully and to appreciate the urgency behind it require that this situation be understood as well. Hence, throughout this chapter the presentation of the program is preceded by a review of the main problems facing the Third World. The second objective of this chapter, then, is to explain the reasons for the developing countries' proposals.

Wherever progress has been made in implementing the program, this is described in conjunction with the relevant discussions. The current state of global negotiation is noted in a concluding section.

The NIEO Approach

One of the main characteristics distinguishing the NIEO program[3] from earlier international economic programs is its basic objectives: to change the purposes, mechanisms, and structures of the international economic system.

The institutions of the present system were designed *by* the developed market economies *for* the developed market economies (DMEs). Their main purpose was to facilitate the reconstruction of the economies devastated by World War II and to integrate them into an open international economic system. The interests, needs, and special conditions of the developing countries (DCs) were largely ignored since most of them were still colonies or under hegemonic domination at the end of that war. It was assumed that the growth of the DMEs would trickle down to the DCs and, further supported by regional and international development efforts, lead to a rapid improvement of the latter's standard of living.

When this did not occur to the extent desired and absolute poverty continued in large parts of the Third World, the DCs could not but conclude that the international economic system itself needed to be changed. This change had to begin with the very purposes that the system was meant to serve and development had to be specifically included among them. In their view, development should no longer be regarded as an indirect by-product of the workings of the international economic system; rather, provisions had to be made to establish an international framework directly supportive of the modernization efforts of the Third World. It was, moreover, explicitly recognized that the required changes "would also contribute to strengthening peace and security in the world,"[4] i.e., were in the overall interest of a comprehensive world security policy.

Against this backdrop, it was stated in the preamble of the Sixth Special Session's "Declaration on the Establishment of a New International Economic Order":

> We, the Members of the United Nations, . . . *solemnly* proclaim our united determination to work urgently for THE ESTABLISHMENT OF A NEW INTERNATIONAL ECONOMIC ORDER based on equity, sovereign equality, interdependence, common interest and co-operation among all States, irrespective of their economic and social systems which shall correct inequalities and redress existing injustices, make it possible to eliminate the widening gap between the developed and the developing countries and ensure steadily accelerating economic and social development and peace and justice for present and future generations.

The "Charter of Economic Rights and Duties of States" repeated these objectives and further elaborated on the developmental ones among them.

Although this passage has already been quoted in the preceding chapter, it is repeated here because it sets the tone, captures the spirit, and indicates the direction of the ensuing NIEO discussions. It also conveys something of the atmosphere of awakening, self-confidence, and departure that characterized the Sixth Special Session and made it a breakthrough experience for the developing countries.

At the same time, the Special Session was a shock for the developed countries. The abrupt politicization of the development issue on the basis of a fully mobilized Third World and in the context of demonstrated assertiveness (the OPEC events) had come too unexpectedly. All of a sudden, the Third World sought to define the international framework in its development effort by itself—or at least to play an active, larger part in its shaping. Consequently, the DMEs found themselves on the defensive. The American ambassador at the United Nations, John A. Scali, for instance, spoke about the "tyranny of the majority,"[5] and warned with reference to the General Assembly that "the steamroller is not the vehicle for solving vital, complex problems."[6] It almost appeared as if the industrialized countries had been confronted with the problem of underdevelopment in all of its dimensions for the first time at a high political level: "We have heard your voices. We embrace your hopes. We will join your efforts. We commit ourselves to our common success."[7]

The Sixth Special Session and the Charter raised the development issue to one of the main purposes of the international economic system. However, if its acceptance is not to remain mere rhetoric but, rather, become the basis of an international development strategy, it has to be translated into changes in the mechanisms governing the interactions between North and South; it must transform the system's present hierarchical structures (which are the result of past and present patterns of interaction) into horizontal ones.[8] Any international development strategy has, therefore, to be founded on the recognition of the special situation of the DCs as historically disadvantaged and structurally dependent underdeveloped economies. These economies have to be protected against the overwhelming preponderance of the DMEs. One way, at least in theory, in which this can be done is by delinking them completely from the North, i.e., by turning the world-market orientation of the prevailing strategy into one of individual and collective self-reliance.

The NIEO program, however, in spite of references to individual and collective self-reliance,[9] has clearly opted for the continuation of the integrative, world-market oriented approach. Hence, the protection of the Third World economies is to be secured by other means. This is exactly what the Charter attempted to achieve when it stipulated:

> With a view to accelerating the economic growth of developing countries and bridging the economic gap between developed and developing countries, developed countries should grant generalized preferential, non-reciprocal and non-discriminatory treatment to developing countries in those fields of international economic co-operation where it may be feasible.[10]

This stipulation can be generalized to mean that not only should selected industries of the DC economies be treated like infant industries, but that the considerations underlying this approach—generalized preferential, nonreciprocal, and nondiscriminatory treatment—should be applied to the DC economies *in their entirety*. If this is the case, the NIEO program advocates a broadened infant-industry approach, within the framework of a market- and world-market orientation, as a means to overcome underdevelopment. Consequently, the economic rights and duties of states have to be allocated asymmetrically. Applied to the trade area, for instance, this approach requires the introduction of a one-way free trade zone[11].

The underdevelopment of the Third World economies and their preferential treatment in economic matters should not be used as a pretext to regard these countries as unequal members of the international system. To reaffirm this, the Charter proclaimed a number of principles that should serve as "fundamentals of international economic relations."[12]

Beyond outlining the general approach for achieving the NIEO, the Charter and the resolutions adopted at the Sixth and Seventh Special Sessions also suggested concrete strategies through which the development objective of the international system is to be translated into new mechanisms and structures in the main areas of North-South interaction: trade and commodities, finance and money, science and technology, industrialization and transnational enterprises, and food and agriculture.[13] Although these areas are discussed individually in the following pages, it is one of the main characteristics of the NIEO program to stress their interdependence. Thus, for instance, the Third World's industrialization target of 25 percent of world manufacturing output by the year 2000 has clear implications for trade, transfer of technology, and finance. It is, in fact, one of the merits of the NIEO program to draw attention to these interrelationships and to deal with the development process as a whole.

I shall now turn to the principal proposals for each of the main areas just identified, giving special attention to trade and commodities (particularly the Integrated Programme for Commodities) and to finance and money since these two areas play a key role in North-South relationships. As already indicated, in an effort to facilitate the understanding of the proposed measures, each will be related to the existing situation in North-South relations.

The NIEO Program

Trade and Commodities

THE SITUATION

The NIEO program builds on past strategies in regarding trade as the engine of development. In this role, trade has two functions: (1) to generate the foreign-exchange earnings necessary to finance the import of capital goods, and (2) to stimulate industrialization. A number of obstacles, however, have impeded the full realization of these objectives.

The share of the DCs in world trade has steadily declined throughout the 1950s and 1960s, from 31 percent in 1950 to 18 percent in 1972 (see table 3.1; all tables to which reference is made in chapter 3 appear in Appendix C). The down-trend only reversed itself in 1973 when the value of OPEC oil exports began to contribute an increasingly larger proportion of the total export earnings of the developing countries. But the share of the non-oil-exporting DCs remained largely unchanged so that in the 1970s they accounted for only somewhat over one-tenth of world exports.

In 1977, close to two-thirds of the exports of the non-OPEC DCs consisted of primary products. Food and raw materials alone accounted for one-half, and fuels for one-seventh. Although these figures indicate progress as compared to 1963 (the share of manufactures in exports increased from one-tenth to one-third), the structure of these exports is still worse than the reverse of that for the DMEs where primary products account for one-fourth (and this share is falling), and manufactures for three-fourths (see fig. 3.1). On the import side of the non-OPEC DCs, more than half consists of manufactured goods, one-fifth of oil, approximately one-seventh of food, and one-sixteenth of raw materials.

This composition of Third World trade explains, to a large extent, its declining share in world commerce. First, the prices of many of the commodities exported by the DCs (especially tropical beverages and agricultural raw materials, but also petroleum) deteriorated throughout the 1950s and most of the 1960s in relation to the prices of the manufactured goods exported by the DMEs (and imported by the DCs) (see fig. 3.2). UNCTAD and World Bank data show that the primary commodities/manufactures terms of trade of the developing countries—that is, the index of unit values of primary commodities (excluding petroleum) exported by the DCs divided by the index of unit values of manufactured goods exported by DMEs—declined at an average annual rate of about 2 percent during the period 1953–1972.[14] As a result, the DCs' overall purchasing power during most of that same period eroded as well, whereas that of the DMEs improved (see table 3.2). Beginning in 1973, the petroleum price changes drastically improved the terms of trade of the oil-exporting countries, but negatively affected those of the DMEs, and further worsened those of the other DCs (although the latter, as a group, benefited from the 1973–1974 commodity boom).

Second, the volume of the main export products of the developing world has grown at a pace considerably slower than that of manufactures (see table 3.3): between the base year of 1963 (= 100) and 1977, the index for agricultural products increased to 165, that of raw materials and fuels to 190, and that of manufactures to 345. The main reasons for

Figure 3.1. Product composition of trade, by country group, 1963 and 1977
(Billion dollars and percent)

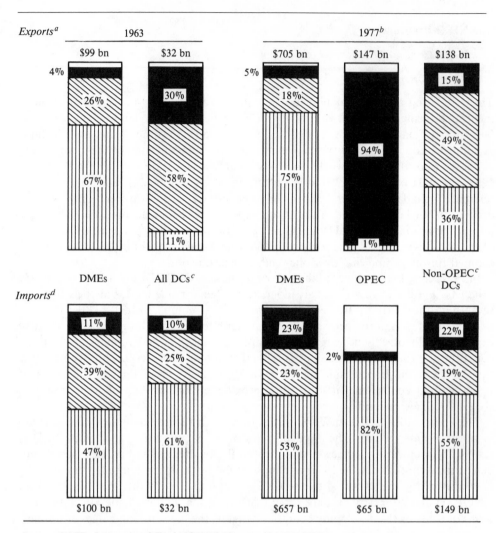

Source: GATT, *International Trade 1977/78* (Geneva: GATT, 1978).

[a]F.o.b.
[b]Provisional.
[c]Including Australia, Israel, New Zealand, and South Africa.
[d]Corresponds to world exports (f.o.b.) to the area reported. Data are for 1963 and 1976.

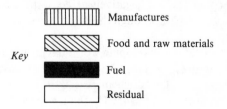

Key

|||||| Manufactures

///// Food and raw materials

■ Fuel

□ Residual

Fig. 3.2. Price indices of primary commodities of particular export interest
to developing countries, 1960–1976[a]

(1963 = 100)

Index of nominal prices

Index of real prices, i.e., primary commodity
terms of trade[b]

Source: UNCTAD, *Monthly Commodity Price Bulletin: 1960–1976 Special Supplement* (Geneva: UNCTAD, 1977).

[a]The price index is a composite of the prices of the four main groups of commodities: (1) food and beverages (wheat, maize, rice, sugar, coffee, cocoa, tea, beef and veal, bananas, pepper); (2) vegetable oilseeds and oils (soybean oil, sunflower oil, groundnuts, groundnut oil, copra, coconut oil, palm kernels, palm kernel oil, palm oil, linseed oil); (3) agricultural raw materials (cotton, wool, sisal, abaca, jute, rubber); and (4) ores and metals (manganese ore, iron ore, aluminum, copper, lead, zinc, tin, tungsten).

[b]Index in current dollars (i.e., nominal prices) divided by the United Nations index of export unit values of manufactured goods.

the slow growth of primary goods include the relative decline of the proportion of raw materials used in production processes (and their partial replacement by synthetics and substitutes), and the low income and price elasticity of demand for agricultural products (aggravated in some instances by protectionist measures of leading developed countries). Given the high export dependence of the DCs on primary products, these two trends have greatly affected the Third World's economic position and are, thus, a major concern to them.

The export dependence of DCs on primary products is further accentuated by their dependence on a very limited number of these products. Excluding oil, a dozen raw materials represent half of all their commodity exports. For many countries, this dependence is even greater. Overall, more than 30 countries during the mid-1970s derived over half of their total export earnings from only one primary material, and about an additional 20 from two (see fig. 3.3). The number of countries that find themselves in high dependence has hardly changed over the last decade. Thus, in 1965, two or more commodities accounted for 50 percent or more of exports for 63 countries; in 1975, the figure was 59 countries. If the threshold is lowered to 30 percent of exports, 84 and 82 countries, respectively, experienced such dependence (see table 3.4).

Furthermore, the annual receipts from these exports often fluctuate considerably, due to short-term changes in volume (for example, poor crops) and prices. Almost one-tenth of the DCs' non-fuel primary commodity exports were subject to price fluctuations of over 15 percent from one year to the next, and another one-fourth to fluctuations of 10–15 percent (see table 3.5). Such instability makes economic planning for development as well as balance-of-payments management extremely difficult and leads to investment cycles that further contribute to supply uncertainties.[15]

For many countries, therefore, the performance of one or two commodities virtually governs the availability of foreign exchange and, to a large extent, even the size of the domestic budget. This, in turn, immediately affects the country's ability to import capital goods, service or repay debts, make domestic investments, and so on. The long-term deterioration of the purchasing power of many primary products, the slow expansion of the trade volume of these products, and the frequent short-term fluctuation of export receipts, thus, directly affect the ability of the DCs to strengthen their economies. In fact, a good percentage of financial assistance merely compensates for the deteriorating purchasing power of many DCs or is used to bridge foreign-exchange gaps created by short-term fluctuations. Any international development program has to take these facts into account.

The preceding discussion has focused on what was identified as the first function of trade: the supply of foreign exchange. The second function, it was suggested earlier, is to stimulate industrialization and, through it, development in general. The obvious starting point is to increase the processing of primary products in the DCs. Although the developing world produces one-third of the world's most important minerals, it processes only about 30 percent of them and consumes only 6 percent (see tables 3.6, 3.7).[16] Most of these minerals, in other words, are supplies for the developed countries where they are processed and fabricated, a division of labor that has not changed significantly during the past three decades.

The situation can be illustrated in further detail for the international bauxite-aluminum industry: the DCs mine three-fifths of the market economies' bauxite, process one-fourth, smelt one-fifteenth, and fabricate one-fiftieth (see table 3.8)—a pattern that is largely the result of the intrafirm division of labor practiced by the major enterprises dominating the industry (see fig. 3.4). This distribution of the various stages of the production process is important because it determines the division of labor between developing and developed countries and, thereby, the division of associated benefits. In the bauxite-aluminum industry, for instance, the amount of value added at each of the four stages of production increases at a ratio of approximately 1:2.5: 8:17. Thus, one ton of semifabricated aluminum yields a gross income about 17 times higher than that created by mining. As a result, for example, only 6 percent of the total value added by the processing of Caribbean metal-grade bauxite is created at the mining level; the rest is created at higher levels in developed countries.[17]

Although detailed comprehensive data do not exist regarding the distribution of benefits between producing and consuming countries, some partial data are available that give an indication of the prevailing pattern. Data on the shares of the prices received by DCs in the final consumer price of commodities exported by them show that there are wide margins between the price obtained by the producing countries and the retail price paid by consumers in DMEs (see table 3.9). To give a few examples: the price the DCs obtained (average 1967–1972) for iron ore was only about 10 percent of the price paid by consumers for the final product, and that of cocoa in the range 12–20 percent (depending on the final market). The share in the final price of aluminum sheets sold in the United States illustrates how the benefits grow with increased processing: it was 5 percent for bauxite, 14 percent for alumina, and 38 percent for aluminum ingot. Partly as a result of the monopolistic or oligopolistic organization of the trading, marketing, and processing stages, the margins between export and consumer prices increased considerably over the past 20 years for many products; even where they remained stable, however, the absolute take of the intermediaries has often risen disproportionately when prices increased. Thus, restraining the share of the intermediaries would allow increases in the export prices without accompanying increases in consumer prices.

More detailed data on the distribution of benefits are also available for selected industries. For instance, the share of the producing countries' economic rent (defined as the price received minus costs)[18] in final consumer prices has been (in 1976) around one-twentieth for bauxite and iron ore, one-eighth for phosphate rock, one-fourth for tin, and one-third for petroleum (see table 3.10). For bauxite (see the breakdown into various economic-rent components contained in table 3.11) and phosphate rocks, the DCs' share in relation to that of the DMEs has deteriorated considerably since 1974, the year the producers had succeeded (through parallel or coordinated actions) in raising significantly their share in the total economic rent. Above all, however, the available data demonstrate the importance of diversifying beyond the mining level—in order to protect gains made in the distribution of the total economic rent between producer and consumer countries and to increase these gains and capture the spin-off effects associated with high value-added processing.

This analysis leads to a consideration of the structures of transportation, marketing, and distribution of primary and other products.[19] These structures are frequently dominated by vertically integrated transnational enterprises (TNEs) (even if, as in the petroleum industry [see table 3.12], ownership at the production level had to be relinquished and control over downstream activities decreased). It is estimated that the share of TNEs in Third World exports (excluding oil) amounts to about 40 percent; moreover, a good percentage of non-TNE exports utilizes their facilities. Thus, in international seaborn trade (an important service industry), the DCs account for over 60 percent of all foods loaded and less than 2 percent unloaded; but their share in world tonnage (ex-

Fig. 3.3. Export dependence of developing countries, by primary product.[a]
(Percentages)

Region and country	Percent and commodity		Percentage of total export earnings

Scale: 0 — 50 — 100

Latin America

Country	Values	Commodity	Percentage
Bolivia	44.8 / 20.9	tin, petroleum	65.7
Chile		copper	66.1
Costa Rica	28.3 / 23.8	coffee, bananas	52.1
Dominican Republic	46.0 / 12.1	sugar, coffee	58.1
Ecuador		petroleum	51.4
El Salvador	47.4 / 10.7	coffee, cotton	58.1
Panama	31.9 / 28.7	refined petroleum, bananas	60.6
Uruguay	26.7 / 23.6	meat, wool	50.3
Venezuela		petroleum	93.5

Caribbean

Country	Values	Commodity	Percentage
Guyana	37.9 / 30.0	sugar, bauxite	67.9
Jamaica	46.6 / 18.6	aluminum, bauxite	65.2
Netherlands Ant.		petroleum	88.4
Suriname	43.7 / 25.2	alumina, bauxite	68.9
Trinidad & Tobago		petroleum	84.8

Africa

Country	Values	Commodity	Percentage
Algeria		petroleum	89.9
Burundi		coffee	86.9
Chad		cotton	65.1
Ethiopia	45.4 / 9.0	coffee, hides & skins	54.4
Gambia		groundnut products	87.9
Ghana		cacao	55.0
Liberia		iron ore	66.8
Libyan Arab Jamahiriya		petroleum	99.9
Malawi	41.7 / 18.3	tobacco, tea	60.0
Mauritania		iron ore	80.7
Mauritius		sugar	87.0
Morocco	41.2 / 8.8	phosphates, citrus fruit	50.0
Niger	37.1 / 15.8	uranium, groundnuts	52.9

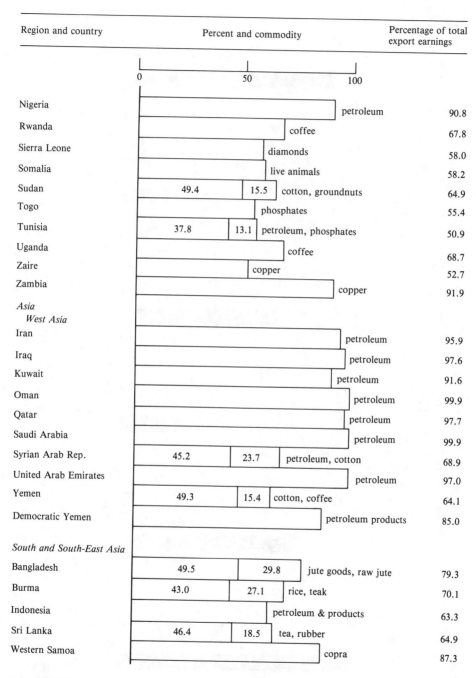

Region and country	Percent and commodity	Percentage of total export earnings

0 — 50 — 100

Nigeria	petroleum	90.8
Rwanda	coffee	67.8
Sierra Leone	diamonds	58.0
Somalia	live animals	58.2
Sudan	49.4 / 15.5 cotton, groundnuts	64.9
Togo	phosphates	55.4
Tunisia	37.8 / 13.1 petroleum, phosphates	50.9
Uganda	coffee	68.7
Zaire	copper	52.7
Zambia	copper	91.9

Asia
  West Asia

Iran	petroleum	95.9
Iraq	petroleum	97.6
Kuwait	petroleum	91.6
Oman	petroleum	99.9
Qatar	petroleum	97.7
Saudi Arabia	petroleum	99.9
Syrian Arab Rep.	45.2 / 23.7 petroleum, cotton	68.9
United Arab Emirates	petroleum	97.0
Yemen	49.3 / 15.4 cotton, coffee	64.1
Democratic Yemen	petroleum products	85.0

South and South-East Asia

Bangladesh	49.5 / 29.8 jute goods, raw jute	79.3
Burma	43.0 / 27.1 rice, teak	70.1
Indonesia	petroleum & products	63.3
Sri Lanka	46.4 / 18.5 tea, rubber	64.9
Western Samoa	copra	87.3

Source: IMF, *International Financial Statistics,* July 1978.
[a]Countries shown are those for which one or two export products account for 50 percent or more of the country's export earnings, taken on a five-year average over the latest five years available.

Fig. 3.4. Intrafirm distribution of production capacities of the main transnational aluminum enterprises: location in developing countries, by stage of processing.[a]

(Percentage)

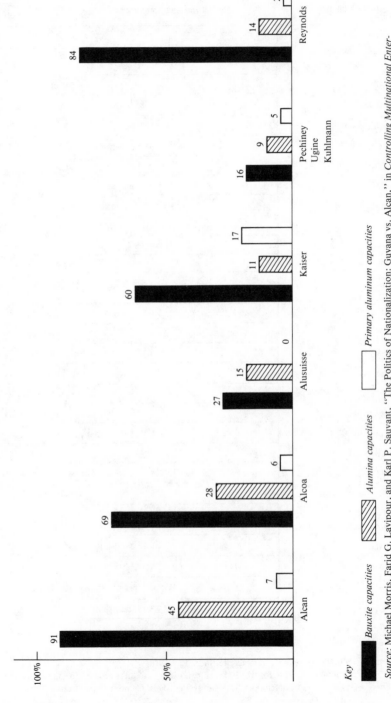

Key

■ Bauxite capacities   ▨ Alumina capacities   □ Primary aluminum capacities

Source: Michael Morris, Farid G. Lavipour, and Karl P. Sauvant, "The Politics of Nationalization: Guyana vs. Alcan," in Controlling Multinational Enterprises: Problems, Strategies, Counterstrategies., ed. Karl P. Sauvant and Farid G. Lavipour (Boulder, Col.: Westview Press, 1976).

[a]Bauxite data are for 1973; all other data for 1971.

cluding Liberia and Panama) is only about 7 percent. At the same time, freight rates for a number of commodities exported by DCs have increased considerably.[20]

In many primary-product industries, the share of transactions controlled by TNEs is even larger. Furthermore, it is coupled with a high degree of concentration, with the same TNEs often occupying a prominent place in several raw material industries (see tables 3.13 to 3.22). To return to the example of the international bauxite-aluminum industry, four North American enterprises account for nearly half of the market economies' bauxite, alumina, and primary aluminum capacity, and all of them are, to a large extent, vertically integrated. In fact, hardly any transactions take place in the industry that are not intrafirm. Prices, therefore, are not determined by the market.[21] Consequently, the aggregated locational decisions of these enterprises play a very important role in determining the division of labor between developed and developing nations. However, it has to be noted that administrative factors, and especially the tariff structure, encourage a certain division of labor. Although tariffs on raw materials average 2 percent in industrial countries, they increase to an average of 8 percent for semifinished manufactures, and to 10 percent for finished goods (see tables 3.8 and 3.23). To these, a host of nontariff barriers (especially for processed and unprocessed food products), "voluntary" export restraint agreements, "orderly marketing arrangements," and other protectionist policies have to be added (see tables 3.24, 3.25).[22] UNCTAD has estimated that the tariffs leveled on goods imported by DMEs from DCs are about 50 percent higher than those faced by imports from DMEs.[23] Clearly, the effect of such a cascading structure of trade obstacles is to impede export-led development. As a result, the industrialization-stimulating effect of trade—as well as its foreign exchange-creating function—remains underutilized.

A final observation of the trade situation of the DCs concerns their dependence on few trading partners and, indeed, companies. In many cases, a substantial share of their exports are absorbed by one developed country (in many cases the former colonial power), for which, however, the products involved constitute only a minor share of its imports (see table 3.26). Thus, in 1975, the most important trading partner absorbed half or more of all exports for 19 DCs (only two of these trading partners were other DCs). For an additional 27 countries, the most important trading partner absorbed between 30 and 49 percent of exports (out of 101 countries for which information was available). On the other hand, for only three of these trading partners did these imports account for more than 2 percent, and most shares were below 1 percent. Although this dependency has increased for a number of DCs over the period 1965–1975, for the DCs as a group it has decreased: in 1965 one trading partner had an export share of 30 percent or more for 65 countries, but by 1975 this number had decreased to 46 (see table 3.27). The already very low import share of the Northern countries frequently declined further, except when these imports originated in OPEC countries. As far as the imports of the DCs are concerned, about six DMEs supply the bulk of imports of the DCs. The asymmetry is obvious: the DCs as a group (let alone individually) have virtually no influence over the terms and conditions of their exports (exempting important products like oil), whereas the DMEs often can control them. It should not be overlooked, moreover, that export or import dependence on a few countries frequently means dependence on a few companies. For instance, approximately 60 percent of Suriname's exports are made up of bauxite; of these, 90 percent are shipped to the United States and 10 percent elsewhere. What these figures disguise is that all transactions are initiated by affiliates of Alcoa and Royal Dutch/Shell, and that most of the exports are sent to affiliates of these companies.[24]

THE INTEGRATED PROGRAM FOR COMMODITIES

The trade and commodity section of the NIEO program addresses itself to all of the problems described above. In the light of the situation faced by the Third World, the focus is necessarily on primary products. Given the magnitude and extent of these problems, that they involve the entire structure of trade relations between North and South, and that the past piecemeal approach has not been successful, it is necessary to develop a set of mechanisms that deals with these problems in a suitably broad and comprehensive manner. UNCTAD's Integrated Programme for Commodities is, so far, the only approach that meets these criteria. Its overall objectives are to introduce "an important element of global resource management in the interests of the development process" and to promote, simultaneously, "a more orderly evolution of commodity supply in the interests of the world economy as a whole."[25] The question is not whether or not resources should be managed—primary product markets have always been managed markets, dominated by monopolies or oligopolies—rather, it is *who* should manage these markets, TNEs (as in the past) or governments, and *in whose interests* they should be managed, those of the developed countries alone (as in the past) or also those of the developing ones? Consistent with the inclusion of development among the principal purposes of the international economic system, and taking into account the new international context discussed earlier, the Integrated Programme leaves no doubt as to the answer.

The "preparation of an overall integrated programme, setting out guidelines and taking into account the current work in this field, for a comprehensive range of commodities of export interest to developing countries" had been mandated by the Programme of Action adopted by the Sixth Special Session in May 1974.[26] The main components and mechanisms of the program were determined by the Seventh Special Session in September 1975. Finally, the concept of an international integrated approach to the commodity problem was endorsed by UNCTAD IV in Nairobi in May 1976.[27]

The commodities to be covered were also selected at UNCTAD IV, after extensive preparations and intensive discussions. The list (see table 3.28) contains 18 commodities of particular export interest to Third World countries. Ten of them (representing roughly three-fourths of the total value of the entire list) have been designated as "core" commodities for which immediate action is required. For each of these ten, the DCs account for more than 50 percent of world exports (see table 3.28). The proceeds from all 18 represent a little over half of all DCs' non-fuel commodity exports; in fact, for the "hard core" least developed countries, the ten commodities alone account for almost half of their export earnings (see table 3.29). Conversely, all 18 commodities represent only 5 percent of the total imports of the DCs and 10 percent of those of the DMEs.

Specifically, the main objectives of the Integrated Programme are (1) to stabilize the conditions of commodity trade, especially regarding fluctuations in prices and export earnings; and (2) to initiate efforts aimed at expanding and diversifying the production capacities and exports of the developing countries. In the words of UNCTAD, the Integrated Programme is designed:

1. To achieve stable conditions in commodity trade, including avoidance of excessive price fluctuations, at levels which would:
   (a) be remunerative and just to producers and equitable to consumers;
   (b) take account of world inflation and changes in the world economic and monetary situations;

(c) promote equilibrium between supply and demand within expanding world commodity trade;

2. To improve and sustain the real income of individual developing countries through increased export earnings, and to protect them from fluctuations in export earnings, especially from commmodities;

3. To seek to improve market access and reliability of supply for primary products and the processed products thereof, bearing in mind the needs and interests of developing countries;

4. To diversify production in developing countries, including food production, and to expand processing of primary products in developing countries with a view to promoting their industrialization and increasing their export earnings;

5. To improve the competitiveness of, and to encourage research and development on the problems of natural products competing with synthetics and substitutes, and to consider the harmonization, where appropriate, of the production of synthetics and substitutes in developed countries with the supply of natural products produced in developing countries;

6. To improve market structures in the field of raw materials and commodities of export interest to developing countries;

7. To improve marketing, distribution and transport systems for commodity exports of developing countries, including an increase in their participation in these activities and their earnings from them.[28]

The two key measures proposed to achieve the first of these objectives involve the establishment of international buffer stocks for a number of commodities[29] (with priority attention to the ten core commodities), and the creation of a Common Fund for the financing of these stocks. The main function of the buffer stocks is to absorb business cycle and other market fluctuations—to balance supply and demand in a rational manner—by stabilizing the prices of the products covered between lower and upper price margins, selling when the upper margins are reached, and buying at the lower ones. Since persistent imbalances cannot be excluded, provisions would have to be made for supply management (for example, export and production quotas). In addition, bilateral and multilateral long and medium-term supply-and-purchase contracts (incorporating, perhaps, elements of the grain agreement between the Soviet Union and the United States[30]) would further contribute to market stability and to a smoother and noncyclical functioning of demand-supply patterns.

The establishment of buffer stocks in the framework of international commodity agreements obviously requires capital. UNCTAD estimated that the costs for financing an optimally operating network of buffer stocks for the ten core commodities would amount to $4.5 to $5 billion.[31] It was envisaged that a Common Fund would manage these monies and provide the required capital to the institutions managing the individual buffer stocks. The Fund, therefore, plays a key role; without it, a system of buffer stocks could not be established and maintained, and markets could not be stabilized. Having its own capital, on the other hand, the Common Fund could play an active catalytic role in bringing about commodity agreements, even though these activities would be restricted by the capital ceiling under which it would have to operate. It was proposed that the capital of the Fund be subscribed by producers and consumers of the commodities involved, and that the Fund be managed by representatives of the funding countries. A key advantage of the Common Fund is that, as long as demand-supply patterns of the individual commodities do not move parallel to each other, costs for one stock can be off-set by gains from the others; hence, the amount of capital needed is less than the sum of capital required for separately held stocks. In addition, such a Fund could be expected to obtain better access to capital markets and more favorable borrowing terms than could individual buffer stocks. Provisions have also been made for commodities not covered by the buffer-stock system; they would be protected by an enlarged and liberalized IMF compensatory financing facility,[32] and, as far as the Third World signatories to the Lomé Convention are concerned, by the scheme for the stabilization of export earnings established under that agreement and the sugar protocol attached to it.

Obviously, the determination of prices (and their adjustment) for the individual commodities covered by the Integrated Programme are crucial issues in this scheme. In a world in which 5 to 10 percent inflation is the rule, any price range agreed upon in nominal terms will soon be eroded in real terms. Periodic adjustments, therefore, are necessary to protect the real prices originally negotiated. Any agreement that does not make provisions for such adjustments would, in fact, be asking the Third World to institutionalize the deterioration of its terms of trade.

In the context of commodity agreements, such an adjustment mechanism could be direct indexation, that is, the direct regulation of market prices in accordance with overall price trends.[33] The initially negotiated price margins could, for instance, be linked to the price of a basket of goods imported by the DCs. In cases where the long-term equilibrium trend of the real market price of a commodity is deteriorating, the negotiated real price has to be supported by the reduction of supply.[34] Buffer stocks would play an important role here since they provide the time necessary for recognizing trends and for facilitating the adjustment process.

Direct indexation, however, is not a suitable mechanism for commodities that exhibit a declining real price trend and that have a high elasticity of demand. In such cases, the price effect obtained by the decrease of supply would tend to be offset by the loss of revenue due to decreased consumer demand (and, thus, decreased export volume). Here, an alternative mechanism could be indirect indexation. Arrangements of this type would not necessitate a regulation of market prices; rather, the purchasing power of commodity exporters would be maintained by direct financial transfers in cases in which market prices do not reach a negotiated real-terms reference price for any particular commodity.[35] Similarly, repayments would be made in years in which market prices are above the reference price. Even here, however, some management of supply (especially export quotas) is required in order to discourage excessive production.

None of these mechanisms, however, fully eliminates short-term fluctuation in commodity export *earnings* in reference to a predetermined target level of real earnings. Such fluctuations, as observed earlier, are the result of short-term changes in export quantitites or short-term *price* fluctuations. (The latter would, however, be contained by the operations of buffer stocks as well as a system of indirect indexation.) To deal with such fluctuations, it is suggested that the existing IMF compensatory financing facility be liberalized and enlarged. UNCTAD has further recommended the creation of a globalized and more comprehensive facility for the stabilization of export earnings, modeled on the STABEX scheme agreed upon in the Lomé Convention (and possibly even incorporating some of its resource-transfer features).[36] Like the STABEX scheme, the UNCTAD system is designed to offset short-term export earnings fluctuations regardless of cause. One modification concerns the product coverage, which is to be extended; another concerns the two thresholds that must be passed, under the Lomé Convention, before a country qualifies for compensation (UNCTAD suggests a single-value threshold). The main modification, however, concerns the reference level that would trigger payments: in the STABEX scheme, this level is defined in terms of nominal earnings around the market trend. The UNCTAD proposal works with real earnings in reference to a minimum real-terms target level that also incorporates an element of growth.[37] Extending the application of the system to general shortfalls in real export earnings, regardless of whether they are caused by primary commodities or by manufactures, is also proposed.

Together, these facilities would provide a "safety net" that could protect the DCs from those instabilities which originate in the DMEs and are transmitted to them through the mechanisms of an integrative aid-by-trade development strategy. Still, the stabilization of export earnings is merely a platform from which other more forward-looking measures can be initiated to diversify the production capacities and exports of the DCs and to capture a greater share in downstream activities and the benefits associated with them.

The second main objective of the Integrated Programme concerns these "other measures," whether to be taken by the eligible international commodity bodies or by governments that have received the endorsement of such bodies. They include international measures aimed at improving the competitiveness of natural products in regard to synthetics and substitutes (through, for instance, productivity improvements, R and D promotion), and measures directed toward the encouragement of vertical diversification. Hence, they aim at broadening the spectrum of DCs' exports and include the improvement of (and greater participation in) transportation, marketing, and distribution facilities.

In a sense, then, the second objective of the Integrated Programme is the more dynamic and future-oriented part of the package. Its purpose is to change the character of the underlying structures through which the DCs are integrated in the international economic system. More concretely, the intention is to transform the DCs from primary-product suppliers into processors and manufacturers. At the same time, dependence would be reduced—in terms of the number of principal traded products, the principal trading partners, and TNEs participating in trade.

UNCTAD estimated that financial resources in the magnitude of $1 to 1.5 billion are necessary to initiate, over a period of several years, a set of meaningful measures to reach these objectives.[38] These financial resources would also be managed by the Common Fund, but through a second account—a "second window," so to speak. The upper limit of the Common Fund was envisaged to be in the order of $6 billion. It was proposed that his amount would be raised through borrowing ($4 billion) and direct government contributions ($2 billion).

UNCTAD IV, with its endorsement of the Integrated Programme, had authorized the commencement of two interrelated sets of activities: (1) the establishment of a Common Fund to finance buffer stocks and other measures in the framework of international commodity agreements, and (2) the negotiation of such individual international commodity agreements.

After a great number of meetings and extensive negotiations, agreement was reached in March 1979 on the fundamental elements of the Common Fund.[39] The Fund, through its first window (but without intervening directly in commodity markets), is to contribute to the financing of buffer stocks established in the framework of international commodity agreements representing producers and consumers. The first window will begin operations with a foundation capital of $400 million from direct government contributions.[40] In addition, the international (producer-consumer) commodity agreements associated with the Common Fund are expected to deposit with it one-third of the funds needed for the financing of their buffer stocks. The Common Fund, in turn, will provide finance (as loans) for up to two-thirds of the value of the stocks to be created under individual commodity agreements associated with it (i.e., the balance required). The Fund, therefore, will act as a banker to each commodity agreement but cannot intervene directly in commodity markets; this will be left to the managers of individual agreements. The target capital for the second window is $350 million.[41]

The administration of the Fund is vested in a Governing Council (aided by a secretariat), overseen by an assembly. Votes in the assembly will be distributed on the basis of the following: Group of 77, 47 percent; DMEs, 42 percent; socialist countries of Eastern Europe, 8 percent; and China, 3 percent. No group, however, will be in a position to impose its preferences on the others since the most important decisions (including constitutional decisions and those with significant financial implications) require a majority of 75 percent of total votes cast.

The present arrangement greatly limits the catalytic role originally envisaged for the Common Fund. Under UNCTAD's 1976 plan, the Fund would have had at its disposal financial resources of $6 billion, of which one-third ($2 billion) would be in the form of direct contributions from *members of the Common Fund*. With these financial means, the Fund could, indeed, have taken the initiative in dealing with unstable commodity markets. Under the present arrangement, the $2 billion will have to be provided by the *members of the individual commmodity agreements as they are being set up*. The Fund's foundation capital will be used to raise the balance of (under UNCTAD's estimate) $4 billion. Nevertheless, modest and limited as these results are, the very establishment of the Common Fund is a step in the direction of implementing the NIEO commodity program. It is a particularly important step because, as UNCTAD observed, "implicit in its creation is the endorsement by the international community of the concept of market regulation on a much wider scale than before."[42]

In the parallel negotiations involving international commodity agreements, progress has been very slow.[43] This may have been, in part, to await the outcome of the negotiations regarding the Common Fund; but, mostly, this reflects a lack of commitment by a number of participating countries to accept commodity arrangements as appropriate instruments for dealing with commodity markets. After numerous preparatory meetings dealing with a dozen commodities included in the Integrated Programme but not yet covered by international commodity agreements, only the discussions about natural rubber reached the stage of a negotiating conference and led, in April 1979, to agreement about the key elements of a market-stabilizing accord that was, in fact, concluded in the fall of 1979. Agreement in principle has been achieved on the need for an arrangement for tea. A relatively advanced stage of the discussion had been reached, by the spring of 1979, for copper, cotton, jute, hard fibers, and tropical timber. As far as manganese, iron ore, phosphates, and vegetable oils are concerned, however, the nature of international action that is required has not yet been sufficiently clarified; for bauxite and bananas, no preparatory work whatsoever has taken place.[44] Progress has been registered for some products already covered by international agreements. Thus, by the spring of 1979, the International Sugar Agreement and the International Olive Oil Agreement had been renewed and negotiations were underway for the extension of the International Cocoa Agreement and the adaptation of agreements for coffee and tin. On the other hand, negotiations for a new wheat agreement (not one of the commodities specified by UNCTAD) were suspended.

THE TRADE PROGRAM

The commodity program flows seamlessly into the NIEO trade (and industrialization) program.[45] The close interrelationship with trade is particularly important since, as in the past, trade is regarded as the engine of development. In fact, given the DCs' very optimistic goal of producing 25 percent of the world's industrial output by the year 2000 (as compared with the present 8 percent), improved trading conditions and the diversification and expansion of trade in manufactures and semimanufactures have become matters of even greater urgency. It has been estimated that the volume of Third World manufactures exports will have to grow at an annual rate of 11 percent for the rest of this century in order to reach this goal.[46] To achieve this target, trade relations must also be intensified among DCs.[47] UNCTAD's proposal to establish a special system of trade preferences among DCs is one of the measures meant to serve this purpose.[48] Most trade, however, is still expected to be directed toward the DMEs.

Trade liberalization and improved access to the markets of the DMEs are, therefore (and in the tradition of past UNCTAD efforts), central planks of the NIEO trade program. The removal, or at least the reduction, of tariff and nontariff barriers is, thus, of special importance. Great attention is also paid to the improvement of the nonreciprocal, nondiscriminatory Generalized System of Preferences (GSP). It is suggested to extend it to all products of export interest to developing nations (including, in particular, agricultural products); to eliminate all safeguards, ceilings, and similar restrictions; to relax, simplify, and harmonize rules of origin; to expand the GSP to cover also nontariff barriers; and to make the GSP a permanent fixture of world trade.[49] Stimulating effects of trade are expected from a commitment of the DMEs to refrain from the application of countervailing duties and to control restrictive business practices through the adoption and enforcement of a set of international rules.[50] Finally, and with increasing urgency, the DCs warn of the proliferation of protectionist policies (including "voluntary" export restraint agreements), which have a negative and potentially serious effect on world trade.[51]

Many of these issues were considered by the "Tokyo Round" of Multilateral Trade Negotiations which were held under the auspices of GATT between 1973 and the spring of 1979. On the urging of the Group of 77, GATT recognized "the importance of the application of differential measures to developing countries in ways which will provide special and more favourable treatment to them."[52] The trade negotiators were entrusted to give special attention to those products of special export interest to the Third World and whose liberalization has tended to lag behind that of products of primary trading interest to industrial nations.

In the end, however, the results of the Tokyo Round greatly disappointed the developing countries. The tariff cuts that were stipulated represented a 33–38 percent reduction from the present tariff levels and are scheduled to be implemented in eight annual stages beginning in January 1980; but the largest reductions will be made in trade among DMEs. Reductions affecting imports from the DCs will average only about 25 percent. This is partly the result of already low tariff levels (e.g., because of privileges obtained under the GSP); however, this also reflects the fact that many of the products exported by DCs are import-sensitive to DMEs (e.g., textiles).[53]

In addition, a number of codes were adopted dealing, among other things, with the use of export and domestic subsidies, customs valuation, and government procurement. However, at the time of the initialing of the results, agreement had not yet been reached on a code to regulate the safeguard measures that might be taken against "disruptive" imports. Under the old régime,[54] a GATT member can take emergency measures to limit imports that cause (or threaten to cause) serious "injury" to domestic industry; these measures have to be applied against all suppliers. In the Tokyo Round negotiations, the European Community in particular insisted that it should also be permissible to apply such measures selectively, i.e., only against a specific "offending" importer. Such an approach has met with strong resistance from the Third World. It is, in fact, one of the expressions of the growing protectionism that the DCs consider as a serious threat to their industrialization efforts.[55] The results of the Tokyo Round, therefore, reinforced the DCs' conviction that fundamental revisions of the principles governing trade relations are necessary.

The NIEO program recognizes that one of the main barriers to trade liberalization is its expected impact on the domestic production of DMEs. The DCs, therefore, increasingly point to the need for anticipatory industrial policies. It is hoped that an industrial policy aimed at such adjustments would gradually soften the main sources of resistance to trade liberalization in developed countries and, in fact, lead to redeployment of certain industrial processes and even whole industries to the Third World.[56] To facilitate the achievement of this goal, a "system of consultations" for the two country groups has been established.[57]

NATIONALIZATION AND PRODUCERS' ASSOCIATIONS

For most DCs, diversification of their economies has to start with their primary products. The Integrated Programme and the trade measures outlined above are designed first to stablilize and then to improve the international framework for these products. However, there exists also an internal component to these efforts which focuses on the primary-product ventures located in the Third World. They must yield a maximum economic rent[58] and must be integrated as far as possible into the local economy to create forward and backward linkages and, thereby, stimulate industrialization.[59] Where and when foreign ventures resist such a policy, or where and when their performance in this regard is perceived to be inadequate, the DCs are prepared to use their right to nationalize the facilities in question and they reserve the right to settle any dispute under domestic law. The objective is to harness the resources—both natural ones and others—of the developing countries as effectively as possible for their own development. As the data cited in chap. 1 indicate, incidents of nationalization have increased, as have renegotiations of contracts.[60]

To legitimize acts of nationalization further, the DCs insisted, in a very strong provision in the Charter of Economic Rights and Duties of States, that:

> Each State has the right: . . . (c) To nationalize, expropriate or transfer ownership of foreign property, in which case appropriate compensation should be paid by the State adopting such measures, taking into account its relevant laws and regulations and all circumstances that the State considers pertinent. In any case where the question of compensation gives rise to a controversy, it shall be settled under the domestic law of the nationalizing State and by its tribunals, unless it is freely and mutually agreed by all States concerned that other peaceful means be sought on the basis of the sovereign equality of States and in accordance with the principle of free choice of means.[61]

The industrial countries do not deny that states—as an expression of the principle of permanent sovereignty over natural resources—have the right of nationalization. But they insist that "prompt, adequate, and effective" compensation be paid and that, in the case of disagreement, the parties can have recourse to international law.

Closely related to this issue is the question of producers' associations. They are another mechanism to capture and improve the potential developmental benefits associated with primary products. In addition, they serve to strengthen the negotiating position of the DCs vis-a-vis the DMEs and their transnational enterprises. As discussed in the preceding chapters, the success of one of these producers' associations, OPEC, was instrumental in launching the NIEO discussions on the international level and in stimulating the expansion of existing associations and the creation of new ones. The Charter, therefore, declared explicitly that "all States have the right to associate in organizations of primary commodity producers"; and the Programme of Action of the Sixth Special Session even provided that "all efforts should be made . . . to facilitate the functioning and to further the aims of producers' associations."[62] The DCs' insistence on the Integrated Programme indicated, however, that they are well aware of the limits of unilateral actions and depend on cooperative measures for the solution of their most important raw material problems.

Finance and Money

FINANCE FOR DEVELOPMENT

The financial resources required to improve the economic situation of the developing countries are tremendous. The greatest part of them (80–90 percent) is generated from domestic savings. But, if visible progress is to be achieved, these have to be supplemented by external resources. This is—and has been—a central tenet of the prevailing international development strategy. To quote the OECD:

> It is important to recall that a central objective of international economic policy has been to encourage deficits by developing countries in order to transfer investment goods and services for their development programmes. This objective is as valid for the future as it has been for the past.[63]

To finance these deficits, the developed and developing countries had agreed, within the framework of the United Nations International Development Strategy, that net capital flows from the developed to the developing countries should reach 1 percent of the GNP of the former; 70 percent of these flows were to take the form of official development assistance (the "0.7 percent target").

Developing countries' need for external finance greatly increased at the beginning of the 1970s, when the sharp escalation of prices for foodstuffs and petroleum, the inflationary price rises in fertilizers and capital goods,[64] and the export-dampening recession in the industrial countries severely aggravated the financial position of the non-oil-exporting developing countries.

The severity of these developments is reflected in the dramatic deterioration of the current-account balance of payments of the non-oil-exporting countries. Thus, the current-account deficits of these countries jumped from $10 billion in 1973 to a peak of $41 billion in 1975 (see table 3.30). Since then, they receded temporarily, but only to reach a new high of over $40 billion in 1979—and this in spite of a certain curtailment of imports (which slows the development effort) and heavy foreign borrowing (which, while helping to sustain the development effort and, incidentally, world demand in a period of recession, burdens the developing economies with interest and amortization payments).

The estimated external finance requirements of the developing countries (excluding the capital surplus oil exporters) to sustain an annual GDP growth rate of 5.2 percent during 1975–1985 reflect this changed situation (see table 3.31). These requirements are projected to increase from $64 billion in 1976 to $283 billion in 1985 (at current prices; $133 billion at 1975 prices). A substantial share of these additional requirements, in fact more than one half, will be needed for debt-service payments (projected for 1985 at $44 billion, current dollars) and the repayment of the principal (projected at $122 billion). These requirements will have to be met through official development assistance (ODA), i.e., concessional official bilateral and multilateral flows for development purposes with a minimum grant element of at least 25 percent; and long-term official and private non-concessional flows, i.e., transactions at commercial terms, mostly export credits, bilateral portfolio investments (including bank lending), and direct investments (including reinvested earnings).

Overall, total net flows to DCs from all donor groups—i.e., the Development Assistance Committee (DAC), OPEC, centrally-planned economies— more than doubled in dollar terms from $36 billion in 1973 to $76 billion in 1977 (see table 3.32).[65] The most notable change in the regional composition of these flows is the emergence of the OPEC countries as major donors: their share in the total increased from 5 to 10 percent during that period.

Concessional Flows

Another notable change in the composition of financial flow is the decreasing share of the concessional component.[66] In fact, to cite a United Nations document: "The distribution of long-term financing between concessional and non-concesisonal flows is almost in exact reverse relation to that envisaged in the Strategy, with ODA flows from developed countries becoming an increasingly less significant component of total flows."[67] Reference is made here to the above-mentioned target of the International Development Strategy that 70 percent of total flows should be at concessional terms and 30 percent at nonconcessional terms, and to the fact that, in 1977, the actual statistics showed the reverse.

ODA flows from all regions amounted to $21 billion in 1977, of which $15 billion originated in the DMEs, $6 billion in the OPEC countries, and less than $1 billion in the centrally planned economies (see fig. 3.5).[68] While flows originating in OPEC countries have increased dramatically since 1973, those from the centrally planned economies have decreased. As a result, OPEC's share in total flows jumped from 11 percent in 1973 to 27 percent in 1977, whereas that of the centrally planned economies slumped from 10 to 3 percent. In terms of GNP, the OPEC countries are now dedicating over 2 percent of their national incomes to the development effort, as opposed to less than 0.5 percent for the centrally planned economies. The DMEs, with 70 percent of total concessional flows in 1977, remain the main donor group. The terms of their ODA transfers have improved over the past seven years: maturities and grace periods became longer, the grant element increased, and interest rates remained relatively stable (see fig. 3.6); but the share of the DMEs in total concessional transfers has decreased, their ODA flows in real terms have remained stable for most of the period since 1961, and the average share of their ODA contributions as a percentage of GNP has stagnated (after a substantial decline during the 1960s) at around 0.33 percent since the beginning of the 1970s (see tables 3.33, 3.34,

Fig. 3.5. Net disbursements of official development assistance, by major groups of donors and as percentage of GNP, 1970, 1973–1977.

(Billion dollars and percent)

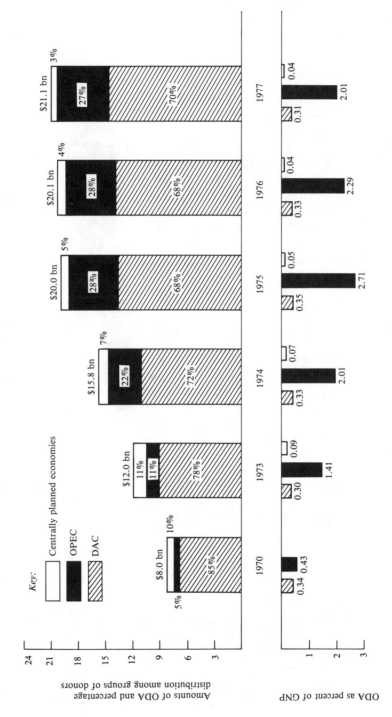

Source: OECD, *Development Co-operation* (Paris: OECD, various years).

99

Fig. 3.6. Average terms of ODA commitments of DAC countries: maturities,
interests, grace periods, grant element, 1971–1977.
(Years and percent)

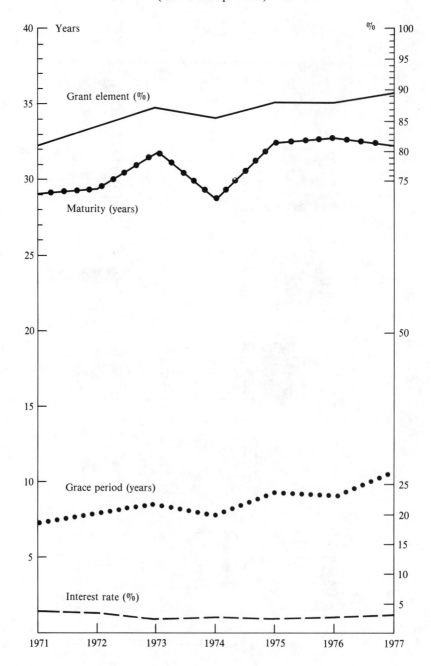

Source: OECD, *Development Co-operation* (Paris: OECD, varoious years).

and fig. 3.7).[69] The shares of some major countries—such as the United States, Japan, Switzerland, and the Federal Republic of Germany—are even below this very low average GNP share (see table 3.34). Concluded the UNCTAD Secretariat:

> These figures suggest that something is basically wrong. The provision of aid, rather than changes in the basic structure and in market mechanisms, was the preferred approach of the developed market-economy countries in response to the development problem. Yet this decline in the relative aid effort took place during a period of unprecedented prosperity and expansion, which saw a rapid improvement in living standards in these countries.[70]

The declining relative importance of ODA in total flows is most dramatically shown by the data pertaining to the DAC member countries which, with 90 percent of all flows, are still by far the most important donors. Looking at the entire period since the beginning of the First Development Decade, the share of ODA in total net flows originating in DAC countries decreased from about 60 percent in 1961 to 24 percent in 1976 (see table 3.33).

The NIEO program reaffirms the importance of ODA and makes its improvement one of its key planks. Specifically, in reaffirming the target set earlier by the International Development Strategy, it stipulates that ODA should reach, at the latest by 1980, 0.7 percent of each donor country's GNP[71] and, as a rule, be untied. Most donor countries, although accepting the target per se, have refused to commit themselves to the target date. And about half of all aid remains tied or partially tied (i.e., procurement is limited to the donor country) (see table 3.35).

One important reason why ODA has not kept its relative position in total financial flows is its voluntary character, making it dependent on changing political and economic situations in individual donor countries. The resolution adopted at the Seventh Special Session states that concessional flows should be made "predictable, assured and continuous."[72] The exploration of other mechanisms that would fulfill these characteristics is encouraged.

In the spirit of these objectives, a number of measures have been suggested.[73] Thus, as far as the improvement of budgetary practices and policies is concerned, suggestions include multiyear aid programming and budgeting (thereby insulating foreign-aid allocations from annual discussions and, thus, allowing longer-term planning and implementation);[74] non-lapsing provisions for aid flows that have already been approved but are not expended during a given fiscal year (in order to avoid arbitrary losses or ill-prepared end-of-the-year spending);[75] recycling of interest and amortization receipts from past development loans (instead of returning them into general revenue)[76]; and aid budgeting in constant prices (in order to maintain the real value of appropriations).[77]

Many of these considerations apply not only to bilateral flows but also to the provision of funds to multilateral financial institutions such as the regional development banks, the World Bank Group (especially the resources of the International Development Association and, while it was still operative, the Bank's Third Window), and the United Nations Development Programme.[78] The facilities provided by these institutions are particularly important since recourse to them frequently helps to smooth fluctuations of financial receipts, whether caused by the instability of development-assistance flows or instability of export earnings. Governments are, therefore, particularly encouraged by the NIEO program to enlarge the resources of, and improve access to, the multilateral financial institutions.

Fig. 3.7. Development assistance committee: ODA net disbursements, in current prices, constant prices, and percent of GNP, 1961–1977.
(1961 = 100).

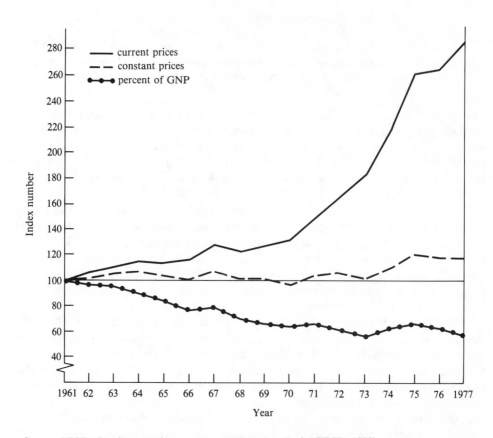

Source: OECD, *Development Co-operation: 1978 Review* (Paris: OECD, 1978).

Among other mechanisms to increase financial flows, the most well-known is the proposal to institute a link between the distribution of special drawing rights (SDRs) by the IMF and development assistance (see below). Another involves the introduction of a development tax, the proceeds of which would be earmarked automatically for the financing of development programs.[79] If such a tax were to be levied on an expanding economic activity, a predictable, assured, continuous, and growing resource flow would be generated. Moreover, if such an economic activity has an international dimension—as does trade—the interest of all countries in stable and continuous world economic growth would be furthered. A tax on internationally traded goods is, in fact, one of the variations that is being discussed in this context. But a progressive income tax or a tax on the consumption of certain luxury goods would serve the same purpose. A third and, at that, quite radical proposal aims at linking a reduction of military expenditures with the provision of development finance. This thought has been the subject of a study by a United Nations group of experts and has also found its way into the

"Declaration" and the "Programme of Action" adopted by the Tenth Special Session of the United Nations General Assembly devoted to disarmament.[80]

Finally, proposals have been made to distribute royalty payments from seabed mining, as well as from the utilization of other international commons, and to use the profits of gold sold by the IMF for development aid. The latter measure has already been implemented through the establishment of the IMF Trust Fund (see below). Some of these proposals are certainly ambitious and far-reaching; all represent efforts to establish a rational system of international financial cooperation in the interest of facilitating the development effort.

Nonconcessional Flows

In the absence of sufficient ODA, DCs increasingly have been compelled to rely on nonconcessional finance. These flows amounted to $53 billion in 1977, nearly all of which originated in industrialized countries (see table 3.32). Among the nonconcessional flows originating in DAC countries, foreign direct investment has kept its share of about one-fourth to one-third, while Eurocurrency credits increased in the mid-1970s to over one-third of all DAC nonconcessional flows. This latter development has made the Eurodollar market one of the most important sources of development finance, a source rivaling total ODA in volume.[81]

Unfortunately, not all DCs have equal access to private international capital markets. Commercial lenders have shown a clear preference for the middle-income countries, i.e., those whose level of development, large export volume, and market size provide them with a certain measure of apparent creditworthiness and profitability (see table 3.36). Consequently, the large majority of DCs has only very limited access to these markets. As a matter of fact, only six to ten countries benefit from most (roughly two-thirds) of the foreign direct-investment flows, export credits, funds raised by international bond issues, and of publicized Eurocurrency credits. Thus, the low-income countries, more than ever before, have to rely on ODA to supplement their domestic resources. The relative decline of ODA, therefore, "has resulted in shifting a disproportionately greater burden of adjustment to poorer countries."[82]

Given the importance of private capital markets as sources of finance, it is not surprising that the NIEO program calls for improved and broader access (under favorable terms). Obstacles that impede such access, apart from considerations of creditworthiness and profitability, mostly involve a host of governmental rules and regulations.[83] Thus, for instance, statutory provisions (e.g., for insurance companies and pension funds) in some DMEs set ceilings on the acquisition of debt issued abroad. Frequently, bond issues of nonnationals also have to comply with stricter regulations than those issued by nationals and, in addition, may be subjected to discriminatory tax treatment (e.g., higher taxes on interest earned and the withholding of certain exemptions granted to domestic issues). Finally, controls on the outflow of capital, likewise, may impede access to capital markets. Beyond abolishing such obstacles, governments can take positive steps to provide—or facilitate—access to nonconcessional development finance. The above-mentioned multilateral financial institutions, some of which have nonconcessional facilities, are of relevance here, as are official guarantees of export credits, an approach that already has a long tradition in DMEs. In the same vein (i.e., combining official efforts with private activities),[84] consideration could be given to providing guarantees for credits granted by the private sector to DCs (e.g., in the context of a multilateral guarantee scheme), to subsidizing the interest rates of borrowings by Third World countries from private capital markets (e.g., along the line of the World Bank's now defunct Third Window), and to encouraging cofinancing arrangements between multilateral institutions and private lenders for specific development projects.[85] All these measures aim at utilizing private capital for development purposes more effectively.

DEBT

The failure of the international financial system to provide (through official channels and under appropriate conditions) the funds required by the DCs for their development effort, and the resulting need for them to turn to private capital markets with their less favorable conditions, have placed a new and rapidly growing burden on the Third World: external indebtedness and the servicing of this debt. From $8 billion in 1955, the external medium- and long-term debt of the developing countries as a whole reached $48 billion in 1967, $114 billion in 1973, and $244 billion in 1977. For the non-oil-exporting countries alone, the figures for the last-mentioned three years were $42 billion, $92 billion, and $205 billion, respectively (see table 3.37 and fig. 3.8).[86]

Within four years, in other words, the nominal value of the external medium and long-term debt of the non-oil-exporting DCs more than doubled. To this, one has to add a short-term debt of $50 billion, most of which consists of self-liquidating trade credits, but some of which is also rolled over.[87] In fact, the total debt obligations of the non-oil-exporting DCs (excluding short-term debt) in 1977 exceeded their total value of exports by nearly 50 percent.

This rapid build-up of the external debt of the non-oil-exporting DCs has not been distributed evenly across country groups. The poorest countries (the 39 with a 1975 per capita GNP of $265 or less) increased their liabilities over the period 1973–1977 by only $17 billion, whereas the middle-income countries (the remaining non-OPEC DCs) increased theirs by $95 billion. The latter group, therefore, accounted for over 80 percent of the new liabilities incurred by the non-oil-exporting developing countries and, at the end of the period, accounted for four-fifths of their total debt (or two-thirds of the debts of all developing countries). Conversely, the share of the low-income non-oil-exporting DCs in total debt (and debt service) has fallen steadily since 1967. The concentration is even greater when the largest debtor countries are singled out. The three largest alone (Brazil, Mexico, and India) owe more than one-fourth of the total debt of all DCs; the 10 largest account for more than one-half (see table 3.38). Such a concentration is also characteristic of the lender's side: over half of the outstanding claims on the non-oil-exporting DCs are held by about 30 banks, most of them based in the United States. About three-fifths of the lending from private financial institutions is derived from this country as well.[88]

The growing role of nonconcessional (and particularly private) flows in providing finance for the developing countries has led to a deterioration of the terms of loan commitments.[89] On the average, maturities have shortened,[90] grace periods have been reduced, the grant element of loans has diminished, and interest rates have risen (see fig. 3.9). These changes are already partly reflected in debt-service payments (amortization plus interest). Such payments, which totaled $3 billion in 1960, increased from $16 billion in 1973 to $37 billion in 1977 for all DCs, and from $13 billion to $29 billion for non-oil-exporting countries alone (see fig. 3.8 and table 3.37). Thus, 1977 debt service payments by all DCs were 60 percent higher than total ODA from all sources and, in fact, absorb-

Fig. 3.8. Total external debt (disbursed) and debt service payments of developing countries,[a] 1960–1977. (Billions of dollars).

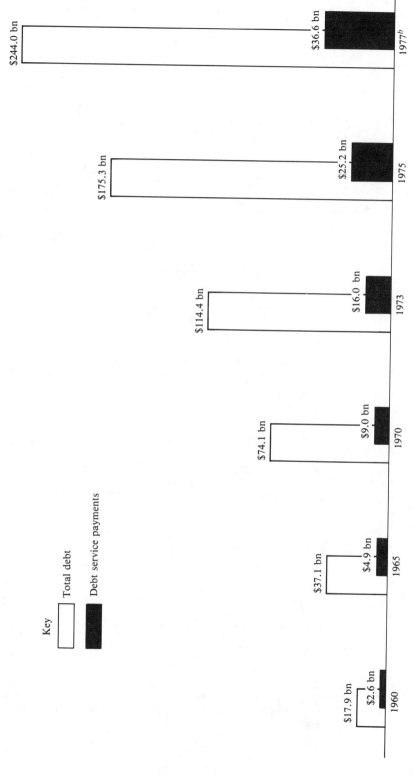

Key

☐ Total debt

■ Debt service payments

Source: OECD, *Development Co-operation: 1978 Review.*
[a]Includes intra-DC and Greece, Israel, Portugal, Spain, Turkey, and Yugoslavia.
[b]Provisional.

Fig. 3.9. Average terms of loan commitments to developing countries:[a] maturities, interests, grace periods, grant element, 1969–1976.
(Years and percent)

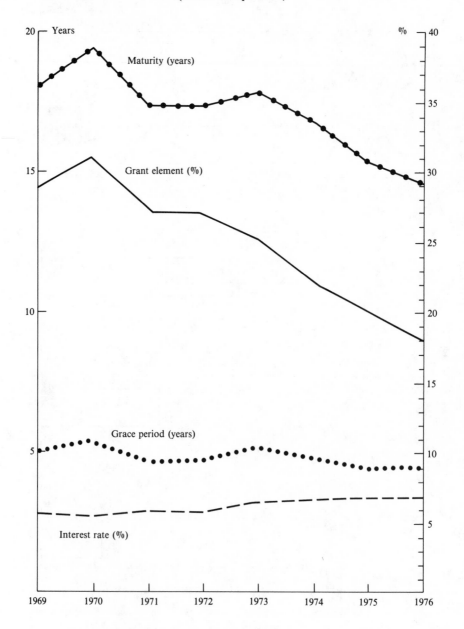

Source: World Bank, *Annual Report* (Washington: World Bank, various years).
[a]Eighty-four developing countries, including Cyprus, Greece, Malta, Portugal, Spain, Turkey, and Yugoslavia. Public debt only (i.e., debt that is a direct obligation of, or has repayment guaranteed by, a public body in the borrowing country).

ed exactly 50 percent of all financial resources made available to all DCs during the same year.

The main burden of these payments is, again, carried by the middle-income countries which, in 1976, had to raise over 90 percent of the debt service payments of all non-oil-exporting countries and over 70 percent of those of all DCs. Parallel to the concentration in the stock of debt, the three largest debtor countries alone account for one-third of all debt service payments, and the ten largest for three-fifths (see table 3.38).[91] Since debt service payments are, in a sense, a charge on export earnings, the burden of these obligations can be roughly appreciated from the debt service ratios of individual countries (see table 3.39). For 27 countries, the debt service ratio was 5–9.9 percent in 1977; for another 22, 10–19.9 percent; and for 8 countries, over 20 percent. Thus, even if in absolute terms debts and debt service payments are highly concentrated, the remaining amounts are still large enough to constitute a serious burden for many DCs.

The full impact of the worsening debt structure, however, will only be felt in the coming years. This is indicated by World Bank projections for public and publicly guaranteed debts of a large sample of developing countries. According to these projections, the average public debt service ratio of the nonsurplus oil-exporting DCs will rise from 12 percent in 1975 to 21 percent in 1985, with the middle-income countries bearing the brunt of the increase. As a result, nearly 5 percent of these countries' GNP, will be required in 1985 to service their external public debt (see table 3.40). If a similar acceleration applies to the servicing of the total debt of the DCs, the burden on the developing countries will be heavy indeed. In a number of cases, this situation may force Third World countries to choose between debt service payments and the pursuit of some of their development projects. This may particularly be the case because service payments are determined according to a fixed schedule that, for instance, does not take into account a country's balance-of-payments performance and, therefore, does not leave much room to maneuver. Furthermore, the debt burden encourages industrialization projects that are geared toward the world market, since they generate the foreign exchange required to service or repay these debts.

It is no wonder, then, that the debt issue has received priority attention by the developing countries, and particularly the non-oil-exporting ones among them. Although different groups of countries have different specific interests (e.g., those that have relatively easy access to capital markets do not wish to jeopardize this access), virtually all of them share a number of common characteristics and are faced with similar problems. First of all, their participation in international financial intermediation is marginal, partly because their individual and regional institutional financial infrastructure is very weak,[92] and partly because representation in international financial bodies is heavily biased in favor of creditors. As the United Nations observed in this context: "Clearly, the system cannot perform adequately in the long-run when the views of major users—whether creditors or debtors—are not fully reflected in decision-making."[93] Second, the difficulties of the non-oil-exporting DCs for the most part originate from the same set of problems, the solutions to which are largely beyond the control of individual Third World states: balance-of-payments deficits, the need to borrow substantially at high costs and under tight conditions in private capital markets, the rigidity of debt service schedules, and the deterioration of their terms of trade. Hence, common across-the-board measures are felt to be necessary.

The remedies advanced by the developing countries are very modest and deal mainly with debt relief in an international framework. More specifically, the Group of 77 has suggested, inter alia,[94] granting relief for official debts to countries seeking such relief in the form of waiving or postponing debt service payments (or components thereof) or canceling the principal; canceling the official debt owed by the least developed, land-locked, and developing island countries in its entirety; and according the same treatment to the most seriously affected countries or, "as a minimum," waiving their debt service payments on official debt "until they cease to be regarded by the United Nations as most seriously affected countries."[95] Subsequently, at UNCTAD IV, the DMEs agreed to take "prompt action to relieve developing countries suffering from debt service difficulties, in particular least developed countries and most seriously affected developing countries."[96] By the end of 1978, 11 industrialized states had acted along the lines of this agreement and canceled (or announced their intention to do so) official debts in the amount of $6.2 billion.[97]

Furthermore, the Group of 77 has proposed the reconsolidation (possibly through a new multilateral financial institution) of the commercial debt of interested DCs and the rescheduling of payments over a period of at least 25 years. In order to provide a common framework for debt relief measures, it is suggested to convene a meeting of major developed creditor and interested debtor countries to devise principles and guidelines governing the renegotiation of debts and leading to the multilateralization of measures aimed at relieving debt servicing pressures.

The DCs' preference for a multilateral approach to the debt problem is based not only on the international nature of the problem to be tackled, but also on the recognition that in case-by-case negotiations—in which one debtor faces a group of creditors—they find themselves in the weakest possible bargaining position.[98] In sum, the measures advanced by the DCs aim chiefly at seeking generalized relief for official debt (especially for the low-income countries among them) in a new international framework of debt renegotiation.

THE INTERNATIONAL MONETARY SYSTEM

Earlier in this section, in the course of the discussion of greater automaticity of development assistance, mention was made of a link between the distribution of SDRs and the allocation of financial resources for development. Since the creation of SDRs in 1968, the DCs have pressed for the establishment of such a link. The proposal is not to create SDRs in order to finance development; rather, it is to allocate a substantial share of SDRs, when they are created according to the needs of the management of the international monetary system, to developing countries. The issue, therefore, is not one of creation but of distribution. Under the current formula, SDRs are distributed on the basis of the quotas of the individual IMF member countries, which are determined by each country's financial circumstances[99] and, hence, are heavily weighted against the DCs (see table 3.41). As a result, those in need of additional finance obtain the least: in the allocation of new SDRs decided in December 1978, the DCs as a group received a share of 32 percent, of which 11 percent belong to OPEC countries alone. The precise purpose of introducing a link is to increase this share.[100] Since most of the funds received by the Third World would be spent for imports from industrial countries, the objective of maintaining sufficient liquidity for world trade as a whole would still be satisfied. At the present time, the distribution of SDRs on the basis of quotas widens, rather than narrows, international wealth inequalities.

The current formula of SDR allocation illustrates an underlying, built-in characteristic of the international monetary system (and, for that matter, of any national monetary system): it is biased against the poor in terms of the creation and distribution of international liquidity as well as access to it.

Before the introduction of SDRs, virtually all new international liquidity (i.e., new additions to international reserves[101]) was created by a few industrial countries (mainly the United States) because their *national* currencies were accepted as *international* reserve currencies. These countries, therefore, not only controlled the creation and growth (see fig. 3.10) of international liquidity (mostly through deficits in their balances of payments), but also were the main beneficiaries of this process, since they did not have to subject themselves to the rigors of the adjustment process which other deficit countries had to undergo. The strength of the DMEs is also reflected in the distribution of international reserves. Their share in the total declined from four-fifths in 1950 to three-fifths in 1977, only after the OPEC countries had asserted themselves; the share of the other developing countries remained relatively constant since World War II, at about one-sixth (see table 3.42).

The introduction of SDRs changed this situation somewhat by vesting in the IMF the decision to create some new international reserve assets. All market economies, including the developing ones, share in the control over the creation of SDRs. But this sharing is weighted, as is any other decision making, in the Fund.[102] Like the distribution of SDRs, it is determined by the quotas.

Although the quotas of the DCs (and their corresponding voting power) have increased substantially—from 20 percent in 1950 to 32 percent in 1981—the DMEs maintain a clearly dominating influence (see table 3.43). Hence, the main industrial countries remain in control of this liquidity-creating process with the United States and the European Community each having sufficient votes to veto any decisions in this matter, and they also remain its major beneficiaries.[103] Furthermore, the introduction of SDRs has not terminated the role of national reserve currencies. On the contrary, of the SDR 183 billion new international liquidity created between the end of 1969 (the year before the first SDRs were allocated) and the end of 1977, national currencies alone accounted for 92 percent. Newly issued SDRs, on the other hand, accounted for a mere 5 percent[104] and, to repeat, only about one-fifth of them were allocated to non-oil-exporting DCs. National reserve currencies thus actually strengthened their role as the most improtant reserve assets, making up three-fourths of total reserves (SDR 260 billion) in 1977.

The second most important reserve asset is gold which, in the international financial statistics of the IMF, continues to be valued at the official price of SDR 35 per ounce. By a decision of the IMF Interim Committee of January 1976 in Kingston,[105] however, it was agreed to abolish the official price of gold and to allow official transactions in gold at market prices.[106] If the 1977 gold holdings of IMF member countries are revaluated at the December 1977 London market price of gold ($164.95 per ounce), their value would increase from SDR 36 billion at the official price of gold to SDR 167 billion at the market price. This not only increases considerably the importance of gold holdings in total reserves but also creates new international liquidity of SDR 131 billion (at the chosen market price). The main beneficiaries of this revaluation are the industrial countries: since they hold over 90 percent of the gold stocks, they also obtain over 90 percent of the newly-created liquidity. As UNCTAD observed, the gold decision constituted, in fact, a "reverse link":[107] a redistribution of international reserves to the disadvantage of the Third World. The outcome is, however, mitigated somewhat by another decision, also taken at Kingston, to establish a Trust Fund whose resources are derived from the profits generated by the auctioning off of one-sixth (25 million ounces) of the IMF's gold holdings (see below). Although this construction may be considered as a partial link between the revaluation of gold and development assistance, the $3–4 billion that is expected to be ultimately available to the Trust Fund through this mechanism has to be

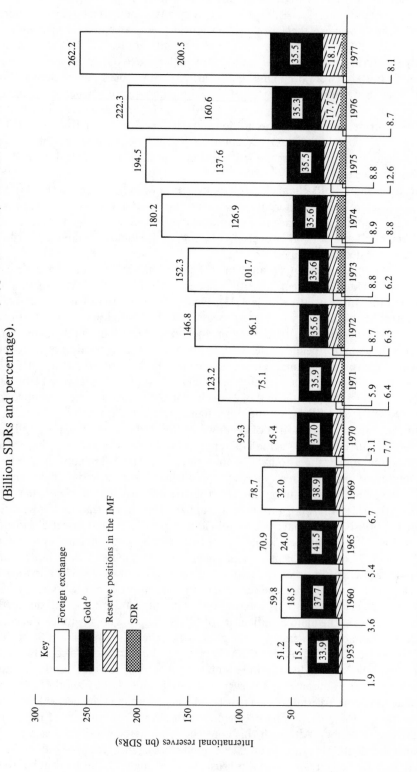

Fig. 3.10. The growth and composition of international reserves, by type of reserve, 1953–1977.[a]
(Billion SDRs and percentage).

Source: IMF, *International Statistics, 1978 Supplement,* 31 (May 1978).
[a]Members of the IMF only.
[b]Gold is valued throughout at SDR 35 per ounce.

seen against the total magnitude of new liquidity created through the revaluation of gold.

Clearly, the international monetary system is still a long way from bringing the creation of liquidity under international control and devising distributive mechanisms that reflect the interests and special needs of all its members. It is against the background of these distributional mechanisms that the DCs support, as one of the key proposals of the NIEO program, phasing out national reserve currencies and gold as international reserve assets and strengthening the role of SDRs as the principal international reserve asset.[108]

Apart from the creation and distribution of international liquidity, the bias of the international monetary system against the poor countries is also visible in the rules governing access to official credit from the IMF. Availability of credit is governed by the size of a country's quota.[109] Hence, the developing nations have only limited access to such credits. This situation, in turn, is the basis for another set of Third World reform proposals, one that aims at increasing credit lines with the Fund. Important proposals in this regard include the following: the absolute increase of quotas[110]; the enlargement of the first (automatic) credit tranche and derestrictions for drawings under the other tranches; the liberalization, enlargement, and general review of various balance-of-payments assistance mechanisms (for example, the compensatory financing facility mentioned above[111]) and, if necessary, the installation of additional ones[112]; and the liberalization of drawings under the buffer-stock financing facility.[113] The various balance-of-payments facilities are of particular importance because of the substantial deficits that the non-OPEC developing countries are presently experiencing and are expected to experience in the foreseeable future due to factors beyond their control.

Progress has been made regarding the implementation of a number of these proposals. One whole set of improvements involves access to balance-of-payments finance.[114] In August 1974, upon the recommendation of the Committee of 20,[115] the Fund established a special "oil facility" to assist members in meeting the increased cost of imports of petroleum and petroleum products. Under the 1974–1976 oil facility, SDR 6.9 billion were made available by oil-exporting and other countries. The oil facility was supplemented by a "subsidy account" (established August 1975) to subsidize the high cost of interest payments on purchases made under the 1975 oil facility by the most seriously affected countries. Since the need for conditional balance-of-payments assistance remained after the discontinuation of the oil facility in 1976, the Interim Committee suggested, in April 1977, to create a "supplementary financing facility" for countries experiencing deficits that are large in relation to their economies and their Fund quotas. The facility was established in August of the same year and became operational in February 1979, when commitments to it reached SDR 7.75 billion. The year 1974 also saw the establishment of an "extended Fund facility" to help overcome structural balance-of-payments maladjustments. Although resources provided under the regular tranche policies of the Fund usually have to be repurchased within three to five years, those made available under the extended facility can be repurchased within four to eight years. In December 1975, accessibility to the "compensatory financing facility" was liberalized, allowing drawings of up to 75 percent of a member's quota (rather than 50 percent as previously permitted), with maximum drawings in any 12-month period limited to 50 percent of quota (raised from 25 percent). Improvements of access were also made to the Fund's "buffer stock facility."[116]

The Fund's decision in 1975/1976 to reduce the role of gold in the international monetary system created additional balance-of-payments finance through the sale of one-sixth of the Fund's gold (25 million ounces) directly to all members at the former official price (of SDR 35 per ounce) and in accordance with each member's quota. Another one-sixth was scheduled for auction at market prices, with the profits (i.e., the difference between the auction price and the official price) going to the above-mentioned "Trust Fund."[117] The Trust Fund was established in May 1976 for the purpose of providing additional balance-of-payments assistance on concessionary terms to eligible developing countries during the period 1976 to 1980. By July 1979, total profits from the gold sales amounted to $2.7 billion.[118]

The Committee of 20 had also proposed, under the Sixth General Review of Quotas, to raise the total of the Fund's quotas from SDR 29.2 billion to SDR 39 billion (which included a doubling of the shares of the major oil exporters). This proposal was endorsed by the Board of Governors in March 1976 and took effect in September 1978.[119] In December 1976, and in the framework of the Seventh General Review of Quotas, the Board of Governors adopted a resolution calling for a renewed increase of quotas by 50 percent to a total of approximately SDR 59 billion (see table 3.41 for the distribution of the quotas if this resolution is adopted by all members before November 1980).[120] Although this quota change increases the total outstanding credit of the Fund and the quota shares of some individual countries, it does not change the controling position of the DMEs in all important issues.

Finally, as previously mentioned, in December 1978, the Fund also decided to make a new allocation of Special Drawing Rights in installments of about SDR 4 billion on January 1, 1979, 1980, and 1981, for a total of SDR 12 billion.

Within the framework of the World Bank, some progress has been made as well. In July 1975, a resolution was adopted by the Executive Directors of the Bank establishing an Intermediate Financing Facility. The "Third Window," as this facility came to be known, was designed to provide development assistance on terms intermediate between those of the Bank and the IDA.[121] The facility became effective in December of the same year; the last loan under it was given in June 1977.[122] At the same time, an Interest Subsidy Fund for the Third Window was devised to facilitate the financing of the Third Window through voluntary contributions. Finally, the mechanisms of coordination between the World Bank and the IMF were strengthened with the establishment, in June 1974, of the Joint Ministerial Committee of the Boards of Governors of the Fund and the Bank, the "Development Committee." The Committee's focus is in the area of the least developed countries and the transfer of real resources for development; it played a major role in the decisions leading to the creation of the Third Window and the Trust Fund.

Important as all these improvements are for assisting the DCs in coping with their immediate problems, progress toward a restructuring of the basic mechanisms determining the creation, distribution, and accessibility of international liquidity is not likely to be achieved without a change in the quota-based influence structure of the IMF. Third World countries are, therefore, pressing for a democratization (although not necessarily to the extent of majority rule) of the decision-making processes of the Fund. Greater weight and effective participation in the IMF would also give them a greater role in the management of the international monetary system as a whole—a system, after all, that constitutes the framework for their trade transactions and their development efforts. Again, the main purpose is to remove the framework's inequities and bias against development by changing mechanisms in such a way as to make the system more responsive to the special needs of the Third World, thereby bringing it into conformity with the overall development objective of the New International Economic Order.

Science and Technology

Technology is a strategic factor of economic development; it may well be the single most important contributor to economic growth. The industrialization process in the DCs, however, has not been accompanied by a corresponding expansion of the scientific and technological capacity in the Third World. Some observers have even concluded that the main area of southern dependence is shifting from the production of goods and services to the production of technology.[123]

TECHNOLOGICAL DEPENDENCE

In fact, the dependence of the developing on the developed countries is perhaps nowhere more pronounced than in the area of science and technology. Virtually all world research and development (R and D) expenditures are made by the North: of the total amount of $96 billion spent for these purposes in 1973, the DMEs accounted for 66 percent,[124] the socialist countries for 31 percent, and the DCs for 3 percent[125] (see table 3.44 and fig. 3.11). Not quite as strong, but equally impressive, is the global imbalance of scientific personnel: of the total number of 2.3 million R and D scientists and engineers, 55 percent work in the DMEs, 32 percent in the socialist countries, and 13 percent in the DCs (see table 3.45 and fig. 3.12). The United States and the USSR alone spend over half of the world's R and D funds; together with Japan, the Federal Republic of Germany, France, and the United Kingdom, this share increases to more than four-fifths. These six countries employ over two-thirds of the world's R and D personnel.[126]

If the figures are standardized, the imbalance becomes even more pronounced. Thus, the R and D expenditures of the North are approximately $182 per economically active person and represent 2.3 percent of their GNP, whereas the corresponding figures for the South are $3 and 0.4 percent, respectively. As far as personnel is concerned, however, the North counts 3,900 R and D scientists and engineers per million economically active persons, the South 310. Although the personnel data demonstrate that the actual R and D effort of the DCs may be larger than suggested by the financial indicators, they also show that the North–South technological imbalance is of a very fundamental nature: beyond the very low level of science and technology expenditures, it is the lack of the broad diffusion of technology (including that not protected by patents) and training, of skills at all levels, and of technological knowledge—in short, the inadequacy of the entire scientific and technological infrastructure—that is the basis of this dependence.

The imbalances extend themselves to within the Third World. Asia alone, for instance, accounts for three-fourths of the DCs' R and D personnel and nearly three-fifths of their expenditures. Africa's share, on the other hand, is in the neighborhood of one-tenth, although the standardized figures are closer together (see tables 3.44 and 3.45). On the level of individual countries, the variations are again very pronounced, with a number of countries undertaking a negligible R and D effort indeed.[127]

The dynamics of the educational situation, however, indicate a growing R and D potential for the Third World (see table 3.46). During the period 1960 to 1974, the number of students receiving higher education in the DCs, and the number of teachers providing it, increased at a faster rate than in the developed countries. As a result, the share of the DCs in the world's third-level student enrollment improved from 18 to 25 percent.

Naturally, only a small percentage of the 8.5 million students in the DCs in 1974 will become scientists and engineers. In addition, a number of them can be expected to

Fig. 3.11. Absolute R and D expenditures and expenditures per economically active person, by region, 1973

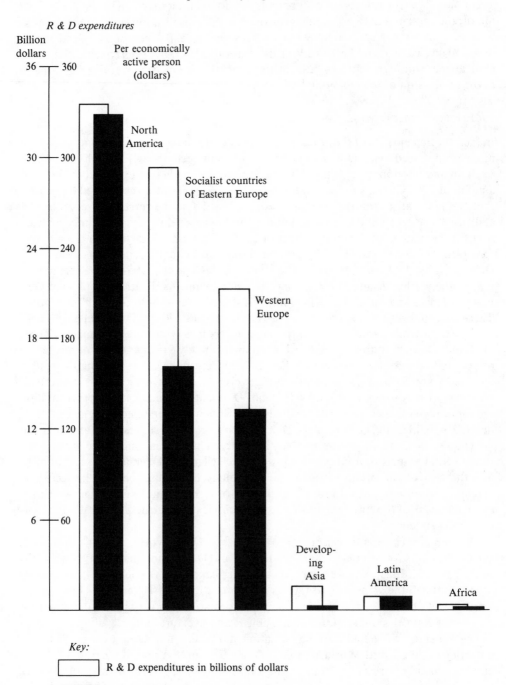

Source: Based on table 3.44.

Fig. 3.12. R and D scientists and engineers, by region, 1973.

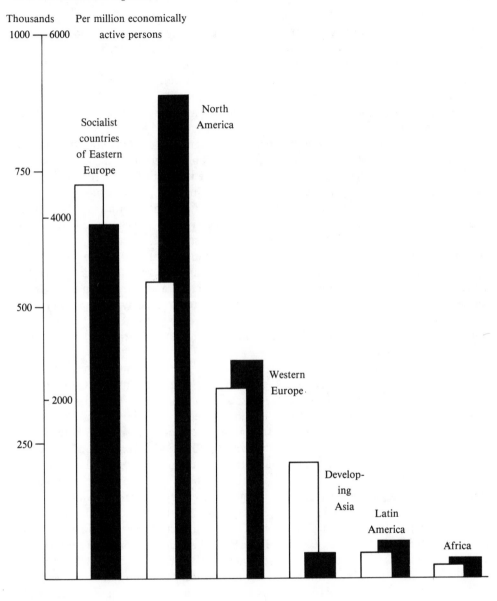

R & D scientists and engineers

Thousands   Per million economically active persons

Key:

R & D scientists and engineers in thousands

R & D scientists per million economically active persons

Source: Based on table 3.45.

migrate to the DMEs. The brain drain is, in fact, a serious problem for the DCs and has assumed considerable proportions (see table 3.47).[128] But the DC potential is replenished to a certain extent by Third World students enrolled in universities of the DMEs and persons obtaining training in the same countries.[129] For the time being, however, the gap between North and South has hardly narrowed—even if one includes the R and D conducted by foreign affiliates in the DCs as part of the national effort.

Such an inclusion, although made in national statistics, is questionable: R and D conducted in foreign affiliates is mostly mere adaptation, i.e., neither basic nor even applied research.[130] The little basic and applied research that is being undertaken, moreover, is mostly oriented toward (and integrated into) the global requirements of the transnational enterprise system as a whole and, thus, is not geared to the needs of the host country.[131] In fact, the research pursued in foreign affiliates may not even enter the host economy. A statistical illusion can result: the R and D effort of a country may appear to be increasing whereas, in reality, only the extension of a foreign corporate R and D effort located on the country's territory is expanding.

Even so, the R and D effort of foreign affiliates, if compared with that of the enterprise system as a whole, is very small: R and D is centralized in the home country. Data on industrial R and D spending by United States transnational enterprises indicate that, in the early 1970s, over 90 percent of their expenditures were made at home (see table 3.48). Of the 7 percent spent abroad, nearly two-thirds were effected in the United Kingdom, the Federal Republic of Germany, and Canada, and 3 percent in the DCs as a whole.[132] Since most R and D in the business sector is undertaken by transnational enterprises, the strong preference of these enterprises for centralized R and D in the home country tends to cement the existing global inequalities in the distribution of scientific-technological capacities.

Data on receipts and payments of royalties and fees mirror this situation (see fig. 3.13 and table 3.49). For foreign affiliates located in the Federal Republic of Germany and the United Kingdom, the balance of these transactions has consistently been negative (although positive for domestic firms). The imbalance is particularly impressive in the Federal Republic of Germany. There, foreign affiliates accounted for 5 percent ($13 million) of the receipts in 1975, and their payments for imports represent 77 percent (a substantial $451 million). Regardless of industry, foreign affiliates hardly export scientific and technological know-how.[133] Although both countries have a developed scientific–technological infrastructure, transnational enterprises prefer to locate their R and D facilities at home. The United States, however, is an exception: there, even foreign affiliates engage in sizable R and D and, in fact, export considerably more technology than they import (see table 3.50).[134] The combination of these preferences further strengthens the scientific technological leadership position of the United States.

Conversely, the DCs must budget large expenditures for imported technology (see table 3.51). Brazil's payments for royalties and fees were more than half of those of the United States (1976), Argentina's were one-third (1974), and Mexico almost matched United States payments (1971).[135] Payments by all DCs are estimated to have been $3 to $5 billion in 1975[136] (or about one-fifth of their ODA receipts during the same year). These costs can be expected to escalate with the further industrialization of the developing countries and the further transnationalization of their industries.

The imbalances described so far are corroborated by the distribution of patent holdings. In 1972, approximately 3.5 million patents were in force, 94 percent of which were held by individuals or organizations in developed countries (over half of them

Fig. 3.13. FRG receipts and payments of royalties and fees from and to affiliated
and nonaffiliated firms, 1975.
(Millions of dollars and percent).

Total receipts and payments

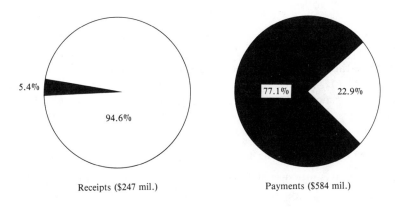

Receipts ($247 mil.)   Payments ($584 mil.)

By major industry (balance of receipts and payments)

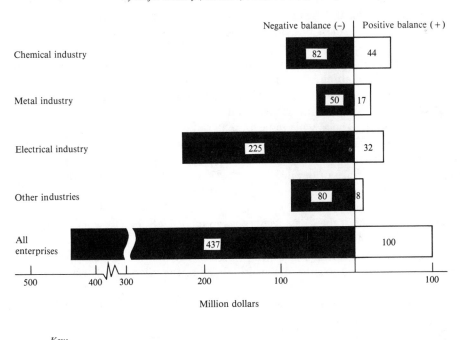

Million dollars

Key:

☐ Domestic enterprises

■ Foreign affiliates

Source: Deutsche Bundesbank, *Monachtsberichte der Deutschen Bundesbank,* April 1976.

residing in the United States or the Federal Republic of Germany). Of the 6 percent held in DCs, 84 percent were owned by foreigners (again, over half of them residing in the United States or the FRG), of which, in turn, 90 to 95 percent were not used. (It is suspected that many of these patents were obtained merely for the purpose of protecting markets by preventing the emergence of local competition.) Overall, then, less than 1 percent of the world's stock of patents is held by Third World nationals (see table 3.52).[137]

Conversely, the number of patents held by DC residents in DMEs is miniscule. In the United States, the DC share in all patents granted during the period 1890–1976 never exceeded one-third of 1 percent (see table 3.53). The share of patents granted to residents from other DMEs, on the other hand, rose from one-tenth before 1950 to over one-third since 1975; residents from only five countries divide over two-thirds of them among themselves.

THE SCIENCE AND TECHNOLOGY PROGRAM

It is only very recently that the importance of science and technology for economic progress in general and industrialization in particular has come to be fully appreciated, and the attention of national and international bodies has begun to focus on these matters. The impetus came from the Sputnik experience and later especially from studies of the costs of technological dependence: the burden of financial payments, the widespread use of restrictive business practices embodied in transfer of technology agreements,[138] the inappropriate character of some of the technology transferred,[139] the lack of control over the host country's technological development, and hence (and most fundamentally) the costs of the absence of an effective indigenous scientific-technological capacity through which innovations can be absorbed, disseminated, and reproduced.[140]

UNCTAD, which had undertaken pioneering work in this area since the end of the 1960s, brought together a wide range of material bearing on these matters. UNCTAD's work soon expanded into all aspects of the technology transfer process, from information about technology, through its acquisition and appropriate adaptation, to its application in the service of development.[141] Also stimulated by this work were extensive investigations into the functioning of the international patent system, especially as it relates to developing countries.

Given the nature of the world technology market, UNCTAD's work so far has focused primarily on the transfer of technology and, especially, on ways and means to improve the terms and conditions under which DCs acquire it. The NIEO program reflects this focus: compared to other issues in this area, the question of technology transfer receives by far the greatest attention.

The first objective of the program is to restructure the existing legal and juridical environment in which technology transactions take place to make it more beneficial to DCs.[142] The core proposal is an International Code of Conduct on the Transfer of Technology. Since, for the time being, the transfer of technology is the only way through which the Third World can obtain the scientific know-how required for its development, the conditions under which the transfer takes place are obviously very important. The main objectives of the code are, therefore, to facilitate and encourage and, hence, accelerate the transfer of technology at fair and reasonable terms, conditions, and prices by curbing restrictive, unreasonable, and unfair business practices in this area and by strengthening national laws and administrative procedures relevant to these transactions. Accordingly, the code focuses on the right of countries to regulate the transfer process in all its aspects: restrictive business practices; guarantees, responsibilities, and obligations of the technology-supplying and receiving parties; special treatment of the DCs; and international cooperation in matters related to the transfer of technology.

Although the NIEO program had foreseen the adoption of a code prior to the end of 1977, negotiations were still underway at the middle of 1979. They were conducted in the framework of a United Nations Conference on an International Code of Conduct on the Transfer of Technology, whose first session was held in Geneva during October/November 1978.[143]

Since the industrial property system constitutes another part of the legal framework for the international transfer of technology, the NIEO program also seeks a review of the international conventions on patents and trademarks with the purpose of making them more responsive to the needs of the DCs. Preparations have begun in the World Intellectual Property Organisation for a revision of the Paris Convention for the Protection of Industrial Property, and work is underway on a Model Law for Developing countries on Inventions.

Naturally, the restructuring of the legal framework for the technology does not, by itself, change the underlying technological dependence. The NIEO program, especially since the Seventh Special Session, reflects the realization that technology transfer, although important, is only a stopgap mechanism and that the long-term objective must be the development of indigenous technological capacities. In fact, the main obstacle for the achievement of greater technological self-reliance may not be difficulties with access to technology as much as the lack of its diffusion in, and absorption by, the DCs.

For this reason, the NIEO program adopts a dual approach to the problem. In addition to dealing with the improvement of the terms and conditions of transfer, it addresses itself to the need for indigenous scientific and technological capacities.[144] At the present time, the main emphasis is still on policy formulation and institution building as the preconditions for effective national efforts. The creation and strengthening of institutional structures, usually in the form of technology centers at the national, subregional, regional, and interregional levels is, therefore, strongly encouraged. The function of such centers of technology is not only to monitor the transfer of technology and to achieve control over its import, but also (and especially) to be the focal points for the establishment of indigenous capacities to generate and apply technology. A number of countries have already received UNCTAD assistance in setting up national centers,[145] and efforts are being made to establish subregional and regional ones.[146]

Thus, although the primary emphasis of the NIEO's science and technology program is still on the transfer of technology, attention is increasingly being paid to the sources of technological dependence. In this context, the greater emphasis placed on technical cooperation among developing countries has added to the mobilization of the DCs' own resources and the establishment of indigenous capabilities.[147] DMEs are requested to support the DCs in their efforts through, inter alia, an industrial technological information bank,[148] increased direct support to the science and technology programs of the DCs, and greater R and D endeavors in favor of technologies appropriate for DCs.

The United Nations Conference on Science and Technology, held in Vienna August 20 to September 1, 1979, provided new impetus to the DCs' efforts to improve their technological situation. The conference underlined the need to restructure the legal framework for the acquisition of technology, establish an appropriate information system on technology, and create or strengthen indigenous scientific and technological capacities. Pending the establishment of long-term financial arrangements, a voluntary interim fund with a target of at least $250 million for 1980–1981 is to be established. A newly-formed high-level Intergovernmental Committee on Science and Technology is to assist the General Assembly in harmonizing the United Nations' policies in this area.[149]

Industrialization and Transnational Enterprises

Industrialization remains the basic objective of the DCs. For most of them, it is the quintessence of development. Industrialization is expected to create employment and income; end undernourishment; provide adequate housing, health care, and education; and ultimately secure an acceptable standard of living. In this spirit, the 1975 Second General Conference of the United Nations Industrial Development Organization (UNIDO) declared in its "Lima Declaration and Plan of Action on Industrial Development and Co-operation" its "firm conviction of the role of industry as a dynamic instrument of growth essential to the rapid economic and social development of the developing countries."[150]

INDUSTRIALIZATION

The industrialization of the Third World requires a fundamental restructuring of the world economy and a far-reaching transformation of the DCs' economies. Excluding China, the DCs accounted for two-thirds of the world's population in 1975 but produced less than 10 percent of the world's value-added in the manufacturing sector (see fig. 3.14). In absolute figures, this represented an output of $130 billion (in 1972 dollars)—roughly equivalent to that produced by the Federal Republic of Germany. In 1975, considerably over half of the DCs' manufacturing output originated in Latin America, over one-third in Asia, and less than one-tenth in Africa; this distribution has barely changed since 1960 (see table 3.54). These figures are themselves an indication of the great disparity of levels of industrialization among developing nations. But as aggregate data, they obscure the fact that actually only four countries—India, Brazil, Argentina, and Mexico—account for more than half of the Third World's manufacturing output (and these four countries also contributed half of the increase in manufacturing value-added of all DCs during the period 1966-1975).[151]

During 1960–1972, the DCs' total output grew at a respectable average annual growth rate of 7 percent—compared to 6 percent for the DMEs and 9 percent for the socialist countries of Eastern Europe.[152] During 1971–1975, the DCs' rate of growth further increased to 8 percent (see table 3.55). These average rates conceal, however, a wide range of specific performances. A number of countries achieved rates between 10 and 20 percent, but more performed considerably below the average. The latter included the lower-income countries as a group, whose industrial production as a whole, as well as its manufacturing component, grew at below–average rates. The average manufacturing growth rate for this group of countries was 5.0 percent during the second half of the 1960s and declined to 4.7 percent during the first half of the 1970s.

As a result of these different growth rates, the disparities in degree of industrialization among the DCs increased further. Although the share of manufacturing in total GNP in 1975 equaled 19 percent for the DCs as a group, it amounted to only 13 percent for the middle-income countries; the higher–income countries, with 23 percent, were visibly above average. Geographically, Africa showed the lowest rate, 5 percent, whereas in Latin America manufacturing contributed nearly 25 percent to the GNP (see table 3.55). The performance of individual countries varies to an even greater extent.

Growth patterns also differ among industries, thereby causing changes in the in-

Fig. 3.14. World manufacturing output by region, 1960–1975.
(Percent)

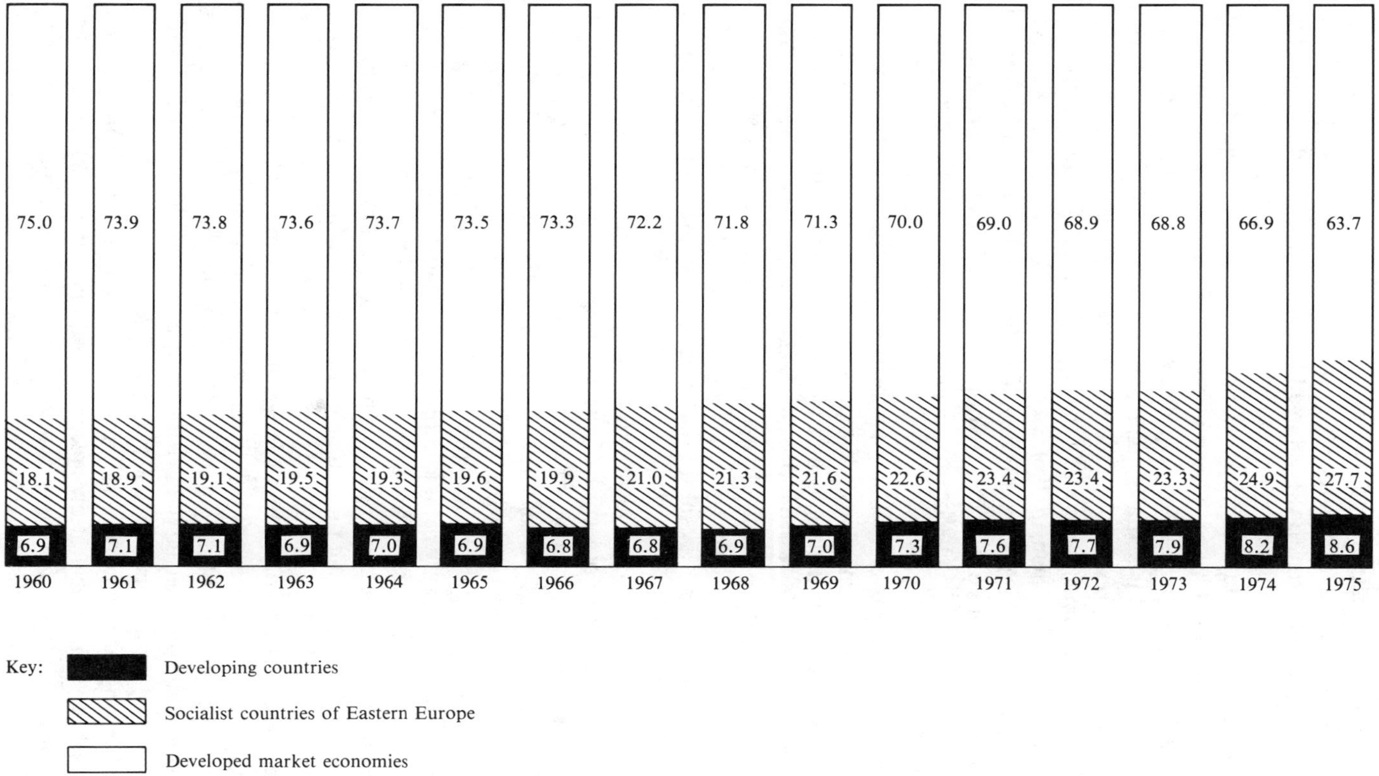

Key:

Developing countries

Socialist countries of Eastern Europe

Developed market economies

Source: UNIDO, *World Industry Since 1960: Progress and Prospects. Special Issue of the Industrial Development Survey for the Third General Conference of UNIDO* (New York: United Nations, 1979).

dustrial structures of the DCs. Output in heavy manufacturing (chemicals, machinery, transport equipment, etc.) grew with an average annual growth rate of 9 percent over the period 1960–1972, as compared to that in light industry (food processing, textiles, cloth, etc.) which rose at a rate of 5 percent (see table 3.56). Hence, by 1972, heavy industry contributed about as much to the value-added in manufacturing as did light industry (see table 3.57). The structure of industrial output, thus, has become more similar to that in the developed countries where heavy industry provides over two-thirds and light industry less than one-third of value-added.

In selected areas of production, especially in mining and light industries, the DCs' share in the world total is actually quite high (see table 3.58); but in the crucial capital goods industry, as represented by the metal and engineering industries (tools, plant equipment, durable consumer goods), the DCs' share in 1970 was a mere 3 percent, one percentage point more than in 1966 (see table 3.59).[153] Furthermore, five countries alone—Brazil, India, Argentina, Mexico, and the Republic of Korea—produce 80 percent of the capital goods of the Third World, with an additional seven countries producing another 12 percent.[154] On the other hand, some 110 countries and territories report no capital-goods industry.[155]

Put differently, the overwhelming majority of the DCs does not even have an embryonic capacity of autonomous self-reproduction, i.e., most DCs do not possess any means to produce goods that contribute to fixed-capital formation. Whatever industrial growth they achieve is borrowed and, hence, dependent growth. Continued industrialization on this basis only strengthens their dependence; moreover, the lack of a capital-goods industry is a very serious handicap for the absorption and adaptation of imported technology and its subsequent regeneration through indigenous innovative processes. Clearly, the growth of the manufacturing sector has not as yet put most DCs in a position to pursue independent development.

Thus, it is a declared objective of the NIEO program, as enunciated in the Lima Declaration, to increase the DCs' share in world manufacturing output from the present 10 percent to at least 25 percent in the year 2000. Expressed in absolute figures, the target output is estimated to be $1,400 billion (in 1972 dollars), or somewhat higher than the manufacturing output of the entire world in 1972 ($1,300 billion). Ambitious (and arbitrary) as this target may be, it is not necessarily impossible to achieve. According to UNCTAD's calculations, it assumes for the period 1972–2000 average annual manufacturing-output growth rates of 5 percent for the developed countries (about one percentage point lower than the combined average growth rates of the DMEs and centrally planned economies during the period 1960–1972))[156] and 10 percent for the DCs (up three percentage points from their average rate during 1960–1972).[157]

The Lima target requires not only accelerated manufacturing output, but also radical changes in the structure of output in the DCs. Most importantly, the share of heavy industry as a whole is projected to have to increase to nearly two-thirds of total manufacturing value-added by the year 2000 (see table 3.57). This implies growth rates of 10–12 percent for most heavy industries, compared to 8–10 percent for most light industries. In line with the Lima Declaration's recommendation "that developing countries should devote particular attention to the development of basic industries such as steel, chemicals, petrochemicals, and engineering,"[158] the highest growth rates are envisaged for engineering industries in order to create indigenous capital goods industries.

Unquestionably, the efforts required to achieve these targets are enormous. The improvement of the external framework within which they can take place is the essence of the NIEO program. The purpose of restructuring the international trade, commodity, finance, money, and science and technology systems is precisely to serve industrialization. The problems and measures discussed earlier in these areas of North-South interaction are, for this reason, directly or indirectly relevant to industrialization.[159]

The NIEO program, however, has also suggested mechanisms that deal directly with the industrialization process. Most innovative and important among them are the idea of setting up a "system of consultations" and the concept of redeployment. The system of consultations would function at the global, regional, interregional, and sectoral levels between developing and developed countries, as well as among DCs themselves, "in order to facilitate the achievement of the goals set forth in the field of industrialisation."[160] It is being designed as a "catalytic scheme to fully mobilize international co-operation with the aim of facilitating, through negotiations and agreements, the sharing of world industrial capacity and the transfer of know-how, management and capital resources so as to bring about a significant increase of industrial production in developing countries."[161]

The sectoral system of consultations was launched with the participation of representatives from labor, industry, governments, and consumer groups in 1977 within the framework of UNIDO (which has a coordinating role in the United Nations system in the field of industrial development[162]). Meetings have been held concerning fertilizers, iron and steel, leather and leather products, petrochemicals, and vegetable oils and fats; initial work has been undertaken on agro-based industries, capital goods, and the pharmaceutical industry. At the beginning of 1979, consultations were also planned for agricultural machinery.[163] This represented the first time that future global developments in these industries had been discussed; the fact that this was done from the point of view of the DCs is especially significant. Since all interested parties were represented at these meetings, and since agreement has been reached to monitor further developments in these sectors, any concrete and specific proposals that may eventually emerge stand a better chance of being adopted and implemented.

Closely linked to these consultations is the question of redeploying from developed countries those of their productive capacities that are "less competitive internationally" to DCs, "thus leading to structural adjustments in the former and a higher degree of utilization of natural and human resources in the latter."[164] In fact, it is partly through such a redeployment process that the Lima industrialization target is expected to be achieved.

What lies at the heart of this concept is the vision of a "rational, just and equitable international division of labour."[165] In strict application of liberal economic theories, the NIEO program recommends an international industrialization strategy that has as its aim an international division of labor in which DCs concentrate on industries determined by their present comparative advantage (that is, usually labor-intensive, low-technology industries), whereas "the industrial structures of the developed countries themselves evolve in a complementary fashion."[166] Similarly, in a preparatory document for UNCTAD V, it was pointed out that "a new international division of labour will necessitate not only the expansion of industrial export capacity in the developing countries, but also complementary structural changes in the productive sectors of the developed market-economy countries."[167] Although the resulting division of labor is labeled "new," it appears to be more accurate to describe it as a "cleaner" form of the old one, i.e., a division that is undistorted by existing administrative impediments (e.g., subsidies, tariff and nontariff barriers) or considerations of political expediency (e.g., temporary unemployment associated with internal structural adjustments).[168]

Thus, the industrialization process of the Third World is thought to proceed within the framework of an international division of labor in which developing and developed states each produce on the basis of their respective comparative advantages. In such a division of labor, care must be taken that the exchange mechanisms among the countries involved function properly and equitably. It is here that the industrialization program feeds back into the other areas of the NIEO program.

TRANSNATIONAL ENTERPRISES

In the industrial restructing envisaged by the NIEO program, particularly in the process of redeployment, transnational enterprises (TNEs) by necessity are of crucial importance.

To be sure, the NIEO program is addressed to governments. Governments, undoubtedly, can independently implement a number of the program's provisions (e.g., the establishment of the Common Fund, the abolition of tariff and nontariff barriers). However, for many others, they can only create—in market economies—a framework (which, of course, can contain various incentives and disincentives) whose potential must then be translated and actualized by important private actors; if this is not done, the framework remains empty and the desired behavioral changes do not take place. In market economies, these actors are enterprises and, in an international context, especially transnational ones. Their strength is precisely that they can combine the various factors needed for industrialization, particularly if this industrialization is export-led.

In fact, TNEs already play a major role in all dimensions of North-South interaction. For some of these dimensions (primary products, finance, transfer of technology) this role has already been documented in earlier sections of this chapter. What remains is to provide some overall data on the importance of TNEs.[169]

An estimated 20,000–30,000 TNEs control some 80,000 foreign affiliates which represented, by the end of 1978, a book value of nearly $300 billion (see table 3.60). Over 90 percent of the stock of international direct investment originates in the DMEs. The international production associated with it is estimated (for 1976) at about $830 billion,[170] compared with aggregate exports of DMEs of $660 billion during the same year. Thus, for the DMEs as a group, sales by foreign affiliates have surpassed exports as the most important means of delivering goods and services to foreign markets. In addition, a substantial part of this trade consists of transnational intracompany transactions (i.e., is not trade between independent sellers and buyers) and, hence, is potentially subject to arbitrary price manipulation (see fig. 3.15).

Although all DMEs (as well as some DCs and socialist states) have outward foreign direct investment, nearly half of the total originates directly[171] in the United States, and nearly another one-third in the United Kingdom, Japan, the FRG, and Switzerland. Concentration in international direct investment extends, however, beyond the country level: although the absolute number of TNEs is high, only about 150–200 of them (virtually all of which are headquartered in the five countries just listed) are estimated to control approximately half of the total international direct investment (see table 3.61). With a few exceptions, all parent enterprises are owned and controlled by home-country nationals, even if a substantial share of their sales, production assets, earnings, and employment is located abroad (see tables 3.62 and 3.63).[172]

The overwhelming part of the activities of the TNEs takes place in DMEs: nearly three-fourths of the stock of international direct investment is located there, and this share has been growing (see table 3.64). Of the $68 billion located in the DCs in 1975, one-fifth was located in OPEC countries, one-eighth in tax havens, and the rest (nearly

Fig. 3.15. The importance of intracompany transactions in
international trade, selected home countries.

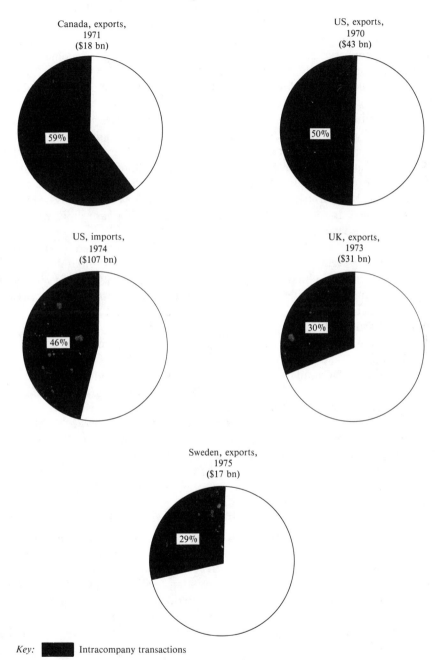

Canada, exports,
1971
($18 bn)

59%

US, exports,
1970
($43 bn)

50%

US, imports,
1974
($107 bn)

46%

UK, exports,
1973
($31 bn)

30%

Sweden, exports,
1975
($17 bn)

29%

Key: ▮ Intracompany transactions

Source: United Nations, *Transnational Corporations in World Development: A Re-examination* (New York:
United Nations, 1978); and United Nations, *Statistical Yearbook 1976* (New York: United Nations, 1977).

two-thirds) in the remaining DCs (see table 3.65). Five host countries alone accounted for more than one-third of all direct investments in the Third World, with this share increasing to over one-half for the 10 most attractive host countries. These are usually the richer countries with large internal markets, a preference which is also reflected in the distribution of foreign direct investment by income group of countries; excluding high-income OPEC countries and tax havens, countries with per capita income of $1000 or more had attracted nearly half of all foreign direct investments in 1975 (see table 3.66). For them, as well as the next lower group, these funds represented nearly 10 percent of GNP.

One further observation must be made about the distribution pattern of book value and foreign affiliates across DCs. Although this pattern is changing, it still strongly reflects the past colonial ties or hemispheric interests of the main investor countries, especially the United Kingdom, France, and the United States. The overwhelming majority of their foreign affiliates and the largest share of their investments in the Third World are located in countries that at one point or another were formally or informally dependent on them. In fact, these home countries are the dominant suppliers in most of their former dependencies.[173]

If the major home countries' direct investment in DCs is examined by industrial sector, a restructuring seems to be taking place (see table 3.67). Most notably, the share of extractive industries is declining (except for countries like the FRG whose share in these industries was small to begin with), whereas that of manufacturing and services is increasing. These changes reflect, on the one hand, nationalizations in the extractive industries (and particularly in the petroleum sector)[174] and, on the other hand, the expanding role of non-equity arrangements[175] as well the growing importance of the TNEs in the industrialization process of the DCs.

Data for selected DCs indicate that this importance is substantial indeed (see table 3.68), including in a number of their key manufacturing industries (see tables 3.69–3.71) and such service industries as insurance (see table 3.72) and advertising (see table 3.73). The role of foreign banks can be illustrated by the fact that the world's largest banks have established a widespread foreign affiliate network in the Third World (see table 3.74). The foreign presence also extends to the communication industries. To illustrate, only three news agencies with global scope exist (the American agencies AP and UPI and the British Reuters), and virtually all market economies are heavily dependent on them for foreign news—and for their selection of what is newsworthy.[176]

Evidence indicates that the role of TNEs in the industrialization process has become more important. For instance, these enterprises increased their share in the Mexican manufacturing industry from 20 percent in 1962 to 28 percent in 1970, and in that of Argentina from 21 percent in 1960 to 31 percent in 1972.[177] Increasingly, this growing role has proceeded through the takeover of existing facilities. Thus, although acquisitions accounted for a third of the new entries into the parent system of the most important U.S. manufacturing TNEs during 1951–1960, this share was one half during 1966–1971 (see table 3.75). At the same time, the preference for wholly-owned affiliates remained at well over two-thirds of all new affiliates. It should be noted that these data only capture influence that is based on outright ownership through equity; they do not take into account various forms of nonequity relationships that can make the foreign partners fully dependent on the parent enterprises involved and, thus, turn them into quasi foreign affiliates.[178]

Naturally, TNEs are also important in DMEs (and increasingly so in socialist countries);[179] but in the case of most DCs, they frequently occupy a better bargaining position and often have a relatively greater impact. As a result, they may exercise considerable influence on the form and content of the industrialization (and development) path of the countries involved, especially as regards the orientation of industrial production (e.g., toward fulfilling the demands of the world market and its extension to the local elites and middle classes versus satisfying the needs of the domestic market and the great majority of the population); hence, the type of goods and services that are being produced (e.g., high-income consumer goods versus mass consumption goods and capital goods); and, therefore, the kind of processes used (e.g., capital versus labor intensive technologies[180]); and, finally, the location of production facilities (e.g., urban versus rural sites). In other words, TNEs are influential in shaping the nature of the industrial apparatus of the DCs, including the extent to which they contribute to the development of a coherent economy with fully integrated production circuits which also include the agricultural sector and, hence, the great majority of the population.

It is precisely the ability of TNEs to combine the various resources required for development and to allocate (or withhold) them worldwide that makes them powerful institutions with great impact. Two aspects of this allocation process are of particular concern to host countries. First, DCs have very limited means for influencing who gets what, when, and how—especially in the area of manufacturing facilities and particularly under conditions of competition among host countries. Second (and in relation to the purpose these allocations are meant to serve once they have been made), although host countries perceive these allocations as serving primarily their national economic objectives, TNEs perceive them, quite naturally, as serving their global corporate objectives. Since DCs (precisely because of their status as *developing*) have only a limited capacity to monitor the activities of TNEs, they fear that their own objectives tend to be disregarded.

The role of TNEs is recognized by the NIEO program, although not to the extent that their importance to an export-led development effort might warrant. However, the underlying approach of the program and its expression in the concrete changes that are being sought does not leave any doubt that the active cooperation of TNEs is sought in order to arrive at the expansion of North-South interactions desired by the DCs. In fact, a number of provisions of the NIEO program specifically solicit the cooperation of TNEs. The Programme of Action of the Sixth Special Session, for instance, called for "urgent measures" to promote foreign investment in the DCs and, for this purpose, asked the DMEs to "encourage investors to finance industrial production projects, particularly export-oriented production, in developing countries."[181] The resolution adopted at the Seventh Special Session strongly echoed these exhortations while simultaneously insisting (as did the earlier statements) that TNEs have to operate in the framework of the DCs' development plans and in accordance with the laws and regulations of the host countries.[182]

The formal involvement of TNEs in the implementation of the NIEO program has taken its most concrete expression in the area of industrialization. Mention has already been made of the participation of industry representatives in the "system of consultations." Perhaps more important, however, are the efforts aimed at redeployment. In UNIDO's work on the potential for redeployment, the organization conducted a survey of some 8,000 enterprises in eight DMEs in order to ascertain, inter alia, "the attitudes of companies as autonomous bodies towards redeployment."[183] The initial findings indicated that "at an enterprise level, there would appear to be significant interest among the industrialists approached to redeploy certain parts of their companies' production and, through transfer of technology, capital and/or resources or services, to participate in establishing manufacturing capacities in developing countries.''[184] A good part of redeployment, it therefore appears, can be expected to take place within the framework of the transnational system of business enterprises and, hence, on the basis of an international intracompany division of labor with all its associated characteristics.[185]

It is the prevalence of TNEs in the economic life of Third World states, their relevance for all main areas of the NIEO, and the limited influence of host countries over the allocation process of the TNEs that are at the root of the DCs' quest for greater control over TNEs and their insistence on the principle of permanent sovereignty of every state over its natural resources and all its economic activities. The Declaration of the Sixth Special Session, in fact, stated that the right to control these enterprises is one of the fundamental principles of the new order, and the Programme of Action dedicated a whole section to this subject.[186] The Charter of Economic Rights and Duties of States further affirmed this in very strong language[187] and made a similarly unambiguous statement (cited above) regarding the question of nationalization.

Although the control issue has receded somewhat into the background since then—the resolution adopted at the Seventh Special Session, for instance, did not mention it at all—a number of efforts have been initiated or continued to control TNEs or aspects of their activities.[188] To date, most control efforts are still taking place at the national level.[189] Some are also pursued at the regional and interregional levels, for example, in the framework of the Andean Common Market and the OECD.[190] Finally, international issue-specific attempts were underway in mid-1979 in the areas of restrictive business practices and transfer of technology (see above), corrupt practices, taxation, accounting and reporting, and social policy.[191] Only the last of these efforts had produced, before the fall of 1979, an internationally accepted instrument.

The main international activity regarding TNEs is, however, that undertaken by the United Nations Commission and Centre on Transnational Corporations. The Commission held its first meeting in March 1975, and the Centre began its work in November of the same year. The work priorities of both bodies include the formulation of a code of conduct, the establishment of an information system, research, and technical cooperation in all matters relating to TNEs. Highest priority has been given to the code of conduct, the formulation of which has been assigned to an Intergovernmental Working Group on the Code of Conduct, a subcommittee of the Commission.[192]

Originally it had been hoped that the code would be adopted at the beginning of 1978. However, this deadline could not be met, although the chairperson of the Working Group had succeeded in obtaining a mandate to prepare, for its January 1979 session, a document that contained what will probably be the substantive content of the code.[193] The code will deal, in a comprehensive manner, with all issues related to TNEs and their activities. As such, it will contribute to a clarification of the relationship between DCs and TNEs, including the role these enterprises are expected to play in the industrialization process of the Third World.

Food and Agriculture

The discussions of the strategy to achieve the Lima industrialization target contributed to a reassessment of the role of agriculture in economic development. It was realized that general growth can only be achieved if agriculture, as the key sector of most DCs, grows as well; that, in fact, a close linkage between industrialization and agriculture can constitute an important stimulus for the development process. In addition, of course, a vitalized agricultural sector is an important source of employment. Furthermore, it increases food supply and alleviates the growing dependence on food imports (and its costs for the balance of payments); at the same time, a strengthened agricultural sector contributes to total foreign exchange earnings if surplus production is exported.

THE SITUATION

Agriculture plays a crucial role in most economies of the developing countries. Excluding oil exporters, value-added in agriculture, fishing, hunting, and forestry (i.e., agricultural production) accounted for somewhat over 25 percent of the 1975 GDP of the DCs (as compared to 5 percent in the DMEs).[194] More importantly, however, the great majority of the population in DCs derives its livelihood from agriculture and the absolute number of persons dependent on this sector is growing: in 1960, agricultural population was 1.4 billion, in 1975 it was 1.8 billion, and the projection for 2000 is 2.1 billion (see table 3.76). Over the same time period, the agricultural labor force is expected to rise from 625 million in 1960, and 709 million in 1975, to 823 million in 2000. However, because of migration movements from rural to urban areas and higher population growth rates in the latter, the share of agricultural labor in the total labor force has declined from 73 percent in 1960 to 63 percent in 1975 (compared with 10 percent in the DMEs) and is expected to recede to 43 percent by the year 2000. (In the DMEs agricultural population and labor, as well as the share of the latter in total labor, has declined consistently.) Thus, overall economic growth of the DCs will remain profoundly influenced by the performance of the agricultural sector.

This performance has, however, slackened over the last decade and a half despite the increased use of high-yield-variety seeds, pesticides, and fertilizers. Agricultural production in the developing countries grew at an annual average rate of 3.1 percent from 1961/65 to 1970 and 2.6 percent from 1970 to 1976 (compared to, respectively, 1.9 and 2.2 percent for the DMEs) (see table 3.77). Since population continued to grow at a yearly rate of 2.6 percent during the entire period, the margin between the two (that is, per capita agricultural growth) has narrowed from 0.5 percent to zero. Population growth in the DMEs, on the other hand, has been declining. In spite of the higher production growth rates of the DCs, therefore, the per capita performance of the DMEs has been superior, with the result that the difference in level of per capita production between North and South widened further during the 1960s and 1970s. As always, these figures disguise great variations among groups of countries, individual countries, and years. For the MSA and African countries, for instance, per capita production during the 1970s actually experienced a negative growth rate, falling to catastrophic proportions for a number of countries during certain years (especially 1971 and 1972).[195]

As previously indicated, even stronger divergent trends characterize the changes in the agricultural production and labor force in the two groups of countries. Often because of insufficient investment in essential inputs, growth rates of output per agricultural worker in DCs have been considerably lower than in DMEs, and have been declining.[196] These figures do not reveal, however, the prevailing substantial differences in the levels of productivity. Thus, to take the extreme cases, agricultural productivity in North America during 1974/76 was 135 times higher than in Africa and the developing Far East (compared to somewhat less than 90 times higher in 1964/66) (see table 3.78). To a large extent, these differences—which are also reflected in crop yields twice as high on the average in developed than in developing countries—are the result of highly uneven use of capital and essential inputs. The ratio of agricultural investment to output, the degree of mechanization, or the consumption of fertilizers are only a fraction of that in DMEs (see tables 3.79 and 3.80).

Low productivity is particularly disturbing because a declining proportion of the labor force has to produce an increased supply of food if consumption levels are to be at least maintained without higher imports (or if unavoidable imports are to be paid by agricultural exports).

The growth of food production in the developing countries—especially cereals (wheat, rice, coarse grains) which, as the main food staple, provide over half of total energy supplies of food—has proceeded at a pace somewhat higher than that of agriculture as a whole: it reached a yearly rate of 3.3 percent during the 1960s and 2.8 percent during the beginning of 1970s (see table 3.81).[197] Per capita food production for these countries, therefore, improved somewhat (even if at a slow pace), although the margin between the growth of population and food supply has been narrowing. But for some country groups—most notably Africa and the MSA group—the average level of per capita food production of the 1960s has not been sustained, and average domestic food supply declined during the 1970s. Food production in the DMEs, on the other hand, registered higher growth rates in the 1970s than in the 1960s, both for total production as well as on a per capita basis. Consequently, "the already large difference in the actual level of per capita food production between the two groups of countries has widened still further."[198]

Finally, on the individual country level, 56 out of 128 DCs experienced a per capita food production decline during the 1960s; 69 countries were in the same position in the 1970s, including such highly populated states as Egypt, Mexico, India, and Pakistan.[199]

At the last level of disaggregation, that of the individual, these figures translate into the dimensions of hunger observed in chap. 1: conservatively estimated, over 400 million persons (over 20 percent of the total population) in developing countries remained undernourished during 1974/76—compared to 360 million in 1969/71.[200] Even if imports are added to domestic food supplies, the average daily intake of somewhat over 2,000 kilocalories per person improved only marginally in the DCs. As far as Africa, the Far East, and the MSA countries are concerned, this amount remained (in 1972/74) about 10 percent below acceptable nutritional requirements (see table 3.82).[201] Food supply per capita in the developed countries, on the other hand, improved steadily at a level of somewhat over 3,000 kilocalories and reached more than 130 percent of requirements in 1972/1974. As in the past, food supply for domestic consumption per capita in the North is 50 percent above that in the South.

This disappointing performance necessitated the rapid expansion of food imports by many countries in order to sustain even low consumption levels. This is dramatically demonstrated by the rise of imports of cereals: from 20 million tons in 1960/61, imports rose to 70 million tons in 1977/78 and if present trends continue, may reach 120 to 145 million tons by 1990.[202] Export volumes, on the other hand, were nearly stagnant so that the DCs' average net balance of cereal imports and exports in the years 1974/76 amounted to a deficit of 33 million tons (see table 3.83).[203] Widely fluctuating prices—the export price of wheat, for instance, more than doubled between 1972 and 1974 (see fig. 3.16)—further burden the DCs and contribute to a destabilization of their economies.

To this, another concern has to be added: the international supply of cereals has progressively become concentrated in North America (see table 3.84) to the extent that, in 1978, the United States and Canada supplied, respectively, 52 and 26 percent of the exports of the major net wheat-exporting countries.[204] This structure of the world's grain

Fig. 3.16. Wheat export prices, 1967–1978.

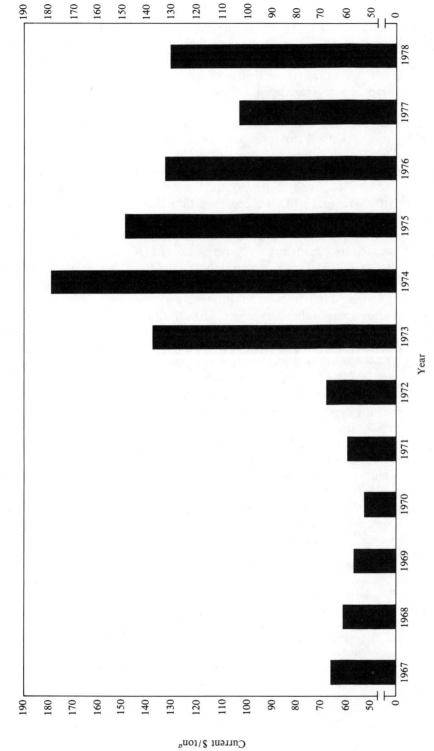

Year

Current $/ton[a]

Source: United Nations, World Food Council, "World Food Security for the 1980s: Report by the Executive Director" WFC/1979/5, April 26, 1979.
[a]U.S. No. 2 Hard Red Winter, f.o.b. Gulf.

131

trade entails serious risks for the importing countries, not only because this situation may become a basis for political pressure in a time of crisis, but also because, from the point of view of food security, a crop failure in one region would have deep ramifications throughout the world. Dependence, in fact, can be disaggregated further: two U.S. transnational trading enterprises—Cargill Inc. and Continental Grains—together control half of the world's grain trade.[205]

The trend of widening deficits also extends to such basic foodstuffs as meat and milk/milk products. Others, for instance sugar, and particularly also some agricultural raw material (e.g., cotton), however, produce continued, albeit frequently declining, export surpluses. Extrapolation suggests that the agricultural trade balance of many DCs will worsen further. As already indicated, this most notably affects cereals, for which the ratio of self-sufficiency of DCs is projected to decline from 96 percent in 1961/65 and 92 percent in 1975 to 85 percent in 1990.[206] Processing of agricultural raw material has, however, increased in DCs. In spite of an unfavorable tariff structure, processed products accounted for approximately 35 percent of the DCs total agricultural exports in 1975.[207] Here as well, TNEs play a central role.[208] In fact, TNEs in this sector are progressively moving out of direct investments in agricultural raw material production and into processing where differentiation constitutes a major barrier to entry.[209]

These, then, are some of the main aspects of DCs' situation in food and agriculture. For most DCs, the majority of the population depends for its livelihood on agriculture; but because of international and especially domestic social and economic conditions, the growth of agricultural and food production has barely kept pace with the growth of population. Widespread and endemic malnutrition, therefore, persists in many countries, to the extent that over 400 million people suffer from acute protein deficiencies. At the same time, the dependence on food (especially wheat) imports increases—not to mention the costs thereof. The highly concentrated nature of international supply contributes furthermore to a high fragility of the world food security system. On the other hand, possibilities of accelerated foreign exchange earnings from TNE-dominated exports of raw and processed agricultural products are limited by a cascading tariff and nontariff barrier structure.

Hence, the overall picture in food and agriculture is similar to that in other areas discussed earlier; absolute levels of performance in the South are unsatisfactory and the gap between North and South is widening. To quote the Food and Agriculture Organization:

> The major lesson of this production experience is no less important for being obvious: past policies have signally failed to raise the performance of agriculture in developing countries sufficiently to make any appreciable dent on the yawning gaps between levels of average productivity of the agricultures of the rich and the poor countries. Internal changes to enable the great majority of farmers in developing countries to apply more productive technologies have not been widely achieved. External assistance to the same end has not been generous. Since most of the world's food is eaten in countries where it is produced, typical nutritional conditions in developing countries remained much inferior to those in developed countries. Thus, by the late seventies the divergent trends in agricultural productivity and inequalities in food consumption were not significantly different from what they had been 20 or 25 years earlier.[210]

Given the dominant role of agriculture in most developing countries, the persistent weakness of this sector cannot but impede economic prospects in general and worsen the burden of dependence on the North. A better balance in development between agriculture and other sectors is necessary if the future is to be less somber.

THE FOOD AND AGRICULTURE PROGRAM

It is in this context that the food and agriculture section of the NIEO program has been formulated. Largely elaborated by the 1974 World Food Conference,[211] it was subsequently endorsed by the Seventh Special Session.

Recognizing that food aid is not a long-term answer, the program urges, first of all, a notable and rapid expansion of agricultural production in the DCs. National and international measures should be directed toward this objective. Among the latter, emphasis is placed on more assistance for capital and other production inputs (particularly fertilizers), but also on easier access to export markets.

The second aspect of the program is an international food-security system to protect all countries, including the developed ones, against temporary food deficits and to create a mechanism for rational market management. As far as the DCs are concerned, improved food aid should ensure—by providing (as transitional arrangement) guaranteed supplies at reasonable prices—that fluctuations do not cause unnecessary hardships.

The program also provides for an international institutional framework to monitor the world food economy and to follow up the measures suggested. Finally, attention is drawn to the need for reforms within countries.

Production

Expansion of agricultural production requires, first of all, better availability of capital. In 1974, the World Food Conference estimated that a growth target of about 4 percent per annum (to match the projected 3.6 percent demand increase) would require annual flows of investment in agriculture of $16–$18 billion (in 1972 prices) over the period 1975 to 1980.[212] Built into this estimate was an external (mostly concessional-terms) public assistance component of $5–6 billion (in 1972 prices; $8–9 billion in 1975 prices), roughly one-third of the total. Both estimates represent a doubling of 1972-level annual flows.

Accordingly, it is urged that the volume of assistance to DCs for the expansion of agricultural production be stepped up. This has, in fact, occurred and quite substantially so: official commitments to agriculture increased by 70 percent between 1973 and 1977, from $2.5 to $4.3 billion (in 1975 prices). More than half of these resources were provided by multilateral agencies, in particular the World Bank.[213] Nevertheless, this was barely half of the requirements identified by the World Food Conference and subsequently reaffirmed by the World Food Council. Similarly, total internal agricultural investments in DCs remained at about 50 percent of requirements, although indications are that agriculture, and especially food production, is accorded a higher priority in national development plans.[214]

To provide a central focus for international assistance and mobilize additional external resources for agricultural development projects, the NIEO program stipulated the establishment of the International Fund for Agricultural Development. This was urged to take place before the end of 1975, with initial resources of SDR 1 billion and periodic replenishing thereafter. The Fund began operations in December 1977 somewhat below this target with an initial capital of slightly more than $1 billion. It is the only major international financial institution exclusively for agricultural investment.[215]Nearly half of its funds were pledged by OPEC member countries.[216] Voting rights are shared equally between the DMEs, OPEC, and non-OPEC developing countries, making it the first international institution of this kind (apart from the Common Fund) that reflects the interests of the DCs. Even if the Fund cannot bridge the investment gap,[217] its establishment signals the international recognition of the importance of agriculture for development.[218]

Agreement on the Fund represents the main innovation to spur production. Too, measures have been encouraged—even if to date with very limited and insufficient follow-up—to improve food supplies through a reduction of food losses, agricultural research, easier availability of fertilizers and pesticides, and the development and more widespread use of high-yield seed varieties.[219] The 1977 United Nations conference on Desertification, furthermore, called for increased assistance to countries suffering from desertification, and the 1977 United Nations Water Conference dealt, inter alia, with improvements in water development, especially irrigation.[220]

World Food Security

The measures discussed so far primarily concern international action to accelerate production; another set of issues involves world food security and food aid to protect countries from disturbances in prices and supplies.

The crux of world food security is wheat, the most widely traded food staple.[221] The main mechanism of food security is a system of internationally coordinated national reserves. Discussions on this matter—which also bear on the stabilization of the international grain trade[222]—have been under way for several years in the framework of the negotiations regarding a new international grains arrangement. However, the negotiating conference called by UNCTAD for a first session in February 1978 (which was preceded by two years of preparatory discussions under the auspices of the International Wheat Council), by end-1979, had not yet led to a replacement of the 1971 International Wheat Agreement. As in the case of the Integrated Programme for Commodities, fundamental disagreements exist over the extent to which stocks should be used for the rational management of markets. This disagreement over the market-intervention function of the stocking system has blocked the realization of the system's second function, i.e., to provide food security.[223]

The reserve stock system is a central element of the International Undertaking on World Food Security, recommended by the World Food Conference, adopted in 1975 by the Food and Agriculture Organization of the United Nations (FAO), and endorsed by the Seventh Special Session. The Undertaking, to which over 70 countries had subscribed by mid-1978, also includes provisions for periodic intergovernmental consultations and reviews on food security problems, the orderly disposal of surpluses, special assistance to the DCs to promote their agricultural production and stock programs, and the establishment of a global food information system. The requested consultations were institutionalized in 1975 in the FAO Committee on World Food Security which oversees the implementation of the Undertaking. In addition, over 90 countries participated in 1979 in FAO's newly established Global Information and Early Warning System on Food and Agriculture which is charged with alerting governments to impending supply difficulties and crises. Too, the FAO has established a Food Security Assistance Scheme to help DCs in the formulation of relevant national policies and the mobilization of required external aid.

The failure to agree on an international stocking system for cereals has made provisions for emergency situations all the more important. In fact, the Seventh Special Session had already recommended the establishment of an International Emergency Food Reserve of not less than 500,000 tons of cereals to be placed at the disposal of the United Nations/FAO World Food Programme. Later, in 1978, the World Food Council decided that this emergency reserve should be continued, even after the conclusion of a wheat agreement, as a contingency fund for local food emergencies whose global impact was not sufficient to trigger releases from the international stocking scheme. The Emergency Food Reserve became operational in 1977, but reached only 70 percent of its minimum target in the subsequent two years.[224]

Until indigenous production is sufficient, measures will be necessary to bridge the gap between domestic demand and supply. Increased and improved food aid has a key role to play here. Since food aid has frequently been a commercial and political tool as well as a method of surplus disposal, it has often not reached those countries that needed it most; moreover, its volume has tended to increase when cereals were abundant and decrease when they were most needed.[225] This inverse relationship between the need and allocation of food aid and its unsatisfactory level are the reasons for the NIEO program's recommendation to adopt minimum food aid targets, more forward planning in aid commitments, the use of objective criteria for assessing the requirements of the recipient countries, and greater reliance on multilateral channels (especially the World Food Programme).

The global food aid target was fixed at a minimum of 10 million tons of grain a year. During the negotiations of a new Food Aid Convention during 1978–79, commitments for food aid were made and were projected to reach 9.5 million tons for 1979 (compared to 4.2 million tons under the 1971 Convention).[226] However, since the adoption of the Convention was made contingent on acceptance of a new International Wheat Agreement, by mid-1979 only individual countries had formalized their commitments. Guidelines were drawn up by the Committee on Food Aid Policies and Programmes to specify objective and rational criteria for the allocation and coordination of food aid and the minimization of its negative side effects.

Institutional Arrangements

The Committee on Food Aid Policies and Programmes is part of a comprehensive international institutional arrangement recommended by the World Food Conference and endorsed by the Seventh Special Session. Its objective was to give international efforts in the area of food and agriculture a permanent framework within which the world food economy can be monitored and appropriate action can be taken. Four institutions comprise this framework.

The first is its centerpiece, the World Food Council. Established in December 1974 by the General Assembly and consisting of 36 governmental representatives at the ministerial level, it is "to serve as a co-ordinating mechanism to provide over-all, integrated and continuing attention for the successful co-ordination and follow-up of policies concerning food production, nutrition, food security, food trade and food aid, as well as other related matters, by all the agencies of the United Nations system."[227] Hence, the Council was set up to ensure the general supervision of the world food problem and to mobilize the necessary political support for its alleviation.

The earliest major achievement of the World Food Council was the establishment of the International Fund for Agricultural Development as a specialized United Nations Agency.

The third institutional innovation was the Committe on World Food Security, which monitors the implementation of the International Undertaking on World Food Security, the Food Security Assistance Scheme, and the Global Information and Early Warning System. It is a standing committee of the FAO Council.

Finally, the task of reviewing and coordinating bilateral, multilateral, and nongovernmental food aid programs (including the World Food Programme and the International Emergency Reserve) has been assigned to the Committee on Food Aid Policies and Programmes. The Committee is a joint United Nations/FAO body, but also submits reports to the World Food Council.

If this institutional framework can establish smooth working relationships and mobilize the required resources and political support, the basis may have been laid for the successful improvement of the world food economy.

National Action

These institutional arrangements indicate that a new emphasis has been given to agricultural development and that the need to make the international environment as conducive as possible to this has been recognized. However, the problem is not simply institutional in nature; nor is it primarily technical—there exist no major physical or technological obstacles to alleviate hunger and malnutrition over the next generation. The main obstacles are inequalities within countries.

This internal dimension was recognized by the Seventh Special Session (as well as the World Food Conference): "it is a responsibility of each State concerned . . . to promote interaction between expansion of food production and socio-economic reforms. . . ."[228] The subsequent work of the World Food Council and especially the 1979 Conference on Agrarian Reform and Rural Development,[229] as well as the broader discussion of the concept on basic needs, put this international dimension into a stronger focus. This was not meant to distract from the international dimension of the agricultural development process—it is, after all, in relation to the internal environment that this process takes place—but, rather, to ensure that the international efforts become as effective as possible and, furthermore, reach the proper target groups.

Hence, agrarian reform questions, in spite of being a very sensitive internal matter, belong to the few important domestic questions that are now being discussed at the international level. The scope of this problem is broad, as the introductory paragraph of the "Programme of Action" of the World Conference on Agrarian Reform and Rural Development indicates:

> The goal of agrarian reform and rural development is transformation of rural life and activities in all their economic, social, cultural, institutional, environmental and human aspects. National objectives and strategies to achieve this transformation should focus on eradication of poverty, including nutritional improvement, and be governed by policies for attaining growth with equity, redistribution of economic and political power, and people's participation. These strategies should include the imposition of ceilings on the size of private holdings, resource mobilization for increased investment, expansion of production and employment, strengthening of the economic base for small farmers, organization of farmers' associations, cooperatives and other groups of the rural poor as well as state farms, introduction of technical innovations, efficiency in the use of resources through adequate incentives and prices, balanced development of rural and urban areas and equity and justice in the sharing of productive resources and the benefits of progress.[230]

The heart of agrarian reform is to achieve better access, through redistribution if need be, to land, water, and other resources, and to ensure broad popular participation in the rural development process. Fundamental changes in the economic, social, and political structures of most DCs are required to achieve these objectives.

Given the focus of the NIEO program on international relations, few allusions are made in it to the need for internal change; but, to repeat, the issues have reached the international level[231] and will undoubtedly be reflected more explicitly in future programmatic documents.

Continuing Negotiations

This, in broad strokes, is the program for the NIEO, the background against which it was formulated, and the concrete steps that have been taken toward its implementation. Progress, it has been seen, has been slow, tedious, and limited. Measures have frequently been agreed upon, but implementation has been delayed or has been very restricted in scope—if it has been undertaken at all. Where progress was achieved, it has mostly confined itself to the most pressing immediate problems of the Third World. In a sense, large parts of the NIEO program have the character of a holding operation designed to prevent a deterioration of the economic situation of the developing countries. At best, they seek to improve the framework for the Third World's pursuit of its development effort. But this may simply be insufficient to bring about the fundamental changes that are being sought.

But the NIEO program is evolving. One of its main achievements is, after all, that structural changes are sought, even if most of its current concrete action proposals have more limited objectives. However, it can be expected that in the future more emphasis will be placed on structural transformation, possibly even on the basis of a different development model. The increasing attention that is being paid to individual and collective self-reliance points in this direction.[232]

The continuing evolution of the program will occur, as in the years since 1974, in numerous regional and international conferences. Thus, for instance, within three months after the Sixth Special Session, the 46 ACP developing countries negotiating the Lomé Convention with the European Community presented the Kingston memorandum to their European interlocutors. This, in the spirit of the NIEO, suddenly revitalized the negotiations and led, on February 28, 1975, to their relatively rapid conclusion—along the lines proposed by the 46. The Lomé Convention pioneers a number of progressive mechanisms, including an export-earnings stabilization fund and free access (as far as formal tariffs are concerned), without reciprocity, to the Community's market for nearly all export goods of the associates. Moreover, the establishment of several institutions charged with implementing the Convention (especially regarding its Industrial Co-operation Title) provides the ACP states with new avenues of access to, and means for pressure on, the EC countries.[233] During 1979, negotiations were finalized to extend the Convention beyond 1980 on the basis of improved terms for the 57 developing countries party to it.[234]

On the international level, a major round of negotiations was undertaken in the framework of the Paris "Conference on International Economic Cooperation." Called upon the initiative of the President of France in October 1974 to deal with energy, its agenda was broadened to questions of energy, raw materials, development, and related financial issues. Representatives of 19 DCs and 8 DMEs negotiated between December 1975 and June 1977 on a wide range of North-South issues. Although the conference remained without tangible follow-up, it contributed greatly to the elaboration of the developing countries' position.[235]

Within the United Nations system, a number of major conferences held subsequent to the Sixth Special Session were also infused with the spirit of the NIEO. Although these conferences had originally been envisaged as dealing with more specialized topics, they were now politicized and geared to the overall objective of development. Less than two months after the end of the Sixth Special Session, the first substantive session of the Third Conference of the United Nations on the Law of the Sea offered an opportunity to implement parts of the NIEO program. The opportunity was, indeed, seized (especially regarding the international authority issue); in fact, the experience of the Sixth Special Session played an important role in effecting rapid agreement on a common Third World bargaining position.[236] A number of other major conferences followed and were also characterized by the new assertiveness of the DCs and their attempts to integrate them into the NIEO framework.[237]

The United Nations remains the main forum in which the NIEO program will be developed further and its implementation will be pressed. Since February 1978, the "Committee Established under General Assembly Resolution 32/174" (the "Committee of the Whole," which is open to the participation of all states) has been meeting between the regular sessions of the General Assembly to assist the Assembly by acting as a focal point on:

> (a) Overseeing and monitoring the implementation of decisions and arrangements reached in the negotiations on the establishment of the new international economic order in the appropriate bodies of the United Nations system;
> (b) Providing impetus for resolving difficulties in negotiations and for encouraging the continuing work in these bodies;
> (c) Serving, where appropriate, as a forum for facilitating and expediting agreement on the resolution of outstanding issues;
> (d) Exploring and exchanging views on global economic problems and priorities.[238]

In establishing the Committee of the Whole, the General Assembly explicitly reaffirmed that "all negotiations of a global nature relating to the establishment of the new international economic order should take place within the framework of the United Nations system," and further reaffirmed that, in the negotiations, "the international community should, with a sense of urgency, make new and resolute efforts to secure positive and concrete results within agreed and specific time-frames."[239] At the same time, the General Assembly decided to convene a special session on development in 1980

> to assess the progress made in the various forums of the United Nations system in the establishment of the new international economic order and, on the basis of that assessment, to take appropriate action for the promotion of the development of developing countries and international economic co-operation, including the adoption of a new international development strategy for the 1980s.[240]

Preparations are being made to ensure that high-level negotiations continue after this special session and after the adoption of the strategy or the Third United Nations Development Decade. The developing countries have proposed that a "round of global and sustained negotiations" be launched at the special session in 1980 to deal with the issues of raw materials, energy, trade, development, money and finance.[241] By including (as in the Paris North-South Conference) the issue of energy in these negotiations, the OPEC countries have not only yielded to the pressure of the oil consumer countries (both developed and developing) to discuss this matter on the international level, but have also reintroduced into the development discussions one of the most important bargaining assets of the Third World.

This unprecedented set of almost continuous negotiations has undoubtedly contributed to an increased acceptance of the NIEO program. It has ensured that the program receives the proper attention, that support for it is being generated, and that the pressure for its implementation is maintained. It demonstrates, in short, that development has become—and will remain—a priority item on the international agenda.

Notes

1. Although public discussion—supported by the composition of the Paris Conference on International Economic Co-operation—tends to equate "North" with the developed market economies (DMEs, or the industrial states), the socialist countries of Eastern Europe, including the Soviet Union, are also the addressees of the "South," i.e., the developing countries (DCs, or the Third World). In this contribution, therefore, "North" generally refers to the developed countries, regardless of whether market or centrally planned economies.

2. "In principle" because many DMEs have registered reservations to the main documents pertaining to the NIEO; the NIEO texts as such generally follow the approach of the DCs, whereas the qualifications have usually been added by DMEs. These reservations and qualifications are often not reflected in my presentation of the NIEO program since the purpose of this chapter is to outline the position of the DCs. See, however, the next chapter as well as Appendix A, at the end of this volume.

For a detailed presentation of the position of the Third World and the DMEs during the negotiations of the Seventh Special Session, as well as the compromises achieved, see Branislav Gosovic and John Gerard Ruggie, "On the Creation of a New International Economic Order: Issue Linkage and the Seventh Special Session of the UN General Assembly," *International Organization* 30 (Spring 1976), esp. pp. 323–45.

An important linguistic compromise reflects the lack of agreement on the character of the changes that are sought. The DCs speak about the establishment of *"the New International Econmic Order"*—an order in which the purposes, mechanisms, and structures of the international economic system have been changed in such a way as also to serve the development process fully. The DMEs, on the other hand, are willing to make certain improvements in the existing order, thereby moving to *"a new international economic order."* The United Nations compromise is either *"a New International Economic Order"* or *"the new international economic order."*

3. I am using "NIEO program" to refer to the proposals and measures contained in the resolutions adopted at the Sixth (1974) and Seventh (1975) Special Sessions of the United Nations General Assembly, entitled "Declaration on the Establishment of a New International Economic Order," and "Programme of Action on the Establishment of a New International Economic Order" (United Nations General Assembly resolutions 3201 [S-VI] and 3202 [S-VI], both adopted May 1, 1974) and "Development and International Economic Co-operation" (United Nations General Assembly resolution 3362 [S-VII], adopted Sept. 16, 1975). Of equal importance is the "Charter of Economic Rights and Duties of States" (United Nations General Assembly resolution 3281 [XXIX], adopted Dec. 12, 1974, by the Regular Twenty-ninth Session of the General Assembly). All three resolutions are reprinted in Appendix A, below.

Aspects of the program were also elaborated in special conferences. Particularly relevant here is the Conference of Developing Countries on Raw Materials which had been prepared by the Non-Aligned Countries and was held February 4–8, 1975, in Dakar; and the Second General Conference of UNIDO, held March 12–26, in Lima. See, respectively, "The Dakar Declaration," "Action Programme," and "Resolutions," reprinted in Odette Jankowitsch and Karl P. Sauvant, eds., *The Third World without Superpowers: The Collected Documents of the Non-Aligned Countries* (Dobbs Ferry, N.Y.: Oceana, 1978), vol. 4, pp. 1989–2057, and "Lima Declaration and Plan of Action on Industrial Development and Co-operation." The UNIDO conference had been preceded by a ministerial conference of the Group of 77 in Algiers, Feb. 15–18, 1975, whose final document, "Declaration and Plan of Action on Industrial Development and Co-operation" became the basis of the later UNIDO document. These documents are reprinted in Karl P. Sauvant, ed., *The Third World without Superpowers,* 2d ser., *The Collected Documents of the Group of 77* (Dobbs Ferry, N.Y.: Oceana, 1980). Finally, also relevant are pertinent materials prepared by UNCTAD and UNIDO (cited below).

A number of documents pertaining to the NIEO and its history are contained in George Moss and Harry N. M. Winton, eds., *A New International Economic Order: Selected Documents 1945–1975* (New York: UNIPUB, n.d.), 2 vols. For the NIEO program, see Karl P. Sauvant and Hajo Hasenpflug, eds., *The New International Economic Order: Confrontation or Cooperation between North and South?* (Boulder, Col.: Westview Press, 1977); and Jyoti Shankar Singh, *A New International Economic Order: Toward a Fair Redistribution of the World's Resources* (New York: Praeger, 1977).

4. Preamble, resolution on "Development and International Economic Co-operation," adopted by the Seventh Special Session.

5. After the adoption of the Charter, as cited in the *New York Times,* Dec. 13, 1974.

6. In his concluding remarks during the Sixth Special Session, contained in the United Nations, *Official Records of the General Assembly, Sixth Special Session, Plenary Meetings, Verbatim Records of Meetings, 9 April-2 May, 1974.*

7. The American Secretary of State, Henry A. Kissinger, in his opening address (read by the American Ambassador at the United Nations, Daniel Moynihan) to the Seventh Special Session, contained in United Na-

tions, *Official Records of the General Assembly, Seventh Special Session, Plenary Meetings.*

8. See the discussion in chap. 1.

9. See the discussion in chaps. 1 and 2.

10. Chapter II, art. 19. Similarly, in the Declaration of the Sixth Special Session (art. 4[n]): "Preferential and non-reciprocal treatment for developing countries, wherever feasible, in all fields of international economic co-operation wherever possible."

11. This has been recognized and accepted in the Lomé Convention.

12. Chapter I: "Economic as well as political and other relations among States shall be governed, *inter alia,* by the following principles: (a) Sovereignty, territorial integrity and political independence of States; (b) Sovereign equality of all States; (c) Non-aggression; (d) Non-intervention; (e) Mutual and equitable benefit; (f) Peaceful coexistence;(g) Equal rights and self-determination of peoples; (h) Peaceful settlement of disputes; (i) Remedying of injustices which have been brought about by force and which deprive a nation of the natural means necessary for its normal development; (j) Fulfillment in good faith of international obligations; (k) Respect for human rights and fundamental freedoms; (l) No attempt to seek hegemony and spheres of influence; (m) Promotion of international social justice; (n) International co-operation for development; (o) Free access to and from the sea by land-locked countries within the framework of the above principles."

13. The program also includes measures concerning the least developed, landlocked, and island developing countries, as well as the restructuring of the United Nations system. These issues will not be examined here because they do not relate to the core of the North-South relationship. For relevant material see UNCTAD, "Least Developed among Developing Countries: Outline for a Substantial New Programme of Action for the 1980s for the Least Developed Countries. Report by the Secretary-General of UNCTAD" (TD/240), February 13, 1979; UNCTAD, "Least Developed Among Developing Countries: Basic Data on the Least Developed Countries. Report by the UNCTAD Secretariat" (TD/240/Supp. 1), April 10, 1979; UNCTAD, "Specific Action Related to the Particular Needs and Problems of Land-Locked Developing Countries: Issues for Consideration. Report by the UNCTAD Secretariat" (TD/241), February 20, 1979, and (TD/242), February 19, 1979; and United Nations, "A New United Nations Structure for Global Economic Co-operation: Report of the Group of Experts on the Structure of the United Nations System" (E/AC. 62/9), May 28, 1975. Most measures of the NIEO program also contain special provisions for the least developed, island, and landlocked developing countries.

Also not included is a discussion of economic cooperation among developing countries since this area is not primarily a question of North-South relations. See, however, UNCTAD, "Economic Co-operation among Developing Countries: Priority Areas for Action. Issues and Approaches. Report by the UNCTAD Secretariat" (TD/244), April 11, 1979.

14. UNCTAD, "Indexation: Report by the Secretary-General of UNCTAD" (TD/B/563), July 7, 1975.

15. See also UNCTAD, "Action on Export Earnings Stabilization and Developmental Aspects of Commodity Policy: Report by the UNCTAD Secretariat" (TD/229), March 8, 1979.

16. For a detailed discussion, see UNCTAD, "The Processing before Export of Primary Commodities: Areas for Further International Co-operation. Report by the UNCTAD Secretariat" (TD/229/Supp. 2), March 20, 1979; Rex Bosson and Bension Varon, *The Mining Industry and the Developing Countries* (New York: Oxford University Press, 1977); and UNIDO, "Transnational Corporations and the Processing of Raw Materials: Impact on Developing Countries. Report by the United Nations Centre on Transnational Corporations" (ID/B/209), April 21, 1978. For an example of a detailed industry study, see Wolfgang Gluschke, Joseph Shaw, and Bension Varon, *Copper: The Next Fifteen Years* (Dordrecht: Reidel, 1978).

17. See Norman Girvan, *The Caribbean Bauxite Industry* (Jamaica: University of the West Indies, 1967), pp. 3, 11. Of the income created in the Caribbean, one would have to subtract net profits, dividends, and interests repatriated by the enterprises involved.

18. For further details, see the footnotes to table 3.10. See also UNCTAD, "Commodities: Proportion between Export Prices and Consumer Prices of Selected Commodities Exported by Developing Countries. Study by the UNCTAD Secretariat" (TD/184/Supp. 3), January 14, 1976.

19. See UNCTAD, "Marketing and Distribution of Primary Commodities: Areas for Further International Co-operation. Report by the UNCTAD Secretariat" (TD/229/Supp. 3),March 8, 1979.

20. See UNCTAD, "Review of Maritime Transport, 1976" (TD/B/C.4/169), March 25, 1977; UNCTAD, "Shipping: Participation of Developing Countries in World Shipping and the Development of Their Merchant Marines. Merchant Fleet Development. Report by the UNCTAD Secretariat" (TD/222), December 18, 1978, and UNCTAD, "Shipping: Participation of Developing Countries in World Shipping and the Development of Their Merchant Marines. Review of Trends 1977/78. Note by the UNCTAD Secretariat" (TD/222/Supp. 6), March 23, 1979.

21. In the case of iron ore, one-third of all transactions originates in mines owned or controlled by major

transnational steel enterprises, approximately another one-third takes place under long-term contracts that specify quantities to be supplied and prices to be paid, and the remaining one-third is channeled through the free market; see UNCTAD, "Interdependence of Problems of Trade, Development Finance and the International Monetary System: World Economic Outlook 1977–1978. Report by the UNCTAD Secretariat" TD/B/665/Add.1 (Part II), July 25, 1977, p. 37.

22. Table 3.25 contains only measures taken that tended to restrict trade; trade-encouraging measures are not included. It is estimated that the trade flows on which new restrictions have been imposed between 1974 and 1977 affect approximately 3–5 percent of world trade; see Richard Blackhurst, Nicholas Marian, and Jan Tumlir, *Trade Liberalization, Protectionism and Interdependence* (Geneva: GATT, 1977), p. 74.

23. UNCTAD, "An Integrated Programme for Commodities: Resources to Expand Processing of Primary Commodities in Developing Countries. Report by the UNCTAD Secretariat" (TD/B/C.1/197), October 23, 1975, Annex, p. 3. The main reason for this situation is that reciprocal tariff reductions among industrial countries have focused on products not of primary export interest to DCs.

24. United Nations, "Problems of Availability and Supply of Natural Resources. Survey of Current Problems in the Fields of Energy and Minerals: The World Mineral Situation. Report of the Secretary-General" (E/C.7/51), February 13, 1975, annex.

25. See UNCTAD, "Commodities: Action on Commodities, Including Decisions on an Integrated Programme, in the Light of the Need for Change in the World Commodity Economy. Report by the UNCTAD Secretariat" (TD/184), March 4, 1976, p. 3. The relevant parts of this document are reprinted in Sauvant and Hasenpflug, *The New International Economic Order*.

26. Part I, 3, para. (a)(iv).

27. UNCTAD IV Conference resolution 93 (IV), adopted by consensus. The resolution is contained in United Nations, *Proceedings of the United Nations Conference on Trade and Development, Fourth Session, Nairobi, 5–31 May 1976*, vol. I, *Report and Annexes* (New York: UN, 1977), pp. 6–9.

28. Ibid., p. 7.

29. Under specified conditions, internationally coordinated national stocks may also be established. This is, for instance, anticipated for grains.

30. The 1976–1981 long-term grain agreement between the United States and the USSR was negotiated with the dual intention of ensuring supplies of wheat and corn to the Soviet Union while lessening the uncertainties of market forces for U.S. producers. The agreement, in setting minimum and maximum amounts of wheat and corn to be sold to the USSR, aimed at the continued development of the Soviet market for U.S. grains while monitoring sales to prevent excessively large Soviet purchases, such as those which contributed to the disruption of domestic markets during 1973–1974. Under the terms of the agreement, the USSR is committed to purchase 6–8 million metric tons of U.S. wheat and corn in each of the five crop years beginning October 1, 1976. However, these total quantities can be reduced if the total estimated U.S. grain supply is less than a specified amount. Government-to-government consultations are required if the USSR wishes to purchase more than eight million tons in any one crop year. See United States, Department of Agriculture, *Foreign Agriculture*, Nov. 3, 1975, and Dec. 1, 1975.

31. See UNCTAD, "Consideration of Issues Relating to the Establishment and Operation of a Common Fund: Financial Requirements. Note by the UNCTAD Secretariat" (TD/B/IPC/CF/L.2), December 29, 1976. Estimates of the capital requirements for the establishment of buffer stocks for the 10 core commodities are difficult to make and therefore tend to vary, depending on the source of the estimate. The OECD has estimated costs in the range $3.8 to $11.94 billion. The OECD figures, however, do not take into account savings that can be realized from offsetting costs/gains associated with the operation of one buffer stock against costs/gains from that of another one; these savings, the OECD estimates, may range from 23 to 43 percent. Cited in Commonwealth Technical Group, *The Common Fund* (London: Commonwealth Secretariat, 1977), p. 40.

32. The IMF compensatory financing facility was established in 1963 to provide financial assistance to members, particularly primary-producing countries, experiencing balance-of-payments difficulties caused by temporary export shortfalls. Preconditions for support are that the adverse situation is short term and beyond the member's control and that the member country cooperates with the IMF in efforts to find appropriate solutions for its balance-of-payments difficulties.

33. " 'Indexation' is an agreed procedure for the automatic adjustment of a nominal target price or price range, so as to ensure that, in conditions of inflation, this always expresses correctly in current money units the real target price or price range specified for the commodity concerned. In conditions of world inflation, therefore, indexation is a procedure particularly relevant to the objective of preserving the purchasing power of developing countries through defence of terms of trade of their export commodities." Quoted from UNCTAD, "Commodities: Preservation of the Purchasing Power of Developing Countries' Exports. Report

by the UNCTAD Secretariat'' (TD/184/Supp. 2), March 5, 1976, p. 12. This document contains a very useful and clear discussion of various mechanisms aimed at maintaining and improving the purchasing power of the developing countries.

34. Efforts to expand the markets for natural products in relation to synthetics and substitutes are also encouraged; see below the discussion of ''other measures.''

35. Under this scheme, payments would be made directly to governments which, in turn, could (if they so choose) compensate the individual raw material enterprises. Under the conditions of direct indexation, enterprises would benefit directly since prices are maintained at a certain level. Considering that TNEs hold an important position in many primary-product industries, direct indexation appears also to be to the advantage of these enterprises.

36. ''ACP-EEC Convention of Lomé,'' contained in United Nations document (A/AC.176/7), September 16, 1975. This Convention was signed on February 28, 1975, by the members of the EC and 46 *A*frican, *C*aribbean, and *P*acific States (11 additional states had acceded to the Convention by the middle of 1979). For a discussion of the Convention, see Isebill V. Gruhn, ''The Lomé Convention: Inching toward Interdependence,'' *International Organization* 30 (Spring 1976): 241–62; see also Hajo Hasenpflug, ''The Stabilization of Export Earnings in the Lomé Convention: A Model Case?'' in Sauvant and Hasenpflug, *The New International Economic Order.*

37. UNCTAD, ''Preservation of Purchasing Power,'' pp. 22–27. UNCTAD has also suggested the reconsideration of the supplementary financing system drafted several years ago. The objective of this system is to compensate countries for unexpected shortfalls in their real export earnings as measured against medium-term forecasts for these earnings. See also UNCTAD, ''Compensatory Financing: Issues and Proposals for Further Action. Report by the UNCTAD Secretariat,'' (TD/229/Supp. 1), March 7, 1979.

38. See UNCTAD, ''Common Fund: Financial Requirements.'' For details see UNCTAD document (TD/B/IPC/CF/L.3), Dec. 29, 1976.

39. See UNCTAD, ''Report of the United Nations Negotiating Conference on a Common Fund under the Integrated Programme for Commodities on Its Third Session'' (TD/IPC/CF/CONF/19), March 28, 1979. This agreement is the basis for the drafting of the actual Articles of Agreement of the Common Fund, to be undertaken by an Interim Committee of the ''United Nations Programme for Commodities,'' which began meeting in the fall of 1979. It is, therefore, unlikely that the fund will become operational before the end of 1980.

40. Each member state is to contribute $1 million; assuming the participation of 150 countries, $150 million will be derived from this source (OPEC has agreed to assume the share of the 28 least developed countries). Another $150 million will be contributed as capital on call and $100 million as government guarantees. The amounts in addition to the $1 million per state levy will be distributed among the various country groups as follows: Group of 77, 10 percent; DMEs, 68 percent; socialist countries of Eastern Europe, 17 percent; and China, 5 percent.

41. Of this $350 million, at least $70 million will come from direct government assessments, out of the $1 million per state levy mentioned above; the balance will be financed mainly from voluntary contributions.

42. UNCTAD, ''Restructuring the International Economic Framework: Report by the Secretary-General of UNCTAD to the Conference'' (TD/221), April 6, 1979, p. 7.

43. For a progress report, see UNCTAD, ''Review of Implementations and Follow-up Action, Including the On-going Preparatory Work and Negotiations: Report by the UNCTAD Secretariat'' (TD/228), March 12, 1979, and Add. 1 of March 13, 1979.

44. Discussions have, however, continued in FAO on bananas as well as on a number of other agricultural commodities.

45. See also, UNCTAD, ''Comprehensive Measures Required to Expand and Diversify the Export Trade of Developing Countries in Manufactures and Semi-Manufactures: Report by the UNCTAD Secretariat'' (TD/230), February 17, 1979.

46. UNCTAD, ''Manufactures and Semi-Manufactures: The Dimensions of the Required Restructuring of World Manufacturing Output and Trade in Order to Reach the Lima Target. Report by the UNCTAD Secretariat (TD/185/Supp. 1), April 12, 1976. See also the earlier UNCTAD document, ''Manufactures and Semi-manufactures: A Comprehensive Strategy for Expanding and Diversifying the Export Trade of the Developing Countries in Manufactures and Semi-manufactures. Report by the UNCTAD Secretariat'' (TD/185), December 30, 1975.

47. Also with the centrally planned economies which, at the present time, account for only approximately 5 percent of the Third World's trade. See, in this context UNCTAD, ''Trade Relations among Countries having Different Economic and Social Systems: Multilateral Action for Expanding the Trade and Economic Rela-

tions between Countries with Different Economic and Social Systems, in Particular Action which would Contribute to the Development of Developing Countries. Report by the UNCTAD Secretariat'' (TD/193), February 12, 1976; and UNCTAD, ''Trade Relations among Countries having Different Economic and Social Systems: Report by the UNCTAD Secretariat'' (TD/243), February 8, 1979, and its supporting papers.

48. See in this context UNCTAD, ''Economic Co-operation among Developing Countries: Report by the UNCTAD Secretariat'' (TD/192), December 22, 1975 (relevant parts of this document are reprinted in Sauvant and Hasenpflug, *The New International Economic Order*); and UNCTAD, ''Economic Co-operation among Developing Countries: Elements of a Programme of Economic Co-operation among Developing Countries. Report by the UNCTAD Secretariat'' (TD/192/Supp. 1), March 26, 1976. See also the more recent UNCTAD, ''Economic Co-operation among Developing Countries: Priority Areas for Action.''

49. See, UNCTAD, ''Review and Evaluation of the Generalized System of Preferences: Report by the UNCTAD Secretariat'' (TD/232), January 9, 1979. A critical review of the GSP is contained in Peter J. Ginman and Tracy Murray, ''The Generalized System of Preferences: A Review and Appraisal,'' in Sauvant and Hasenpflug, *The New International Economic Order*. Since the first preferential schemes were introduced, some progress has been made through extending the list of beneficiary countries, expanding product coverage, increasing the depth of tariff cuts, and simplifying the rules of origin.

50. Considerable progress has been made toward the adoption of ''A Set of Multilaterally Agreed Equitable Principles and Rules for the Control of Restrictive Business Practices having Adverse Effects in International Trade, Particularly that of Developing Countries, and on the Economic Development of these Countries.'' For a review, see UNCTAD, ''Report of the Third Ad hoc Group of Experts on Restrictive Business Practices on Its Fifth Session'' (TD/B/C.2/AC.6/18), July 27, 1978. It is expected that a negotiating conference, called for November-December 1979, will negotiate and adopt, on the basis of the work of the Third Ad hoc Group of Experts, a set of rules on this subject matter. The emphasis of these rules is, however, not so much on restrictive business practices (these are one of the main topics of the code on transfer of technology), but rather on establishing worldwide antitrust rules dealing with the abuse of dominant market positions. See also UNCTAD, ''Principles and Rules and Other Issues Relating to Restrictive Business Practices: Report by the UNCTAD Secretariat'' (TD/231), January 8, 1979.

51. See, UNCTAD, ''Implications for Developing Countries of the New Protectionism in Developed Countries: Report by the UNCTAD Secretariat'' (TD/226), March 6, 1979.

52. ''The Tokyo Declaration. Declaration Issued at the End of the Ministerial Meeting Held in Tokyo, September 12-14, 1973,'' para. 5, contained in GATT, *GATT Activities in 1973* (Geneva: GATT, 1974).

53. The highest cuts will be in non-electrical machinery, wood products, chemicals, and transport equipment. On the other hand, average cuts on textiles and clothing will be about 20 percent and those on leather, rubber footwear, and travel goods about 16 percent. For a preliminary evaluation of the results of the Tokyo Round, see UNCTAD, ''Multilateral Trade Negotiations: Evaluation and Further Recommendations Arising Therefrom: Report by the UNCTAD Secretariat'' (TD/227), April 2, 1979.

54. Art. 19 of GATT.

55. According to FAO estimates, ''a 50% reduction in protection in the OECD countries on 79 primary and processed agricultural products would have added some $3,000 million to the agricultural export earnings of the 57 most populous developing countries in 1970-74.'' See Food and Agriculture Organization of the United Nations, ''Statement by Nurul Islam before the United Nations General Assembly Preparatory Committee for the New International Development Strategy, Second Session, New York, 11-22 June 1979,'' mimeo, p. 2. At the same time, these protectionist measures entail heavy costs for consumers in DMEs. To quote from the same statement: '' . . . the protectionist measures imposed in the United States in 1975-77 cost consumers $660 million for sugar and $400 to $800 million for meat.''

56. See below. In this context, it has been suggested to establish a national adjustment fund in each DME to facilitate structural changes.

57. See below.

58. In this context, gains from transportation are also important—the reason why the DCs insisted on the negotiation of a liner code, which intends to guarantee the DCs a significantly bigger share of international non-bulk cargo shipping. The ''Convention on a Code of Conduct for Liner Conferences'' was adopted on April 6, 1974; with the European Community's agreement in May 1979 to ratify it—and assuming the Convention will be ratified by the national parliaments—enough countries (accounting for a sufficiently large proportion of world liner tonnage) have agreed to ratification to bring the Convention into force.

59. See also the materials on processing cited earlier as well as H. W. Singer, *The Expansion of Processing in Developing Countries and International Policy Requirements* (London: Commonwealth Secretariat, 1978).

60. See Thomas W. Wälde, ''Revision of Transnational Investment Agreements: Contractual Flexibility in

Natural Resource Development," *Lawyer of the Americas* 10 (1978):265–98; and his "Transnationale Investitionsverträge: Rohstoffvorhaben in Entwicklungsländern," *Rabels Zeitschrift für ausländisches und internationales Privatrecht* 42 (1978): 28–86.

61. Chapter II, Art. 2, para. 2(c).

62. Chapter II, Art. 5 and Part I, para. 1(c), respectively.

63. OECD, *Development Co-operation: 1977 Review* (Paris: OECD, 1977), p. 31.

64. The unit value index of food products exported by the DMEs to the DCs increased from 100 in 1970 to 232 in 1974. During the same period, the unit value index of fuels exported from all market economies to the DCs increased from 100 to 528. In 1973, 11 percent of the imports of the non-oil-exporting countries consisted of fuels and 18 percent of food.

On the other hand, prices for agricultural and mineral commodities exported by the DCs also increased, especially during the 1973/1974 commodity boom, thereby bringing some relief to a number of DCs. The unit value index of food exported by the DCs to all market economies increased from 100 in 1970 to 109 in 1972 and 204 in 1974; that of raw materials increased from 100 in 1970 to 105 in 1972 and 192 in 1974. See United Nations, *1977 Statistical Yearbook* (New York: United Nations, 1978).

The unit value index of machinery exported by the DMEs to the DCs increased from 100 in 1970 to 165 in 1974, and that of other manufactures from 100 to 177. See ibid.

65. Australia, Austria, Belgium, Canada, Denmark, Finland, France, Federal Republic of Germany, Italy, Japan, the Netherlands, New Zealand, Norway, Sweden, Switzerland, the United Kingdom, the United States, and the Commission of the European Community. The IBRD and the IMF are observers.

66. Virtually all concessional flows are ODA flows; the DAC countries, however, are also the source of grants by private voluntary agencies which reached $1.5 billion in 1977.

67. United Nations, "Transfer of Resources in Real Terms to Developing Countries: Note by the Secretariat" (A/AC.191/7), April 13, 1978, p. 10.

68. Concessional flows in 1976 decreased as compared to 1975, due to lessened efforts on the part of all groups. In 1977, ODA increased again in current dollar terms—mostly due to the performance of DAC countries—but remained roughly unchanged in real terms, i.e., when inflation is taken into account.

69. In 1977, in fact, ODA from DAC countries "slipped back as a share of GNP from 0.33 percent in 1976 to 0.31 percent in 1977, the second lowest ratio in the 1970s and, indeed, since statistics on aid flows were first collected in the mid-1950s." Quoted from OECD, "Press Release: Resources for Developing Countries 1977 and Recent Trends," June 19, 1978.

70. UNCTAD, "New Directions and New Structures for Trade and Development: Report by the Secretary-General of UNCTAD to the Conference" (TD/183), April 14, 1976, p. 50.

71. In 1977, only Sweden, the Netherlands, and Norway had reached or exceeded this target.

72. Art. II, 1.

73. For a discussion of a number of them, see United Nations, "Ways and Means of Accelerating the Transfer of Real Resources to Developing Countries on a Predictable, Assured and Continuous Basis: Report of the Secretary-General" (A/31/186), September 21, 1976. For the views of the DAC member countries on some of these measures, as well as a review of the extent to which some of them are already implemented in individual countries, see United Nations, "Acceleration of the Transfer of Real Resources to Developing Countries: Report of the Secretary-General" (A/32/149), August 18, 1977.

74. In a number of countries, multi-year budgeting for selective domestic purposes is an established practice. Some countries apply this practice also to components of their development finance (e.g., technical assistance in the cases of France, Italy, and Switzerland), to commitments to individual recipients (e.g., through legislative approval as in the case of the Federal Republic of Germany), or to the over-all targets of their assistance programs (e.g., Sweden's effort to reach a specified level of financial flows).

75. A number of countries have more or less flexible carry-forward practices, but only Sweden has automatic carry-forward flexibility for all its aid appropriations.

76. This, for instance, is done by the Caisse centrale de coopération économique in France and, as far as amortization receipts are concerned, by the Kreditanstalt für Wiederaufbau in the Federal Republic of Germany.

77. This is done by Denmark, Norway, Finland, and the United Kingdom.

78. UNDP works with 150 governments and 26 international agencies to promote higher standards of living and faster economic growth in the Third World. At the beginning of 1979, UNDP provided financial and technical support to 3,500 projects, on the basis of a budget of $739 million.

79. Norway has had such a tax which financed most of its aid programs between 1964 and 1974. The tax, however, was abolished since it was seen to have an adverse impact on public support for the country's aid pro-

gram. It should be noted that task- or program-specific taxes are used in many countries for domestic purposes.

80. See, respectively, United Nations, *Reduction of the Military Budgets of States Permanent Members of the Security Council by 10 percent and Utilization of Part of the Funds Thus Saved to Provide Assistance to Developing Countries* (New York: United Nations, 1975); and "Final Document of the Tenth Special Session of the General Assembly" (A/RES/S-10/2), July 13, 1978.

81. Some governments seeking loans may have preferred private capital markets to bilateral and multilateral official lending institutions in order to avoid the conditionality that is frequently associated with access to funds from the latter. It should also be noted that a number of governments utilized the Eurodollar market, or other sources, to build up their monetary reserves.

82. United Nations, "Transfer of Resources in Real Terms," p. 11.

83. See United Nations, "Ways and Means," pp. 21–22.

84. See ibid., pp. 22–28 for a more detailed discussion.

85. Techniques of this kind have been employed by the World Bank Group.

86. The subsequent figures exclude debts to the IMF, short-term debts (i.e., debts repayable to external creditors in foreign currency, goods or services with an original or extended maturity of less than one year) and, as a rule, military debt. OECD data have been taken in preference to World Bank data since they are more comprehensive (see, for an exposition of the sources and methodology of both institutions, OECD, *Development Co-operation: 1978 Review,* p. 251). All data refer to disbursed debts only. It should also be noted that in the OECD and World Bank classifications, Greece, Israel, Portugal, Spain, Turkey, and Yugoslavia are classified as developing countries.

87. See Helen Hughes et al., "Prospects for Developing Countries, 1978–85" (Washington: World Bank, 1977), mimeo, p. 71. An UNCTAD report has estimated that the total short, medium, and long-term debt (including loans committed but not yet disbursed) of the non-oil-exporting DCs had reached $250 billion in 1976 and $300 billion in 1977; and those of all DCs, $340 billion at the end of 1977; see UNCTAD, "The External Indebtedness of Developing Countries: A Background Statistical Note. Note by the UNCTAD Secretariat" (TD/B/695), February 27, 1978.

Trade credits are usually liquidated when the imported goods, for which they have been taken up, are sold. Since most of the short-term debts are of this nature, they are not included in subsequent discussions.

88. See Hughes et al., "Prospects," p. 53; and World Bank, *World Development Report, 1978* (Washington: World Bank, 1978), p. 24.

89. Debt owed to official creditors usually has relatively favorable conditions, including a relatively high grant element. Compare in particular the term of ODA transfers (fig. 3.6) with those of loan commitments (fig. 3.9).

90. This has led to a serious bunching of repayment obligations. Nearly half of the DCs' total debt outstanding at the end of 1977 is scheduled for repayment during 1978–1982; see World Bank, *World Development Report, 1979* (Washington: World Bank, 1979), p. 30.

91. The 10 largest debtor countries are not necessarily also the 10 largest debt service payers since the absolute amount of such payments depends on the structure of debts. In 1977, the 10 countries with the highest debt service payments were (in descending order): Brazil, Mexico, Iran, Argentina, Yugoslavia, Algeria, Indonesia, Spain, Republic of Korea, and Egypt, accounting together for two-thirds of the total debt service payments of the DCs.

92. This is illustrated, for example, by the role private DME institutions play in recycling petrodollars. It is also illustrated by the fact that in 1977 non-oil-exporting DCs, with $63 billion, accounted for 15 percent of the external liabilities (net of double-counting due to redepositing among reporting banks) of banks of the Group of Ten Countries and Switzerland, and of the offshore branches of U.S. banks; oil-exporting DCs accounted for another 19 percent. See *IMF Survey* 7 (July 31, 1978):231. The members of the Group of Ten are Belgium and Luxembourg, Canada, France, the Federal Republic of Germany, Italy, Japan, the Netherlands, Sweden, the United Kingdom, and the United States.

93. United Nations, "Transfer of Resources in Real Terms," p. 6.

94. See, Third Ministerial Meeting of the Group of 77, "Manila Declaration and Programme of Action," in Sauvant, *Documents of the Group of 77.* Apart from the measures listed in the text, the Group of 77 has also proposed that multilateral financial institutions provide program assistance to each DC "in an amount no less than its debt service payments to these institutions" (ibid).

95. Ibid. The category of the "most seriously affected countries" had been established in the mid-1970s to include those low-income countries that had been hardest hit by balance-of-payments difficulties. They include the following 45 countries: Afghanistan, Bangladesh, Burma, Burundi, Cape Verde, the Central African

Republic, Chad, Dahomey, Democratic Kampuchea, Democratic Yemen, Egypt, El Salvador, Ethiopia, Gambia, Ghana, Guatemala, Guinea, Guinea-Bissau, Guyana, Haiti, Honduras, India, the Ivory Coast, Kenya, Laos, Lesotho, Madagascar, Mali, Mauritania, Mozambique, Nepal, Niger, Pakistan, Rwanda, Senegal, Sierra Leone, Somalia, Sri Lanka, the Sudan, Uganda, the United Republic of Cameroon, the United Republic of Tanzania, Upper Volta, Western Samoa, and Yemen.

96. Resolution 94 (IV) "Debt Problems of Developing Countries," adopted on May 31, 1976, by UNCTAD IV; contained in United Nations, *Proceedings of the Fourth Session*, p. 17.

97. The main countries are: Federal Republic of Germany ($2.3 billion), United Kingdom ($1.87 billion), Japan ($1.2 billion), Canada ($254 million), Sweden ($200 million), Netherlands ($133 million), Switzerland ($120 million), Denmark ($105 million), and Finland ($47 million). Belgium has canceled the interest on past ODA loans for a number of countries and refinanced 75 percent of the debt services on past ODA loans for some other countries. The savings in debt servicing costs associated with these cancellations represent approximately $300 million per year for the next 20 years. See United Nations press release (TAD/834), November, 1980. France announced in May 1979 that it would cancel $650 million of debts owed to it.

98. An argument could be made that the increased indebtedness of the DCs during the middle of the 1970s has enabled them to maintain largely their import levels, thereby supporting the otherwise faltering conjunctural trend in the industrial states. In a sense, then, at least a part of the debts could be considered as a kind of international deficit spending by the industrial countries and might, therefore, receive more favorable treatment.

99. The formulas used to calculate quotas take into account national income, international reserves, imports, export variability, and the ratio of exports to national income.

100. For a discussion of the various forms of the link, see UNCTAD, "SDR Creation and Development Assistance," in UNCTAD, *Money, Finance and Development: Papers on International Monetary Reform* (New York: United Nations, 1974).

101. The principal function of reserves is to provide countries with liquid assets with which possible future balance-of-payments deficits can be financed. In addition, private lenders often take the size of reserves as an indicator of the creditworthiness of a given country; hence, even if a country intends to finance temporary deficits through external borrowing (and thus could be content with low reserves), the very availability of private external finance may be a function of possessing high reserves. (This partially explains the build-up of reserves by the DCs during the mid-1970s.) Apart from considerations related to private-market confidence, a certain level of reserves is also required to conduct, should the need arise, foreign exchange-market interventions.

102. For voting purposes, each member of the Fund has 250 votes plus one additional vote for each part of its quota equivalent to $100,000. Special majorities, frequently requiring 85 percent of the votes, are required for an increasing number of decisions. See Joseph Gold, *Voting Majorities in the Fund: Effects of Second Amendment of the Articles* (Washington: IMF, 1977). Voting in the World Bank is also weighted. As in the IMF, each member has 250 votes plus one additional vote for each $100,000 of capital stock subscribed by it. Canada, France, the FRG, Italy, Japan, the United Kingdom, and the United States (which, in addition to India, are the largest shareholders) together have more than one-half of all votes and, hence, can defeat any issue requiring a simple majority (the normal requirement for decisions). See table 3.41 for the distribution of subscriptions. Given the formula governing voting power, each quota or subscription increase (which is mostly financed by the rich countries) lessens the importance of the original 250 votes and, hence, increases the voting power of the rich countries. On the other hand, almost all important decisions are taken by consensus in the governing bodies.

103. To date, two decisions to allocate SDRs have been made, involving a total of SDR 21.3 billion. The first was at the end of 1969, and allocations involving SDR 9.3 billion were made during 1970-1972. The second decision was made in December 1978 and involved SDR 12 billion to be allocated by the beginning of 1981.

104. It should be noted that no new SDRs were issued between 1973 and 1978—exactly because international liquidity was growing independently at a sufficient rate.

105. These decisions were incorporated in the Second Amendment to the Fund's Articles of Agreement which entered into force on April 1, 1978. For a review of the Kingston decision, see Tom de Vries, "Jamaica, or the Non-Reform of the International Monetary System," *Foreign Affairs*, 54 (April 1976): 577-605.

106. The objective of this decision was to reduce the role of gold in the international monetary system.

107. UNCTAD, "Money and Finance and Transfer of Real Resources for Development: International Monetary Issues. Problems of Reform. Report by the UNCTAD Secretariat" (TD/189), March 11, 1976, p. 18.

108. Since most of the reserve holdings of the DCs are in dollar and sterling deposits, the value of these

holdings has decreased with the depreciation of its principal components. Exchange-rate stability is, therefore, another objective of the DCs.

109. For a tabular presentation of the various IMF facilities and their conditionality, see UNCTAD, "International Monetary Issues: Report by the UNCTAD Secretariat" (TD/233), March 8, 1979.

110. Under the IMF's Articles of Agreement (Art. III, section 2), "The Fund shall at intervals of not more than five years conduct a general review, and if it deems it appropriate propose an adjustment of the quotas of the members. It may also, if it thinks fit, consider at any other time the adjustment of any particular quota at the request of the member concerned." An 85 percent majority of the total voting power is required for any change in quotas in the context of a general review, and 80 percent for any other quota changes.

111. See note 32.

112. For example, the Fourth Ministerial Meeting of the Group of 77 (held in February 1979 in Arusha) suggested the establishment of a long-term facility for financing purchases of capital goods by DCs. See "Arusha Programme for Collective Self-Reliance and Framework for Negotiations," in Sauvant, *The Documents of the Group of 77.*

113. The buffer stock financing facility was established in 1969 to assist in financing contributions to buffer stock arrangements, accepted as suitable by the Fund, by members having balance-of-payments difficulties.

114. For a review of the role of the Fund in financing balance-of-payments deficits, see "A Profile of 1967–76: Role Played by Resources of Fund in Financing Payments Needs," *IMF Survey* (June 5, 1978).

115. The Committee of 20 had been established by a resolution of the Fund on July 26, 1972 in order to elaborate proposals for the reform of the international monetary system. It completed its work in 1974 with the publication of a report entitled "Outline of Reform" and was replaced by an advisory committee of the Board of Governors, the Interim Committee.

116. After the Fund had decided in April 1973 to provide financial assistance in connection with loans to the International Cocoa Council, it agreed in June 1976 and December 1977 that its buffer stock facility could also be used for, respectively, buffer stocks to be established under the Fifth International Tin Agreement and the International Sugar Agreement. The Second Amendment provides that drawings under this facility are fully additional to those under the reserve tranche (formerly the gold tranche); purchases can be made up to 50 percent of a member's quota. Since market prices of tin and cocoa remained above the level at which stocks could be purchased under the terms of the agreements, the only purchases under this facility since 1975 were made during 1978/79 in connection with the establishment of sugar stocks.

117. The auctioning of the gold was scheduled to take place July 1976 to June 1978 and July 1978 to June 1980. During each of the two periods, 12.5 million ounces of gold were sold.

118. See IMF, *Annual Report 1979* (Washington: IMF, 1979): p. 86–87. Out of this total, $759 million were directly distributed to the DCs on the basis of their quotas, and the balance was available for low-interest (0.5 percent) loans, to be repaid within 10 years after disbursement. The IMF can make further gold sales, provided that members holding 85 percent of the total votes concur.

119. Until the effective date of the quota increase under the Sixth General Review, the size of each credit tranche was enlarged by 45 percent on a temporary basis. The implementation of the Sixth General Review was tied to acceptance of the Second Amendment to the Fund's Articles of Agreement which became effective on April 1, 1978. The Amendment was an effort to adapt the IMF to the international monetary events since 1971. It deals, inter alia, with the management of exchange rates, the gradual reduction in the role of gold in the international monetary system, the use of SDRs, the possible establishment of a Council for the IMF, and improvements in a number of organizational aspects of the Fund. (The First Amendment concerned the introduction of SDRs in 1969.)

120. Since a country's quota cannot be changed without its consent, this figure assumes that all countries will agree to the enlargment. During the Sixth General Review, only Democratic Kampuchea did not consent to the increase of its quota within the period provided, which was then extended; and Singapore consented to an increase that was less than the full amount specified by the resolution of the Board of Governors.

121. As a rule, Third Window lending was restricted to countries with 1972 average per capita income of less than $375.

122. Since then, various international forums have suggested to reactivate and expand the Third Window; see, e.g., the United Nations Committee Established under General Assembly resolution 32/174, in United Nations, "Agreed Conclusions on some Aspects of the Transfer of Resources in Real Terms to Developing Countries: Note by the Secretariat" (A/AC. 191/32), February 5, 1979.

123. See Charles-Albert Michalet, *Le capitalism mondiale* (Paris: Presses Universitaires de France, 1976); and his "From Unequal Industrial Development to Unequal Scientific and Technological Development: the Role of Multinational Corporations in the 'International' Transfer of Technology," in *The New International*

Division of Labour, Technology and Underdevelopment: Consequences for the Third World, ed. Dieter Ernst (Frankfurt: Campus, 1980); see also Bernadette Madeuf, "Technological Dependence in the World Economic System," ibid. The volume edited by Ernst provides an extensive overview of many of the questions pertaining to technological dependence. See in this context also UNCTAD, "Towards the Technological Transformation of the Developing Countries: Report by the UNCTAD Secretariat" (TD/238), March 15, 1979.

124. The level of industrial R and D expenditures has remained fairly constant during the past decade, but the geographic distribution of expenditures has undergone major changes. Most importantly, the shares of the United States and the United Kingdom have declined and those of the Federal Republic of Germany and Japan have increased. See OECD, *International Statistical Year 1975: International Survey of the Resources Devoted to R and D by OECD Member Countries, International Volume* (Paris: OECD, 1979); for an analysis, see, "Industrial R and D in the OECD Area in 1975: A Bird's Eye View," *Science Resources Newsletter* (Winter 1977/78).

125. If some selective data are indicative, R and D (which includes adaption) in many DCs is partly financed by foreign funds, including funds from transnational enterprises; see United Nations, "The role of the Public Sector in Promoting the Economic Development of Developing Countries: Report of the Secretary-General" (E/5690/Add. 1), June 5, 1975, p. 29. In other words, even the already very meager research effort of the DCs may be partly controlled from abroad.

126. See Jan Annerstedt, "Technological Dependence: A Permanent Phenomena of World Inequality?" in Ernst, *The New International Division of Labour.* Annerstedt observed further: "The six countries mentioned spend almost six times as much on military R and D than all developing countries spend on all types of R and D."

127. See the data reported in UNESCO, *Statistical Yearbook.*

128. For a discussion, see UNCTAD, "Technology: Development Aspects of the Reverse Transfer of Technology. Study by the UNCTAD Secretariat" (TD/239), January 29, 1979.

129. In 1974, 98,162 students and trainees were pursuing their education in DAC countries on publicly financed fellowships. In addition, 9,010 persons had received fellowships from multilateral technical cooperation programs. See OECD, *Development Co-operation: 1977 Review* (Paris: OECD, 1977): 216, 222.

130. To quote from an OECD study: "whatever the sector or country of establishment, laboratories situated in the developing countries rarely undertake basic or applied research." See Dimitri Germidis, ed., *Transfer of Technology by Multinational Corporations,* vol. 1, *A Synthesis and Country Case Study* (Paris: OECD, 1977), p. 24.

131. Ibid., p. 26. The OECD report describes this phenomenon as " 'brain drain' *within the host country.*"

132. See Daniel Creamer, Anthony D. Apostolides, and Selina L. Wang, *Overseas Research and Development by United States Multinationals, 1966–1975: Estimates of Expenditures and a Statistical Profile* (New York: The Conference Board, 1976), pp. 4–5.

133. Virtually all payments were made to other DMEs (with the United States receiving over half of total payments); of the receipts, on the other hand, one-fourth originated in the DCs. See Deutsche Bundesbank, *Monatsberichte der Deutschen Bundesbank,* April 1976, p. 20.

134. The data show that about four-fifths of the US receipts are on an intracompany basis.

135. Eighty percent of Mexico's total payments were made by foreign affiliates of transnational enterprises; see F. Fajnzylber and T. M. Tarrago, *Las empresas transnacionales* (Mexico: Fondo de Cultura Economica, 1976).

136. See UNCTAD, "New Direction," p. 41. For some 15 DCs, annual (mostly 1970) transfer-of-technology payments averaged 3.8 percent of exports; see UNCTAD, *Major Issues Arising from the Transfer of Technology to Developing Countries* (New York: United Nations, 1975), p. 26.

137. For a summary of some of the main findings of the study on which these data are based and a discussion of some related matters, see the articles by Surendra J. Patel, Pedro Roffe, and Peter O'Brien in the special issue of *World Development* 2 (September 1974): 3–39.

138. The "Draft International Code of Conduct on the Transfer of Technology" as discussed at the end of 1978 by the United Nations Conference on an International Code on the Transfer of Technology, TD/CODE TOT/9, November 27, 1978, identified the following restrictive practices: grant-back provisions; challenges to validity; exclusive dealing; restrictions on research; restrictions on the use of personnel; price fixing; restrictions on adaptions; exclusive sales or representation agreements; tying arrangements; export restrictions; cartels/patent pool or cross-licensing agreements; restrictions on publicity; payments and other obligations after expiration of industrial property rights; restrictions after expiration of arrangement; limitations on volume, scope, etc.; use of quality controls; obligations to use trade marks; requirements to provide equity or participation in management; unlimited or unduly long duration of arrangements; and limitations upon use of technology already imported. Most common among all these restrictive business practices associated with

transfer of technology arrangements appear to be the tying of purchase of imported inputs, equipment, and spare parts to a particular source (usually the parent firm), restrictions on exports and sources of supply, and transfer pricing.

139. Given the structure of the world's R and D capacities as described above, technology is developed by enterprises of the DMEs for the markets of the DMEs. It reflects, therefore, primarily the factor endowments and needs of the developed and not the developing countries. Most notably it is capital (not labor) intensive and geared toward the production of medium and high-income consumption products. Research appropriate for the DCs, on the other hand, "may be said to cover those technologies that produce essential commodities, increase the productivity of poor populations in rural and urban areas and generate employment. It also covers technologies suitable for small scale application and those that make maximum use of local material and human resources." Quoted from OECD, *Development Co-operation: 1978 Review* (Paris: OECD, 1978), pp. 57–58.

140. For a discussion of these costs, see Frances Stewart, *Technology and Underemployment* (Boulder, Col.: Westview Press, 1977).

141. For a listing of UNCTAD's work in this area (as well as for other relevant material), see Economic Commission for Europe (ECE) and UNCTAD, "Technology Transfer: A Bibliography of Materials Available in the ECE/UNCTAD Reference Unit, Including a Complete List of UNCTAD Publications, 1964–1974," bibliography No. 9, rev. ed. (Geneva: ECE/UNCTAD, Reference Unit, 1975), mimeographed; and UNCTAD, "Select Bibliography of Documents on Transfer and Development of Technology that have been Prepared by or for the UNCTAD Secretariat" (TD/B/C.6/INF.2/Rev. 1), July 12, 1979. For a more recent bibliography on the entire subject matter, see Taghi Saghafi-nejad and Robert Belfield, "The Transnational Corporations and Transfer of Technology: A Bibliography" (New York: Pergamon Press, 1980). For a brief review of the United Nations work on science and technology, see Klaus-Heinrich Standke, "Wissenschaft und Technologie im System der Vereinten Nationen," *Vereinte Nationen* 24 (February 1976): 8–12.

142. See UNCTAD, "Restructuring the Legal and Juridical Environment: Issues under Negotiations. Report by the UNCTAD Secretariat" (TD/237), January 29, 1979, and Add. 1 of April 12, 1979.

143. Although efforts to formulate and adopt a code of conduct on the transfer of technology date back to 1964, concrete steps were taken only since UNCTAD III (May 1972) with a resolution requesting an examination of the possibilities for new international legislation in this field. For a summary of the intensive activities that took place in the following years, see UNCTAD, "United Nations Conference on an International Code of Conduct on the Transfer of Technology: Background Note by The UNCTAD Secretariat" (TD/CODE TOT/4), September 6, 1978. This document also describes the major features of the draft code prepared in six sessions between November 1976 and July 1978 by an Intergovernmental Group of Experts; this draft code constituted the basis of the negotiations of the international conference. For the text of the draft code as it stood at the adjournment of the first session of the conference on November 11, 1978, see UNCTAD, "Draft International Code of Conduct on the Transfer of Technology" (TD/CODE TOT/9), November 27, 1978. For a critical review of UNCTAD's code efforts, see Dieter Ernst, "A Code of Conduct on the Transfer of Technology: Establishing New Rules or Codifying the Status Quo?" in Sauvant and Hasenpflug, *The New International Economic Order.*

144. See also in this context UNCTAD, "Transfer of Technology: Action to Strengthen the Technological Capacity of Developing Countries. Policies and Institutions. Report by the UNCTAD Secretariat" (TD/190/Supp. 1) February 3, 1976; and UNCTAD, "Technology Planning in Developing Countries: Study by the UNCTAD Secretariat" (TD/238/Supp. 1), January 8, 1979.

145. For instance, national centers have been set up in Afghanistan, Ethiopia, Iraq, Sri Lanka, and Venezuela. The essential functions of such centers are summarized by a UNCTAD document as follows:

(a) To lay the foundations for the formulation of a technology plan by supplying the technological component of national development plans; (b) to lay the foundations for a co-ordinated set of policies for the implementation of the technology plan; (c) to assist in the evaluation and selection of appropriate technologies for the different jobs to be done, with the emphasis on decision-making, which is the most critical stage in the whole process; (d) to assist in the unpacking of imported technology, including assessment of suitability, the direct and indirect costs and the conditions attached; (e) to assist in the negotiation of the best possible terms and conditions for the technology to be imported, including arrangements for registration, evaluation and approval of agreements for its transfer; (f) to promote and assist absorption and adaptation of foreign technology and generation of indigenous technology, linked specifically to design/engineering, research and development; (g) to promote the diffusion among users of technology already assimilated, whether indigenous or foreign.

See UNCTAD, "Strengthening the Technological Capacity of Developing Countries: Advisory Service on Transfer of Technology (ASTT). Progress Report by the UNCTAD Secretariat" (TD/B/C.6/33), September 15, 1978, pp. 4–5. For a detailed country study see, for instance, UNCTAD, "Transfer and Development of

Technology in Iraq: Report by an UNCTAD Mission'' (UNCTAD/TT/AS/2), June 5, 1978. See also, UNCTAD, "Advisory Service on Technology: Report by the UNCTAD Secretariat on Its Activities and Future Resources Requirements" (TD/238/Supp.2), April 5, 1979.

146. A center for the development and transfer of technology has also been established for the Asian and Pacific Region.

147. See especially the United Nations Conference on Technical Co-operation among Developing Countries, held in Buenos Aires from August 30 to September 12, 1978. The report of the conference is contained in A/CONF. 79/13/Rev.1, New York, 1978. It stated, inter alia, that technical co-operation among developing countries "is a vital force for initiating, designing, organising and promoting co-operation among developing countries so that they can create, acquire, adopt, transfer and pool knowledge and experience for their mutual benefit and for achieving national and collective self-reliance, which are essential for their social and economic development" (p. 3). As this quote indicates, technical co-operation among developing countries has to be seen in the broader context of self-reliance.

148. The pilot operation for this information bank was established in 1977 by UNIDO as a complement to the Information and Advisory Services provided by UNIDO.

149. See United Nations, *Report of the United Nations Conference on Science and Technology for Development, Vienna, 20–31 August 1979* (New York: United Nations, 1979).

150. Paragraph 23. The document is reprinted in Sauvant, *Documents of the Group of 77*. UNIDO II was "entrusted with establishing the main principles of industrialisation and defining the means by which the international community as a whole might take action of a broad nature in the field of industrial development within the framework of new forms of international co-operation, with a view to the establishment of a new international economic order" (para. 1).

151. See UNIDO, *World Industry Since 1960: Progress and Prospects. Special Issue of the Industrial Development Survey for the Third General Conference of UNIDO* (New York: United Nations, 1979), p. 42. This publication contains a comprehensive review of the industrialization achievements of the DCs. It is supplemented by a more policy-oriented document, also prepared by UNIDO, entitled "Industrialisation for the Year 2000: New Dimensions. Joint Study on International Industrial Co-operation" (Vienna: UNIDO, 1979).

152. See United Nations, *Restructuring of World Industry: New Dimensions for Trade Co-operation* (New York: United Nations, 1978), p. 3.

153. Since the statistics used for this calculation include durable consumer goods, (e.g., automobiles), the share of the DCs in the production of capital goods is even lower than the 3 percent cited in the text, possibly as low as 1–2 percent of world production. See, Economic Commission for Europe, *Role and Place of Engineering Industries in National and World Economies* (New York: United Nations, 1974).

154. Ibid. These shares are determined on the basis of the number of workers in the mechanical-machinery industry.

155. Ibid. Among these, 52 have less than 1 million inhabitants, 50 have 1 to 10 million, and 12 have more than 10 million.

These figures underline the fact that import substitution as a development strategy has mainly aimed at substituting the import of *consumption* goods by local production, and even this production has frequently come under the control of foreign capital interests.

156. Structural reasons why the developed countries' industrial output rates can be expected to decrease in the future include the generally declining growth of these countries, the increasing share of the service sector in their economies, the need for investments for energy and environmental protection, and efforts to avoid inflationary developments. It should be noted that the centrally-planned economies increased their share in world manufacturing value-added from 18 percent in 1960 to 28 percent in 1975 without causing major market disruptions. UNIDO concluded, therefore: "The fact that the world industrial structure was able to accommodate changes of such magnitude suggests considerable flexibility in the adjustment process." See , UNIDO, *World Industry*, p. 52.

157. Assuming a growth rate of 5 percent of manufacturing value-added in the developed countries during 1975–2000 and a growth rate of 7–8 percent for the DCs—i.e., their average growth during the period 1960–1975—the share of the Third World in world manufacturing value-added would still increase to some 15 percent in the year 2000. See, United Nations, "Lima Declaration and Plan of Action on Industrial Development and Co-operation and Strengthening of the Industrial Capacity of Developing Countries: Note by the Secretariat" (A/AC.191/36), March 2, 1979, p. 6.

158. Para. 52 of the Lima Declaration; see also para. 58(f) of the Lima Plan of Action.

159. See, for instance, UNCTAD, *Restructuring of World Industry*, p. 8: "trade expansion and diversification become preconditions for achieving the industrial growth that is required." Also, UNCTAD, "New Directions," p. 12: "a sound commodity sector has to serve as a spring board for the dynamic transformation of their economies, a transformation that must point inevitably in the direction of industrialization."

160. Section IV, para. 3, of the resolution adopted at the Seventh Special Session. The "system of consultations" was originally proposed in the Lima Declaration, para. 26.

161. United Nations, "Overseeing and Monitoring the Implication of Decisions and Agreements Reached in the Negotiations on the Establishment of the New International Economic Order in the Appropriate Bodies of the United Nations System: Note by the Secretariat" (A/AC.191/11), April 17, 1978, p. 3

162. To strengthen UNIDO's role, the Lima Declaration (later supported by the Seventh Special Session) had recommended in 1975 that UNIDO be converted into a specialized agency, thus giving it more autonomy in (and a budget of its own for) the pursuit of its tasks. After laborious negotiations, this objective had finally been achieved in April 1979. It may, however, still take another two or three years before this decision is ratified by the required number of states and UNIDO can actually function as a specialized agency. Apart from its budget, UNIDO will also be able to draw on an Industrial Development Fund whose establishment was also recommended in the Lima Declaration.

163. See the first report about these consultations contained in UNIDO, "Establishment of a System of Consultations in the Field of Industry: Progress Made between April 1977 and March 1978 and the Experience thus Acquired. Report by the Executive Director" (ID/B/204), March 31, 1978.

164. Section IV, para. 2 of the resolution adopted at the Seventh Special Session. This idea as well was contained in the Lima Declaration.

165. Programme of Action on the Establishment of a New International Economic Order, part I, 3(a) vii. In order to obtain this objective, the developed countries were urged at the same place to "make appropriate adjustments in their economies so as to facilitate the expansion and diversification of imports from developing countries."

166. UNCTAD, "New Directions," p. 38.

167. UNCTAD, "Evaluation of the World Trade and Economic Situation and Consideration of Issues, Policies and Appropriate Measures to Facilitate Structural Changes in the International Economy: Report by the UNCTAD Secretariat" (TD/224), March 28, 1979, p. 9. UNCTAD is, however, aware that the existing vertical division of labor has to be transformed; see ibid.

168. To quote from a UNIDO document:

> During the past decade, cost structures and labour market conditions in the developed countries have led firms to redeploy industrial capacity to the developing countries in order to retain international competitiveness. High labour costs, costly Government regulation, newly levied environmental costs, and rising raw material and energy costs in developed countries have combined to make a growing number of developing countries more attractive as locations for certain industrial activities. Such developing countries offer an abundant supply of cheap and well-disciplined labour, greater access to raw materials, lower energy and antipollution costs, lower building and grounds costs, and growing access to modern world-wide transport and communications facilities.

From this, UNIDO concluded for the international division of labor:

> Barring the introduction of protectionist policies or other measures by the developed countries, which would change this new emerging attractiveness of industrial sites in the developing countries, the international division of labour will most probably continue to develop along the lines established during the past decade: continued growth of labour intensive and raw material intensive industry in the developing countries; increasing redeployment of capital intensive production in the late stages of the product cycle to the developing countries; maintenance of capital intensive sectors in the early stages of the production cycle in the developed countries; and maintenance and expansion of human capital intensive industry—industry requiring a sophisticated service sector, R and D facilities, and a highly qualified and flexible labour force—in the developed countries. These trends can be expected to lead to an ever-increasing intra-branch division of labour on a world-wide scale and to ever-increasing regional specialization within the international division of labour.

See, United Nations, "Industrial Redeployment in Favour of Developing Countries: Report of the Executive Director of the United Nations Industrial Development Organization" (A/34/288), June 20, 1979, pp. 7–8.

169. Main data sources are United Nations, *Transnational Corporations in World Development: A Reexamination* (New York: United Nations, 1978); OECD, *Pénétration des entreprises multinationales dans l'industrie manufacturière des pays membres* (Paris: OECD, 1977); and J. P. Curhan, W. H. Davidson, and R. Suri, *Tracing the Multinationals* (Cambridge: Ballinger, 1977); for further references, see United Nations, *Bibliography on Transnational Corporations* (New York: United Nations, 1979).

170. United Nations, *Transnational Corporations,* p. 35.

171. "Directly" because *foreign affiliates* also undertake foreign direct investments. These indirect foreign direct investments, although ultimately controlled by the parent enterprises in their home country, nevertheless appear as foreign direct investments in the statistics of the respective host countries in which these affiliates are located. Thus, for instance, over one-fourth of Canada's foreign direct investment is controlled by United States affiliates in Canada. Similarly, the Deutsche Bundesbank has estimated that at the end of 1976 the total stock of foreign direct investment of the FRG abroad was about 10 percent higher (and that of foreigners in the FRG abroad 20 percent higher) if such indirect foreign investments were added. See Deutsche Bundesbank, "Stand der Direktinvestitionen Ende 1976," *Monatsberichte,* April 1979, pp. 31 and 34.

172. For instance, a 1972 survey of the Conference Board found that of the 10,760 directors of 855 large United States enterprises only 146 (or 1.4 percent) were not citizens of the United States. See Jeremy Bacon, *Corporate Directorship Practices: Membership and Committees of the Board* (New York: The Conference Board, 1973).

In fact, in a number of countries, legal provisions make the takeover of TNEs by non-nationals very difficult, if not impossible. Where multinational ownership or control exists, it is virtually entirely limited to nationals of a few developed countries.

173. At the end of the 1960s, approximately 70 percent of France's DC affiliates were located in Africa, and 90 percent of these in former French colonies. Of the United Kingdom's affiliates in the Third World, 89 percent of those in Africa, 47 percent of those in Latin America, and 73 percent of those in Asia were in former colonies. Finally, foreign affiliates in Latin America represented 75 percent of the United States' DC affiliate network. More generally speaking, one single home country supplied at least 75 percent of the stock of foreign direct investment in about half of the developing nations and over 50 percent in about four-fifths of them. See, *Yearbook of International Organisations,* 13th ed., 1970–1971 and OECD, *Stock of Private Direct Investments by DAC Countries in Developing Countries, End 1967* (Paris: OECD, 1972).

174. Even where production facilities are nationalized, however, the former host countries frequently remain dependent on the former parent enterprises (or on other TNEs) for the management of the production facilities involved (e.g., the copper mines in Zambia), for transportation, marketing and distribution, and for supply of technology. This continued dependence is an important factor for explaining the low incidence of nationalization reported in chap. 1. Nevertheless, a certain fear of nationalization (especially in natural resource industries) exists. The proposal of U.S. Secretary of State Henry A. Kissinger at UNCTAD IV in Nairobi (May 1976) to establish an International Resource Bank to finance natural resource development projects in the Third World was largely born out of this fear. Observed Samir Amin: "Pour le sécrétaire d'Etat, il ne s'agit pas d'améliorer et de protéger les revenues des exportateurs, mais de minimiser les risques des multinationales." See his article "Sept propositions pour le Tiers monde," *Jeune Afrique* 801 (May 14, 1976):40.

175. See United Nations, *Transnational Corporations.*

176. See, e.g., Juan Somavia, "The Transnational Power Structure and International Information: Elements of a Third World Policy for Transnational News Agencies," *Development Dialogue,* no. 2, 1976, pp. 15–28.

177. United Nations, *Transnational Corporations,* pp. 269, 270.

178. Such nonequity arrangements include licensing, franchising, management contracts, leasing of plants, contract manufacturing, subcontracting joint research and development, coproduction, specialization, comarketing, and the like.

179. Given the subject of this chapter, the preceding discussion has focused on DCs. For a worldwide analysis of the role of TNEs, see United Nations, *Transnational Corporations.*

180. It must be recalled that the R and D underlying the technology used by TNEs, and the product mix favored by them, is produced in the home country in response to conditions that, of course, are quite different from those in the DCs.

181. Section II, 2(e) and section III(b).

182. Section IV, 6 of the resolution adopted at the Seventh Special Session reads:

> Developed countries should whenever possible, encourage their enterprises to participate in investment projects within the framework of the development plans and programmes of the developing countries which so desire; such participation should be carried out in accordance with the laws and regulations of the developing countries concerned.

183. UNIDO, "The Redeployment of Industries from Developed to Developing Countries: Note Prepared by the Secretariat of UNIDO" (ID/B/190), April 27, 1977, p. 4. See also United Nations, "Industrial Redeployment in Favour of Developing Countries: Report of the Executive Director of the United Nations Industrial Development Organization" (A/33/182), September 19, 1978 and (A/34/288) June 20, 1979.

184. United Nations, "Strengthening the Industrial Capacity of Developing Countries," p. 8. Interest in redeployment was found to exist in all industrial branches. The survey seemed to have confirmed much of what is known about the reasons for foreign direct investment and the patterns that characterize it.

It is worth noting in this context that TNEs may well become strong allies of the Third World for some purposes—for instance, as tax collectors (as for the members of OPEC and other producers' associations), in the sense of agreeing to higher prices and passing them on to consumers in developed countries, or as lobbyists for the redeployment of industries.

185. It should be noted that the Committee on Industrial Co-operation and the Centre for Industrial Development, both of which have been established in the framework of the Lomé Convention, are also engaged in activities that encourage redeployment.

186. Para. 4(g) and Section V, respectively.

187. Chapter II, art. 2,2:

> Each State has the right:
> (a) To regulate and exercise authority over foreign investment within its national jurisdiction in accordance with its laws and regulations and in conformity with its national objectives and priorities. No State shall be compelled to grant preferential treatment to foreign investment;
> (b) To regulate and supervise the activities of transnational corporations within its national jurisdiction and take measures to ensure that such activities comply with its laws, rules and regulations and conform with its economic and social policies. Transnational corporations shall not intervene in the internal affairs of a host State. Every State should, with full regard for its sovereign rights, co-operate with other States in the exercise of the right set forth in this subparagraph.

188. For a review of host country efforts at the national, regional and international levels as well as the role of labor unions, see Karl P. Sauvant, "Controlling Transnational Enterprises: A Review and Some Further Thoughts," in Sauvant and Hasenpflug, *The New International Economic Order.* See also Robert Black and Elizabeth C. Hanson, *Multinationals in Contention: Responses at Government and International Levels* (New York: The Conference Board, 1978). Extensive documentary material is contained in United Nations, *Transnational Corporations: Material Relevant to the Formulation of a Code of Conduct* (New York: United Nations, 1977), and *Transnational Corporations: Issues Involved in the Formulation of a Code of Conduct* (New York: United Nations, 1976). For a discussion of a number of issues relating to the legal consequences of codes of conduct, see Norbert Horn and E. R. Lanier, eds., *Legal Problems of Codes of Conduct for Multinational Enterprises* (forthcoming).

189. See United Nations, *National Legislation and Regulations Relating to Transnational Corporations* (New York: United Nations, 1978).

190. See, respectively, Decision 24 (as amended) of the Junta del Acuerdo de Cartagena on "Common Treatment of Foreign Capital, Trademarks, Patents, Licensing Agreements and Royalties in the Andean Common Market," reprinted in the *Journal of Common Market Studies* 10 (June 1972): 339-59; and the OECD "Declaration of International Investment and Multinational Enterprises" which includes the "Guidelines for Multinational Enterprises" and is contained in OECD, *International Investment and Multinational Enterprises* (Paris: OECD, 1976). The OECD guidelines, which are voluntary and were adopted on June 21, 1976, are only indirectly relevant to DCs.

191. The Ad Hoc Intergovernmental Working Group on the Problem of Corrupt Practices is negotiating under the aegis of ECOSOC, an "International Agreement to Prevent and Eliminate Illicit Payments in Connexion with International Commerce Transactions" (see the report of the Working Group on its fourth, fifth, and resumed fifth sessions, contained in E/1978/115 of July 7, 1978); the United Nations Group of Experts on Tax Treaties between Developed and Developing Countries is dealing with international tax relations (including double taxation and tax evasion and avoidance) (see United Nations, "Transnational Corporations: The Work of the Group of Experts on Tax Treaties Relevant to the Formulation of a Code of Conduct. Note of the Secretariat" (E/C.10/AC.2/10), January 4, 1979); an Ad Hoc Intergovernmental Working Group of Experts is scheduled to begin work in 1980 on international standards of accounting and reporting (see, in this context, United Nations, *International Standards of Accounting and Reporting for Transnational Corporations* [New York: United Nations, 1977]); and the International Labour Organisation adopted, in 1977, the "Tripartite Declaration of Principles Concerning Multinational Enterprises and Social Policy" (Geneva: ILO, 1977).

192. For the Working Group's reports on its first two sessions, see E/C.10/31 of May 4, 1977; on its third and fourth sessions, see E/C.10/36 of April 20, 1978; and on its fifth, sixth and seventh sessions, see E/C.10/46 of April 11, 1979.

193. See, United Nations, "Transnational Corporations: Code of Conduct. Formulations by the Chairman" E/C.10/AC.2/8, December 13, 1978. This document covers the following issues:

I. Activities of transnational corporations.
   A. General and political: respect for national sovereignty and observance of domestic laws, regulations, and administrative practices; adherence to economic goals and development objectives, policies and priorities; adherence to socio-cultural objectives and values; respect for human and fundamental freedoms; noninterference in internal political affairs; noninterference in intergovernmental relations; abstention from corrupt practices.
   B. Economic, financial, and social: ownership and control; balance of payments and financing; transfer pricing; taxation; competition and restrictive business practices; transfer of technology; employment and labour; consumer protection; environmental protection.
   C. Disclosure of information.
II. Treatment of transnational corporations.
   A. General treatment of transnational corporations by the countries in which they operate.
   B. Nationalisation and compensation.
   C. Jurisdiction
III. Intergovernmental co-operation.

194. Food and Agriculture Organization, *Agriculture: Toward 2000* (Rome: FAO, 1979), p. xxi; if the major oil exporters are included, this percentage was 21; see ibid., p. 37. (Hereinafter referred to as *AT:2000*.)

195. During the first half of the 1970s, the growth of agricultural output was lower than population growth in 51 countries, comprising almost 70 percent of the DCs' total population (and 95 percent of the population of the MSA countries); see United Nations, "Review of Progress Made in the Implementation of the International Development Strategy and in Relation to General Assembly Resolutions 3202 (S-VI), 3281 (XXIX) and 3262 (S-VII): Report Prepared by the Secretariat" (E/AC.54/22), March 16, 1979, p. 9. Production instability (in the form of a drop in food production of 5 percent or more) was experienced twice or more by 51 countries and at least in one year by 36 countries during the period 1960–1978; see FAO, *AT: 2000*, p. 3.

196. It is, possible, of course, that some countries pursue a policy to expand employment in agriculture, even at the cost of productivity as measured by output per agricultural worker. In such cases, the productivity measure used here is not appropriate since it does not capture the social benefits of reduced unemployment. Furthermore, if productivity is measured by output per unit of land, increased employment may well lead to improved productivity.

197. The average annual rates of growth of cereal production alone were somewhat higher: 3.7 percent during the 1960s and 3.0 percent during the early 1970s. As a result, per capita cereal production was also somewhat more favorable; see Food and Agriculture Organization, *The Fourth World Food Survey* (Rome: FAO, 1977), p. 7.

198. Ibid., p. 3.

199. Ibid., p. 6.

200. FAO, *AT: 2000*, p. 2.

201. To reemphasize: these figures are averages, i.e., do not take into account the highly skewed income distribution that greatly limits actual access to food for a large proportion of the population (especially women and children).

202. United Nations, World Food Council, "Food Production, Nutrition and Investment in Developing Countries: Report by the Executive Director" (WFC/1979/7), May 7, 1979, p. 1. Approximately 80 million tons of the projected 1990 deficit will involve the low-income countries of Asia and Africa. International food supplies and food aid became plentiful beginning in the mid-1950s, a factor that probably contributed to a certain neglect of agriculture in the DCs.

203. As rice and coarse grain imports and exports largely compensate each other, these data reflect almost exclusively the growing dependence of the DCs on wheat imports. The importance of this dependence is further magnified by the high "essentiality" of these imports for many DCs: bottlenecks in international supply can mean starvation. Here as well, wide variations exist. Dependence is highest for countries with per capita GDP in 1970 of $200 to $400: this group's average ratio of net imports of cereals to apparent consumption averaged 24 percent during 1971–1975. See, United Nations, "Development Trends since 1960 and Their Implications for a New International Development Strategy: Paper Presented by the Secretariat" (E/AC.54/L.98), February 13, 1978, p. 37.

204. United Nations, World Food Council, "World Food Security for the 1980s: Report by the Executive Director" (WFC/1979/5), April 26, 1979, p. 7. The other main net exporters are Australia (18 percent) and Argentina (4 percent).

205. UNCTAD, "Technological Policies in the Food Industry: Issues for Research. Report by the UNCTAD Secretariat" (TD/B/C/.6/40), November, 16, 1978, p. 23.

206. FAO, *AT: 2000*, p. 26.

207. Ibid., p. 82. Excluded are manufactures and semi-manufactures based on agricultural materials (e.g., leather goods, textiles).

208. See Sanja Lall, "Private Foreign Investment and the Transfer of Technology in Food Processing" (Geneva: ILO, 1978). 50 of the 60 leading TNEs in food processing and related sectors are based in the United States or the United Kingdom. The DCs' total food and beverage industry had, in 1975, an estimated sales volume of $60 billion, of which around one-sixth was produced by foreign affiliates. See United Nations, "Transnational Corporations in Food and Beverage Processing" (E/C.10/70), April 17, 1980, and the supporting technical paper ST/CTC/19.

The food industry accounts on the average for 16–19 percent of manufacturing employment in each of the developing regions and for 20–26 percent of manufacturing output. See UNCTAD, "Food Industry," p. 1.

209. See United Nations, "Transnational Corporations in Food and Beverage Processing."The reasons include the high capital intensity of foreign direct investment in agriculture, the sensitivity of host countries about foreign ownership of land and agricultural resources, and the production risks related to agriculture (e.g., weather, insects, diseases). Direct investment is, however, frequently replaced by contract farming. For a thorough analysis of the role of the TNEs in the international food and beverage industry, and especially also the problems this role creates for DCs, see ibid.

210. FAO, *AT: 2000*, pp. 4–6.

211. See United Nations, *World Food Conference, Rome, 5–16 November 1974: Report* (New York: United Nations, 1975).

212. See, United Nations, World Food Council, "Investment Requirements for Food Production: Report by the Executive Director" (WFC/1979/4), April 26, 1979, pp. 1–2. Major investment costs involve land development, soil and water conservation, flood control, irrigation development and improvement, establishment of permanent tree crops, and mechanization. Not included in these estimates are investments needed for fertilizer plants and other agricultural input industries, agro-industries, rural communication and transport, and for multipurpose river basin projects. A recent estimate, which takes into account these and related requirements as well as depreciation charges, arrives at total gross investment estimates of $41 billion in 1975; see FAO *AT: 2000*, p. 10.

213. Ibid., p. 24.

214. See United Nations, Centre for Development Planning, Projections and Policies, "Planning for Development: Goals and Policies of Developing Countries for the Second Half of the 1970s," *Journal of Development Planning*, no. 11 (1977).

215. Other institutions provide finance for agriculture as well, but not in an exclusive manner. Foremost among them is the World Bank Group which has identified agriculture as a target sector for its activities and has provided, in 1979, $2.5 billion (one-quarter of its total lending) for agriculture and rural development. See World Bank, *1979 Annual Report* (Washington: World Bank, 1979), p. 30.

216. Of the initial pledges, OECD countries contributed 56.5 percent, OPEC countries 43.5 percent, and other developing countries 2 percent; see United Nations, "Measures Regarding World Food Problems and Agricultural Development: Note by the Secretariat" (A/AC.191/38), March 19, 1979, p. 1.

217. For 1979, the Executive Board of the Fund has set a commitment target of $375 million, benefiting mainly small farmers; see ibid., p. 5.

218. On recommendation of the World Food Conference, a Consultative Group on Food Production and Investment in Developing Countries had been created to assist countries in formulating and implementing specific programs and projects for increasing food production. This Group was discontinued, however, with the establishment of the International Fund for Agricultural Development.

219. For a summary of the activities in this area, see United Nations, World Food Council, "Toward a World without Hunger: Progress and Prospects for Completing the Unfinished Agenda of the World Food Conference. Report by the Executive Director" (WFC/1979/3), March 23, 1979.

220. See, United Nations, *United Nations Conference on Desertification, Nairobi, 29 August–9 September 1977: Report* (New York: United Nations, 1977); and United Nations, *United Nations Water Conference, Mar del Plata, 14–25 March 1977: Report* (New York: United Nations, 1977).

221. See United Nations, World Food Council, "World Food Security for the 1980s."

222. The issues here are the same as for other raw materials discussed earlier, i.e., improvement of terms of trade, diversification of production capacity, and stabilization of world markets.

223. More specifically, disagreements focused on the level of the trigger prices at which reserve stocks should be bought and released, the size and distribution of the reserve stocks, and the question of special treatment of the DCs in financing reserve stocks.

224. Ibid., p. 27.

225. Food aid during the 1972–75 food crisis was about one-third of that during the surplus years of the 1960s. Food aid and its specific characteristics can also have a number of undesirable side effects. To quote the World Food Council:

> The most widely debated side-effects have been the discouragement of investment in local food production, the development of consumption patterns which tend to establish a permanent dependency on imported food commodities, particularly wheat, and the unfair competition by those food exporting countries who could afford financing an aggressive marketing effort to displace and discourage those who could not.

"World Food Security for the 1980s," p. 16.

226. Ibid., p. 26. Since it was recognized that a 10-million-tons minimum is insufficient, discussions were initiated to increase it to 50 million tons.

227. World Food Conference resolution XXII, para. 5, as later endorsed by General Assembly resolution 3348 (XXIX) of December 17, 1974.

228. Section V, para. 3.

229. See, FAO, *World Conference on Agrarian Reform and Rural Development, Rome, 12–20 July 1979: Report* (Rome: FAO, 1979).

230. Ibid., p. 4.

231. The question of land reform has not entirely escaped international attention in the past. See, most notably, United Nations, *Progress in Land Reform: Sixth Report* (New York: United Nations, 1976); and the earlier reports.

232. See chapters 1 and 2.

233. See, "ACP-EEC Convention of Lomé" contained in United Nations document A/AC.176 of September 16, 1975; also, Steven J. Warnecke, "The Lomé Convention and Industrial Cooperation: A New Relationship between the European Community and the ACP States?" in Sauvant and Hasenpflug, *The New International Economic Order.* Third World countries also lobbied for support and acceptance of the NIEO program in another interregional context: a conference of the Commonwealth Heads of Government (April/May 1975). See, Commonwealth Secretariat, "Towards a New International Economic Order," contained in United Nations document A/AC.176/5 of September 8, 1975; and Commonwealth Secretariat, *Towards a New International Economic Order: A Further Report by a Commonwealth Experts' Group* (London: Commonwealth Secretariat, 1976).

234. Since 1975, 11 additional DCs had acceded to the Convention. The second Lomé Convention was signed on October 31, 1979; it has a duration of five years, beginning March 1, 1980.

235. The relevant DC documents of the conference, including its final report, are contained in Sauvant, *Documents of the Group of 77.*

236. See Michael Morris, "The New International Economic Order and the New Law of the Sea," in Sauvant and Hasenpflug, *The New International Economic Order.*

237. See chap. 1 for a listing of these conferences. The various United Nations conferences mentioned elsewhere in this chapter (e.g., UNCTAD IV and V, UNIDO II) as well as various conferences of the Group of 77 and the Non-Aligned Countries should be added to this list.

238. General Assembly resolution 32/174 of December 19, 1977.

239. Ibid.

240. Ibid. For the reports on the meetings of the Committee of the Whole, see, General Assembly, *Official Records: Thirty-third Session, Supplement No. 34, Report of the Committee Established Under General Assembly Resolution 32/174* (A/33/34).

241. Draft resolution A/AC.191/L.4 of September 13, 1979.

4

The Position of the Industrialized Countries

Baron Rudiger von Wechmar

Introduction

Demands by the oil-producing and developing countries for a New International Economic Order caused a serious confrontation between industrialized countries and the Third World during the Sixth Special Session of the General Assembly. Under heavy political pressure from the developing countries, that session adopted in 1974 a "Declaration" and a "Programme of Action" on the establishment of such a New International Economic Order, although all industrialized countries lodged more or less comprehensive reservations against these decisions (see Appendix A). Since then, the question of establishing a New International Economic Order has been at the center of the international discussion on economic policies. While the divergences of opinions between industrialized countries and developing countries continue to persist in many substantive questions, it proved possible, following the Seventh Special Session of the General Assembly in 1975, to render the discussion more businesslike and to continue it in the form of a dialogue between partners. Above all, the subsequent Conference on International Economic Co-operation in Paris contributed to this result.

In order to facilitate the continuation of the dialogue and to further a better understanding of the respective views, this chapter explains the major objections and reservations the industrialized countries have lodged against the Declaration and the Programme of Action on the Establishment of a New International Economic Order.

The documents relating to the New International Economic Order claim to put the economic relations among all countries around the globe on a new basis. In reality, however, the debates in, and resolutions by, the United Nations General Assembly address themselves only to a partial reshuffling of economic relations, namely those between industrialized and developing countries. While the industrialized countries as well as the so-called socialist states remain free to arrange their economic relations among themselves on the basis of their own rules, both these groups are called upon to develop their relations with the Third World according to new rules embodied in the Declaration and the Programme of Action on the Establishment of a New International Economic Order and the Charter of Economic Rights and Duties of States.

Since the Third World's share in international economic exchanges has so far been relatively modest (about 20 percent of world trade), the bulk of world economic relations remains for the time being, therefore, outside of this new order. In effect, the new economic order confines itself to a new order of economic relations between the Third World and Western industrialized countries. The socialist states offer the Third World political support and oral promises of assistance, but when it comes to trade and other elements of economic relations, these states strictly insist on the principle of mutual advantage. The Third World seems to have resigned itself to this fact.

Whereas, in the past, East-West problems dominated the political scene, it appears that today the economic problems between North and South—or, to be more precise, between West and South—have moved toward the center of the debate, if not of world events.

The emergence of an alliance of oil-producing and other developing countries as a result of the oil crisis some five years ago has resulted in a comprehensive catalogue of demands by the Third World addressed to the industrialized nations that basically aims at a redistribution of wealth in favor of developing countries. In their view, a key to this redistribution is their potential of oil and other natural resources. The catalogue of demands comprises, inter alia, the following:

- commodity agreements providing price and quota regulations, purchase guarantees, financing of surplus production, and automatic compensation for diminishing earnings
- a link between the developing countries' export prices and their import prices (indexation)
- preferential treatment of the developing countries in all sectors
- transfer of industrial production from the industrialized countries to the developing countries
- transfer of modern technologies to the developing countries on preferential conditions
- tailoring of the international monetary system to the needs of the developing countries (e.g., creation of SDRs by the IMF to suit targets of development policy)
- rescheduling of debts, debt relief, and interest subsidies

The Western industrialized countries have registered substantial reservations with respect to these far-reaching demands since they believe such changes would abolish market economy principles and gradually replace them with a predominantly controlled world economy. Furthermore, they would put too heavy a burden on their economies.

Yet, criticism and reservations alone are no remedy, nor is a mere reference to the essential merits of the market economy system for the coordination of the world economy. The industrialized countries must accept the challenge of the developing countries instead of simply paying lip service to their own principles. Market economy principles have been—and still are—too often violated by industrialized nations at the expense of the developing countries.

Both sides must continue to speak frankly to one another. Spelling out our individual or group interests is the best method for avoiding misunderstandings. Many Third World countries regard the articulation of such interests as a sign of their political maturity, and so do we. However, we all know from experience: to be mature is not a pleasure, but a responsibility.

Industrialized and developing countries are today, more than ever, economically interdependent. The industrialized countries do not need only raw materials and oil, the developing countries do not need only capital and technology: we both need each other's markets. None of us can gain from confrontation. We are in the same boat and must, together, try to keep it from capsizing. To achieve this we have to continue a dialogue in which all aspects of the economic relations between industrialized and developing countries are discussed.

Developing countries assert that the market economy system benefits only the industrialized West and offers capital and influence exclusively to rich countries, while the young nations would remain economically dependent and weak; for this reason they urge that new rules replace the old order. In their view, economic relations, and trade in particular, should be governed by dirigistic means as laid down in the decisions of the Sixth Special Session. Such a new order would correspond to the economic system in some countries, where most or all economic activities are planned and regulated by governments.

Before taking any decisions, the accomplishments of the various economic systems should be compared, especially from the point of view of the results they have yielded for the developing countries. One might ask, for instance: why is it that the Western industrialized countries' share in the total volume of the developing countries' trade amounts to 75 percent, while the socialist countries' share is less than 5 percent, although the latter countries claim to conduct their trade with the developing countries on the basis of strict equality?

I cannot agree with what I consider to be the erroneous thesis that a market economy system operates only in favor of the industrialized countries. On the contrary, such a system, if well understood and implemented, benefits all countries. Worldwide dirigism on the other hand would result in substantial losses, failures, and the wrong channeling of resources. It would, therefore, produce disadvantages for all. In addition, it would lead to the creation of a vast international bureaucracy, strangle initiative, perpetuate obsolete structures, and hamper economic growth. A look at the economic performance of several socialist countries will prove this point.

Rather, we should try to shape the international economic order along lines that favor a restructuring of the international economy to the benefit of the developing countries. Their share in agricultural and industrial production, as well as in world trade, is too low and must be raised to enable them to fulfill their task of affording their citizens a life free from hunger and need.

We cannot create a better and more equitable international economic order by totally destroying the existing one. We shall achieve our aims only by constantly improving the existing system, notably where imbalances warrant change, and by preserving those elements that have worked well to the advantage of all and that have proved their efficiency. Considerations of equity would, however, require structural changes in favor of the developing countries, to enhance their position and strengthen their capacity to participate in the world economy through accelerated development. The new has to do justice to all. It must provide for rights and duties in a balanced proportion. A departure from this rule should be permitted only where duties impose too heavy a burden on individual countries or groups of countries. Where privileges are granted, these should invariably serve to enable the beneficiaries to assume, as soon as possible, their normal duties. The experience of the past should have taught us that arrangements that accord more privileges than duties to specific countries or groups of countries are of short duration. We must not lapse into such errors again.

Criticisms

It appears to be the developing countries' objective to gain from a restructuring of the international economic order those financial means which they need to accelerate the development of their economies. The major part of the Third World's foreign exchange revenues results from trade, whereas the share of development aid has been constantly receding. This development will continue. Therefore, and in order to integrate the developing countries more closely into the international economy and to enable them to earn the necessary foreign exchange funds themselves, a restructuring of international trade is particularly important. This raises the question, however, whether the measures proposed by the developing countries are really conducive to the attainment of these objectives.

Commodities

In their considerations, the developing countries proceed from the fact that the major part of their exports consists of commodities. They believe they can increase their foreign exchange earnings considerably by stabilizing and increasing their commodity prices. This target should be achieved, in their view, by the establishment of producers' associations, the Integrated Programme for Commodities, and indexation.

PRODUCERS' ASSOCIATIONS

The raw material producers demanding the establishment of producers' associations intend to emulate the success of the OPEC countries. They want to increase their foreign exchange earnings through increases in raw material prices. This objective can be attained only in cases of low demand elasticity, i.e., the decline in the demand for a commodity must be smaller than a possible relative price increase.

Apart from the fundamental objections against producers' associations for the regulation of supplies of raw materials, the potential members of such associations will have to ask themselves whether the conditions are as favorable in their case as in that of the oil-producing countries. Substitution of one commodity for another is possible for both agricultural and mineral resources. In the case of mineral resources, moreover, the larger share of production is accounted for by developed countries. The main producers are the United States, the Soviet Union, Canada, Australia, and South Africa. Only in the cases of tin, cobalt, and niobium does the developing countries' share exceed two-thirds, and in the case of bauxite one-half, of world production. Furthermore, recycling is of growing importance. Depending on the price structure, there will also be increasing pressure from synthetics which, in turn, will stimulate the development of commodity-saving technologies. One can safely assume that, in the long run, the market mechanism will have repercussions on producers' associations which will lead to a much less intensive exchange of goods with developing countries. This can cause foreign exchange earnings from commodity sales to drop below even their former level.

In the same context, the following basic rule should be recalled: economic growth cannot be achieved through supply limitation and built-in price increases. The poorest among the developing countries would suffer most since, apart from being unable to meet the higher raw material costs, they would also be confronted with higher prices for finished goods.

THE INTEGRATED PROGRAMME FOR COMMODITIES

In order to avoid a decline in foreign exchange earnings from commodity exports and also to guard against the risk of a collapse of the foundation on which producers' associations are based, developing countries support commodity agreements in which producers and consumers participate. This is exemplified by UNCTAD's Integrated Programme for Commodities that proposes a network of such agreements for all raw materials exported by developing countries, as well as the establishment of a Common Fund to provide the necessary financial means for commodity agreements.

This is a two-pronged approach: on the one hand, commodity prices are to be stabilized and price fluctuations to be eliminated; on the other hand, commodity prices are to be increased in the long run. Such action creates particular hardship for two groups of countries:

● those developing countries that dispose of no or only insufficient commodity resources and depend on raw material imports; to this category belong not only the least developed countries and the most seriously affected countries, but also such countries as South Korea, Hong Kong, and Singapore; and
● industrialized countries with no or only limited raw material resources as well as economies which, owing to a high foreign trade share, are closely integrated into the international economy, particularly most European countries and Japan.

Consequently, a dirigistic redistribution of wealth through the suggested method of the artificially high pricing of raw materials without regard to long-term market trends would weaken the position of such important partners in world trade as Europe and Japan. At the same time, such an approach would strengthen, in the long run, those industrial countries which themselves own large raw material deposits, like the USSR and the United States (i.e., the superpowers), as well as Canada, Australia, and South Africa. Such a result could be neither in the economic nor in the political interest of the developing countries.

The industrialized countries have, however, declared their preparedness to conclude, where appropriate, individual commodity agreements to eliminate the causes of major price fluctuations. They are prepared to do so in order to contribute to a stabilization of the developing countries' export proceeds. A more suitable means for achieving this objective, however, would be a system for the stabilization of earnings from commodity exports. In its approach and effect, the stabilization of export earnings is in conformity with market economy principles since it does not influence world market prices. Furthermore, with regard to commodities exported by both developing and industrialized countries, it has the advantage of permitting a selective application. Hence, it could be operated to the exclusive benefit of the developing countries, thus avoiding the paradoxical effect caused by giving commodity-exporting industrialized countries additional income at the expense of commodity-importing countries—whether industrialized or developing.

INDEXATION

A scheme for the stabilization of export earnings guarantees continuous foreign exchange revenues to the developing countries and, thus, the uninterrupted implementation of their development projects. While its point of departure is commodities, which today are still the most important export goods of the developing countries, it is ultimately designed to promote structural changes, including further processing and manufacturing. In this respect, the government of the Federal Republic of Germany, for instance, has submitted relevant suggestions. But the Conference on International Economic Co-operation could agree only to invite the Development Committee of the World Bank and the International Monetary Fund to prepare a study dealing with all facets of the problem.

An Integrated Commodity Programme designed to fix and defend commodity prices above the long-term equilibrium level and to link these prices, by means of indexation, to the prices for the export goods of the industrialized countries, gives rise to substantial objections: if implemented on a worldwide scale, it would meet with insurmountable difficulties, especially as far as indexation is concerned. Such a link of raw material prices with prices for manufactured goods must lead to a distortion of conditions for healthy competition, must cement obsolete economic structures, and must result in automatic inflation. The corrective function of prices would be abolished. The implementation of indexation would, no doubt, require an avalanche of tight administrative measures and an army of international bureaucrats. Yet, the greatest danger in the long run would be surplus production and, consequently, a misallocation of resources.

In addition to accumulations of unsold agricultural products in the European Community there would, for instance, soon exist international mountains of lead, zinc, copper, and bananas of immense proportions. This would probably lead to financial burdens of unknown magnitude for all concerned because, unlike the regional commodity agreements, the Integrated Programme would lack outlets to the world market. Since surplus production cannot be dumped on the world market, it must be destroyed, stored, or used for purposes other than free trade.

Furthermore, if this approach were implemented, the developing countries would lose interest in adjusting raw material production to existing demand. The larger the amount of raw materials they produce, the higher will be their earnings. The original aim of achieving industrialization on a broad scale, thus, would become of secondary concern. It would be easier for them to continue to supply raw materials—thus remaining, in most cases, a one-product economy with little incentive to raise levels of skills and technology—instead of upgrading resources and promoting industrialization. Despite higher prices for their products and assured markets, an even greater disparity in growth and prosperity between North and South would become practically inevitable. Each of these alternatives, however, will cause severe losses to the world economy.

Additionally, such a system would be inappropriate as a means to redistribute wealth from the rich to the poor. More than half of the international raw material exports originate in such industrialized countries as the United States, Canada, the Soviet Union, the Republic of South Africa, and Australia. Any subsidizing mechanisms would, therefore, largely benefit these countries and not the developing ones.

Apart from the stabilization of commodity earnings, the industrialized nations also support the aim of preventing excessive commodity price fluctuations. This is in the in-

terest of consumers and producers alike. The industrialized countries, therefore, are willing to envisage international commodity agreements in cases where:
- these are capable of preventing excessive price fluctuations in a commodity market;
- these keep prices at levels likely to balance supply and demand in the long term; and
- there is a reasonable cost/benefit ratio.

COMMODITY SUPPLIES

Even in the present situation of stagnation and declining commodity consumption, we must not lose sight of the problem of ensuring future commodity supplies. An expanding world economy and rapid population growth inevitably lead to increasing commodity consumption. We must, therefore, look well ahead in order to ensure the future availability of adequate production capacities. This includes exploration and the development of new raw material resources, as well as the establishment of an infrastructure to bring these commodities to the market. The task of ensuring a continuous commodity supply can be solved only through cooperation between industrialized and developing countries. Cooperation assures that the commodities of a developing country are exploited to the benefit of the producing country.

For a number of commodities, and not only grain, the problem of continuous supplies could, indeed, become the crucial problem of the future. The question of how to finance and organize the necessary cooperation between industrialized and developing countries and of how to find new and appropriate forms of cooperation should receive due attention in the discussions on commodities between industrialized and developing countries. Another topic of such talks must be the question of how a parallel development of commodity production and industrialization can be attained in the developing countries. Without such parallel development, these countries are constantly faced with the danger of serious economic setbacks—particularly when their raw material resources are exhausted or when technological developments make particular commodities superfluous.

Trade

Further economic progress of the developing countries requires an increase of their exports of semimanufactures and manufactures. These products have constituted the most dynamic sector of world trade in the past—and will continue to do so in the future. It is here, therefore, where the Third World has the greatest opportunities for increasing its exports; and, in particular, it is here where the markets of the industrialized countries should be made even more accessible to the developing countries than they already are. It is no longer justifiable that the existing tariffs in the industrialized countries are, in spite of many improvements, generally lower for primary products than for manufactures and semimanufactures. Such a tariff structure hampers the export of manufactured products from the developing countries.

The rules governing world trade may, in part, be obsolete, but they are certainly capable of being improved. It is not the system as such which is unsatisfactory, but the way in which it is being applied. It is essential to continue to dismantle trade barriers, to increase the efficiency of our economies through market mechanisms, to liberalize world trade even further, to offer easier access to markets, to achieve a more rational division of labor, and to avoid protectionist measures. In short, what is needed are changes in the world trading system—but not its replacement.

Essential steps in this direction have already been taken, the most significant being the introduction and continuous improvement of the Generalized System of Preferences by the member states of the European Community and other industrialized countries at the beginning of the 1970s. This system has been one of the reasons why the import of semimanufactures and manufactures from developing countries by the Federal Republic of Germany rose considerably faster in percentage terms than the imports of such goods from industrialized countries. It also contributed to the surplus in export earnings obtained by the non-oil-exporting developing countries from their trade with the Federal Republic of Germany in 1976 and 1977. This surplus continues to rise steadily.

The multilateral trade negotiations conducted on the basis of the 1973 Tokyo Declaration offered an opportunity to move in this direction. Protectionist measures, which have recently gained in strength, may bring some relief in the short run for national industries and their labor force; but, in the long run, they are detrimental to all. They force other countries to react and, thus, cause an escalation of protectionist measures. Furthermore, they hamper necessary structural changes and adjustments and reduce economic growth so that, in the end, employment opportunities are curtailed everywhere.

Yet, the developing countries should not only look at their trade relations with industrialized countries. With three-quarters of their trade being conducted with the industrialized world, they are leaning too heavily on these countries in their foreign trade and are, thus, extremely vulnerable to cyclical fluctuations in the developed part of the world. This dependence must be reduced. Developing countries should, therefore, also focus on enhancing economic relations among themselves. Exports from industries in developing countries should also be geared to the markets of other developing countries and not merely to those of the industrialized nations, which do not have unlimited absorptive capacity. If all developing countries channel the bulk of their products into the markets of the industrialized countries, these will soon be oversaturated. The textile sector already offers an example of competition among developing countries for markets in the industrialized world.

Another problem is the low volume of trade between the developing and the socialist countries. The latter contend that access to their markets for products from the Third World is in no way hampered by tariffs or other trade barriers; that their trade with the developing countries is conducted on a "democratic, just and mutually advantageous basis"; and that they do not exploit the developing countries. This, however, raises the question of why the share of the socialist states in the foreign trade of the Third World continues to amount to less than 5 percent. Is this due to the monopolistic organization of state-owned foreign trade corporations, to their dependence on five-year plans, or to the fact that the quality of their goods does not meet international standards? An objective comparison between the results of free as distinct from state-controlled foreign trade will easily reveal their respective merits and disadvantages.

Industrialization

Better access to markets alone is not sufficient to encourage and promote structural changes and to integrate developing countries more closely into the world economy. It must be supplemented by the establishment of efficient industries in the developing countries.

STRUCTURAL ADJUSTMENTS

This does not mean however, that political negotiations are the proper framework within which to decide the reallocation of industrial production from developed to developing countries, as some developing countries demand. The socialist states provide ample proof that, given the complexity and ramifications of industrial production, optimal planning is almost impossible. The inevitable outcome is a waste of scarce resources. Many industrialized countries, therefore, are against an anticipatory structural policy in which decisions are made solely by administrations. They consider a policy of promoting structural adjustments through market mechanisms and of supporting the industrialization of developing countries through government incentives to offer the better solution.

Developing countries themselves are primarily responsible for taking initiatives to set up efficient industries in their countries. This will be supported by continuing capital aid and technical assistance from the developed countries. It is true that the volume of official development assistance from some industrialized countries has not reached the developing countries' expectations and that efforts must be intensified in this respect. But official development assistance alone cannot meet the vast financial requirements of the Third World. It must be supplemented by private investments which can considerably accelerate the developing countries' economic growth, as a few well-known examples have shown. Yet, the propensity of enterprises to invest does not depend on the existence of instruments of promotion in the industrialized countries. Entrepreneurial interest in the Third World is determined in the first place by the conditions and the climate for foreign investments in host countries. If a government wishes foreign investors to provide capital at reasonable terms, to reinvest profits instead of rapidly transferring them abroad, to regard their investment as a long-term commitment, and to behave like citizens of the host country, it must create an atmosphere of confidence.

Such a favorable climate will not be brought about by a United Nations resolution in which the developing countries, disregarding the rules of international law, claim the right to control foreign investments only pursuant to their domestic legislation, which can be altered at any time. We respect the sovereign decision of some countries to allow only a limited amount of private investment, if any, and, thereby, to exclude a significant growth factor. But these countries should not try to hold others responsible for the results of their own decisions.

SCIENCE AND TECHNOLOGY

Science and technology have to assume an important role in the industrialization of the Third World and the acceleration of the development process. Therefore, the scientific-technological infrastructure of the developing countries has to be strengthened through partnership within a bilateral and multilateral framework. These measures give the developing countries a greater capacity to absorb technology, particularly to enable them to develop technology creatively and to adapt it to their own economic needs. In many spheres it will be necessary to replace the capital-intensive production methods of the industrialized countries with equally modern but labor-intensive methods.

The developing countries regard the transfer of technology as the main problem in this field, and demand the elimination of all obstacles in industrialized countries which could hamper the transfer of technology to them. Moreover, they demand preferential conditions for the acquisition of technology. These problems are to be settled in a code of conduct currently being elaborated within UNCTAD.

Provided that rights and duties are distributed evenly among the parties concerned, such a code of conduct can promote the transfer of technology. Unilateral rights in favor of developing countries and to the disadvantage of private enterprises will no doubt reflect negatively on the latters' willingness to transfer technology. Preferential conditions for the transfer of technology are, as a rule, excluded if technology originates from a private enterprise. Technology is not a natural resource. In most cases, it must be generated by enterprises at considerable expense and without any prior guarantee that their efforts will lead to success. This is why private enterprises, when transferring technology, must see to it that they recover their expenditures.

In focusing their attention on the problem of the transfer of technology, the developing countries fail to realize that the real problem lies elsewhere. An essential part of the technological know-how of the industrialized countries is freely available. Patents, it is true, are protected for a period of up to twenty years. Most patents, however, are waived after a few years as their returns are out of proportion with increasing patent fees. Only a small number of significant basic patents are claimed by industry for the whole duration of the protection period.

The main problem is the innovative and absorptive capacity of the developing countries. This capacity has to be enhanced, and this requires the improvement of the scientific and technological infrastructure of the Third World. Only indigenous scientific and technological institutions are in a position to find appropriate solutions for the physical and social problems of the developing countries and to adapt the technologies of the industrialized countries to the needs of the Third World. The mere transfer of technology may create more problems than it solves.

INDUSTRIAL COOPERATION

Frequently, industrialization and transfer of technology can best be accelerated through industrial cooperation between developing countries and companies from industrialized countries. In some cases, the developing countries will also want such firms to engage in joint ventures. The two basic requirements for joint ventures are mutual trust and the assurance that such cooperation enjoys long-term legal protection. Both sides must be able to rely on safeguards of international law. Creating forms of industrial cooperation which meet both these conditions is of decisive importance in promoting development in the Third World.

Money and Finance

The development of the Third World requires financial resources that cannot be raised by the developing countries alone. In fact, their financial situation has deteriorated considerably because of the drastic increase in oil prices and of widespread inflation.

RESTRUCTURING THE INTERNATIONAL MONETARY SYSTEM

It is, therefore, not surprising that the developing countries, within the context of their demand for the establishment of a New International Economic Order, should also have presented proposals with regard to a restructuring of the international monetary system. They ask that it be tailored to their needs. We believe, however, that monetary mechanisms must continue to remain problem- and purpose-oriented. It was not without reason that the tasks of securing international liquidity and of providing long-term funds for economic development have been entrusted to two different institutions—the International Monetary Fund and the World Bank. It is inappropriate in the interest of long-term stability to turn monetary policy into an instrument of development policy. A link between the creation of Special Drawing Rights and development aid must, therefore, be rejected.

The rise in demand resulting from such a link would increase inflationary pressures on a worldwide scale and, under the additional impact of the multiplier and accelerator effects of other demand stimulants, would reach disproportionate dimensions. Such an increase in inflation would undermine confidence in the Special Drawing Rights on which their very functioning as an international reserve instrument depends and, in a wider sense, the functioning of the entire international monetary system.

At the same time, inflation jeopardizes the objective of the link, to obtain a growing transfer of real resources to the developing countries. The increase in the price of goods would, in fact, cancel the benefits of SDR distributions which, in turn, would lead to ever-increasing demands for the allocation of new Special Drawing Rights.

A transfer of resources, therefore, can be achieved only if the industrialized countries are prepared—and are in a position—to provide capital from their internal savings. The problem that the developing countries insist on attacking through a link between development aid and SDRs remains to be solved by the donor countries: to provide an increasing amount of real resources for development. If the industrialized countries are prepared to provide these resources at the expense of their own economies, we do not need the link; if not, the link will not be a means of effecting the desired redistribution. This, then, is the core of the problem: what is required is a direct real transfer of resources from the industrialized to the developing countries.

At the same time, we must realize that resources transferred to other countries are no longer available for distribution in the donor country. This is a simple, indisputable fact, which cannot be concealed by demands for indirect transfer mechanisms. Monetary policy, therefore, should neither be abused as a tool for safeguarding the interests of individual countries nor be degraded into an instrument of an international distribution struggle. Rather, its aim should be a stability-oriented adjustment of the international monetary system which allows for the specific requirements of the developing countries.

The world monetary system must make available the necessary liquidity for the growth of our world economy and world trade. Such a system must be equipped to maintain the value of resources and to combat inflation. But to reemphasize: international monetary policy is not a substitute for development policy. A monetary financing of development aid must be avoided. Developing countries need real resources to finance their development and not a nominal inflationary capital increase.

DEBT PROBLEMS

The developing countries' demand for an alleviation of their growing debt burden—either through cancellation or rescheduling of their official and commercial debts—aims at an immediate improvement of their financial situation. Given the high amounts involved and the consequences of a general cancellation or rescheduling of the developing countries' official and commercial debts, it is neither possible nor advisable to fulfill this demand. Solutions for the existing problems have to take into account the different reasons for the indebtedness of the countries involved, their economic situation, and their economic prospects. Hence, it is appropriate to seek solutions only on a case-by-case basis.

Moreover, the demand for a general alleviation of debts meets with the following objections.

1. The debt burden is unevenly distributed among the developing countries. The most heavily indebted among them would benefit from an overall cancellation of debts, whereas those that have restricted their borrowings to their capacity to pay would be placed at a disadvantage. The donor countries, for their part, would also have to shoulder widely differing financial burdens.

2. The developing countries will continue to depend, for years to come, on loans from private creditors. Even if the 0.7 percent target is reached, official development assistance will not be nearly sufficient to meet the capital needs of the developing countries. However, private loans are granted only on a basis of confidence between creditor and debtor. Yet this confidence is badly shaken by demands for the cancellation of debts. The likely result is that the Third World will be unable to find any creditors. Some developing countries, which have raised substantial loans on international financial markets in the past and are likely to continue to do so, realize this danger and have cautiously dissociated themselves from the demand for an overall cancellation of debts.

The industrialized countries, for their part, are well aware of the significance of the debt problem for the developing countries and, in particular, the least developed among them; they try to assist these countries within the limits of their resources. A decisive step forward was made in this respect at the March 1978 ministerial meeting of UNCTAD Trade and Development Board. At that meeting, the industrialized countries promised to take measures to adjust the terms of past official development assistance in order to bring them into line with softer terms, as a means of improving the net flow of official development assistance. A number of industrialized countries have already, in line with this commitment, converted loans given to least developed countries into grants and have provided capital aid to these countries in the form of grants. The Trade and Development Board agreed, furthermore, that detailed features for future operations relating to debt problems of interested developing countries should be elaborated.

Conclusions

Let me make one thing quite clear: we fully understand the concerns of the Third World and their basic demand to reduce the gap between the tremendous wealth of a few countries and the poverty of many member states of the United Nations. This is a premise that we accepted long ago. If not, why would we have spent billions of dollars of taxpayers' money for development aid, why would we have sent thousands of experts to Third World countries? I believe that this entitles us to say "no" when we think that programs and plans offered during the debates of the past few years appeared to suggest a wrong approach to the solution of mutual problems. A simple redistribution of wealth leads nowhere. Development will only be accelerated in an expanding world economy. Scarce resources must be used economically.

More balanced and more equitable economic relations between developing and industrialized countries cannot be achieved at one single conference. This is a process which will continue to dominate international politics in the years ahead. We participate in this process in a sincere spirit of partnership and cooperation. We welcome and promote dialogue between the industrialized and developing countries with the aim of achieving an equitable balance of interests. We want to proceed beyond this dialogue to joint practical action.

Economic power has been abused again and again—just as political and military power has been abused. Those who possess power must not be at liberty to use it unrestrictedly. Therefore, a world economic order based on fair cooperation requires clear rules that provide rights and duties in a balanced proportion.

The economic capacity of all states on earth together, no matter how big it may be, is, nevertheless, not unlimited. Perhaps it is just big enough to solve our most severe problems by the end of the twentieth century: to overcome underdevelopment, hunger, disease, and poverty. But one thing is certain: our combined economic strength will not be enough if the individual states use their economic potential against each other instead of for each other's benefit and for joint peaceful development.

The demands of the Third World for the establishment of a New International Economic Order, as embodied in United Nations' resolutions, cannot be met in practice. At the same time, the present economic order cannot remain as it is. However, this dilemma should not lead to a fruitless and dangerous confrontation; rather, it should prompt us to strive for détente in economic relations. Economic détente means preventing nations embittered by the inequitable structures of the world economy from being driven to use what may be their only resources as weapons of economic warfare.

The First and the Third Worlds have spelled out their interests. The identification of interests is essential to finding a basis for common action. If it is necessary to achieve compromises for détente—and it is imperative—they can be reached only if each side knows its position, so that each side knows when and where to stop compromising.

Political détente has shaped international relations for the last decade. Economic détente, it is my conviction, will have to shape international relations in the coming decades if the world is to avoid a confrontation almost as dangerous as the Cold War. We will have to go through a long and painful process, a period of successes and setbacks, to find solutions that are acceptable to all. But in our search for a New International Economic Order, we should not forget that growth rates stem from industrial productivity and that a subsistence economy does not grow. And there cannot be any industrial productivity without capital, know-how, and trained labor.

The industrialized countries of the West have struggled for more than a century to reach the present level of mass production, mass consumption, employment, social security, and economic stability. What the Third World regards as our achievement was not accomplished in one generation. We are still in the process of development, and there appears to be no check list of criteria by which one could evaluate whether a country's development is completed.

We shall achieve nothing if we merely draft a New International Economic Order on United Nations paper. We shall achieve nothing if we set our standards on the basis of what was attained in a historically different situation. Nor do we achieve anything by denying deficiencies of the market system or by clinging to privileges.

Economic détente and adjusted international and national market mechanisms have to be brought about not against the will or over the heads of nations but by cooperation and consensus. What has to be done can only be achieved by all countries together in a permanent dialogue. Steps in the right direction have been taken. The Paris Conference on International Economic Co-operation is but one of many moves of this kind. Economic détente is a matter of active, peaceful interaction between rich and poor.

Our determined will to avoid costly confrontations in favor of constructive cooperation must not invite either industrialized or developing countries to fall for phoney compromises, but must, on the contrary, see us prepared for frank exchanges of views, some of which will no doubt find us on the opposite ends of the table.

Let us, therefore, speak out, argue with the hope of convincing, strive for consensus rather than voting victories. And, above all, let us keep in mind which economic order created the fortunate conditions of the industrialized countries and why it is that all members of the United Nations with a planned economy have yet to prove that government dirigism is better than a free economy.

Appendix A — The Basic Documents of the NIEO Program

A. Sixth Special Session of the United Nations General Assembly:

1. Declaration and Programme of Action on the Establishment of a New International Economic Order

3201 (S-VI). Declaration on the Establishment of a New International Economic Order

The General Assembly
Adopts the following Declaration:

DECLARATION ON THE ESTABLISHMENT OF A NEW INTERNATIONAL ECONOMIC ORDER

We, the Members of the United Nations,

Having convened a special session of the General Assembly to study for the first time the problems of raw materials and development, devoted to the consideration of the most important economic problems facing the world community,

Bearing in mind the spirit, purposes and principles of the Charter of the United Nations to promote the economic advancement and social progress of all peoples,

Solemnly proclaim our united determination to work urgently for THE ESTABLISHMENT OF A NEW INTER-NATIONAL ECONOMIC ORDER based on equity, sovereign equality, interdependence, common interest and co-operation among all States, irrespective of their economic and social systems which shall correct inequalities and redress existing injustices, make it possible to eliminate the widening gap between the developed and the developing countries and ensure steadily accelerating economic and social development and peace and justice for present and future generations, and, to that end, declare:

1. The greatest and most significant achievement during the last decades has been the independence from co-lonial and alien domination of a large number of peoples and nations which has enabled them to become members of the community of free peoples. Technological progress has also been made in all spheres of economic activities in the last three decades, thus providing a solid potential for improving the well-being of all peoples. However, the remaining vestiges of alien and colonial domination, foreign occupation, racial discrimination, *apartheid* and neo-colonialism in all its forms continue to be among the greatest obstacles to the full emancipation and progress of the developing countries and all the peoples involved. The benefits of technological progress are not shared equitably by all members of the international community. The develop-ing countries, which constitute 70 per cent of the world's population, account for only 30 per cent of the world's income. It has proved impossible to achieve an even and balanced development of the international community under the existing international economic order. The gap between the developed and the develop-ing countries continues to widen in a system which was established at a time when most of the developing coun-tries did not even exist as independent States and which perpetuates inequality.

2. The present international economic order is in direct conflict with current developments in international political and economic relations. Since 1970, the world economy has experienced a series of grave crises which have had severe repercussions, especially on the developing countries because of their generally greater vulnerability to external economic impulses. The developing world has become a powerful factor that makes its influence felt in all fields of international activity. These irreversible changes in the relationship of forces in the

171

world necessitate the active, full and equal participation of the developing countries in the formulation and application of all decisions that concern the international community.

3. All these changes have thrust into prominence the reality of interdependence of all the members of the world community. Current events have brought into sharp focus the realization that the interests of the developed countries and those of the developing countries can no longer be isolated from each other, that there is a close interrelationship between the prosperity of the developed countries and the growth and development of the developing countries, and that the prosperity of the international community as a whole depends upon the prosperity of its constituent parts. International co-operation for development is the shared goal and common duty of all countries. Thus the political, economic and social well-being of present and future generations depends more than ever on co-operation between all the members of the international community on the basis of sovereign equality and the removal of the disequilibrium that exists between them.

4. The new international economic order should be founded on full respect for the following principles:

(*a*) Sovereign equality of States, self-determination of all peoples, inadmissibility of the acquisition of territories by force, territorial integrity and non-interference in the internal affairs of other States;

(*b*) The broadest co-operation of all the States members of the international community, based on equity, whereby the prevailing disparities in the world may be banished and prosperity secured for all;

(*c*) Full and effective participation on the basis of equality of all countries in the solving of world economic problems in the common interest of all countries, bearing in mind the necessity to ensure the accelerated development of all the developing countries, while devoting particular attention to the adoption of special measures in favour of the least developed, land-locked and island developing countries as well as those developing countries most seriously affected by economic crises and natural calamities, without losing sight of the interests of other developing countries;

(*d*) The right of every country to adopt the economic and social system that it deems the most appropriate for its own development and not to be subjected to discrimination of any kind as a result;

(*e*) Full permanent sovereignty of every State over its natural resources and all economic activities. In order to safeguard these resources, each State is entitled to exercise effective control over them and their exploitation with means suitable to its own situation, including the right to nationalization or transfer of ownership to its nationals, this right being an expression of the full permanent sovereignty of the State. No State may be subjected to economic, political or any other type of coercion to prevent the free and full exercise of this inalienable right;

(*f*) The right of all States, territories and peoples under foreign occupation, alien and colonial domination or *apartheid* to restitution and full compensation for the exploitation and depletion of, and damages to, the natural resources and all other resources of those States, territories and peoples;

(*g*) Regulation and supervision of the activities of transnational corporations by taking measures in the interest of the national economies of the countries where such transnational corporations operate on the basis of the full sovereignty of those countries;

(*h*) The right of the developing countries and the peoples of territories under colonial and racial domination and foreign occupation to achieve their liberation and to regain effective control over their natural resources and economic activities;

(*i*) The extending of assistance to developing countries, peoples and territories which are under colonial and alien domination, foreign occupation, racial discrimination or *apartheid* or are subjected to economic, political or any other type of coercive measures to obtain from them the subordination of the exercise of their sovereign rights and to secure from them advantages of any kind, and to neo-colonialism in all its forms, and which have established or are endeavouring to establish effective control over their natural resources and economic activities that have been or are still under foreign control;

(*j*) Just and equitable relationship between the prices of raw materials, primary commodities, manufactured and semi-manufactured goods exported by developing countries and the prices of raw materials, primary commodities, manufactures, capital goods and equipment imported by them with the aim of bringing about sustained improvement in their unsatisfactory terms of trade and the expansion of the world economy;

(*k*) Extension of active assistance to developing countries by the whole international community, free of any political or military conditions;

(*l*) Ensuring that one of the main aims of the reformed international monetary system shall be the promotion of the development of the developing countries and the adequate flow of real resources to them;

(*m*) Improving the competitiveness of natural materials facing competition from synthetic substitutes;

(*n*) Preferential and non-reciprocal treatment for developing countries, wherever feasible, in all fields of international economic co-operation whenever possible;

(*o*) Securing favourable conditions for the transfer of financial resources to developing countries;

(*p*) Giving to the developing countries access to the achievements of modern science and technology, and promoting the transfer of technology and the creation of indigenous technology for the benefit of the developing countries in forms and in accordance with procedures which are suited to their economies;

(*q*) The need for all States to put an end to the waste of natural resources, including food products;

(*r*) The need for developing countries to concentrate all their resources for the cause of development;

(*s*) The strengthening, through individual and collective actions, of mutual economic, trade, financial and technical co-operation among the developing countries, mainly on a preferential basis;

(*t*) Facilitating the role which producers' associations may play within the framework of international co-operation and, in pursuance of their aims, *inter alia* assisting in the promotion of sustained growth of the world economy and accelerating the development of developing countries.

5. The unanimous adoption of the International Development Strategy for the Second United Nations Development Decade* was an important step in the promotion of international economic co-operation on a just and equitable basis. The accelerated implementation of obligations and commitments assumed by the international community within the framework of the Strategy, particularly those concerning imperative development needs of developing countries, would contribute significantly to the fulfilment of the aims and objectives of the present Declaration.

6. The United Nations as a universal organization should be capable of dealing with problems of international economic co-operation in a comprehensive manner and ensuring equally the interests of all countries. It must have an even greater role in the establishment of a new international economic order. The Charter of Economic Rights and Duties of States, for the preparation of which the present Declaration will provide an additional source of inspiration, will constitute a significant contribution in this respect. All the States Members of the United Nations are therefore called upon to exert maximum efforts with a view to securing the implementation of the present Declaration, which is one of the principal guarantees for the creation of better conditions for all peoples to reach a life worthy of human dignity.

7. The present Declaration on the Establishment of a New International Economic Order shall be one of the most important bases of economic relations between all peoples and all nations.

2229th plenary meeting
1 May 1974

3202 (S-VI). Programme of Action on the Establishment of a New International Economic Order

The General Assembly
Adopts the following Programme of Action:

PROGRAMME OF ACTION ON THE ESTABLISHMENT OF A NEW INTERNATIONAL ECONOMIC ORDER

CONTENTS

*Resolution 2626 (XXV).

INTRODUCTION

1. In view of the continuing severe economic imbalance in the relations between developed and developing countries, and in the context of the constant and continuing aggravation of the imbalance of the economies of the developing countries and the consequent need for the mitigation of their current economic difficulties, urgent and effective measures need to be taken by the international community to assist the developing countries, while devoting paticular attention to the least developed, land-locked and island developing countries and those developing countries most seriously affected by economic crises and natural calamities leading to serious retardation of development processes.

2. With a view to ensuring the application of the Declaration on the Establishment of a New International Economic Order,* it will be necessary to adopt and implement within a specified period a programme of action of unprecedented scope and to bring about maximum economic co-operation and understanding among all States, particularly between developed and developing countries, based on the principles of dignity and sovereign equality.

I. FUNDAMENTAL PROBLEMS OF RAW MATERIALS AND PRIMARY COMMODITIES AS RELATED TO TRADE AND DEVELOPMENT

1. *Raw materials*

All efforts should be made:

(*a*) To put an end to all forms of foreign occupation, racial discrimination, *apartheid*, colonial, neo-colonial and alien domination and exploitation through the exercise of permanent sovereignty over natural resources;

(*b*) To take measures for the recovery, exploitation, development, marketing and distribution of natural resources, particularly of developing countries, to serve their national interests, to promote collective self-reliance among them and to strengthen mutually beneficial international economic co-operation with a view to bringing about the accelerated development of developing countries;

(*c*) To facilitate the functioning and to further the aims of producers' associations, including their joint marketing arrangements, orderly commodity trading, improvement in the export income of producing developing countries and in their terms of trade, and sustained growth of the world economy for the benefit of all;

(*d*) To evolve a just and equitable relationship between the prices of raw materials, primary commodities, manufactured and semi-manufactured goods exported by developing countries and the prices of raw materials, primary commodities, food, manufactured and semi-manufactured goods and capital equipment imported by them, and to work for a link between the prices of exports of developing countries and the prices of their imports from developed countries;

(*e*) To take measures to reverse the continued trend of stagnation or decline in the real price of several commodities exported by developing countries, despite a general rise in commodity prices, resulting in a decline in the export earnings of these developing countries;

(*f*) To take measures to expand the markets for natural products in relation to synthetics, taking into account the interests of the developing countries, and to utilize fully the ecological advantages of these products;

(*g*) To take measures to promote the processing of raw materials in the producer developing countries.

2. *Food*

All efforts should be made:

(*a*) To take full account of specific problems of developing countries, particularly in times of food shortages, in the international efforts connected with the food problem;

(*b*) To take into account that, owing to lack of means, some developing countries have vast potentialities of unexploited or underexploited land which, if reclaimed and put into practical use, would contribute considerably to the solution of the food crisis;

(*c*) By the international community to undertake concrete and speedy measures with a view to arresting desertification, salination and damage by locusts or any other similar phenomenon involving several developing countries, particularly in Africa, and gravely affecting the agricultural production capacity of these countries, and also to assist the developing countries affected by any such phenomenon to develop the affected zones with a view to contributing to the solution of their food problems;

(*d*) To refrain from damaging or deteriorating natural resources and food resources, especially those deriv-

---

*Resolution 3201 (S-VI).

ed from the sea, by preventing pollution and taking appropriate steps to protect and reconsitute those resources;

(*e*) By developed countries, in evolving their policies relating to production, stocks, imports and exports of food, to take full account of the interests of:

(i) Developing importing countries which cannot afford high prices for their imports;

(ii) Developing exporting countries which need increased market opportunities for their exports;

(*f*) To ensure that developing countries can import the necessary quantity of food without undue strain on their foreign exchange resources and without unpredictable deterioration in their balance of payments, and, in this context, that special measures are taken in respect of the least developed, land-locked and island developing countries as well as those developing countries most seriously affected by economic crises and natural calamities;

(*g*) To ensure that concrete measures to increase food production and storage facilities in developing countries are introduced, *inter alia,* by ensuring an increase in all available essential inputs, including fertilizers, from developed countries on favourable terms;

(*h*) To promote exports of food products of developing countries through just and equitable arrangements, *inter alia,* by the progressive elimination of such protective and other measures as constitute unfair competition.

3. General trade

All efforts should be made:

(*a*) To take the following measures for the amelioration of terms of trade of developing countries and concrete steps to eliminate chronic trade deficits of developing countries:

(i) Fulfilment of relevant commitments already undertaken in the United Nations Conference on Trade and Development and in the International Development Strategy for the Second United Nations Development Decade;*

(ii) Improved access to markets in developed countries through the progressive removal of tariff and non-tariff barriers and of restrictive business practices;

(iii) Expeditious formulation of commodity agreements where appropriate, in order to regulate as necessary and to stabilize the world markets for raw materials and primary commodities;

(iv) Preparation of an over-all integrated programme, setting out guidelines and taking into account the current work in this field, for a comprehensive range of commodities of export interest to developing countries;

(v) Where products of developing countries compete with the domestic production in developed countries, each developed country should facilitate the expansion of imports from developing countries and provide a fair and reasonable opportunity to the developing countries to share in the growth of the market;

(vi) When the importing developed countries derive receipts from customs duties, taxes and other protective measures applied to imports of these products, consideration should be given to the claim of the developing countries that these receipts should be reimbursed in full to the exporting developing countries or devoted to providing additional resources to meet their development needs;

(vii) Developed countries should make appropriate adjustments in their economies so as to facilitate the expansion and diversification of imports from developing countries and thereby permit a rational, just and equitable international division of labour;

(viii) Setting up general principles for pricing policy for exports of commodities of developing countries, with a view to rectifying and achieving satisfactory terms of trade for them;

(ix) Until satisfactory terms of trade are achieved for all developing countries, consideration should be given to alternative means, including improved compensatory financing schemes for meeting the development needs of the developing countries concerned;

(x) Implementation, improvement and enlargement of the generalized system of preferences for exports of agricultural primary commodities, manufactures and semi-manufactures from developing to developed countries and consideration of its extension to commodities, including those which are processed or semi-processed; developing countries which are or will be sharing their existing tariff advantages in some developed countries as the result of the introduction and eventual enlargement of the generalized system of preferences should, as a matter of urgency, be granted new openings in the markets of other developed countries which should offer them export opportunities that at least compensate for the sharing of those advantages;

*Resolution 2626 (XXV).

(xi) The setting up of buffer stocks within the framework of commodity arrangements and their financing by international financial institutions, wherever necessary, by the developed countries and, when they are able to do so, by the developing countries, with the aim of favouring the producer developing and consumer developing countries and of contributing to the expansion of world trade as a whole;

(xii) In cases where natural materials can satisfy the requirements of the market, new investment for the expansion of the capacity to produce synthetic materials and substitutes should not be made;

(b) To be guided by the principles of non-reciprocity and preferential treatment of developing countries in multilateral trade negotiations between developed and developing countries, and to seek sustained and additional benefits for the international trade of developing countries so as to achieve a substantial increase in their foreign exchange earnings, diversification of their exports and acceleration of the rate of their economic growth.

4. *Transportation and insurance*

All efforts should be made:

(a) To promote an increasing and equitable participation of developing countries in the world shipping tonnage;

(b) To arrest and reduce the ever-increasing freight rates in order to reduce the costs of imports to, and exports from, the developing countries;

(c) To minimize the cost of insurance and reinsurance for developing countries and to assist the growth of domestic insurance and reinsurance markets in developing countries and the establishment to this end, where appropriate, of institutions in these countries or at the regional level;

(d) To ensure the early implementation of the code of conduct for liner conferences;

(e) To take urgent measures to increase the import and export capability of the least developed countries and to offset the disadvantages of the adverse geographic situation of land-locked countries, particularly with regard to their transportation and transit costs, as well as developing island countries in order to increase their trading ability;

(f) By the developed countries to refrain from imposing measures or implementing policies designed to prevent the importation, at equitable prices, of commodities from the developing countries or from frustrating the implementation of legitimate measures and policies adopted by the developing countries in order to improve prices and encourage the export of such commodities.

II. INTERNATIONAL MONETARY SYSTEM AND FINANCING OF THE DEVELOPMENT OF DEVELOPING COUNTRIES

1. *Objectives*

All efforts should be made to reform the international monetary system with, *inter alia,* the following objectives:

(a) Measures to check the inflation already experienced by the developed countries, to prevent it from being transferred to developing countries and to study and devise possible arrangements within the International Monetary Fund to mitigate the effects of inflation in developed countries on the economies of developing countries;

(b) Measures to eliminate the instability of the international monetary system, in particular the uncertainty of the exchange rates, especially as it affects adversely the trade in commodities;

(c) Maintenance of the real value of the currency reserves of the developing countries by preventing their erosion from inflation and exchange rate depreciation of reserve currencies;

(d) Full and effective participation of developing countries in all phases of decision-making for the formulation of an equitable and durable monetary system and adequate participation of developing countries in all bodies entrusted with this reform and, particularly, in the proposed Council of Governors of the International Monetary Fund;

(e) Adequate and orderly creation of additional liquidity with particular regard to the needs of the developing countries through the additional allocation of special drawing rights based on the concept of world liquidity needs to be appropriately revised in the light of the new international environment; any creation of international liquidity should be made through international multilateral mechanisms;

(f) Early establishment of a link between special drawing rights and additional development financing in the interest of developing countries, consistent with the monetary characteristics of special drawing rights;

(*g*) Review by the International Monetary Fund of the relevant provisions in order to ensure effective participation by developing countries in the decision-making process;

(*h*) Arrangements to promote an increasing net transfer of real resources from the developed to the developing countries;

(*i*) Review of the methods of operation of the International Monetary Fund, in particular the terms for both credit repayments and "stand-by" arrangements, the system of compensatory financing, and the terms of the financing of commodity buffer stocks, so as to enable the developing countries to make more effective use of them.

2. *Measures*

All efforts should be made to take the following urgent measures to finance the development of developing countries and to meet the balance-of-payment crises in the developing world:

(*a*) Implementation at an accelerated pace by the developed countries of the time-bound programme, as already laid down in the International Development Strategy for the Second United Nations Development Decade, for the net amount of financial resource transfers to developing countries; increase in the official component of the net amount of financial resource transfers to developing countries so as to meet and even to exceed the target of the Strategy;

(*b*) International financing institutions should effectively play their role as development financing banks without discrimination on account of the political or economic system of any member country, assistance being untied;

(*c*) More effective participation by developing countries, whether recipients or contributors, in the decision-making process in the competent organs of the International Bank for Reconstruction and Development and the International Development Association, through the establishment of a more equitable pattern of voting rights;

(*d*) Exemption, wherever possible, of the developing countries from all import and capital outflow controls imposed by the developed countries;

(*e*) Promotion of foreign investment, both public and private, from developed to developing countries in accordance with the needs and requirements in sectors of their economies as determined by the recipient countries;

(*f*) Appropriate urgent measures, including international action, should be taken to mitigate adverse consequences for the current and future development of developing countries arising from the burden of external debt contracted on hard terms;

(*g*) Debt renegotiation on a case-by-case basis with a view to concluding agreements on debt cancellation, moratorium, rescheduling or interest subsidization;

(*h*) International financial institutions should take into account the special situation of each developing country in reorienting their lending policies to suit these urgent needs; there is also need for improvement in practices of international financial institutions in regard to, *inter alia*, development financing and international monetary problems;

(*i*) Appropriate steps should be taken to give priority to the least developed, land-locked and island developing countries and to the countries most seriously affected by economic crises and natural calamities, in the availability of loans for development purposes which should include more favourable terms and conditions.

III. INDUSTRIALIZATION

All efforts should be made by the international community to take measures to encourage the industrialization of the developing countries, and to this end:

(*a*) The developed countries should respond favourably, within the framework of their official aid as well as international financial institutions, to the requests of developing countries for the financing of industrial projects;

(*b*) The developed countries should encourage investors to finance industrial production projects, particularly export-oriented production, in developing countries, in agreement with the latter and within the context of their laws and regulations;

(*c*) With a view to bringing about a new international economic structure which should increase the share of the developing countries in world industrial production, the developed countries and the agencies of the United Nations system, in co-operation with the developing countries, should contribute to setting up new industrial capacities including raw materials and commodity-transforming facilities as a matter of priority in the developing countries that produce those raw materials and commodities;

(*d*) The international community should continue and expand, with the aid of the developed countries and the international institutions, the operational and instruction-oriented technical assistance programmes, including vocational training and management development of national personnel of the developing countries, in the light of their special development requirements.

IV. TRANSFER OF TECHNOLOGY

All efforts should be made:

(*a*) To formulate an international code of conduct for the transfer of technology corresponding to needs and conditions prevalent in developing countries;

(*b*) To give access on improved terms to modern technology and to adapt that technology, as appropriate, to specific economic, social and ecological conditions and varying stages of development in developing countries;

(*c*) To expand significantly the assistance from developed to developing countries in research and development programmes and in the creation of suitable indigenous technology;

(*d*) To adapt commercial practices governing transfer of technology to the requirements of the developing countries and to prevent abuse of the rights of sellers;

(*e*) To promote international co-operation in research and development in exploration and exploitation, conservation and the legitimate utilization of natural resources and all sources of energy.

In taking the above measures, the special needs of the least developed and land-locked countries should be borne in mind.

V. REGULATION AND CONTROL OVER THE ACTIVITIES OF TRANSNATIONAL CORPORATIONS

All efforts should be made to formulate, adopt and implement an international code of conduct for transnational corporations:

(*a*) To prevent interference in the internal affairs of the countries where they operate and their collaboration with racist régimes and colonial administrations;

(*b*) To regulate their activities in host countries, to eliminate restrictive business practices and to conform to the national development plans and objectives of developing countries, and in this context facilitate, as necessary, the review and revision of previously concluded arrangements;

(*c*) To bring about assistance, transfer of technology and management skills to developing countries on equitable and favourable terms;

(*d*) To regulate the repatriation of the profits accruing from their operations, taking into account the legitimate interests of all parties concerned;

(*e*) To promote reinvestment of their profits in developing countries.

VI. CHARTER OF ECONOMIC RIGHTS AND DUTIES OF STATES

The Charter of Economic Rights and Duties of States, the draft of which is being prepared by a working group of the United Nations and which the General Assembly has already expressed the intention of adopting at its twenty-ninth regular session, shall constitute an effective instrument towards the establishment of a new system of international economic relations based on equity, sovereign equality, and interdependence of the interests of developed and developing countries. It is therefore of vital importance that the aforementiond Charter be adopted by the General Assembly at its twenty-ninth session.

VII. PROMOTION OF CO-OPERATION AMONG DEVELOPING COUNTRIES

1. Collective self-reliance and growing co-operation among developing countries will further strengthen their role in the new international economic order. Developing countries, with a view to expanding co-operation at the regional, subregional and interregional levels, should take further steps, *inter alia:*

(*a*) To support the establishment and/or improvement of an appropriate mechanism to defend the prices of their exportable commodities and to improve access to and stabilize markets for them. In this context the increasingly effective mobilization by the whole group of oil-exporting countries of their natural resources for the benefit of their economic development is to be welcomed. At the same time there is the paramount need for co-operation among the developing countries in evolving urgently and in a spirit of solidarity all possible means to assist developing countries to cope with the immediate problems resulting from this legitimate and perfectly justified action. The measures already taken in this regard are a positive indication of the evolving co-operation between developing countries;

(*b*) To protect their inalienable right to permanent sovereignty over their natural resources;

(*c*) To promote, establish or strengthen economic integration at the regional and subregional levels;

(*d*) To increase considerably their imports from other developing countries;

(*e*) To ensure that no developing country accords to imports from developed countries more favourable treatment than that accorded to imports from developing countries. Taking into account the existing international agreements, current limitations and possibilities and also their future evolution, preferential treatment should be given to the procurement of import requirements from other developing countries. Wherever possible, preferential treatment should be given to imports from developing countries and the exports of those countries;

(*f*) To promote close co-operation in the fields of finance, credit relations and monetary issues, including the development of credit relations on a preferential basis and on favourable terms;

(*g*) To strengthen efforts which are already being made by developing countries to utilize available financial resources for financing development in the developing countries through investment, financing of export-oriented and emergency projects and other long-term assistance;

(*h*) To promote and establish effective instruments of co-operation in the fields of industry, science and technology, transport, shipping and mass communication media.

2. Developed countries should support initiatives in the regional, subregional and interregional co-operation of developing countries through the extension of financial and technical assistance by more effective and concrete actions, particulary in the field of commercial policy.

VIII. ASSISTANCE IN THE EXERCISE OF PERMANENT SOVEREIGNTY OF STATES OVER NATURAL RESOURCES

All efforts should be made:

(*a*) To defeat attempts to prevent the free and effective exercise of the rights of every State to full and permanent sovereignty over its natural resources;

(*b*) To insure that competent agencies of the United Nations system meet requests for assistance from developing countries in connexion with the operation of nationalized means of production.

IX. STRENGTHENING THE ROLE OF THE UNITED NATIONS SYSTEM IN THE FIELD OF INTERNATIONAL ECONOMIC CO-OPERATION

1. In furtherance of the objectives of the International Development Strategy for the Second United Nations Development Decade and in accordance with the aims and objectives of the Declaration on the Establishment of a New International Economic Order, all Member States pledge to make full use of the United Nations system in the implementation of the present Programme of Action, jointly adopted by them in working for the establishment of a new international economic order and thereby strengthening the role of the United Nations in the field of world-wide co-operation for economic and social development.

2. The General Assembly of the United Nations shall conduct an over-all review of the implementation of the Programme of Action as a priority item. All the activities of the United Nations system to be undertaken under the Programme of Action as well as those already planned, such as the World Population Conference, 1974, the World Food Conference, the Second General Conference of the United Nations Industrial Development Organization and the mid-term review and appraisal of the International Development Strategy for the Second United Nations Development Decade should be so directed as to enable the special session of the General Assembly on development, called for under Assembly resolution 3172 (XXVIII) of 17 December 1973, to make its full contribution to the establishment of the new international economic order. All Member States are urged, jointly and individually, to direct their efforts and policies towards the success of that special session.

3. The Economic and Social Council shall define the policy framework and co-ordinate the activities of all organizations, institutions and subsidiary bodies within the United Nations system which shall be entrusted with the task of implementing the present Programme of Action. In order to enable the Economic and Social Council to carry out its tasks effectively:

(*a*) All organizations, institutions and subsidiary bodies concerned within the United Nations system shall submit to the Economic and Social Council progress reports on the implementation of the Programme of Action within their respective fields of competence as often as necessary, but not less than once a year;

(*b*) The Economic and Social Council shall examine the progress reports as a matter of urgency, to which end it may be convened, as necessary, in special session or, if need be, may function continuously. It shall draw the attention of the General Assembly to the problems and difficulties arising in connexion with the implementation of the Programme of Action.

4. All organizations, institutions, subsidiary bodies and conferences of the United Nations system are entrusted with the implementation of the Programme of Action. The activities of the United Nations Conference

on Trade and Development, as set forth in General Assembly resolution 1995 (XIX) of 30 December 1964, should be strengthened for the purpose of following in collaboration with other competent organizations the development of international trade in raw materials throughout the world.

5. Urgent and effective measures should be taken to review the lending policies of international financial institutions, taking into account the special situation of each developing country, to suit urgent needs, to improve the practices of these institutions in regard to, *inter alia*, development financing and international monetary problems, and to ensure more effective participation by developing countries—whether recipients or contributors—in the decision-making process through appropriate revision of the pattern of voting rights.

6. The developed countries and others in a position to do so should contribute substantially to the various organizations, programmes and funds established within the United Nations system for the purpose of accelerating economic and social development in developing countries.

7. The present Programme of Action complements and strengthens the goals and objectives embodied in the International Development Strategy for the Second United Nations Development Decade as well as the new measures formulated by the General Assembly at its twenty-eighth session to offset the shortfalls in achieving those goals and objectives.

8. The implementation of the Programme of Action should be taken into account at the time of the mid-term review and appraisal of the International Development Strategy for the Second United Nations Development Decade. New commitments, changes, additions and adaptations in the Strategy should be made, as appropriate, taking into account the Declaration on the Establishment of a New International Economic Order and the present Programme of Action.

X. SPECIAL PROGRAMME

The General Assembly adopts the following Special Programme, including particularly emergency measures to mitigate the difficulties of the developing countries most seriously affected by economic crisis, bearing in mind the particular problem of the least developed and land-locked countries:

The General Assembly,
Taking into account the following considerations:

(*a*) The sharp increase in the prices of their essential imports such as food, fertilizers, energy products, capital goods, equipment and services, including transportation and transit costs, has gravely exacerbated the increasingly adverse terms of trade of a number of developing countries, added to the burden of their foreign debt and, cumulatively, created a situation which, if left untended, will make it impossible for them to finance their essential imports and development and result in a further deterioration in the levels and conditions of life in these countries. The present crisis is the outcome of all the problems that have accumulated over the years: in the field of trade, in monetary reform, the world-wide inflationary situation, inadequacy and delay in provision of financial assistance and many other similar problems in the economic and developmental fields. In facing the crisis, this complex situation must be borne in mind so as to ensure that the Special Programme adopted by the international community provides emergency relief and timely assistance to the most seriously affected countries. Simultaneously, steps are being taken to resolve these outstanding problems through a fundamental restructuring of the world economic system, in order to allow these countries while solving the present difficulties to reach an acceptable level of development.

(*b*) The special measures adopted to assist the most seriously affected countries must encompass not only the relief which they require on an emergency basis to maintain their import requirements, but also beyond that, steps to consciously promote the capacity of these countries to produce and earn more. Unless such a comprehensive approach is adopted, there is every likelihood that the difficulties of the most seriously affected countries may be perpetuated. Nevertheless, the first and most pressing task of the international community is to enable these countries to meet the shortfall in their balance-of-payments positions. But this must be simultaneously supplemented by additional development assistance to maintain and thereafter accelerate their rate of economic development.

(*c*) The countries which have been most seriously affected are precisely those which are at the greatest disadvantage in the world economy: the least developed, the land-locked and other low-income developing countries as well as other developing countries whose economies have been seriously dislocated as a result of the present economic crisis, natural calamities, and foreign aggression and occupation. An indication of the countries thus affected, the level of the impact on their economies and the kind of relief and assistance they require can be assessed on the basis, *inter alia,* of the following criteria:

    (i) Low *per capita* income as a reflection of relative poverty, low productivity, low level of technology and development;

(ii) Sharp increase in their import cost of essentials relative to export earnings;

(iii) High ratio of debt servicing to export earnings;

(iv) Insufficiency in export earnings, comparative inelasticity of export incomes and unavailability of exportable surplus;

(v) Low level of foreign exchange reserves or their inadequacy for requirements;

(vi) Adverse impact of higher transportation and transit costs;

(vii) Relative importance of foreign trade in the development process.

(*d*) The assessment of the extent and nature of the impact on the economies of the most seriously affected countries must be made flexible, keeping in mind the present uncertainty in the world economy, the adjustment policies that may be adopted by the developed countries and the flow of capital and investment. Estimates of the payments situation and needs of these countries can be assessed and projected reliably only on the basis of their average performance over a number of years. Long-term projections, at this time, cannot but be uncertain.

(*e*) It is important that, in the special measures to mitigate the difficulties of the most seriously affected countries, all the developed countries as well as the developing countries should contribute according to their level of development and the capacity and strength of their economies. It is notable that some developing countries, despite their own difficulties and development needs, have shown a willingness to play a concrete and helpful role in ameliorating the difficulties faced by the poorer developing countries. The various initiatives and measures taken recently by certain developing countries with adequate resources on a bilateral and multilateral basis to contribute to alleviating the difficulties of other developing countries are a reflection of their commitment to the principle of effective economic co-operation among developing countries.

(*f*) The response of the developed countries which have by far the greater capacity to assist the affected countries in overcoming their present difficulties must be commensurate with their responsibilities. Their assistance should be in addition to the presently available levels of aid. They should fulfil and if possible exceed the targets of the International Development Strategy for the Second United Nations Development Decade on financial assistance to the developing countries, especially that relating to official development assistance. They should also give serious consideration to the cancellation of the external debts of the most seriously affected countries. This would provide the simplest and quickest relief to the affected countries. Favourable consideration should also be given to debt moratorium and rescheduling. The current situation should not lead the industrialized countries to adopt what will ultimately prove to be a self-defeating policy aggravating the present crisis.

Recalling the constructive proposals made by His Imperial Majesty the Shahanshah of Iran* and His Excellency Mr. Houari Boumediène, President of the People's Democratic Republic of Algeria,**

1. *Decides* to launch a Special Programme to provide emergency relief and development assistance to the developing countries most seriously affected, as a matter of urgency, and for the period of time necessary, at least until the end of the Second United Nations Development Decade, to help them overcome their present difficulties and to achieve self-sustaining economic development;

2. *Decides* as a first step in the Special Programme to request the Secretary-General to launch an emergency operation to provide timely relief to the most seriously affected developing countries, as defined in subparagraph (*c*) above, with the aim of maintaining unimpaired essential imports for the duration of the coming twelve months and to invite the industrialized countries and other potential contributors to announce their contributions for emergency assistance, or intimate their intention to do so, by 15 June 1974 to be provided through bilateral or multilateral channels, taking into account the commitments and measures of assistance announced or already taken by some countries, and further requests the Secretary-General to report the progress of the emergency operation to the General Assembly at its twenty-ninth session, through the Economic and Social Council at its fifty-seventh session;

3. *Calls upon* the industrialized countries and other potential contributors to extend to the most seriously affected countries immediate relief and assistance which must be of an order of magnitude that is commensurate with the needs of these countries. Such assistance should be in addition to the existing level of aid and provided at a very early date to the maximum possible extent on a grant basis and, where not possible, on soft terms. The disbursement and relevant operational procedures and terms must reflect this exceptional situation. The assistance could be provided either through bilateral or multilateral channels, including such new institutions and facilities that have been or are to be set up. The special measures may include the following:

---

*A/9548, annex.

**Official Records of the General Assembly, Sixth Special Session, Plenary Meetings, 2208th meeting, paras. 3-152.

(*a*) Special arrangements on particularly favourable terms and conditions including possible subsidies for and assured supplies of essential commodities and goods;

(*b*) Deferred payments for all or part of imports of essential commodities and goods;

(*c*) Commodity assistance, including food aid, on a grant basis or deferred payments in local currencies, bearing in mind that this should not adversely affect the exports of developing countries;

(*d*) Long-term suppliers' credits on easy terms;

(*e*) Long-term financial assistance on concessionary terms;

(*f*) Drawings from special International Monetary Fund facilities on consessional terms;

(*g*) Establishment of a link between the creation of special drawing rights and development assistance, taking into account the additional financial requirements of the most seriously affected countries;

(*h*) Subsidies, provided bilaterally or multilaterally, for interest on funds available on commercial terms borrowed by the most seriously affected countries;

(*i*) Debt renegotiation on a case-by-case basis with a view to concluding agreements on debt cancellation, moratorium or rescheduling;

(*j*) Provision on more favourable terms of capital goods and technical assistance to accelerate the industrialization of the affected countries;

(*k*) Investment in industrial and development projects on favourable terms;

(*l*) Subsidizing the additional transit and transport costs, especially of the land-locked countries;

4. *Appeals* to the developed countries to consider favourably the cancellation, moratorium or rescheduling of the debts of the most seriously affected developing countriess, on their request, as an important contribution to mitigating the grave and urgent difficulties of these countries;

5. *Decides* to establish a Special Fund under the auspices of the United Nations, through voluntary contributions from industrialized countries and other potential contributors, as a part of the Special Programme, to provide emergency relief and development assistance, which will commence its operations at the latest by 1 January 1975;

6. *Establishes* an *Ad Hoc* Committee on the Special Programme, composed of thiry-six Member States appointed by the President of the General Assembly, after appropriate consultations, bearing in mind the purposes of the Special Fund and its terms of reference:

(*a*) To make recommendations, *inter alia,* on the scope, machinery and modes of operation of the Special Fund, taking into account the need for:

    (i) Equitable representation on its governing body;

    (ii) Equitable distribution of its resources;

    (iii) Full utilization of the services and facilities of existing international organizations;

    (iv) The possibility of merging the United Nations Capital Development Fund with the operations of the Special Fund;

    (v) A central monitoring body to oversee the various measures being taken both bilaterally and multilaterally;

and, to this end, bearing in mind the different ideas and proposals submitted at the sixth special session, including those put forward by Iran* and those made at the 2208th plenary meeting, and the comments thereon, and the possibility of utilizing the Special Fund to provide an alternative channel for normal development assistance after the emergency period;

(*b*) To monitor, pending commencement of the operations of the Special Fund, the various measures being taken both bilaterally and multilaterally to assist the most seriously affected countries;

(*c*) To prepare, on the basis of information provided by the countries concerned and by appropriate agencies of the United Nations system, a broad assessment of:

    (i) The magnitude of the difficulties facing the most seriously affected countries;

    (ii) The kind and quantities of the commodities and goods essentially required by them;

    (iii) Their need for financial assistance;

    (iv) Their technical assistance requirements, including especially access to technology;

7. *Requests* the Secretary-General of the United Nations, the Secretary-General of the United Nations Conference on Trade and Development, the President of the International Bank for Reconstruction and Development, the Managing Director of the International Monetary Fund, the Administrator of the United Nations Development Programme and the heads of the other competent international organizations to assist the *Ad Hoc* Committee on the Special Programme in peforming the functions assigned to it under paragraph 6 above, and to help, as appropriate, in the operation of the Special Fund;

8. *Requests* the International Monetary Fund to expedite decisions on:

---

*A/AC.166/L.15; see also A/9548, annex.

(*a*) The establishment of an extended special facility with a view to enabling the most seriously affected developing countries to participate in it on favourable terms;

(*b*) The creation of special drawing rights and the early establishment of the link between their allocation and development financing;

(*c*) The establishment and operation of the proposed new special facility to extend credits and subsidize interest charges on commercial funds borrowed by Member States, bearing in mind the interests of the developing countries and especially the additional financial requirements of the most seriously affected countries;

9. *Requests* the World Bank Group and the International Monetary Fund to place their managerial, financial and technical services at the disposal of Governments contributing to emergency financial relief so as to enable them to assist without delay in channelling funds to the recipients, making such institutional and procedural changes as may be required;

10. *Invites* the United Nations Development Programme to take the necessary steps, particularly at the country level, to respond on an emergency basis to requests for additional assistance which it may be called upon to render within the framework of the Special Programme;

11. *Requests* the *Ad Hoc* Committee on the Special Programme to submit its report and recommendations to the Economic and Social Council at its fifty-seventh session and invites the Council, on the basis of its consideration of that report, to submit suitable recommendations to the General Assembly at its twenty-ninth session;

12. *Decides* to consider as a matter of high priority at its twenty-ninth session, within the framework of a new international economic order, the question of special measures for the most seriously affected countries.

2229th plenary meeting
1 May 1974

2. Reservations

Sixth Special Session of the United Nations General Assembly

[The resolutions 3201 (S-VI) and 3202 (S-VI) were adopted by consensus by the Sixth Special Session on May 1, 1974. After the adoption of the resolutions, a number of delegations made statements which also contain the reservations made by representatives of the developed market economies. These are reproduced below.*]

United Nations, General Assembly, Sixth Special Session:
2229th Plenary Meeting, Wednesday, May 1, 1974

. . .

20. The PRESIDENT (interpretation from Spanish): Several representatives have expressed the wish to make comments on the decisions just taken by the General Assembly. I shall now call on them in turn.

. . .

75. Mr. HANEKOM (South Africa): There are certain passages in the Declaration on the Establishment of a New International Economic Order and the Programme of Action which are unacceptable to my delegation. The Assembly will know which they are, so I need not identify them.

76. Because of this, I wish formally to place on record that my delegation is obliged to dissociate itself from the Declaration and the Programme of Action. We regret this, as we support, and are ready to contribute to, the over-all objective of securing a new economic order which would correct the economic imbalances of today and of rendering aid to the disadvantaged countries. However, we have been left with no other alternative.

77. Mr. SCALI (United States of America): As this session of the Assembly draws to a close it is time to take stock. Much good has been done. The world community, represented by its leading statesmen, has devoted several weeks of intensive attention to the critical situation which has arisen in the international economic area. We believe that this was right, proper and useful. Many constructive suggestions were made on how to cope with the range of problems in this field.

78. We are—I must confess—disappointed that it was not possible to emerge from our deliberations with unanimous agreement on how these problems can best be solved. Over the years we have negotiated our differences on complicated economic and development questions in various other appropriate forums. We

---

*United Nations, *Official Records of the General Assembly, Sixth Special Session, Plenary Meeting, Verbatim Records of Meetings, 9 April–2 May, 1974,* 2229th, 2230th and 2231st meetings.

seriously question what value there is in adopting statements on difficult and controversial questions that represent the views of only one faction.

79. Some have referred to the procedure by which these documents have been formulated as that of "consensus". My delegation believes that the word "consensus" cannot be applied in this case. The document which will be printed as the written product of this special session of the General Assembly does not in fact—whatever it is called—represent a consensus in the accepted meaning of that term. My delegation did not choose to voice objection to the resolution presented to us this evening even though, at the last moment, it was presented without mention of the word "consensus".

80. The intent, however, was clear. This was intended as a consensus procedure, but our objecting at the last second would only have served to exacerbate the divisions that we have worked to the best of our ability to bridge during the past weeks.

81. The document in question contains elements supported by all United Nations Members. It also contains elements which many Members of the United Nations—large and small, and on every continent—do not endorse. The United States delegation, like many others, strongly disapproves of some provisions in the document and has in no sense endorsed them. The document we have produced is a signifiant political document, but it does not represent unanimity of opinion in this Assembly. To label some of these highly controversial conclusions as "agreed" is not only idle; it is self-deceiving. In this house, the steamroller is not the vehicle for solving vital, complex problems.

82. The major concern of my own Government has been to assure some immediate and effective relief to those developing countries which have been most adversely affected by the recent changes in the world economy. While a Programme of Action has been adopted, we are frankly not convinced that it will respond to these immediate needs. I would draw the Assembly's attention to the fact that just yesterday my own delegation advanced a number of ideas in the *Ad Hoc* Committee which were addressed primarily to this area of most critical need. We regret that the shortage of time made it impossible to obtain agreement. I wish to assure the Assembly, however, that my own Government is examining carefully what additional measures it can take to provide assistance to those countries which have suffered most.

83. The United States remains deeply concerned about the need for a co-operative effort to resolve the difficulties which face the international community on a whole range of issues, including commodity prices, aid, trade, energy, food and monetary stability. We remain committed to seeking solutions to these issues on a co-operative basis and through true consensus rather than through confrontation.

84. The sixth special session has acknowledged mankind's common destiny. Our nations met in a global forum to come to grips with what once were considered national problems: inflation, economic growth, feeding the hungry and uplifting the impoverished.

85. The challenge has been to accept our mutual dependence and to agree on an agenda for common action to improve the quality of life acrosss the globe. Success cannot be determined by one nation or by one group of nations seeking to impose its will. Nor will it result from one session of the General Assembly.

86. Too often in the past this Organization has been the forum for unrealistic promises and unfulfilled commitments. The ideal has been substituted too often for the attainable, and the results have been often no more than increased frustration and disappointment. Historically, the United States has not made commitments that we did not intend to fulfil. Thus, as Secretary of State Kissinger recently told the Foreign Ministers of Latin America and the Caribbean, the United States will promise only what it can deliver. And we will make what we can deliver count.

87. In this spirit, on behalf of President Nixon, Secretary Kissinger, in his address to this Assembly two weeks ago [*2214th meeting*], pledged the United States to a major effort in support of development. He stated that the United States would make a substantial contribution to the special needs of the poorest nations.

88. We have set forth our specific proposals and commitments to help assure an abundant supply of energy at an equitable price, to achieve a more stable balance between raw materials supply and demand, to narrow the gap between food and population growth, to build a trade monetary and investment system that encourages economic growth rather than economic warfare, and to bring the best minds of all nations to apply science to meet the problems that science has helped to create.

89. It is easy to agree to yet another set of principles, to another programme of action, to more steps that other nations should take. But each nation must ask itself what it can do, what contribution it can make. The needs of the poor will not be met by empty promises; the needs of an expanding global economy will not be met by new restrictions on supply and demand; the growing interdependence of all nations cannot be managed on the basis of confrontation.

90. There are provisions in the Declaration and the Programme of Action to which the United States Government cannot lend its support. I will deal here only with our most important reservations.

91. Perhaps the most difficult subject which the Declaration addresses is that of permanent sovereignty over

natural resources. It will be recalled that this problem was successfully dealt with by the General Assembly in 1962, when, in a meeting of minds of developing and developed countries, widespread agreement was achieved on the terms of resolution 1803 (XVII). The United States delegation regrets that the compromise solution which resolution 1803 (XVII) embodies was not reproduced in this Declaration. If it had been, on this count the United States would gladly have lent its support. Resolution 1803 (XVII) provides, among other things, that, where foreign property is nationalized, appropriate compensation shall be paid in accordance with national and international law; it also provides that foreign-investment agreements by and between States shall be observed in good faith. By way of contrast, the present Declaration does not couple the assertion of the right to nationalize with the duty to pay compensation in accordance with international law. For this reason, we do not find this formulation complete or acceptable. The governing international law cannot be, and is not, prejudiced by the passage of this resolution.

92. The United States does not support the provisions of the Declaration which refer only to the exertion of economic pressure for some ends, but which do not condemn generally the exercise of economic pressure. In this respect, the Declaration contrasts unfavourably with the Declaration on Principles of International Law concerning Friendly Relations and Co-operation among States in accordance with the Charter of the United Nations[*resolution 2625(XXV)*]. Nor does the United States support the provisions of the resolution that refer to restitution and full compensation for exploitation of, and damage to, certain resources and peoples.

93. Neither can the United States accept the idea of producer associations as a viable means of promoting development, or of fixing a relationship between import and export prices. Artificial attempts to manage markets which ignore economic realities and the legitimate interests of consumers as well as producers run the risk of political confrontation on the one hand and economic failure on the other.

94. I also wish to make mention of that part of the Declaration dealing with the regulation and supervision of the activities of multinational corporations. The United States is of the view that multinational corporations must act as good corporate citizens of the States in which they operate, and that multinational corporations are subject to the regulation and supervision of the countries in which they operate, but such regulation and supervision must be non-discriminatory and otherwise conform to the norms of international law.

95. The Programme of Action has too many objectionable features, from our point of view, to permit a detailed listing and explanation in a brief statement. Among their features are the emphasis on marketing arrangements for primary products which exclude the interests of consumers and the impractical proposals to establish artificial and fixed price relationships between prices of exports and imports of developing countries. Our scepticism about commodity agreements is well known, but we are prepared to consider them on a case-by-case basis. The current negotiations within the framework of the General Agreement on Tariffs and Trade (*GATT*) and other actions we support can increase the trade of developing countries, but it is out of the question for us to allocate a specified share of our market for the developing countries. We object to the Assembly's making recommendations now on the provisions related to the link between special drawing rights and development finance, the provisions to reform the international financial institutions, and subsidization of interest payments and other involved questions that should be left to the IMF.

96. As this special session of the General Assembly nears its close, there is one central concern in the minds of all of us. Many of the less developed nations of the world are afflicted with the most serious and debilitating economic ills of their lifetime. There are parallel economic dislocations in the industrialized world, but it is better prepared to recover.

97. Before the special session began, the United States delegation said it would negotiate in a spirit of compromise and conciliation. This is still our attitude. It will continue to be, as the United Nations and its individual States seek ways to lighten the burdens of the less developed countries.

98. Unfortunately, the time to consider programmes for the neediest countries has been short. We nevertheless regret that ways were not found, even though the hour was late, to explore varying proposals of substance.

99. I wish to point out an obvious truth. Despite scores of public speeches, hundreds of hours of detailed discussion and thousands of hours of consultations, we have not yet agreed on the kind of co-ordinated action which will provide the immediate emergency relief that is indispensable in the present crisis.

100. Words cannot feed the starving nor help the impoverished. The sudden increased cost of life is still being borne by the poor. This moment demands more of us than words—more of us than promises, which may materialize many months from now, if ever. Have we measured up to the challenge?

101. While this Assembly has not been without accomplishment, we must not go home in the belief that we have already met the central task before us.

102. Let us go home, each nation determined to do its part to meet the immediate crisis that challenges our interdependent world community.

103. I can assure this Assembly that the United States will do its share.

104. Mr. GEHLHOFF (Federal Republic of Germany): For the first time in the history of the United Nations a special session of the General Assembly has been convened for the exclusive purpose of discussing economic and development questions. The United Nations thus is making a new and determined effort to promote, as set forth in the Charter, "social progress and better standards of life in larger freedom" and to employ international machinery in furthering the economic and social advancement of all peoples. My Government strongly endorses these efforts. It has been the policy of my Government in the past to foster economic co-operation with the developing countries and their integration into the world economy. My Government is determined to support all measures and actions which lead to an improvement of the international economic order.

105. This special session had to face difficult tasks, but, thanks to the work of all delegations and to the prevailing spirit of co-operation, it has been possible to make important progress. I particularly want to express my delegation's gratitude for the enlightened leadership shown by the President of the General Assembly and for the untiring efforts of the Chairman of the *Ad Hoc* Committee in bringing about a compromise.

106. Permit me to refer in some detail to the documents we have adopted. My delegation welcomes the adoption of the declaration of principles [*resolution 3201 (S-VI)*], which, we are convinced, will pave the way for a new economic order. My Government recognizes the right of permanent sovereignty of States over their natural resources, including the right of nationalization. This right is vested in the rules of international law. It should, in our view, be exercised in accordance with these rules. My Government considers it necessary to secure fair and equitable prices for exported and imported goods. Fixed price relationships, however, are liable to suspend the market mechanism, which is indispensable for the orderly functioning of the world economy.

107. My Government has also certain apprehensions regarding producer associations. This does not apply to their existence as such. My Government is concerned, however, lest the policy of such associations might lead to new dependencies and might be detrimental to an unhampered exchange of goods.

108. With regard to the Programme of Action, considerable progress has been made during the past few days in approximating positions which were originally far apart. The Programme now at hand contains a number of proposals to which my delegation fully subscribes. On the other hand, a number of measures are suggested which do not seem to us feasible or appropriate for achieving the envisaged aim of closer international economic co-operation. It is no lack of political will which prompts me to state this view. On the contrary, it is our conviction that political determination is best applied when based on reality.

109. I do not want to expound here the reservations of my delegation on the Programme of Action. They will have to be dealt with when the relevant items are discussed in the competent United Nations bodies. I should like, however, to refer briefly to some important points.

110. Concerning section I of resolution 3202 (S-VI), I am obliged to state that conditions in the commodity markets obviously vary so much that measures in respect to individual commodities can be taken only after examination on a case-by-case basis. We are in favour of structural adjustments which serve to integrate the developing countries more closely and equitably into the international division of labour. Structural measures must not lead, however, to sacrificing sound and competitive branches of the economy. The implementation of the code of conduct for liner conferences has, in the view of my Government, to be considered at the twenty-ninth session of the General Assembly. With regard to freight and insurance, I wish to emphasize that my Government has no means of establishing or subsidizing freight rates or of influencing insurance costs.

111. With regard to section II, I have to state the following. First, the reform of the international monetary system was the subject of an intensive discussion at the twenty-eighth session of the General Assembly, the result of which was reflected in resolution 3084 (XXVIII). We consider the formulation arrived at, after thorough negotiations, to be a well-balanced compromise. We do not want to anticipate further decisions in the bodies of IMF entrusted with this reform. We believe in the necessity of world-wide measures to check inflation. Isolated measures to prevent a transfer of inflation are either impossible or unsuited to check inflation as a whole. My Government does not see any possibility of devising means of guaranteeing the real value of currency reserves. The creation of special drawing rights as a whole should be based on criteria of a stability-oriented world-wide need for liquidity. Special drawing rights established without regard for these criteria would not be of use to the developing countries either.

112. Secondly, regarding the implementation of the International Development Strategy concerning transfer of resources. I wish to recall the reservations made by my delegation on its adoption. Moreover, nothing should be done here to anticipate the results of the examination in the World Bank regarding the improvement of its decision-making process. My delegation states that we cannot influence private credit contracts with the aim of reducing the external debt of developing countries.

113. The Federal Republic of Germany takes a positive view of the Special Programme. It will endeavour to increase further its total assistance to the developing countries in order to provide additional means for special measures beyond the scope of the assistance granted so far.

114. We cannot, of course, forestall the budget procedures applied in a democratic State like ours. In our view, not all the measures listed under paragraph 3 of the Special Program in section X of the resolution are feasible. We shall concentrate on those items which we consider to be the most effective; these include the fertilizer and food assistance programme.

115. I will say a few words on behalf of the European Economic Community. The Community through the President of its Council stated right at the outset of this special session [*2209th meeting*] its awareness of the magnitude of the problems for which the session was convened and of the need to find urgent solutions to the present instabilities and disruptions of trade flows. The objective is to achieve an international economic system equitable to all nations and based on their increasing interdependence. The Community, as well as its member States, have, throughout this session, endeavoured to take an active and constructive part in the discussions. The Community and the member States have been doing so in a spirit of open-mindedness and wanted to underline their will to further develop a partnership with the developing countries.

116. With regard to the texts the General Assembly has adopted, we would like to make the following reservations and interpretations.

117. First, the European Economic Community and its member States wish to increase their aid to the developing countries but cannot envisage the automatic transfer of revenues from their import policy or their tax systems.

118. Second, the European Economic Community has regularly improved and extended the generalized preferences scheme, which it applies. It considers, however, that the situation of commodities on the international markets requires other solutions.

119. The European Economic Community has always accepted the examination of the possibilities for compensatory financing within the competent international bodies; it considers, however, that this matter should continue to be dealt with in those bodies.

120. While recognizing that buffer stocks in the framework of commodity agreements can, in appropriate cases, be a useful factor, it is of the opinion that, since the aim of such stocks is to assist the stabilization of these markets, they are in themselves favourable to all countries, in particular to both producing and consuming developing countries.

121. With regard to multilateral trade negotiations, the Community subscribed to the Declaration of Tokyo,* under the terms of which these negotiations would be conducted on the basis of the principles of mutual advantage, mutual commitment and global reciprocity with respect for the most-favoured-nation clause, while not expecting reciprocity of commitments from the developing countries and recognizing the need to take differential measures in respect of such countries to ensure special and more favourable treatment for them.

122. With regard, finally, to the emergency measures, the European Economic Community and its member States are aware of the critical situation resulting from the latest developments in the prices of imported products which are, particularly for some developing countries, essential. They thus wish to express their determination, in conjunction with all interested States and international organizations, forthwith to examine the most effective procedures for an exceptional international aid project to overcome the difficulties of such developing countries. The Community and its member States would, for their part, be prepared to play an active part in these efforts and to make a substantial contribution provided the other members of the Community of nations were willing to join them.

123. Mr. RYDBECK (Sweden): The two documents adopted through the consensus decision taken tonight on the establishment of a new international economic order are of the highest importance. Through them the States Members of the United Nations have declared their intention to achieve a more equitable distribution of the world's resources and to narrow the widening gap between the developed and the developing countries. We pay our tribute to the untiring efforts of the representatives who have been active in the preparation of these documents, in particular to the Chairman of the *Ad Hoc* Committee.

124. In our view this Assembly signifies a milestone in the history of the United Nations. Member States have demonstrated a spirit of co-operation that is greatly encouraging. They have, from sometimes strongly conflicting positions of interest, made sacrifices with the aim of creating a solid foundation for the forthcoming efforts to design a more just and equitable relationship between nations.

125. The results of this Assembly will carry with them the hope that future work in other spheres of United Nations activities will lead to similar accomplishments achieved through negotiation and co-operation for the benefit of Member States.

---

*Declaration of 14 September 1973, approved by the Ministerial Meeting of the Contracting Parties to the General Agreement on Tariffs and Trade held in Tokyo.

126. I want now to make just a few brief remarks regarding some specific points in the documents just adopted.

127. Our delegation certainly supports the aim of achieving a more just and equitable relationship between, on the one hand, prices of products exported by the developing countries and, on the other hand, prices of products imported by the same countries, but we do not believe that it would be technically and practically feasible to establish a specific link. We do share the belief that producers' co-operation among the developing countries should be facilitated within a broader international framework where the legitimate interests of all countries will be taken into account.

128. There are some points in the Programme of Action, and specifically in sections I, II and VIII, on which we would have wished for further improvements. I want specifically to mention those on the reimbursement of receipts from custom duties, taxes, on new investment for production of synthetic materials and also paragraph 3 (*b*) of section I under the title "general trade". We believe furthermore that it is important that the compromise wording achieved in the Tokyo Declaration should be adhered to and that we should avoid changes in the agreed objectives of these negotiations. As regards the paragraphs on transportation, our position on the code of conduct for a liner conference has been made clear at the Geneva conference,* where for reasons stated there we had to vote against the code.

129. We have accepted section II on monetary matters in the Programme of Action on the understanding that any reform should be based on the concept of global liquidity needs and on the availability of financial resources and that it should aim at the creation of monetary stability.

130. As regards the question of an increase in the official component of the net amount of financial resource transfers to developing countries, our Minister for Trade pointed out in the general debate [*2219th meeting*] that some additional $8,000 million would be put at the disposal of the poorer countries if the developed countries fulfilled the target laid down in the International Development Strategy of official assistance equal to 0.7 per cent of the gross national product within the next year. That, in our view, is a real aid target.

131. A clear distinction must be made between flows of private capital and official investments in developing countries. The development effects of private investment could be ascertained only after a careful political and economic analysis on a case-by-case basis.

132. We regard the Programme of Action as an important general guideline for the efforts to be made by Member States and the United Nations family of organizations in the follow-up of the principles laid down in the Declaration. For our part, we will from now on, in co-operation with all States Members of the United Nations, do our best to respond to it.

133. We are indeed very happy that it proved possible, despite the short time available, to reach agreement on a special programme, including, in particular, emergency measures to mitigate the difficulties of the developing countries most seriously affected by the economic crisis. Without that accomplishment, the special session of the General Assembly could not have been said to have achieved the goals it had been convened to reach.

134. Mr. KARHILO (Finland): The Finnish Government was among the very first to support the Algerian initiative to convene the General Assembly in special session to try for the first time to tackle the problems of raw materials and development in an integrated and comprehensive manner. I am now authorized to state that the Government of Finland accepts, and indeed lends its full support to, the conclusion of our work as presented in the documents before the Assembly. My Government particularly welcomes the manifestation of a joint and determined political will by the world community to work together to solve the economic problems facing us; it welcomes the resolve to work urgently for the establishment of a new international economic order, which is expressed in the Declaration adopted by the Assembly and which has the unreserved support of my Government.

135. Similarly, Finland gives its support to the Programme of Action, which in our view is a prerequisite for making the principles of the Declaration truly meaningful. Some of the measures recommended in the Programme will present Finland, an industrialized, but none the less a capital-importing, country with obvious problems. However, my delegation sees the Programme as the start of an important process that will make the new economic order operational. In the course of that process within the United Nations system, we shall have an opportunity to elaborate the problems which arise out of our particular position.

136. In conclusion, I should like to refer to the Special Programme and the urgent measures contained in section X of the Programme of Action in favour of the developing countries most seriously affected by economic crisis. My Government welcomes the Special Programme as a recognition of the principle of the interdependence of all nations which must form the corner-stone of the new international economic order. It is in

---

*United Nations Conference of Plenipotentiaries on a Code of Conduct for Liner Conferences, held at Geneva from 12 November to 15 December 1973 (first part) and from 11 March to 6 April 1974 (second part).

that spirit that the Finnish Government has already committed itself to that Programme and has undertaken urgent action to determine how best it could participate with additional measures in the implementation of the Special Programme.

137. Mr. RAE (Canada): The Canadian delegation has joined in the decision which has marked the conclusion of this special session. We have done so in order to signify Canada's firm support for the basic objective of the session—namely, an acceleration in the rate of development of developing countries and a more equitable distribution of the world's economic resources.

138. It is, however, necessary for my delegation to comment on certain of the specific provisions of the documents. I turn first to the Declaration.

139. Our discussion of paragraph 4(*e*), on permanent sovereignty and nationalization, revealed general agreement on the fundamental principle that each State enjoys permanent sovereignty over its natural resources and all economic activities within its territory. The problem we were unable to resolve relates to identifying those legal principles which are to apply when a State, in the exercise of its permanent sovereignty, adopts measures of nationalization. My delegation considers that a State's right to undertake nationalization must be exercised in accordance with the generally accepted rules of international law and practice governing such an act.

140. The Canadian delegation wishes to enter a reservation with respect to paragraph 4(*f*), which, as worded, appears to be at variance with international practice.

141. With respect to paragraph 4(*j*), the Canadian delegation supports the objective of just and equitable prices for goods traded by developing countries and understands that to be the intention of this paragraph.

142. My delegation is able to support paragraph 4(*s*), but we would expect co-operation among developing countries to be consistent with their international obligations.

143. With respect to paragraph 4(*t*), my delegation recognizes the right of countries which are exporters of raw materials to seek an equitable return for their resources, just as consumers may associate in order to protect their interests. But in the view of the Canadian delegation the principle which flows from recognition of the economic interdependence of States, which is the basis of this entire Declaration, is the need for mutually beneficial co-operation between producing and consuming States. This paragraph does not, in our view, accurately reflect that principle.

144. I turn now to the Programme of Action.

145. The Canadian delegation recognizes the need for urgent action to mitigate the immediate difficulties of the developing countries most seriously affected by economic crises. Canada considers such action to be vitally necessary, and it will be recalled that in this special session's general debate the Secretary of State for External Affairs, the Honourable Mitchell Sharp, announced a number of concrete measures Canada itself is taking in that direction [*2211th meeting*]. It is our expectation that other advantaged countries and the international community as a whole will take a similarly positive and forthcoming attitude.

146. We do have problems, however, with the Programme of Action contained in the documents we have just adopted. Had there been a separate vote on the Programme of Action, my delegation would have been constrained to abstain. Our reservation stems from the fact that in the time available to this special session, it was not possible to refine in the text economic, trade and monetary issues which will have long-term implications for all members of the international community. Nor was it possible, again because of the lack of time, either to harmonize the text of the Programme of Action with that of the Declaration, or to reconcile the inconsistencies and contradictions within the Programme. I think it would be counter-productive to go into these problems in detail at this late stage.

147. It is my delegation's sincere hope and expectation that work on these important issues might continue in other appropriate organizations and bodies, both within and outside the United Nations. Indeed, we believe that the discussion begun here, the views we have exchanged, the hard work we have done, will enable Governments to address these questions more vigorously in more specialized bodies. It is our hope also that these discusions will give further impetus to bilateral and multilateral steps to bring immediate relief to those developing countries most seriously affected by recent economic disorders.

148. I should like to make certain additional comments, briefly, directed specifically to section X of the Programme of Action.

149. The Canadian delegation supports section X, the Special Programme, including in particular the emergency measures. We do so in the light of our perception of a need for urgent action to assist the developing countries most seriously affected by economic crisis.

150. Immediately prior to this special session, the Canadian Government decided to provide an additional $100 million over and above originally projected development assistance programmes to meet the emergency needs of the hardest hit developing countries, particularly in the food and fertilizer areas. These funds are now being disbursed. We have stressed at this session that a renewed effort of international co-operation is called

for in which full use should be made of those established and recognized international institutions which have experience and expertise in supporting development. The United Nations Development Programme, [*UNDP*], the World Food Programme, the International Bank for Reconstruction and Development and the regional development banks are repositories of the technical skills now available to the international community. As such, they offer a ready means of securing early and effective action.

151. We support the call for an emergency effort to be launched by the Secretary-General—who has shown such concern for all these problems in the course of the past weeks—as outlined in paragraph 2 of the Special Programme. We consider that the scope of this Programme would have had more attraction had it concentrated on urgent measures for the emergency period rather than on more general problems of development. In this connexion we find less than satisfactory the formula in paragraph 1 linking the time-frame of the Special Fund to the remainder of the Second Development Decade. Regarding the Special Fund which is introduced in paragraph 5, some Governments, particularly those which have not traditionally offered financial support to existing United Nations institutions, may find this Fund a more attractive channel for emergency and development assitance to developing countries most seriously affected by recent economic events. In our view maximum use should be made of the existing international development institutions. Canada for its part has agreed to a contribution of $276 million to the fourth replenishment of the International Development Association.

152. The text of this section does go somewhat beyond the scope of the special measures which in our view were first contemplated. In paragraphs 3 and 8, a number of monetary issues are raised. We would not wish it to be thought that our positions on a series of ongoing consultations on monetary issues, under the auspices of IMF, are prejudged by acceptance of this Special Programme as a whole. We look forward to an early decision on the establishment and the operation of the proposed new special credit facility now under consideration in the IMF to alleviate the deteriorating balance-of-payments situation of the developing countries, especially those most seriously affected by recent economic events. Regarding paragraph 4, Canada will continue to give sympathetic consideration to the debt problems of developing countries.

153. Our support for section X as a whole should be seen as a reflection of our determination to make every effort to respond to the urgent and immediate needs of developing countries hardest hit by economic disasters.

154. Finally, may I conclude by observing that the extensive negotiations which have taken place on these documents throughout the special session have clearly shown the possibility for a higher degree of co-operation between developed and developing, producer and consumer countries, on the issues with which these documents deal than has ever been achieved in the past. It is our sincere hope and expectation that our work together, the progress made towards co-operation achieved at this special session, will be carried further into other bodies, both within and outside the family of the United Nations.

155. Mr. LONGERSTAEY (Belgium) (*interpretation from French*): The spokesman for the European Economic Community has entered the reservations and expressed the comments of our group that we felt were necessary for inclusion in the record. It goes without saying that the delegations of Belgium and of the Grand Duchy of Luxembourg, on whose behalf I speak also, support the comments made.

156. With regard to the Declaration, the acceptance by the delegations of Belgium and Luxembourg of paragraph 4(*e*), which speaks to the sovereignty of States over their natural resources, must be understood in accordance with the attitude that the States members of the European Economic Community adopted during the third session of the Working Group on the Charter of Economic Rights and Duties of States.

157. Moreover, the intentions and principles mentioned in that Declaration deserve to be clarified within the context of the discussions on the Charter I mentioned before, since Belgium and Luxembourg adhere to all the principles and since we voted in favour of them at the third session of the United Nations Conference on Trade and Development [*UNCTAD*] in Santiago. It is thus that we read the terms of paragraph 6 which states that "the present Declaration will provide an additional source of inspiration" in the preparation of that Charter.

158. With regard to the Programme of Action, I should like to make the following comments. As far as we are concerned, section I, paragraph 1 (*c*), which speaks of producers' associations, must be understood within the framework of international co-operation explicitly as mentioned in paragraph 4 (*t*) of the Declaration.

159. With regard to paragraph 1 (*d*) of the Programme of Action, we continue to believe that the establishment of a direct link between import prices and export prices would create serious difficulties.

160. In the Programme of Action, we particularly support those provisions that are intended to assure a favourable evolution of the market in raw materials, which is the main subject of discussion of the present session of the Assembly.

161. However, in order to achieve a harmonious functioning of international markets, we must not lose sight of the fact that an important element in the stability of the markets lies in regular supply on equitable conditions, as Mr. Walter Scheel, President of the Council of Ministers of the European Economic Community stated when he spoke on behalf of the Community [*2209th meeting*].

162. We understand, furthermore, that the provisions contained in section 1, paragraph 4 (*f*), covering certain measures that the developed countries should abstain from imposing can in no way prejudice the commitments assumed by Belgium and Luxembourg in an international or European framework.

163. With reference to section II, efforts to reform the international monetary system and to finance development—as contained in paragraphs 1 and 2—should take fully into account the work under way in these fields in the appropriate international forums.

164. By the same token, the provisions covering the transfer of technology in section IV and the activities of transnational corporations in section V should also be carried out in harmony with the work and research now under way in, respectively, UNCTAD and the United Nations in these two fields.

165. With regard to section VIII, we understand that the preamble will be drafted in accordance with the terminology of most of the paragraphs, namely, "all efforts should be made . . .". We contend, furthermore, that the assistance required in subparagraph (*b*) cannot be greater than that which is normally given to the new industrial development projects.

166. And, finally, on section X, entitled "Special Programme," including emergency measures, the Belgian delegation would like to make the following comments, which, I believe, will make clear how and under what conditions we accept this part of the Programme of Action.

167. In the course of the debates, we have noted unanimously that the present economic situation in the world, flowing from the rise in the prices of certain raw materials, has seriously affected the fate of certain developing countries.

168. As far as Belgium is concerned, in the statement that we made in the plenary Assembly [*2212th meeting*], we said that emergency assistance to these countries is imperative and, therefore, a clear distinction should be made between the short-term and longer-term efforts. Naturally, this aid may be fitted into a more general context which is less temporary but still part of the development policies. However, Belgium and Luxembourg feel that priority should be granted today to the solution of problems that at present threaten the survival of entire populations.

169. Therefore, without underestimating the import of the Programme of Action which will inspire our long-term efforts, what is more necessary today is the adoption of urgent decisions, particularly in the field of essential raw materials, fertilizers and financial resources in favour of those countries most directly affected.

170. So far as Belgium and Luxembourg are concerned, we intend with our partners in the European Economic Community to participate in all this and we believe that all those who feel as we do will participate in such concentrated and speedy action, because this action will be all the more efficient if we do not dilute or uselessly delay it.

171. In conclusion, I regret that we have been unable to examine and, hence, to adopt concrete measures contained in a series of draft resolutions that we believe have been discussed too hastily. It is a shame, for example, that we have been unable to decide upon urgent action in the matter of fertilizers. We can only hope that the Economic and Social Council will be able to fill this gap.

172. Mr. DE GUIRINGAUD (France) (*interpretation from French*): My statement will contain specific explanations and a number of thoughts with regard to the events of which our Organization has been the theatre during the course of the last three weeks, and first of all, the event itself—the fact that this session has taken place. Surprising though it may seem, the sixth special session of the General Assembly, which is about to conclude, is the first one that has been devoted to international economic relations in the last 29 years. It was particularly important for us to succeed in a task as important and novel as this one. It was clear from the outset that we were about to create precedents for future special sessions of the Assembly of this nature—the one for the fall of 1975, for example—as well for the work of the Second Committee at regular sessions of the General Assembly.

173. I cannot fail to hail the consensus that has marked the adoption of the basic documents that were discussed. The United Nations has committed itself to the right course by avoiding any final confrontation, which would not have failed to create a difficult atmosphere for future deliberations on topics in the economic field. I whole-heartedly and most sincerely congratulate those who were responsible for this success, in particular the President of the General Assembly and the indefatigable Chairman of our *Ad Hoc* Committee, who was also chairman of many meetings, including restricted and confidential plenary meetings, which have been taking place here over the last four weeks, and our friend and conciliator the Ambassador of His Majesty the Emperor of Iran, without whom we would not have been able to maintain the serene and constructive atmosphere so necessary for the progress of our deliberations.

174. The consensus on which this session is about to conclude does not, however, mean that we have succeeded in reaching an understanding on all issues. Those who initiated our session proposed that we examine the first foundations of a new and more equitable international economic order. This programme naturally has

the approval of a country such as France, which is not unaware of how history is made up of revolutions and often positive reforms, but which also assesses the danger which sterile confrontations might cause for the most legitimate causes. The idea of a new order has meaning only if we fully understand that we must all work at achieving it. And I say "all" without any exception and without ulterior motives because it is true that no arbiter is here to decide between us; there is no doctor for civilization, for we are all our own doctors, entrusted with the task of using reason and conciliation to contain the selfish inclinations of our very nature.

175. Two or three fundamental rules seem to have been on our mind in the last few days in certain conditions which, I hope, will not remain precarious. First of all, the countries that have numbers on their side finally decided not to use their automatic majority in their favour. Undoubtedly, they have understood that the very edifice of the United Nations would not resist this kind of exercise and that the importance of the problems on which there exist here differences of interest or of ideology made it necessary that the difficulties which arise should not be decided in an unrealistic manner. And I say "unrealistic" because it is all too clear that the structures that serve as the framework for trade among States and economic entitites are only what they are—they cannot be changed by simple votes—and that the prestige of our Organization as well as its possibilities for action would be affected for a long time if an attempt was made here to force the acceptance of extreme claims against the will of a considerable minority.

176. That simple rule leads me to mention another, which, I hope, will continue to be observed—a rule in accordance with which there is nothing realistic except that which can be achieved. In other words, we must relentlessly distinguish between that which is possible and that which is not, so as to proceed in accordance with stages truly accepted by those that have the means to implement them. This simple appeal or, rather, reminder of the laws of genuine international progress does not, of course, imply that we can disregard the notion of that which is desirable. It is clearly necessary for the United Nations to continue to be a centre for active thought in determining those ideals that are to guide Member States not only in the fields of peace, security and disarmament but also, and increasingly, in determining the conditions in which a more satisfactory economic order ought to be established.

177. That is the direction in which our Assembly, in our view, seems to have gone by having achieved this consensus today. Having hailed the skills of those who have so well hoped to achieve these results, I shall be all the more at ease mentioning some regret as to the state of mind which at times prevailed in our discussions with regard to procedure. What took place in the last few days, the manner in which at least six important draft resolutions were left out of the discussions, constitutes a disquieting sign. I should be very happy if authoritative voices would point out the fact that no one has tried to stifle the discussions that have time and again been requested by well-meaning delegations.

178. My delegation would like to stress the fact that the Declaration of principles and the Programme of Action seem to make a very important contribution to the definition of a new international economic order, which we hope to see most sincerely very soon. For example, the preamble of the Declaration includes a very clear statement as to the spirit which henceforth will have to prevail in international economic relations. But this is also the case of many more concrete sections such as, for instance, those dealing with the organization of markets or the international division of labour.

179. With regard to a number of points, however, my delegation wishes to express a number of reservations and believes it is useful to explain how it interprets certain given provisions.

180. First of all, I shall of course confirm the reservations and the statements of interpretation made by the representative of the Federal Republic of Germany as the representative of a country which at present is exercising the presidency of the Council of the Community regarding, in particular, the paragraphs of the Programme of Action on general trade.

181. As to the Declaration of principles, the French delegation, with regard to paragraph 4(e) on the exercise of the right of nationalization, maintains the position which was explained on behalf of our Government as well as the other eight Governments of the countries members of the European Economic Community in the work done on the preparation of the Charter of Economic Rights and Duties of States.

182. Furthermore, the French delegation cannot associate itself with paragraph 4 (f).

183. With regard to the Programme of Action, my delegation would like to say the following.

184. In Section I, on "Fundamental problems of raw materials and primary commodities as related to trade and development", paragraph 1, "Raw materials", subparagraph (b), the French delegation has a reservation on the word "recovery".

185. In the same section, in connexion with paragraph 1(c) and (d). we feel like other States of the European Community, that suitable relations must be sought between the prices of exported goods and those of products imported by the developing countries. However, we believe that the establishment of a formal link between them would be difficult to achieve. We should also like to state that we feel that the role of producers' associa-

tions should be as it was defined in the Declaration on the Establishment of a New International Economic Order.

186. In paragraph 3, "General trade", the French delegation has a reservation on subparagraph (*a*) (xii), which, in our opinion, does not duly take into account the needs of economic development and it wishes to specify, with regard to subparagraph (*a*) (v), that we must take into account the social conditions flowing from the measures envisaged.

187. With regard to section II relating to the international monetary system and the financing of development, I wish to recall the fact that the French Government has always been in favour of a more active and wider participation of the developing countries in the international monetary system. We believe that, if most of the provisions envisaged in the Programme of Action go along the lines of this needed evolution, we must not prejudge the result of the work under way in the framework of the financial organizations. In the circumstances, my delegation has to make a general reservation on paragraph I of this section as a whole.

188. In section II, paragraph 2(*a*), the French delegation interprets the phrase "and even to exceed it" as the expression of an objective to be achieved, in so far as possible.

189. For reasons already expressed with regard to the international financial institutions, my delegation has to note its reservation on paragraph 2(*c*).

190. In connexion with paragraph 2(*g*), if we are to accept the idea of a renegotiation of debts on a case-by-case basis, my delegation feels that such measures should only accrue to the benefit of countries that find themselves in a crisis, and should not turn into solutions that would tend to ensure the automatic refinancing of debts.

191. In section IV, "Transfer of technology," the French delegation would have preferred, in subparagraph (*a*), to see the word "directives" rather than the expression "code of conduct," an expression which prejudges the results of the work currently under way in other organs of the United Nations system.

192. The French delegation is unable to take a position on section V, "Regulation and control over the activities of transnational corporations", until the studies currently being carried out in the United Nations have been completed.

193. With reference to section VII, "Promotion of co-operation among developing countries", it goes without saying that the reference in subparagraph (*e*) to existing international agreements must be understood as applying to the whole paragraph.

194. In section VIII, "Assistance in the exercise of permanent sovereignty of States over natural resources", the French delegation wishes, with respect to subparagraph (*a*), to refer to the reservation it has made in connexion with pragraph 4(*e*) of the Declaration.

195. As to subparagraph (*b*), in the view of the French delegation, the role of the United Nations is to assist the developing countries in defining and implementing their own development programmes, in strict respect for the procedures and decisions of competent bodies, and in the framework of programmes established by the countries concerned themselves.

196. With regard to section IX, on institutional arrangements, the French delegation has serious misgivings, from the standpoint of both legality and effectiveness, as to the possibility mentioned in paragraph 3(*b*) of the Economic and Social Council meeting on a permanent basis.

197. Paragraph 5 of the same section prompts the same reservation as the one we expressed in connexion with paragraphs 1 and 2(*c*) of section II.

198. Finally, in connexion with emergency measures, section X, the French Government believes that the Special Programme included in the Programme of Action is a very constructive contribution to the search for and implementation of solutions to benefit the most seriously affected countries. If, in view of the wide number of provisions and commitments in this programme, we do not consider ourselves bound by all these proposals, my Government, however, obviously confirms its readiness to participate in the activities of the international community to benefit those countries in the spirit just recalled by my German colleague on behalf of the European Economic Community and its member States.

199. The reservations and comments I have just voiced on the documents on which we have reached our consensus today in no way interfere with the satisfaction which I have referred to earlier in my statement. The principles which we have adopted, the action which we have agreed to undertake to the best of our ability, the assitance which we envisage giving, to the extent possible and as our own problems permit, are three elements of a policy which France will be glad to endorse in the same way as its European partners. The European Economic Community does not ignore the responsibilities stemming from its position in the areas of industry, agriculture and world trade. France, which is a member of that Community, plays a role in it, and guides its own action towards as constructive an effort as possible, welcomes the conclusion of this session as a positive and essential contribution to the new spirit of agreement and solidarity which is to prevail among our States.

The times make it necessary for this spirit to prevail, and it should exist as follows: first, a short-term concrete solidarity—that is to say, the implementation of emergency measures, in which, I repeat, France, as well as Europe, will participate, in spite of the fact that right now it is one of the countries most seriously affected by the present crisis—to be accompanied later by a more effective search for ways and means of preventing further crises and of controlling the present situation, while achieving a more equitable economic order in the context of the principles adopted today.

200. May I in conclusion recall the fact that France was the first to suggest that our Organization should deal with one of the most burning problems in the serious difficulties that occured last fall in the important sector of energy. That was the starting point, the first idea; but it needs to be followed up. The French delegation, in this connexion, has suggested certain practical procedures which we would not want to be forgotten.

201. I hope no one will take my last few words as criticism: we have concluded the most general part of our work, and thus perhaps the easiest of the tasks called for by the present imperfect economic situation. This imposes other, more concrete, and thus perhaps even more difficult tasks, and it would be highly desirable for our Organization to deal with them as soon as possible, in the spirit of dialogue which my country has untiringly advocated and always will.

202. Sir Laurence McINTYRE (Australia): In his statement from this podium on 22 April [*2224th meeting*], the Secretary of the Australian Department of Foreign Affairs, speaking on behalf of my Government, welcomed the initiative of President Boumediène of Algeria in asking that this special session be convened, and promised the fullest possible co-operation of the Australian Government in working towards the purposes of that initiative.

203. It has been an arduous special session of the General Assembly, as we all know. In recognizing the essential part that you yourself, Mr. President, have played in the direction of our work, I must also pay a full tribute to the unflagging, patient and ultimately successful efforts of the Ambassador of Iran to encourage many among us to work night and day, as he has said, to narrow the differences that inevitably existed when we assembled here on 9 April and to bring this session to a generally satisfactory conclusion.

204. There is no point in disguising the difficulties that a number of delegations have had in reaching the present substantial measure of agreement. Their difficulty has arisen over important questions of principle and equally important matters of substance. There will still be disappointments. No delegation is going to be fully satisfied with the results of the session. But this, after all, is what the United Nations is all about. Compromises and concessions have to be made, if the purposes of this Organization are to prosper, and compromises have been made in the course of the numerous discussions and consultations that we have had over the past few weeks. There was, nevertheless, unity from the beginning in the conviction that the special problems of the developing countries most gravely affected by current trends in the world economic situation were a matter of urgent and direct concern to all of us, and it has been this unanimous conviction that has enabled us to reach decisions and to agree upon targets to which my Government is able to subscribe—and I have in mind, not least of all, the special programme of emergency measures for the relief of the hardest-hit countries.

205. Like other delegations that have spoken tonight, my delegation has certain reservations about one aspect or another of the Declaration and the Programme of Action that we have now accepted, and these reservations I should like be allowed to state briefly.

206. Turning first of all to the Declaration contained in resolution 3201 (S-VI) let me first draw attention to its paragraph 4(*e*), which refers to the right of any country to full permanent sovereignty over its natural resource and its right of nationalization. My Government does not question either of these rights, but it is bound to interpret that paragraph to mean that any act of nationalization should be accompanied by lawful measures for prompt, effective and adequate compensation, as envisaged in resolution 1803 (XVII). Similarly, my Government would interpret the right referred to in paragraph 4(*f*) as a right to be exercised under law. With regard to paragraph 4(*s*) of the Declaration, Australia fully supports efforts by the developing countries to strengthen economic co-operation among themselves. We take it that where such efforts are made on a preferential basis full regard will be paid to other principles in the Declaration and to international obligations.

207. As for the Programme of Action in resolution 3202 (S-VI), my Government will do all it can to help in bringing about those changes that are desirable and necessary in the existing international economic order, while fully cognizant of those features of it that have been of benefit to all countries. In short, Australia's aim will be to ensure that existing arrangements continue to contribute to international co-operation and that, where appropriate, they are improved to reflect the needs of changing circumstances.

208. Again, as a producer and exporter of raw material and primary commodities, Australia is concerned to promote orderly marketing arrangements which take into account the interests of both producers and consumers. There is a place for improving and facilitating co-operation and consultation between producers of raw materials in their mutual and individual national interests, while taking into account the interests of con-

sumers, particularly those of consumer developing countries. In making these remarks, I have in mind especial-ly paragraph 1(c) of section I, dealing with producers' associations, and paragraph 3(a)(xi) of that section, dealing with buffer stocks.

209. As regards paragraphs 1 (d) and 3 (a)(viii). of section I, I must say that we have some doubts about the practicability or usefulness of seeking to establish prices for commodities either according to a general set of principles or through a link with the prices of manufacturers. Similarly, we have doubts about the practical ef-fectiveness of paragraph 3 (a)(vi), on the matter of reimbursement of duties and losses on imports from developing countries, and paragraph 3 (a)(xii) of section I, on investment in the manufacture of synthetics.

210. We interpret paragraph 3(b) of section I of resolution 3202 (S-VI) and paragraph 4(n) of resolution 3201 (S-VI), concerning preferences and non-reciprocity, in the context of the Tokyo Declaration on the multilateral trade negotiations. IMF is at present reviewing the formula for calculation of fund quotas, which *inter alia* determine voting patterns. We should on the whole have preferred that this review be completed before the General Assembly made any pronouncement on this subject. Hence we have reservations about paragraph 1(g) of section II of resolution 3202 (S-VI) and we also have reservations of a similar nature about paragraph 2(c) of the same section.

211. Let me conclude by saying that, notwithstanding these individual points on which we are not entirely happy, my delegation has been able to accept both resolutions in the document before us, whose urgent pur-poses Australia supports and subscribes to and will do its utmost to translate into practical effect in full co-operation with the international community. I can assure this Assembly that the Australian response to the problems before us will be found, as in the past, to be forthcoming.

2230th Plenary Meeting, Thursday, May 2, 1974.

1. The PRESIDENT (interpretation from Spanish): This morning the General Assmbly will, as decided yesterday, continue to hear statements by representatives who have views to put forward.
...

13. Mr. DE PINES (Spain) (interpretation from Spanish): The delegation of Spain has stated its position on this question in the debate at the special session of the General Assembly [*2218th meeting*]. We welcome the conclusions and accept them, by and large.

14. The Declaration and the Programme of Action containing special emergency measures are, to our way of thinking, an important basis for this new international economic order, as the text which we adopted last night says.

15. My delegation cannot fail to state that, for my country, acceptance of paragraph 4(e) of the Declaration presupposes due respect for the rules of international law and recognition of jurisdiction under international law.

16. With regard to paragraph 4(t), we would like due account to be taken of the position of the countries which are consumers of raw materials, especially considering the efforts of those countries to develop and their need to ensure supplies in the future. This is based on a spirit of economic interdependence which has been stressed in the course of this session.

17. I also wish to state that we would have preferred different language for paragraph 1(e) of section VII of the Programme of Action. In our opinion, respect for existing agreements or agreements being negotiated is not made sufficiently clear. We are referring to agreements including countries which, like mine, are not yet fully developed.

18. We are particularly pleased to support urgent action to help the most needy countries and we made an appeal along these lines in the general debate.

19. Mr. PLAJA (Italy): The special session of the General Assembly has been convened to face a critical economic situation affecting all members of the international community and especially many among the developing countries. My delegation believes that the session has proved to be a remarkable effort of the world community to indicate ways and means to cope with the global problems with which it is confronted and to en-courage co-operation among Member States with a view to creating a more just, equitable and stable interna-tional economic order, taking into full account the new realities of today's world.

20. The Italian delegation has participated in this special session in a spirit of full and open-minded co-operation. It has been guided by an awareness of the close interdependence existing among all members of the world community, by the feeling that the interests of all countries are interrelated and that the well-being of one country cannot be dissociated from that of all the others. In this conception the Italian delegation has attached paramount importance to the necessity for the world community to take into due consideration the needs and

the expectations of the developing countries. The Italian Government is convinced that one of the historic tasks of our time is to try to close the gap between the rich and the poor, the "haves" and the "have nots". Not only economic and social progress is at stake here, but so also are peace and security themselves.

21. My delegation was also guided by the sincere desire to see urgent, concrete decisions reached in favour of those countries which have been most gravely affected by the present economic situation and which can be helped only by a major effort of the world community, as was so impressively underlined to us by the Secretary-General [*2207th meeting*] and several heads of delegations in the general debate.

22. The results we have achieved have required the strenuous efforts and the best skills of all those who have been engaged in our difficult negotiations. Special gratitude is due in this respect to you, Mr. President, for presiding so capably over our debates, and my delegation wishes to express particular praise of, and thanks to, the Chairman of the *Ad Hoc* Committee, Ambassador Hoveyda. It is no exaggeration to say that without his most brilliant performance and untiring efforts these results would not have been possible.

23. In the tremendous task with which the special session has been confronted, it is understandable that specific aspects of the documents that we have been called upon to decide call for different interpretations and reservations. Like other delegations, the Italian delegation has its own. They are based in general, firstly, on our belief that provisions contained in resolutions and declarations adopted by the Assembly have to be in accordance with the spirit and letter of the United Nations Charter and with international law; secondly, on our opinion that action of the Assembly should encourage, and not prejudge, activities which, on the matters dealt with by this Assembly, are already under way in or fall within the competence of other institutions of the United Nations system or other multilateral forums; and, thirdly, on the conviction that the best way to serve the purposes that have prompted the convening of this session is to be inspired by some spirit of realism and by the necessity of taking full account of the institutional orders and the economic and social systems on which the States Members of this Organization are based.

24. The representative of the Federal Republic of Germany, in his capacity as representative of the country that is currently occupying the presidency of the European Economic Community, has indicated [*2229th meeting*] the points in the documents I have mentioned which call for reservation on the part of the Community as such. My delegation has considerations it wants to express on some other points also.

25. First, I shall comment on the Declaration on the Establishment of a New International Order.

26. With regard to paragraph 4(*e*), relating to sovereignty over natural resources and economic activities, the Italian Government has constantly asserted the right of each State to exercise permanent sovereignty over its resources and economic activities. At the same time, with reference to nationalization, it has constantly maintained that this right must be exercised in accordance with the rules of international law. I should also like to recall the views expressed by the Italian delegation in the Working Group on the Charter on Economic Rights and Duties of States, a Group to whose activities we attach particular importance. I therefore confirm that the Italian delegation interprets this point in the light of these views.

27. With regard to paragraph 4(*t*) of the Declaration, relating to raw-materials producers' associations, the Italian delegation approves the concept of co-operation as appearing in the text and therefore interprets this subparagraph as implying that co-operation will be a basic aim of these associations.

28. Secondly, with regard to the Programme of Action, the Italian delegation believes that a programme was certainly due and desirable at this time. But many points of the text before us required, in my delegation's opinion, more careful consideration. As a matter of fact, the Italian delegation has been able to concur in the procedures of adopting it in the conviction that the formula adopted means that the elements the programme contains are going to be discussed and developed in future in the appropriate international forums, being but an indication on which to work in order to define the best action to establish the new, more equitable and stable economic order we are striving for.

29. My delegation's comments on specific points of the Programme of Action are as follows.

30. Regarding section I, paragraph 1(*d*), we wonder whether a link between prices such as the one mentioned in the last sentence of this paragraph is really feasible in practice.

31. Regarding section I, paragraph 3 in general, this provision, in my delegation's opinion, does not take into sufficient consideration the particular situation of free-market-economy countries or the fact that in a democratic country limitations on the economic activity of its citizens can be imposed only by law. This applies particularly to paragraph 3(*a*) (xii) and paragraph 4(*b*) and (*d*). With regard to the latter, I should like to recall that Italy had to abstain in the vote on the convention for a code of conduct for liner conferences.

32. Regarding section II, paragraph I(*c*), relating to the guarantee of the real value of the currency reserves of the developing countries, my delegation believes that this is a worthy aim which is very difficult to attain; it has been and still is, especially today, pursued by all countries in the world without finding until now any really effective remedy.

33. Regarding section II, paragraph 2(*a*), relating to the implementation of the Second United Nations Development Decade, I interpret it of course having in mind the three reservations formulated by the Italian delegation at the moment of the adoption of the International Development Strategy for the Second Development Decade.*

34. Section II, paragraph 2(*d*) presents some difficulties for my delegation in its present form owing to the well-known world situation regarding capital movements.

35. With regard to section III, subparagraph (*a*), the Italian delegation feels that the response to the request for financing of industrial projects in developing countries should be given by all countries within their respective contributing capacity.

36. Notwithstanding the observations I have made, and some other doubts the Italian delegation had, my delegation joined in the procedure of adoption of the Declaration and of the Programme of Action. This is meant to be a sincere contribution to our joint efforts to proceed in the constructive dialogue to pave the way for the continuation of a positive process in which all of us will make substantial, speedy progress towards the new international economic order we hope for. I can assure the Assembly that my country will continue to base its participation in this process on the most open spirit of co-operation and on the earnest desire to attain our common objective.

37. Mr. SAITO (Japan): I wish to pay a tribute to the high degree of seriousness with which Member States have sought to find solutions for the problems confronting the world. Since the special session began three weeks ago, every delegation without exception has strenuously worked to devise effective answers to the problems of raw materials and development.

38. The direct responsibility for working out these answers was assigned to our *Ad Hoc* Committee, and we were extremely fortunate to have Mr. Hoveyda of Iran as its Chairman. Mr. Hoveyda worked untiringly not only as the Committee's presiding officer but also in private discussions to achieve solutions which would meet the needs of all our membership.

39. My delegation has done what it could to help solve these world problems through dialogue and co-operation.

40. My delegation would like to express satisfaction that the efforts made by all delegations culminated in the recommendations by the *Ad Hoc* Committee contained in document A/9556, which have now been adopted without a vote. The text is the outcome of a very serious debate in which a co-operative spirit was shown by all parties. My delegation welcomes the adoption of the Declaration. Here we wish to make the following statements.

41. My Government recognizes the principle of permanent sovereignty over natural resources. We believe that this right must be exercised in accordance with international law.

42. The Government of Japan fully recognizes the need to improve the terms of trade of developing countries. However, we consider that it is difficult to reach a workable and comprehensive solution of this question through an approach based on relationships between the prices of various products, which are most complex.

43. In order to promote the economic development of developing countries, Japan is determined to make sincere efforts to provide special and more favourable treatment to the developing countries in economic co-operation, where this is feasible and appropriate.

44. With regard to the Programme of Action—except section X—my delegation would have abstained if a vote had been taken on it. For the reasons already stated in the *Ad Hoc* Committee and in the Working Party meetings, my delegation has difficulties, particularly with the following paragraphs and subparagraphs. Please allow me to mention only the paragraph numbers without explanation: section I, paragraph 1(*c*), (*d*) and (*f*), paragraph 3(*a*) and (*b*), and paragraph 4(*b*) and (*d*); section II, paragraph 1(*a*), (*e*), (*f*) and (*g*) and paragraph 2(*c*), (*d*), (*f*) and (*g*); section IV, subparagraphs (*a*) and (*d*); section VII, paragraph 1(*a*); section VIII; and section IX, paragraph 5.

45. With regard to section X of the Programme of Action, namely, the Special Programme, my delegation supports it fully, and has the following observations to make on it.

46. With regard to paragraph 1, it is the view of my delegation that the Special Programme should be devoted to immediate relief measures for the most seriously affected developing countries and, accordingly, that it should be operative only for the period of time necessary to provide such immediate relief.

47. My delegation wishes to state that the Special Fund, which is a part of the Special Programme, should aim at providing immediate relief for the most seriously affected developing countries.

48. As to paragraph 3, my delegation wishes to repeat our understanding, based on informal consultations

---

*See *Official Records of the General Assembly, Twenty-fifth Session, Annexes,* agenda item 42, document A/8124/Add.1.

with delegations from developing countries, that it will be at the discretion of each Member State to select the measures it will implement and the extent to which it will implement them.

49. As for the specific formulation of some of the measures, my delegation has particular views in the light of the position it has maintained and of the circumstances in which my country finds itself.

50. As regards subparagraph (f) of the first preambular paragraph and paragraph 3 of the Special Programme, my delegation considers that a careful examination should be made by the developed countries of the extent to which each of them will be able to provide assistance, taking into consideration that the effects of the recent economic crisis on the economies of developed countries differ from one country to another.

51. My delegation also entertains difficulties with regard to paragraph 8.

52. The spirit of co-operation, as well as concepts embodied in the Tokyo Declaration on multilateral trade relations,* should be maintained. In all examinations of these questions, both multilaterally and bilaterally, the Government of Japan will neglect no opportunity to help solve problems which involve the welfare and prosperity of the world. It will also continue to implement the policy measures contained in the International Development Strategy as accepted by it.

53. I wish to conclude by stating the fundamental position of the Government of Japan with regard to action to mitigate the difficulties of those developing countries most seriously affected by the current crisis.

54. The recent economic changes have had enormous impact on the world economy, and it is the belief of my Government that this problem can be solved only through international solidarity and co-operation in these days of interdependency.

55. Japan, which is heavily dependent upon other countries for raw materials, has been harder hit than any other developed country. However, my Government has fully recognized the necessity for emergency relief measures for the most seriously affected developing countries, and hopes that a concrete plan for a fund, to be operated effectively in a very practical international framework, can be formulated. To this end, my Government is ready to participate in the examination of a plan in co-operation with other countries concerned and with the related international organizations. When an internationally acceptable plan has been formulated, the Government of Japan intends to make the greatest possible contribution, taking into full account the urgent character of such a fund, provided that other countries possessing the capability also do so.

56. Mr. KAUFMANN (Netherlands): The Netherlands delegation has whole-heartedly joined the consensus on the two principal documents of this special session of the General Assembly on the problems of raw materials and development: the Declaration and the Programme of Action.

57. My delegation is particularly gratified that, despite the limited time available, it has been possible, through the strenuous efforts of all concerned, to come to this consensus. I should like to pay a tribute in particular to the Chairman of the *Ad Hoc* Committee, Ambassador Hoveyda, whose untiring activities have contributed so much to the results achieved.

58. The consensus reflects the importance of the special session as a momentous step forward towards the establishment of a new international economic order, based on interdependence and equity. This new international economic order cannot be established in a single special session. The Programme of Action, in particular, contains a large number of actions which will require efforts by all concerned. My delegation recognizes that the statement, repeatedly found in the Programme of Action, that "all efforts should be made" is an important element of the consensus we have achieved. My delegation wishes to emphasize that this statement is not applicable in all respects. My Government sincerely hopes that the consensus now reached will form the solid basis for our future efforts; and as we see it, these efforts should culminate in and converge towards the special session of the General Assembly in 1975. As the Netherlands Minister for Foreign Affairs, Mr. van der Stoel, stated during the general debate at this special session:

"Between today and September 1975 we have the historic opportunity to lay the foundations of a new system of international economic co-operation." [*2212th meeting, para. 20.*]

59. I shall now address myself to a number of specific points in the Declaration and the Programme of Action.

60. First, with respect to paragraph 4(f) of the Declaration, the Netherlands Government is of the opinion that the application of that paragraph should be considered on a case-by-case basis.

61. Second, with respect to the Programme of Action, section I, paragraph 1(b), the Netherlands delegation has to reserve its position on the inclusion of the word "recovery."

62. Third, with respect to paragraph 1(d) of the same section, the Netherlands can accept the principle con-

---

*Declaration of 14 September 1973, approved by the Ministerial Meeting of the Contracting Parties to the General Agreement on Tariffs and Trade held in Tokyo.

tained therein, but wishes to express the view that the relationship between the prices of exports of developing countries and the prices of their imports should relate to imports from any source.

63. Fourthly, regarding section I, paragraph 4(*d*), on the implementation of the code of conduct for liner conferences, my delegation wishes to recall the Netherlands abstention in the vote that took place on this matter on 6 April 1974, at the conclusion of the United Nations Conference of Plenipotentiaries on a Code of Conduct for Liner Conferences. At that Conference the Netherlands delegation stated that we consider the outcome of that Conference as contrary to its main purpose, namely, the creation of improved conditions for developing countries both with regard to development of their liner shipping and with regard to the transport of their trade. However, the Netherlands Government remains convinced of the desirability of unilateral preferences for developing countries in the field of liner shipping; this conviction will be reflected in the Netherlands shipping policy with regard to developing countries.

64. Fifth, as regards section VIII, subparagraph (*b*), the Netherlands Government considers that the assistance referred to in that subparagraph does not imply financing of compensation in cases of nationalization.

65. Of course, my delegation wishes to associate itself fully with the remarks made, on behalf of the European Community, by the representative of the Federal Republic of Germany [*2229th meeting*].

66. To conclude, my delegation wishes to stress that the Netherlands Government is ready to consider contributing to the proposed Special Programme as contained in section X of the Programme of Action. The Netherlands Government, moreover, has already initiated certain re-arrangements in its development co-operation programme in order to make funds available for immediate relief to the most seriously affected developing countries.

67. Mr. ELIASHIV (Israel): I should like to state, in respect of the documents which were adopted in this Assembly last night, that they contain a number of points on which my delegation has reservations.

68. Mr. TEMPLETON (New Zealand): New Zealand has from the outset recognized the need for positive and constructive action on the urgent problems which led to the summoning of this special session. Therefore my delegation welcomes the very wide measure of agreement that has been reached in regard to the Declaration on the Establishment of a New International Economic Order and the Programme of Action, including the Special Programme of emergency measures. The spirit of compromise which enabled a consensus to be achieved on the two principal documents before us augurs well for their effective implementation.

69. We regard these documents in their present form as essentially hortatory in character. We should have liked in particular to see a more detailed examination of the terms of the Programme of Action. We regard the documents also as subject to accepted norms of international law, wherever these may be applicable. It has been our concern throughout the Assembly to help prepare the ground for a more effective co-operation in international economic affairs. It is our hope and belief that these documents will achieve that purpose.

70. At the same time, my delegation must record its keen disappointment that the proposal it sponsored together with Sri Lanka for the establishment of a fertilizer pool [*see A/9556, para. 10*] was not immediately adopted at this session. This proposal was especially designed as a quick-acting emergency measure to help those developing countries which are short of fertilizer and short of food and which are also short of money to pay for the fertilizer they must import. I understand that the proposal has been welcomed by the Director-General of the Food and Agriculture Organization [*FAO*] and that he stands ready to call an emergency session of the FAO Council to put into effect a plan for the operation of the pool. My Government has indicated willingness to make a substantial cash contribution, and we have every reason to believe that other Governments are prepared to consider contributing to the scheme, either in money or in fertilizer.

71. My delegation is, therefore, very concerned at the possibility that the time-table for giving effect to the proposal may be subject to delay. I scarcely need to emphasize that it is not New Zealand, but the peoples of those countries hardest hit by shortages of food and fertilizer, that will suffer from every day's delay in putting the scheme into operation.

72. It is our understanding, arising from the discussion in the *Ad Hoc* Committee of its recommendation to the Assembly on this matter, that the Economic and Social Council would be requested to give expeditious consideration to the proposal of New Zealand and Sri Lanka at its current session. Should it do so, this would permit the emergency session of the FAO Council to be called in accordance with the time-table envisaged by the Director-General.

73. My delegation has heard no objection of substance to the proposal of New Zealand and Sri Lanka as set out in its revised form in paragraph 10 of document A/9556. We believe that, in fact, there exists a consensus in favour of the proposal. It is in the hope and expectation that the Economic and Social Council will give prompt effect to it now that we have decided to refer it to that body.

74. Mr. KENNEDY (Ireland): Mr. President, as this special session of the General Assembly moves today

towards its successful conclusion, I should like, on behalf of the Irish delegation, to congratulate you on the most able manner in which you have guided our deliberations. It has been an arduous task, in which your wise and influential counsel, reflecting the important role of your country and of Latin America in the United Nations, has been of the greatest significance for the success of our common task.

75. We in the Irish delegation have been greatly encouraged by the substantial progress that has been achieved. In a spirit of consensus, we have all tried here not only to reach a rapid understanding of the urgent needs of the developing world in the present crisis but also to map out a course of longer-term work and study for the achievement of a new international economic order, which the mutually interdependent interests of all our countries demand. Here—since we were unable to do so in the *Ad Hoc* Committee—my delegation would also like to pay a special tribute to its Chairman, Ambassador Hoveyda, whose patience, sense of humor and readiness to search at all hours for the acceptable compromise were so boundless that he has aroused our envious admiration.

76. These efforts and the good-will of the negotiating parties have given us the Declaration on the Establishment of a New International Economic Order. Its historic importance would alone have justified the initiative of President Boumediène of Algeria in convening this special session, and the Declaration is rightly described in its concluding paragraph as "one of the most important bases of economic relations between all peoples and all nations".

77. The spirit of co-operation of this special session has also led to our dealing, in the positive and concrete manner set out in the Special Programme in section X of the Programme of Action, with the grave problems of those developing countries which are the most seriously affected by the current economic crisis. My Government will take an active part in the efforts of the European Economic Community to alleviate, in a practical way, those urgent and pressing problems now facing so many Member States. As you are aware, Mr. President, the delegation of the Federal Republic of Germany has already repeated, last evening, on behalf of the other eight States members of the Community, including, of course, Ireland, that the Community is prepared to make a substantial contribution to assist those developing countries most seriously affected by the current economic crisis, provided, of course, that the other members of the community of nations were also willing to play their part.

78. Of course, we all realize, developing and developed countries alike, the many complex and difficult issues that have to be dealt with in planning our future action in order to implement the Declaration of Principles. Perhaps it was too much to hope that we could have achieved more than we did in the relatively short period of time available to this special session. Nevertheless, significant and encouraging progress was made. That progress was assisted in no small measure by the constructive contribution of the Group of 77 developing countries to the drafting of the final text of the Programme of Action, which was accepted by consensus. It is clear that the work must continue in other bodies, especially in the agencies within our United Nations system. We welcome the progress which has been made but at the same time we must make it clear that there still remain, in the Programme of Action, elements which, in their present form, need some further negotiation before they can become fully acceptable to my delegation. Our position on these issues was made clear during the negotiation meetings of the current session. I should also like, of course, to recall in this connexion that the delegation of the Federal Republic of Germany, speaking on behalf of the nine member States of the Community last evening, has already made a concise statement on behalf of all of us in the Community in this regard.

79. May I say, in conclusion, that the consensus which has been achieved in this special session constitutes a very real encouragement for the future. For it has given us reason to hope that we can achieve here in the United Nations a genuine international solidarity on those fundamental problems with which this General Assembly has had to deal. This, of course, is only the beginning—we are only commencing to create a new international economic order. The hard work must continue long after the speeches are over. But I can assure you, Mr. President, that my Government will co-operate fully in the work which this special session has set in motion and which has been well described in paragraph 6 of the Declaration of principles itself as the "creation of better conditions for all peoples to reach a life worthy of human dignity."

80. Mr. ARVESEN (Norway): My Government had great hopes for this General Assembly and was determined, in constructive and positive co-operation with all other countries, to work for concrete progress and a meaningful break-through towards the establishment of a new and improved economic order in the world.

81. We are therefore pleased to note that it has been possible to elaborate a Declaration on the Establishment of a New International Economic Order, a Declaration which my Government accepts.

82. Furthermore, we support fully the Special Programme of emergency measures which has been agreed upon. With regard to the rest of the Programme of Action, my delegation endorses its main objectives. However, the Programme of Action is a very comprehensive document which, it must be admitted, we have not

had sufficient time to discuss fully. There are a few paragraphs in the Programme of Action that contain concepts and formulations which cause some difficulties for my delegation. My Government is, consequently, not in a position to commit itself at this point with regard to these concepts and formulations. I am referring *inter alia,* as an example, to section I, paragraph 3(*a*)(vi) under the heading "General trade."

83. As regards the provisions of section I, paragraph 4 under the heading "Transportation and insurance", we are *inter alia*, asked to ensure the implementation of the code of conduct for liner conferences. At the recently concluded United Nations Conference in Geneva on this matter, Norway submitted proposals, which, while preserving the multilateral character of international shipping, would have given preferences to developing countries. These proposals were not accepted and the code which emerged from that Conference introduces, in our opinion, the unfortunate principle of bilateralism. My Government's position with regard to these issues remains unchanged.

84. However, as I stated at the outset of my intervention, Norway subscribes to the main objectives of the Programme of Action.

85. My Government for one, is particularly pleased to accept the results arrived at as the basis for further elaboration and implementation of a new international economic order, which will hopefully and eventually secure a more equitable distribution of income and wealth among the nations of the world, thus ensuring accelerated and sustained economic and social progress and development for the peoples of the third world.

. . .

92. Mr. JANKOWITSCH (Austria): My delegation welcomes the consensus which, after long and most difficult negotiations, has been reached on the main documents before this Assembly. In that connexion, may I address a special word of appreciation to the Chairman of the *Ad Hoc* Committee, Ambassador Hoveyda of Iran, for his dedicated efforts during the many hours of intensive consultations?

93. Austria regards yesterday's decision of the General Assembly as an expression of the political will of the international community to work together for the establishment of a more balanced and just world economic order.

94. The Austrian Federal Minister for Foreign Affairs has in his statement in the general debate [*2224th meeting*] already outlined my Government's position on a number of basic issues which now form the subject of the Declaration and the Programme of Action. I can therefore limit my remarks on those documents to the following observations.

95. Concerning the Declaration on the Establishment of a New International Economic Order, my delegation interprets its provisions, particularly the principles enumerated in its paragraph 4, as applicable under the Charter of the United Nations and international law.

96. As to the Programme of Action, my delegation is pleased to see that agreement has been reached on a Special Programme in favour of the developing countries most seriously affected by recent economic events.

97. The Programme of Action, as its Introduction rightly states, is of "unprecedented scope." Its best hope of realization rests on maximum economic co-operation and understanding among States. In responding to this challenge and subscribing to the broad aims of the Programme, my delegation has overcome a number of serious reservations on a number of its provisions. Some of those reservations were met in the course of our deliberations, while others still prevail.

98. In referring specifically to some of our reservations, I wish to make the following comments.

99. We hold the view that in pursuing the objectives set out in section I, paragraphs 1(*c*) and (*d*), due account will have to be taken of the legitimate interests of both producers and consumers of raw materials and other goods. Only thus will there be a chance to maintain equitable and stable prices, on the one hand, and a continuous and orderly supply for consumers, on the other.

100. While fully subscribing to the necessity to explore all possible avenues to provide developing countries with additional resources to meet their development requirements, my delegation entertains considerable doubts as to the viability and practicability of the concept contained in paragraph 3(*a*) (vi) of section I of the Programme of Action.

101. As to matters of general trade, and in particular the ongoing multilateral trade negotiations, my Government's position was outlined by the Austrian Federal Minister of Trade in his statement at the Ministeral Meeting of the Contracting Parties to the General Agreement on Tariffs and Trade in September 1973 in Tokyo, and is based upon the Declaration adopted at that meeting.

102. As far as paragraph 2 of section II is concerned, Austria, within the limits of its financial and budgetary possibilities, will continue to make every effort to increase its assistance to developing countries.

103. In making these observations I wish to stress, however, that they will in no way affect the willingness of my country to join in the common effort which has now been launched by this Assembly.

104. But our work has only begun. I am confident that whatever the forum it will be conducted in a spirit of

understanding of new economic relationships as they emerged in the course of our debate. That awareness of a new phase of economic interdependence will prove to be indispensable if the documents adopted at this special session are to become, as we hope they will, the basis for a more stable economic and social order in peace and justice for all peoples of this world.

. . .

115. Mr. MEGALOKONOMOS (Greece): The Greek delegation has, from the very beginning, supported wholeheartedly the proposal of the developing countries to convene the sixth special session of the General Assembly.

116. Consequently, we welcome with great satisfaction the adoption by the General Assembly of both the Declaration of principles and the Program of Action on the Establishment of a New International Economic Order, which, we are sure, will mark a milestone on the road towards the betterment of human conditions and international relations.

117. Nevertheless, it is only natural that, in a text of such importance and extent, any country might have some remarks and reservations to make. The main reservations under which my delegation accepted the Declaration of Principles and the Programme of Action are the following.

118. Concerning the Declaration and particularly paragraph 4(e), the Greek delegation recognizes fully the permanent sovereignty of every country over its natural resources and economic activities. It believes, nevertheless, that the right to nationalize should be closely interlinked with the obligation to provide prompt, real and equitable compensation, especially when the nationalization aims at small or medium-sized enterprises, in order not to deprive their owners of their sole means of existence.

119. As far as the Programme of Action is concerned, the Greek delegation would like to express the following reservation on section I, paragraph 4(a). We consider that the objectives of that subparagraph, "to promote an increasing and equitable participation of developing countries in the world shipping tonnage", should be implemented through the adoption of such measures as may be appropriate to permit free competition in the international freight market. To be more specific, those measures must respect the principle of the freedom of transactions in the maritime trade, as well as the need to safeguard both legitimate and fair competition and the freedom for everyone to choose the means of transportation of his preference.

120. We would like also to state that, as far as the phrase in paragraph 4(b) is concerned, "to arrest and reduce . . . freight rates" is generally desirable for both developed and developing countries. But, in a free-market system, freight rates depend essentially on the law of supply and demand, and it would be unrealistic to consider possible that any international agreement could modify this basic truth. On the other hand, we should not forget that in times of declining economic activity, quite often shipping operates at a loss in the expectation that world trade will resume its upward trend.

121. With regard to paragraph 4(d), we feel that the code of conduct for liner conferences should be implemented in such a way as not to hamper the free flow of international trade and particularly the transportation of raw materials and food-stuffs. For this reason the code of conduct should take into account the availability and general conditions of shipping.

122. My delegation's last reservation refers to section VII, paragraph 1(e). The first sentence of this paragraph concerns the treatment accorded by developing countries to imports from developed and developing countries. My delegation's reservation consists in the need to condition this disposition to the obligations and rights resulting from already existing international agreements. It is therefore without prejudice to those international agreements that this provision will be applied by my country.

123. The Greek delegation would like to add that Greece welcomes warmly the Special Programme in section X, including emergency measures to mitigate the difficulties of the developing countries most seriously affected by economic crisis. Although now approaching the threshold of industrialization, Greece is to be considered among the European developing countries and it therefore attaches great importance to the system of preferences between developed and developing countries. Greece has had the experience of advancing during the last 30 years, step by step, from the stage of despair resulting from destruction to the stage of hope for reconstruction. This is why we fully realize how long the process of development is and how great the role of assistance from developed countries can prove to be. This is why we are today in a position to appreciate especially the new economic order adopted by this Assembly. The inauguration of a new era in the relations between developing and developed countries which, if implemented with goodwill, if based on the respect of mutual obligations and rights, and if covered with international credibility, will mark, we are sure, a new dawn for the United Nations and for mankind in general.

124. Mr. ISAKSEN (Denmark): Let me at the outset state that my delegation shares the sentiments that the adoption by consensus of a Declaratation on the Establishment of a New International Economic Order and a Programme of Action, including a Special Programme for the developing countries most seriously affected by

the economic crisis, is an important event in the history of the United Nations. This is the first time that the United Nations has taken up in its General Assembly the whole spectrum of economic problems. Seen in this light, it is a great encouragement that this special session has demonstrated a common willingness to deal with the economic questions which are confronting the whole of mankind.

125. The deliberations on the questions raised in the documents now adopted do not end with the closing of this special session. We will certainly have to deal with these problems not only in coming sessions of the General Assembly and especially at the special session to be convened in September 1975 but also in other organs within the United Nations framework.

126. Having said that, permit me on behalf of the Danish Government to make some comments on the documents which we adopted by consensus.

127. With reference to the Declaration, the progress achieved during the very extensive negotiations under the able guidance of Ambassador Hoveyda has removed the necessity for my delegation to make specific reservations to the text. This does not mean that we can fully subscribe to the formulation of all paragraphs in the Declaration, and I should like in particular to explain the Danish position on three paragraphs.

128. First, with regard to paragraph 4(e) of the Declaration, my Government fully supports the principle of permanent sovereignty of every State over its natural resources. We also acknowledge the right of any State to nationalize such resources. We therefore have no objection to the wording of the subparagraph as it stands. As to the question of compensation, the basic criterion should, in our view, be the principle of prompt, complete and effective compensation. We recognize, however, that in practice a solution will often have to be found in a compromise between conflicting interests. Settlement of disputes in this regard which are not solved within national jurisdiction should in all cases be made through arbitration or international adjudication.

129. Secondly, we should have preferred a different wording in paragraph 4(j) concerning the relationship between the prices of the different categories of goods exported and imported by developing countries. Our preference would have been a text which made it clear that the prices should be profitable to producers and fair to consumers and that the aim should be to bring about satisfying terms of trade and the expansion of the world economy.

130. Thirdly, while recognizing that an improvement was made as regards the formulations concerning associations of producers, my delegation feels that the text would have been further improved by a reference to the equally important interests of producers and consumers.

131. The Programme of Action really falls into two separate parts: a first part which I might call the Programme of Action proper and another part containing the emergency measures to be taken to mitigate the difficulties of the developing countries most seriously affected by the economic crisis.

132. Concerning the Programme of Action proper, it would serve no purpose to conceal the fact that there are a number of paragraphs where it has not been possible to find a wording which is acceptable to my delegation. This is not surprising, however, when one realizes that the Programme of Action contains a catalogue of nearly all the economic questions which the different United Nations bodies have dealt with for the last 10 years. The closing of the special session would definitely not be the right time to repeat all Danish positions on the questions raised in the Programme of Action proper which over the years have been stated in the General Assembly, in the United Nations Conference on Trade and Development [UNCTAD], in IMF, in the Working Group on the Charter of Economic Rights and Duties of States and so on. In the future work on the questions raised in the Programme of Action these positions will be our point of departure.

133. Some of the elements in the Declaration of principles which I touched upon earlier are repeated in the Programme of Action. That being so, my earlier comments also cover the Programme of Action.

134. Furthermore, last night the Ambassador of the Federal Republic of Germany made a number of observations on behalf of the European Economic Community and thus also on behalf of Denmark.

135. Against this, I shall limit myself to a reservation on paragraph 4 of section I, concerning transportation and insurance. My Government is in complete sympathy with the wishes of the developing countries to minimize their freight expenditures. We cannot, however, comply with a request to ensure an early implementation of the code of conduct for liner conferences. We feel that this convention will not lead to lower costs but on the contrary will involve higher freight rates, less efficient service and, in general, create increased inconvenience to all.

136. Finally, I should like to turn to the last part of the Programme of Action concerning the Special Programme in favour of the most affected countries. My delegation realizes that many of the developing countries need immediate assistance to overcome their present situation. In recognition of this, the Community and its member States, including Denmark, have declared that they are prepared to make a substantial contribution, provided other members of the community of nations are willing to join them.

137. As to my country's possibility of making contributions beyond this initiative and over and above our

present level of assistance, I shall limit myself to referring to the remarks made by the Danish Minister for Foreign Affairs during the general debate [*2218th meeting*] when he spoke about the future scope of the Danish development assistance programme.

138. May I add that the Danish delegation has noted with satisfaction that the Special Programme foresees the full utilization of the services and facilities of existing international organizations in the operation of the Special Fund.

2231st Plenary Meeting, Thursday, May 2, 1974.

. . .

29. Mr. RICHARD (United Kingdom): We are now very near the end of this very important special session of the General Assembly, and as far as my delegation is concerned we think it is perhaps time for us to try and assess where we now are and what exactly we have achieved in the last four weeks.

30. On the face of it, we have reached a consensus. May I say how much I agreed with Mr. Bouteflika this morning [*2230th meeting*] when he used, I thought, very wise words to this Assembly, and indeed, to the world, when he said consensus is not unanimity. Perhaps what we have achieved could better be described as a collective acquiescence in most of the two documents before us. We have avoided confrontation, we have avoided a vote, and to that extent we are together. But it would be wrong for anyone to assume that the avoidance of a vote is necessarily the same thing as total agreement. My Government has serious reservations on parts of these documents, and our agreement to the procedure we have adopted is, as I made clear yesterday at the 21st meeting of the *Ad Hoc* Committee, without prejudice to those views. As the newly appointed representative of a new Government in Britain which is committed to the strengthening of this Organization—and also, may I say, as a representative making his maiden speech from this rostrum—I should like, if I might, to clarify my Government's position.

31. May I first of all, Mr. President, pay a public tribute to you for the skill and good humour with which you have presided over our proceedings. May I also join in the very well deserved tributes which have been paid to Ambassador Hoveyda, who has worked so hard to achieve this result?

32. From the outset the United Kingdom welcomed the timely initiative of the President of Algeria. The world we knew had changed and we, together with others, shared President Boumediène's desire that the United Nations should give shape and direction to this new age of economic interdependence. Before the session started, therefore, we made several efforts to launch a detailed dialogue which we believed to be essential if we were going to succeed. In doing so we emphasized that new approaches were required. We stressed our collective responsibility for guiding our debates towards partnership and towards co-operation and away from the divergence and the discord which have characterized so much of the past. We agree that the new order which has to be achieved must be not only one in which the developing world will emerge economically but also one in which those countries come to play their proper and rightful role in international decision-making. That means change, but we at least came to this session in what we believed to be a genuine and a realistic attempt to face the new realities as we saw them and to try to assure our collective future. The debate in the plenary Assembly was wide-ranging, serious and constructive. The theme of interdependence and co-operation became the keynote for this session. A break-through indeed seemed close. And yet, at the end of the day now, the result is not a total success despite the very considerable measure of agreement that has been reached.

33. I do not propose to go back over the last three weeks and analyse every turn that our discussions took. I will come straight to what I see as the core of the problem. The Assembly will, I know, expect me to speak frankly on these matters. They are much too important for me to do otherwise.

34. In all honesty, I think the main problem we have to face here is a difference of views on what the concept of economic interdependence should mean in practice. This divergence has been symbolized by the fact that the drafting of a general declaration of principles caused little difficulty, but when we went on to the details of the Programme of Action we immediately ran into serious problems. In brief, I think the difference is this. Some see our future interdependence in terms of the relative strengths of various groupings of interest—developed countries versus developing countries, producers of commodities versus their consumers, and so on. Others put co-operation and partnership first, not envisaging a balance of economic forces but rather—to use an expression which emerged in the Economic and Social Council last year—a collective economic security. As a result of that divergence we were faced with the task of trying in three weeks to negotiate and agree on a document which sometimes looked more like a catalogue of every possible remedy that has ever been advocated for every conceivable economic ill. In the circumstances, it is remarkable that we made the progress that we did, but it is not surprising that we could not really finish in the time that was available.

35. May I turn now to the three main aspects of our work, and first to the Declaration of principles. We support that Declaration because we endorse its broad approach and particularly its commitment to a new international economic order based on co-operative interdependence. We do not, however, interpret the Declaration

as in any way affecting international obligations in relation to States' sovereignty over natural resources, nor do we accept the apparent obligation for compensation referred to in paragraph 4(*f*), and I think it is very well known that we have great doubts about the practicability of price indexation.

36. The Programme of Action we found a less satisfactory document and one upon which we do have a number of major reservations which I would like to state briefly. May I say, first, that I recognize with deep appreciation the concession made in the negotiations which I turned this document from a Programme of Action into one which could more accurately be described as a statement of aims for possible future action. The British Government for its part will continue to work towards those many common goals on which agreement has been reached at this session. We will also continue to work towards solutions to the questions on which some difficulties inevitably remain.

37. I should perhaps emphasize that our inability to accept the Programme of Action in its entirety does not mean that we will not implement as much of it as we have been able to accept in the exhaustive discussions that we have had.

38. Turning to the specific reservations, with regard specifically to section I, paragraph 1(*a*), section VII, paragraph 1(*b*), and section VIII, subparagraph (*a*), of the Programme of Action, we accept, of course, the right of permanent sovereignty over natural resources. But we are not able to accept these subparagraphs in their present form since we believe that this right should only be exercised with due regard for international law.

39. With regard to section I, paragraph 1(*c*), I am afraid, in respect of that provision and also in respect of section VII, paragraph 1(*a*), we cannot agree that it is in the real interests of the expansion of the world economy to encourage the formation of what would be in effect producers' cartels. We still believe that successful economic relationships must hinge primarily on greater co-operation between producers and consumers.

40. With regard to section I, paragraph 1(*d*), as delegations will know, this is being studied at UNCTAD and we do not wish in a document of this sort to prejudge the results of those studies.

41. With regard to section I, paragraph 1(*e*), we find it difficult to believe that it is really in anybody's best interests actively to promote pricing arrangements which are unrealistic.

42. With regard to section I, paragraph 3(*a*) (viii) and (ix), we could not now enter into arrangements of that nature. Furthermore, this matter is already being considered in other international consultations. We feel that the inclusion of these paragraphs would prejudge that work.

43. With regard to section I, paragraph 4(*a*), (*b*) and (*d*), as is well known, we do not find ourselves able to accept the code of conduct for liner conferences, nor can we accept proposals which would involve the subsidizing of shipping.

44. Finally, with regard to section IV, under our existing official aid programme, the United Kingdom already provides significant assistance in the field of transfer of technology. Beyond this we do not accept that commercial transfers of technology should be on terms inconsistent with normal commercial practice.

45. I turn, finally, to the Special Programme in Section X, and particularly to the emergency measures. This special session was called at a time of very real economic difficulty for both developed and developing countries. But some developing ocuntries are suffering grievously, and in our view this was from the start of the Assembly, and still remains, the most urgent of the problems facing us. We therefore welcome the moves that have been made towards emergency relief. They are a concrete expression of the spirit of international co-operation with which my delegation approached this session. We cannot, however, commit ourselves unreservedly to all the recommendations in the document.

46. We should have preferred to see emergency aid directed through established international development institutions which already have the necessary machinery and the necessary expertise, but we do understand and recognize the desire of the developing countries for there to be a new channel under United Nations auspices. In this connexion, I would like to associate myself with the remarks of the Ambassador of the Federal Republic of Germany relating to the European Economic Community contribution to emergency help for the hardest hit countries [*2229th meeting*]. As he said, any contribution would be conditional on the willingness of others to participate.

47. I have felt it right to speak frankly about my delegation's reactions to these proceedings. This session has not achieved as much as we had hoped. Perhaps we all tried to do more than was possible in three weeks. But let us not end this session without recognizing what has in fact been achieved.

48. This session has made us all reassess our economic relationships. It has made many of the attitudes of the past irrelevant. I believe that this Assembly will, in later years, be seen as a turning-point: the United Nations is committing itself to a serious attempt to create a new world economic structure through the processes of rational discussion and orderly change. We have thus proclaimed the agenda of much of the international community's business for the next decade. Things will never be the same again.

49. I believe, too, that this session has done something else. It has demonstrated that the Members of the

United Nations need each other's understanding and help more than ever before. Whether we are developed or developing, whatever point of the compass we come from, the last three weeks have shown that it is only as partners and as equals that we can hope to make real progress.

. . .

B. Twenty-ninth Regular Session of the United Nations General Assembly:

1. Charter of Economic Rights and Duties of States

3281 (XXIX). Charter of Economic Rights and Duties of States

PREAMBLE

THE GENERAL ASSEMBLY,

Reaffirming the fundamental purposes of the United Nations, in particular the maintenance of international peace and security, the development of friendly relations among nations and the achievement of international co-operation in solving international problems in the economic and social fields,

Affirming the need for strengthening international co-operation in these fields,

Reaffirming further the need for strengthening international co-operation for development,

Declaring that it is a fundamental purpose of this Charter to promote the establishment of the new international economic order, based on equity, sovereign equality, interdependence, common interest and co-operation among all States, irrespective of their economic and social systems,

Desirous of contributing to the creation of conditions for:

(a) The attainment of wider prosperity among all countries and of higher standards of living for all peoples,

(b) The promotion by the entire international community of economic and social progress of all countries, especially developing countries,

(c) The encouragement of co-operation, on the basis of mutual advantage and equitable benefits for all peace-loving States which are willing to carry out the provisions of this Charter, in the economic, trade, scientific and technical fields, regardless of political, economic or social systems,

(d) The overcoming of main obstacles in the way of the economic development of the developing countries,

(e) The acceleration of the economic growth of developing countries with a view to bridging the economic gap between developing and developed countries,

(f) The protection, preservation and enhancement of the environment,

Mindful of the need to establish and maintain a just and equitable economic and social order through:

(a) The achievement of more rational and equitable international economic relations and the encouragement of structural changes in the world economy,

(b) The creation of conditions which permit the further expansion of trade and intensification of economic co-operation among all nations,

(c) The strengthening of the economic independence of developing countries,

(d) The establishment and promotion of international economic relations, taking into account the agreed differences in development of the developing countries and their specific needs,

Determined to promote collective economic security for development, in particular of the developing countries, with strict respect for the sovereign equality of each State and through the co-operation of the entire international community,

Considering that genuine co-operation among States, based on joint consideration of and concerted action regarding international economic problems, is essential for fulfilling the international community's common desire to achieve a just and rational development of all parts of the world,

Stressing the importance of ensuring appropriate conditions for the conduct of normal economic relations among all States, irrespective of differences in social and economic systems, and for the full respect for the rights of all peoples, as well as the strengthening of instruments of international economic co-operation as means for the consolidation of peace for the benefit of all,

Convinced of the need to develop a system of international economic relations on the basis of sovereign equality, mutual and equitable benefit and the close interrelationship of the interests of all States,

Reiterating that the responsibility for the development of every country rests primarily upon itself but that concomitant and effective international co-operation is an essential factor for the full achievement of its own development goals,

Firmly convinced of the urgent need to evolve a substantially improved system of international economic relations,

Solemnly adopts the present Charter of Economic Rights and Duties of States.

CHAPTER I

Fundamentals of international economic relations

Economic as well as political and other relations among States shall be governed, *inter alia*, by the following principles:

(a) Sovereignty, territorial integrity and political independence of States;

(b) Sovereign equality of all States;

(c) Non-aggression;

(d) Non-intervention;

(e) Mutual and equitable benefit;

(f) Peaceful coexistence;

(g) Equal rights and self-determination of peoples;

(h) Peaceful settlement of disputes;

(i) Remedying of injustices which have been brought about by force and which deprive a nation of the natural means necessary for its normal development;

(j) Fulfilment in good faith of international obligations;

(k) Respect for human rights and fundamental freedoms;

(l) No attempt to seek hegemony and spheres of influence;

(m) Promotion of international social justice;

(n) International co-operation for development;

(o) Free access to and from the sea by land-locked countries within the framework of the above principles.

CHAPTER II

Economic rights and duties of States

Article 1

Every State has the sovereign and inalienable right to choose its economic system as well as its political, social and cultural systems in accordance with the will of its people, without outside interference, coercion or threat in any form whatsoever.

Article 2

1. Every State has and shall freely exercise full permanent sovereignty, including possession, use and disposal, over all its wealth, natural resources and economic activities.

2. Each State has the right:

(a) To regulate and exercise authority over foreign investment within its national jurisdiction in accordance with its laws and regulations and in conformity with its national objectives and priorities. No State shall be compelled to grant preferential treatment to foreign investment;

(b) To regulate and supervise the activities of transnational corporations within its national jurisdiction and take measures to ensure that such activities comply with its laws, rules and regulations and conform with its economic and social policies.Transnational corporations shall not intervene in the internal affairs of a host State. Every State should, with full regard for its sovereign rights, co-operate with other States in the exercise of the right set forth in this subparagraph;

(c) To nationalize, expropriate or transfer ownership of foreign property, in which case appropriate compensation should be paid by the State adopting such measures, taking into account its relevant laws and regulations and all circumstances that the State considers pertinent. In any case where the question of compensation gives rise to a controversy, it shall be settled under the domestic law of the nationalizing State and by its tribunals, unless it is freely and mutually agreed by all States concerned that other peaceful means be sought on the basis of the sovereign equality of States and in accordance with the principle of free choice of means.

Article 3

In the exploitation of natural resources shared by two or more countries, each State must co-operate on the basis of a system of information and prior consultations in order to achieve optimum use of such resources without causing damage to the legitimate interest of others.

Article 4

Every State has the right to engage in international trade and other forms of economic co-operation irrespective of any differences in political, economic and social systems. No State shall be subjected to discrimination of any kind based solely on such differences. In the pursuit of international trade and other forms of economic co-operation, every State is free to choose the forms of organization of its foreign economic relations and to enter into bilateral and multilateral arrangements consistent with its international obligations and with the needs of international economic co-operation.

Article 5

All States have the right to associate in organizations of primary commodity producers in order to develop their national economies to achieve stable financing for their development, and in pursuance of their aims, to assist in the promotion of sustained growth of the world economy, in particular accelerating the development of developing countries. Correspondingly all States have the duty to respect that right by refraining from applying economic and political measures that would limit it.

Article 6

It is the duty of States to contribute to the development of international trade of goods, particularly by means of arrangements and by the conclusion of long-term multilateral commodity agreements, where appropriate, and taking into account the interests of producers and consumers. All States share the responsibility to promote the regular flow and access of all commercial goods traded at stable, remunerative and equitable prices, thus contributing to the equitable development of the world economy, taking into account, in particular, the interests of developing countries.

Article 7

Every State has the primary responsibility to promote the economic, social and cultural development of its people. To this end, each State has the right and the responsibility to choose its means and goals of development, fully to mobilize and use its resources, to implement progressive economic and social reforms and to ensure the full participation of its people in the process and benefits of development. All States have the duty, individually and collectively, to co-operate in order to eliminate obstacles that hinder such mobilization and use.

Article 8

States should co-operate in facilitating more rational and equitable international economic relations and in encouraging structural changes in the context of a balanced world economy in harmony with the needs and interests of all countries, especially developing countries, and should take appropriate measures to this end.

Article 9

All States have the responsibility to co-operate in the economic, social, cultural, scientific and technological fields for the promotion of economic and social progress throughout the world, especially that of the developing countries.

Article 10

All States are juridically equal and, as equal members of the international community, have the right to participate fully and effectively in the international decision-making process in the solution of world economic, financial and monetary problems, *inter alia,* through the appropriate international organizations in accordance with their existing and evolving rules, and to share equitably in the benefits resulting therefrom.

Article 11

All States should co-operate to strengthen and continuously improve the efficiency of international organizations in implementing measures to stimulate the general economic progress of all countries, particularly of developing countries, and therefore should co-operate to adapt them, when appropriate, to the changing needs of international economic co-operation.

Article 12

1. States have the right, in agreement with the parties concerned, to participate in subregional, regional and

interregional co-operation in the pursuit of their economic and social development. All States engaged in such co-operation have the duty to ensure that the policies of those groupings to which they belong correspond to the provisions of the Charter and are outward-looking, consistent with their international obligations and with the needs of international economic co-operation and have full regard for the legitimate interests of third countries, especially developing countries.

2. In the case of groupings to which the States concerned have transferred or may transfer certain competences as regards matters that come within the scope of the present Charter, its provisions shall also apply to those groupings, in regard to such matters, consistent with the responsibilities of such States as members of such groupings. Those States shall co-operate in the observance by the groupings of the provisions of this Charter.

Article 13

1. Every State has the right to benefit from the advances and developments in science and technology for the acceleration of its economic and social development.

2. All States should promote international scientific and technological co-operation and the transfer of technology, with proper regard for all legitimate interests including, *inter alia,* the rights and duties of holders, suppliers and recipients of technology. In particular, all States should facilitate the access of developing countries to the achievements of modern science and technology, the transfer of technology and the creation of indigenous technology for the benefit of the developing countries in forms and in accordance with procedures which are suited to their economies and their needs.

3. Accordingly, developed countries should co-operate with the developing countries in the establishment, strengthening and development of their scientific and technological infrastructures and their scientific research and technologial activities so as to help to expand and transform the economies of developing countries.

4. All States should co-operate in exploring with a view to evolving further internationally accepted guidelines or regulations for the transfer of technology, taking fully into account the interests of developing countries.

Article 14

Every State has the duty to co-operate in promoting a steady and increasing expansion and liberalization of world trade and an improvement in the welfare and living standards of all peoples, in particular those of developing countries. Accordingly, all States should co-operate, *inter alia,* towards the progressive dismantling of obstacles to trade and the improvement of the international framework for the conduct of world trade and, to these ends, co-ordinated efforts shall be made to solve in an equitable way the trade problems of all countries, taking into account the specific trade problems of the developing countries. In this connexion, States shall take measures aimed at securing additional benefits for the international trade of developing countries so as to achieve a substantial increase in their foreign exchange earnings, the diversification of their exports, the acceleration of the rate of growth of their trade, taking into account their development needs, an improvement in the possibilities for these countries to participate in the expansion of world trade and a balance more favourable to developing countries in the sharing of the advantages resulting from this expansion, through in the largest possible measure, a substantial improvement in the conditions of access for the products of interest to the developing countries and, wherever appropriate, measures designed to attain stable, equitable and remunerative prices for primary products.

Article 15

All States have the duty to promote the achievement of general and complete disarmament under effective international control and to utilize the resources freed by effective disarmament measures for the economic and social development of countries, allocating a substantial portion of such resources as additional means for the development needs of developing countries.

Article 16

1. It is the right and duty of all States, individually and collectively, to eliminate colonialism, *apartheid,* racial discrimination, neo-colonialism and all forms of foreign aggression, occupation and domination, and the economic and social consequences thereof, as a prerequisite for development. States which practise such coercive policies are economically responsible to the countries, territories and peoples affected for the restitution and full compensation for the exploitation and depletion of, and damages to, the natural and all other resources of those countries, territories and peoples. It is the duty of all States to extend assistance to them.

2. No State has the right to promote or encourage investments that may constitute an obstacle to the liberation of a territory occupied by force.

Article 17

International co-operation for development is the shared goal and common duty of all States. Every State should co-operate with the efforts of developing countries to accelerate their economic and social development by providing favourable external conditions and by extending active assistance to them, consistent with their development needs and objectives, with strict respect for the sovereign equality of States and free of any conditions derogating from their sovereignty.

Article 18

Developed countries should extend, improve and enlarge the system of generalized non-reciprocal and non-discriminatory tariff preferences to the developing countries consistent with the relevant agreed conclusions and relevant decisions as adopted on this subject, in the framework of the competent international organizations. Developed countries should also give serious consideration to the adoption of other differential measures, in areas where this is feasible and appropriate and in ways which will provide special and more favourable treatment, in order to meet the trade and development needs of developing countries. In the conduct of international economic relations the developed countries should endeavour to avoid measures having a negative effect on the development of the national economies of the developing countries, as promoted by generalized tariff preferences and other generally agreed differential measures in their favour.

Article 19

With a view to accelerating the economic growth of developing countries and bridging the economic gap between developed and developing countries, developed countries should grant generalized preferential, non-reciprocal and non-discriminatory treatment to developing countries in those fields of international economic co-operation where it may be feasible.

Article 20

Developing countries should, in their efforts to increase their over-all trade, give due attention to the possibility of expanding their trade with socialist countries, by granting to these countries conditions for trade not inferior to those granted normally to the developed market economy countries.

Article 21

Developing countries should endeavour to promote the expansion of their mutual trade and to this end may, in accordance with the existing and evolving provisions and procedures of international agreements where applicable, grant trade preferences to other developing countries without being obliged to extend such preferences to developed countries, provided these arrangements do not constitute an impediment to general trade liberalization and expansion.

Article 22

1. All States should respond to the generally recognized or mutually agreed development needs and objectives of developing countries by promoting increased net flows of real resources to the developing countries from all sources, taking into account any obligations and commitments undertaken by the States concerned, in order to reinforce the efforts of developing countries to accelerate their economic and social development.

2. In this context, consistent with the aims and objectives mentioned above and taking into account any obligations and commitments undertaken in this regard, it should be their endeavour to increase the net amount of financial flows from official sources to developing countries and to improve the terms and conditions thereof.

3. The flow of development assistance resources should include economic and technical assistance.

Article 23

To enhance the effective mobilization of their own resources, the developing countries should strengthen their economic co-operation and expand their mutual trade so as to accelerate their economic and social development. All countries, especially developed countries, individually as well as through the competent international organizations of which they are members, should provide appropriate and effective support and co-operation.

Article 24

All States have the duty to conduct their mutual economic relations in a manner which takes into account the interests of other countries. In particular, all States should avoid prejudicing the interests of developing countries.

Article 25

In furtherance of world economic development, the international community, especially its developed members, shall pay special attention to the particular needs and problems of the least developed among the developing countries, of land-locked developing countries and also island developing countries, with a view to helping them to overcome their particular difficulties and thus contribute to their economic and social development.

Article 26

All States have the duty to coexist in tolerance and live together in peace, irrespective of differences in political, economic, social and cultural systems, and to facilitate trade between States having different economic and social systems. International trade should be conducted without prejudice to generalized non-discriminatory and non-reciprocal preferences in favour of developing countries, on the basis of mutual advantage, equitable benefits and the exchange of most-favoured-nation treatment.

Article 27

1. Every State has the right to enjoy fully the benefits of world invisible trade and to engage in the expansion of such trade.

2. World invisible trade, based on efficiency and mutual and equitable benefit, furthering the expansion of the world economoy, is the common goal of all States. The role of developing countries in world invisible trade should be enhanced and strengthened consistent with the above objectives, particular attention being paid to the special needs of developing countries.

3. All States should co-operate with developing countries in their endeavours to increase their capacity to earn foreign exchange from invisible transactions, in accordance with the potential and needs of each developing country and consistent with the objectives mentioned above.

Article 28

All States have the duty to co-operate in achieving adjustments in the prices of exports of developing countries in relation to prices of their imports so as to promote just and equitable terms of trade for them, in a manner which is remunerative for producers and equitable for producers and consumers.

CHAPTER III

Common responsibilities towards the international community

Article 29

The sea-bed and ocean floor and the subsoil thereof, beyond the limits of national jurisdiction, as well as the resources of the area, are the common heritage of mankind. On the basis of the principles adopted by the General Assembly in resolution 2749 (XXV) of 17 December 1970, all States shall ensure that the exploration of the area and exploitation of its resources are carried out exclusively for peaceful purposes and that the benefits derived therefrom are shared equitably by all States, taking into account the particular interests and needs of developing countries; an international régime applying to the area and its resources and including appropriate international machinery to give effect to its provisions shall be established by an international treaty of a universal character, generally agreed upon.

Article 30

The protection, preservation and the enhancement of the environment for the present and future generations is the responsibility of all States. All States shall endeavour to establish their own environmental and developmental policies in conformity with such responsibility. The environmental policies of all States should enhance and not adversely affect the present and future development potential of developing countries. All States have the responsibility to ensure that activities within their jurisdiction or control do not cause damage to the environment of other States or of areas beyond the limits of national jurisdiction. All States should co-operate in evolving international norms and regulations in the field of the environment.

CHAPTER IV

Final provisions

Article 31

All States have the duty to contribute to the balanced expansion of the world economy, taking duly into account the close interrelationship between the well-being of the developed countries and the growth and development of the developing countries, and the fact that the prosperity of the international community as a whole depends upon the prosperity of its constituent parts.

Article 32

No State may use or encourage the use of economic, political or any other type of measures to coerce another State in order to obtain from it the subordination of the exercise of its sovereign rights.

Article 33

1. Nothing in the present Charter shall be construed as impairing or derogating from the provisions of the Charter of the United Nations or actions taken in pursuance thereof.

2. In their interpretation and application, the provisions of the present Charter are interrelated and each provision should be construed in the context of the other provisions.

Article 34

An item on the Charter of Economic Rights and Duties of States shall be inscribed in the agenda of the General Assembly at its thirtieth session, and thereafter on the agenda of every fifth session. In this way a systematic and comprehensive consideration of the implementation of the Charter, covering both progress achieved and any improvements and additions which might become necessary, would be carried out and appropriate measures recommended. Such consideration should take into account the evolution of all the economic, social, legal and other factors related to the principles upon which the present Charter is based and on its purpose.

2. Reservations

[The final drafting of the Charter of Economic Rights and Duties of States was undertaken in the Second Committee of the General Assembly during the Assembly's Twenty-ninth Regular Session. The draft Charter as a whole was adopted there by 115 votes to 6, with 10 abstentions. After the vote, a number of delegations made statements which also contain the reservations made by representatives of the developed market economies. These are reproduced below.*

The Charter was adopted by the General Assembly on December 12, 1974 by a vote of 120 votes to 6, with 10 abstentions. Before and after the vote, a number of delegations made statements which also contain the reservations made by representatives of the developed market economies. These are reproduced below as well.†]

United Nations, General Assembly, Twenty-ninth Session, Second Committee: 1649th meeting, Friday, December 6, 1974

. . .

---

*United Nations, *Official Records of the General Assembly, Twenty-ninth Session, Second Committee, Summary Records of Meetings 18 September–11 December 1974,* 1649th and 1650th meetings.

†United Nations, *Provisional Verbatim Records of the General Assembly, Twenty-ninth Session,* 2315th and 2316th meetings.

13. Mr. KARHILO (Finland) said that his Government's position on the Charter of Economic Rights and Duties of States reflected the conviction that the opening of avenues towards a new international economic order required new thinking. Consequently, his Government had decided to vote in favour of the text as a whole for the same reaon that it had joined the consensus on the Declaration and the Programme of Action adopted at the sixth special session without any specific reservations. In view of the amount of work that had been done on the draft Charter, he regretted that the negotiation process had not culminated in a decison by consensus. Such a decision would certainly have increased the impact of the Charter. His delegation had abstained in the vote on the procedural proposal for postponement of a decision, because it had recognized the strong desire to have the Charter adopted at the twenty-ninth session of the General Assembly.

14. His delegation had been obliged to abstain in the vote on article 2, paragraph 2(c). His Government largely agreed with the position of the sponsors but felt that there did not seem to be adequate provision for dealing with questions of compensation in the event of nationalization. Reasonable arrangements for settling questions of compensation were absolutely essential; leaving the disagreement unresolved weakened the general significance of the Charter.

15. His delegation had voted in favour of all the other articles of the Charter. In so doing, it had interpreted article 5 as implying that the interests of consumers were not forgotten when the rights of primary commodity producers to associate organizations was recognized. In supporting article 28, his Government continued to support efforts to improve the terms of trade of the developing countries but had not committed itself to any particular means of doing so.

16. Mr. TEMBOURY (Spain) said that the results of the work done on drafting a Charter of Economic Rights and Duties of States, in which his delegation had participated actively, had surpassed all expectations. Nevertheless, his delegation's feeling that there was still work to be done had led it to vote in favour of draft resolution A/C.2//L.1419; the rejection of that draft resolution marked an unfortunate breakdown in the pursuit of widely sought objectives. The text of the draft resolution that had been adopted was very different from the text that had emerged from the fourth session of the Working Group in Mexico. His delegation understood perfectly well that, where it had not been possible to reach a compromise on the changes, each delegation had to state its position. But a charter of economic rights and duties of states that did not enjoy at least support by consensus was a document of very relative value. The text before the Committee did not have the necessary balance. His delegation found itself obliged to state its position clearly, because of the change in the spirit of compromise.

17. His delegation had voted in favour of the amendments in documents A/C.2/L.1401–1405, 1407, 1409, and 1412–1414. It had abstained in voting on the amendment contained in document A/C.2/L.1406, calling for the deletion of article 5, because it had felt that the text should be more detailed. In the voting on the draft Charter paragraph by paragraph, his delegation had abstained on the introductory paragraph and subparagraph (f) of chapter I and would have abstained if a vote had been taken on subparagraph (i) of that chapter. It had abstained in the vote on article 2, paragraph 2(a) and had voted against paragraph 2(c) of that article. It had abstained in the vote on article 3 and would have abstained had a vote been held on articles 5, 19 and 28. Although it had voted for article 18, it would have preferred to see more account taken of countries that suffered more than others because of their stage of development. His delegation had voted against the automatic granting of most-favoured-nation treatment in article 26. In the voting on the draft Charter as a whole, his delegation had abstained because of the lack of balance in the text.

18. His delegation regretted very sincerely that the unnecessarily precipitated decision to proceed to a vote had spoilt the results of a great deal of effort and had reduced the effectiveness of a document that could undoubtedly have been an important factor in the new international economic order. Had the Charter been adopted at the thirtieth session, the decision would have been timely and the text more mature.

. . .

23. Mr. ARVESEN (Norway) said his delegation regretted that a final decision on the various provisions and articles and on the Charter as a whole in its present form had had to be taken at the current session, and had hoped that a decision on a matter of such importance could have been postponed so that further consultations might have been held with a view to arriving at a text which could have been adopted by consensus.

24. His Government had always supported the idea of drawing up a Charter of Economic Rights and Duties of States and it agreed with most of the concepts embodied in the Charter as adopted. The Charter was a very comprehensive document which did, however, contain certain concepts to which his Government could not commit itself. His delegation had therefore voted against article 2, paragraph 2(c), because it was of the opinion that possible disputes arising out of questions of compensation in cases of nationalization or expropriation had specific international aspects and should be settled according to relevant international legal criteria. It had also voted against article 26 because it had been able to accept the reference in that provision to most-

favoured-nation treatment. It had voted in favour of the deletion of article 5 and 16; if those two articles had been put to a separate vote, it would have abstained. The wording of article 5 did not take fully into account the legitimate interests of consumer countries. Article 16 was irrelevant and out of place in that particular context. His delegation had, however, been able to accept article 28 because it supported the principle that the terms of trade of developing countries should be substantially improved.

25. For all the reasons to which he had referred, his delegation had been compelled to abstain in the vote on the Charter as a whole. His Government regretted that it had had to adopt that position, but it had hoped that the final decision could be postponed until the crucial mid-term review and appraisal of the International Development Strategy in 1975. At that time, it would be logical to consider making some changes in the International Development Strategy in the light of the developments which had taken place and the decisions which had been taken by the General Assembly with regard to international development co-operation. After the review had been carried out and the decisions taken at the seventh special session of the General Assembly had been carefully studied, consideration could be given to standards relating to the economic rights and duties of States to be embodied in a charter. In that connexion, he stressed that his Government continued to consider itself morally and politically committed to the International Development Strategy.

26. Mr. KJELDGAARD-OLESEN (Denmark) said that his country had supported the idea of a charter containing comprehensive rules for economic and trade relations between States, on the understanding that such a charter would reflect a true balance of the interests and aspirations of all States Members of the United Nations and thus provide a stabilizing factor in their economic relations. The text of the Charter, as adopted, could hardly be considered to contain such rules and, in view of the lengthy discussions which had preceded the vote, his delegation had expected that it would have been possible to arrive at a text which could be adopted by consensus. Such a text would have expressed the point of view of the developing countries, the importance of which his delegation fully recognized, and would also have taken account of the fact that the industrialized and commodity-consuming countries could help to promote the interests of developing countries only in the context of an evolutionary process which would not impede the developed countries' economic stability. His delegation had hoped that the text to be submitted to the General Assembly would constitute a balance between two considerations, but that was not the case with the text which had just been adopted. Thus the negotiations on the Charter could not be considered completed.

27. The purpose of the lengthy discussions on article 2 had been to take into account the legitimate aspirations of Member States to dispose of their own natural wealth and to ensure the observance in good faith of international agreements and other obligations. Sound international rules reflecting the interests of all members of the international community in that important respect would benefit all States, provided that the rules struck a true balance between the interests involved. It was regrettable that the text of article 2 did not meet that requirement. The lack of a reference to international obligations and to international arbitration in cases of disputes would be to the disadvantage of all countries.

28. The wording of article 5 contained no reference to the legitimate interests of consumers of commodities and favoured producer organizations. His delegation regretted that omission, because international trade was based on a mutually acceptable balance between trading partners; neither the text of article 5 nor the text of article 6 reflected that situation. While his delegation supported the objective of article 19 relating to the preferential treatment of developing countries and had shown its willingness to apply such a policy, it felt that the wording of that article was too general and too broad in scope. That particular area of international co-operation lent itself more to selective and carefully considered measures. The adjustment measures for import prices of developing countries advocated in article 28 would have far-reaching consequences for world trade and the world economy. Those measures and their implications were being studied in other bodies, and acceptance of the text of article 28 as it stood would be prejudicial to the studies being carried out. Finally, his delegation hoped that continued discussions and international contacts would make it possible for the Charter to develop in a direction which would make it a true instrument of international economic and trade cooperation.

29. Mr. DITTMANN (Federal Republic of Germany) said that his delegation had taken an active part in the negotiations on the Charter of Economic Rights and Duties of States because it believed that, if the Charter could be accepted by all States, it would be a valuable instrument for progress and co-operation among all countries and would help to create a better, more secure basis for international economic relations and the well-being and economic growth of all. His delegation was glad that it had been possible to find acceptable and satifactory solutions for many articles and believed that, if sufficient time had been available, there would also have been a good chance of finding satisfactory solutions to articles on which full agreement had not been possible. His Government regretted that it had been unable to approve certain articles of the Charter and that, in view of the importance of those articles, it had not been able to support the Charter as a whole. It nevertheless agreed with many of the provisions of the Charter, as it had explained during the voting.

. . .

40. Mr. BERLIS (Canada) paid a tribute to the initiative of the President of Mexico in proposing the Charter of Economic Rights and Duties of States, and to the efforts of the Mexican representatives. The fact that the Working Group had been able to achieve agreement on so many of the issues facing it was a great accomplishment, and the fact that it had not reached complete agreement was an indication of the sensitivity of certain issues.

41. The Canadian Government firmly supported the basic objective of the Charter, namely the formulation of principles to enable the international community to establish and maintain an equitable distribution of the world's wealth.

42. Canada approached article 2 of the Charter from the viewpoint of a country which had investments abroad but itself received a far larger amount of investment from overseas. However, the text of the article raised several difficulties.

43. The United Nations had for a number of years asserted the permanent sovereignty of States over their natural resources, but article 2, paragraph 1, asserted the permanent sovereignty of every State not only over its natural resources but over its wealth and economic activities, without restriction of the territorial application of those concepts. The paragraph was thus open to the interpretation that if a State chose to transfer a portion of its wealth abroad, for example by investing in other countries, it retained full permanent sovereignty over that wealth. He doubted whether many countries, including his own, would accept investment on such terms. Moreover, the unqualified references he had cited contradicted later provisions of article 2 which asserted the primary jurisdiction of the host State in matters of foreign investment.

44. Article 2, paragraph 2(*a*), asserted in its original version that no State should demand privileged treatment for its nationals who invested in a foreign country; the problem was what constituted privileged treatment. His Government did not think that Canadian investors should occupy a privileged position in the economies of the countries in which they invested, but it did maintain that when a host State applied measures against foreign investment it should not discriminate against Canadian foreign investment, and the measures which it applied should be in accordance with its international obligations. If either of those conditions were not met his Government would feel entitled to raise the matter with the Government of the host State and to rely on any relevant principles of international law. He could not consider that as constituting a demand for preferential treatment, but was not at all confident that the sponsors of the text of the Charter shared that view. His problem had not been solved by the revision to the text of the article (A/C.2/L.1386/Corr.6).

45. His delegation fully supported article 2, pragraph 2(*b*), concerning the regulation of transnational corporations.

46. With regard to paragraph 2(*c*), his delegation did not deny the right of a State to nationalize foreign property, subject to the payment of compensation. The question of what amount of compensation was equitable would depend on the circumstances of each case but he could not accept a text seeking to establish the principle that a State could nationalize foreign property without compensation.

47. One of the most important obstacles to his delegation's support of the Charter as a whole was the absence of any references in article 2 to the applicability of international law to the treatment of foreign investment. If the compulsory jurisdiction of the International Court of Justice in the case of disputes between States had not been accepted, or some other agreement made between the parties regarding the settlement of disputes, jurisdiction would rest with the appropriate tribunal of the host State, and its measures must be in conformity with its international legal obligations. There was disagreement as to whether such obligations arose only from treaties, or from principles of customary international law as well. The amendment to article 2 (A/C.2/L.1404) which his delegation had co-sponsored had used the words "international obligations" rather than "international law" so as to permit both groups of States to maintain their positions on the issue.

48. There was disagreement regarding what principles of customary international law were relevant to the treatment of foreign investment. Where old law was unjust or ineffective it must be changed to reflect the present economic interdependence of States and the need for the development of developing countries. His delegation had hoped that the Charter of Economic Rights and Duties would command the consensus necessary for it to contribute to the codification and progressive development of law in that area; unhappily, that was not the case.

49. Although chapter I of the Charter referred to the fulfillment of international obligations, the application of that principle to article 2 in general was seriously impaired by the unqualified reference in paragraph 2(*c*) to the domestic law of the nationalizing State. The new paragraph 3 proposed for article 2 (A/C.2/L.1404) had merely sought to establish that the rule of law would apply among States in respect of foreign investment. That was important because, if an equitable distribution of the world's wealth was to be achieved, an investment flow of private capital from developed to developing countries would be required, and such movement

would take place only in conditions which provided at least a degree of security. His delegation therefore felt that article 2 as adopted would constitute an obstacle to developing countries seeking to attract the funds required for their development, and it was quite unable to support the article.

50. With regard to article 5, he understood the desire of nations to achieve stable and remunerative export earnings; however, Canada, as a major exporter and importer of many commodities, felt that where international action was required to solve commodity problems it should be directly devised and implemented by exporters and importers.

51. Article 6 approximately reflected the Canadian position that exporting nations had a responsibility to promote the flow of commercial goods, and importing nations to facilitate access of goods, including processed and fabricated products.

52. He had voted for article 15 since Canada had long been a staunch supporter of disarmanent measures, though at the present stage of the discussion of a possible link between disarmament and development financing, his Government continued to question the validity of the concept that development funds might be automatically generated by disarmament.

53. His delegation was in sympathy with the aim of article 16 but had abstained in the vote on it in view of its reservations regarding the obligations which it would impose on all States to extend assistance to the countries, territories and peoples mentioned. Moreover, paragraph 2 of the article was capable of far too broad an interpretation, particularly when the important question of the sovereignty of States which were host countries to foreign investments was considered.

54. His delegation had abstained on article 19, while it agreed that generalized preferential treatment to developing countries might be technically feasible, the extension of preferences in some fields might not be appropriate.

55. His delegation would have been able to accept the text of article 26 but for the manner in which most-favoured-nation treatment was referred to; a basis for international trade relations should be worked out between the States themselves.

56. With regard to article 28, his delegation considered that techniques to protect the terms of trade of developing countries deserved detailed examination, but doubted the feasibility of linking the prices of their exports to the prices of their imports. It was premature to include such a concept in the Charter.

57. In general his delegation was disappointed that it had not been possible to reach agreement on a Charter enjoying the general support of the international community. In view of the manner in which the Charter had been adopted, it could not be considered as a basis for the evolution of international law in the controversial areas where it had not achieved general acceptance.

58. Mr. SKOGLUND (Sweden) said that his delegation had voted for the Charter of Economic Rights and Duties of States, which he regarded as an expression of support for the principles of intergovernmental economic relations within the framework of a new international economic order. Nevertheless, it should have been possible with a further effort and in a spirit of compromise on all sides to reach a consensus; he hoped that efforts in that direction would continue. With a few exceptions, he had supported all the articles in the Charter; in a few cases he had abstained and only on one paragraph—article 2, paragraph 2(c), on the settlement of disputes in case of nationalization— had he cast a negative vote.

59. His Government fully supported article 2, paragraphs 1, 2(a) and 2(b). But as regards paragraph 2(c) his Government, while recognizing the sovereign right of States to nationalize foreign property, still held the view, which was in conformity with General Assembly resolution 1803 (XVII), that international disputes following nationalization should be settled by an international court.

60. His Government accepted the principle that primary commodity producers could associate in organizations and that by so doing they might asist the growth of world economy; but that did not necessarily imply that his Government supported all the measures which might be taken by associations of the kind referred to in article 5, and it reserved the right to protect its legitimate interests in that context.

61. His Government agreed with the tenor of article 6 that co-operation between primary commodity producers would be facilitated if it took the form of international co-operation with due regard to the interests of producers and consumers. He noted in particular the statement in the article that all States shared the responsibility to promote the regular flow and access of goods to the market, with particular reference to the interests of developing countries.

62. With regard to article 15, his Government's objective had been to find practical proposals for an end to the arms race, which was diverting enormous human and material resources from peaceful pursuits to unproductive military purposes; nevertheless, disarmament and development must be sought separately and development must not be made dependent on progress in disarmament.

63. He considered that article 19 was a duplication of article 18 in a less satisfactory form.

64. With regard to article 22, a clear distinction should be made between commercial transactions and

development assistance. Private investments might have a positive development effect in the host country, but each case must be examined on its merits and no general opinions could be given.

65. On article 26, his delegation had voted for the amendment proposed in document A/C.2/L.1405 and had abstained with regard to the text in document A/C.2/L.1386. The texts were identical except for the formulation regarding most-favoured-nation treatment. His delegation's vote illustrated its views on that point.

66. Article 28 dealt with import and export prices for developing countries. At the sixth special session, his delegation had supported the principle of a just relationship between those prices and improvements in the terms of trade of developing countries, but had stressed that a direct link was neither appropriate nor feasible: that was still his delegation's view. He recognized the duty of co-operating in achieving equitable price relations, but the best solution to deal with changes in exchange rates and inflation probably lay in world-wide commodity agreements. However, his Government was prepared to study any other proposals that might result from further work in that area.

67. His Government supported the general goal set forth in article 32 but found the wording somewhat inappropriate and had therefore also voted for the amendment proposed in document A/C.2/L.1415.

. . .

73. Mr. PERCY (United States of America) said that his delegation regretted not having been able to support the Charter of Economic Rights and Duties of States.

74. The vision of the President of Mexico Mr. Luis Echeverria, who had initiated the concept of such a charter, had been a worthy one and the United States Government, being convinced that there was a real need for basic improvements in the international economic system, favoured the concept. The United States had worked hard and sincerely with other countries to formulate a Charter that would achieve a balance between the concerns of the industrialized and the developing countries. He expressed appreciation to the Foreign Minister of Mexico for his negotiations, thanks to which agreement had been reached on many important articles which the United States delegation had supported.

75. Agreement had not been reached on a number of other articles; his delegation's views on them were made clear by the amendments which it had proposed, together with certain other countries, but which had been rejected. Many of the provisions on which agreement had been lacking were fundamental and were unacceptable in their present form. They included the treatment of foreign investment in terms which did not fully take into account respect for agreements and international obligations, and the endorsement of the concepts of producer cartels and the indexation of prices.

76. The Charter was therefore unbalanced and failed to achieve the purpose of encouraging harmonious economic relations and necessary development. Indeed, its provisions would tend to discourage the capital flow vital for development.

77. His Government had been prepared to continue negotiations until agreement could be reached on all articles, and had supported the proposal to continue negotiating in 1975 with a view to acting on a generally agreed Charter at the thirtieth session of the General Assembly.

78. For the reasons which he had stated, his Government had been compelled to vote against the Charter as a whole. But it accepted the possibility of reconsideration, if other delegations concluded that an agreed Charter would be preferable to one that was meaningless without the agreement of countries whose numbers might be small but whose significance in international economic relations and development could hardly be ignored.

79. Mr. KANAZAWA (Japan) said that his Government had participated in the work of drafting the Charter of Economic Rights and Duties of States, which it had hoped would be adopted by consensus to the satisfaction of all. His delegation greatly regretted that the Charter had been put to the vote without exploring all possible means for the achievement of consensus. Some articles had obviously required more time for substantive discussion. In an effort to find satisfactory solutions, his delegation had joined in sponsoring a number of amendments. For example, the amendment to article 2 (A/C.2/L.1404) submitted by the delegations of Japan and other developed countries embodied the maximum concession that they could offer in an effort to arrive at an agreement.

80. There were many articles for which his delegation had voted and a number which it had been unable to accept (articles 2, 5, 6, 19 and 28).

81. His delegation appreciated the initiative of President Echeverria in proposing the Charter and was in full agreement with its objectives. Therefore, although he had voted against the important articles which he had enumerated, he had abstained in the vote on the Charter as a whole in the hope that efforts would be made to reach a universally acceptable solution of the economic and social problems facing all States in an era of growing interdependence.

82. His delegation's abstention on the Charter as a whole did not imply any change in its negative votes on individual articles.

The meeting rose at 11.30 p.m.

United Nations, General Assembly, Twenty-ninth Session, Second Committee: 1650th meeting, Monday, December 9, 1974.

1. Mr. MOLITOR (Luxembourg) said that Luxembourg had consistently supported efforts to establish generally accepted international rules with a view to improving international economic co-operation, and in particular the initiative of the President of Mexico in proposing a universal Charter to promote just and equitable economic relations between developed and developing countries. His delegation therefore regretted that it had not been able to vote in favour of the text of draft resolution A/C.2/L.1386 and Corr.6. While many of the provisions in that document were acceptable to his Government, others were incompatible with some of its principles and with certain commitments it had assumed in other forums.

2. His delegation had co-sponsored the proposal, in document A/C.2/L.1419, to continue negotiations with a view to achieving a generally acceptable text, and also certain amendments to make the text of the draft Charter more acceptable. Since those amendments had not been adopted, his delegation wished to state that it shared the reservations of other members of EEC and fully supported the statement which the representative of France would be making on behalf of those countries.

3. Under the terms of article 33, paragraph 1, the text adopted was a recommendation within the meaning of the Charter of the United Nations, and his delegation would have preferred a formulation more in conformity with that basic requirement of the Charter of the United Nations. As stated in article 33, paragraph 2, the provisions of the Charter of Economic Rights and Duties of States were interrelated and each provision should be construed in the context of the others.

4. Mr. MASSONET (Belgium) said that Belgium had always been sympathetic to efforts aimed at improving international economic relations and had supported the initiative of the President of Mexico in proposing a Charter of Economic Rights and Duties of States. However, it had never agreed that such a Charter should be put to a vote, since it could be effective only if adopted unanimously or by consensus. It remained convinced that further progress towards a consensus could have been made. It was therefore regrettable that the draft resolution had been put to the vote as it stood. Although Belgium was well-disposed towards any efforts to reduce imbalances in international economic relations and believed in the interdependence of the interests of all countries, it could not accept a Charter which failed to take into account the legitimate interests of all the parties involved and in particular, articles 2, 4, 5, 6, 16 and 26, which his delegation felt were unbalanced and contrary to the spirit of moderation and co-operation which had guided Belgium's participation in the preparation of the draft Charter.

5. Mr. ROUGE (France) said that, despite its desire to improve relations between developed and developing countries, his delegation had abstained from voting on the draft resolution as a whole. Although it favoured the concept of a Charter of Economic Rights and Duties of States and approved of many of the provisions of the text which had been submitted, it had serious objections to some of the most important ones. The amendments which his delegation had sponsored and the manner in which it had voted clearly demonstrated his country's position.

6. Nevertheless, he wished to clarify two points. The first concerned the text of article 2 as proposed in amendment A/C.2/L.1404. On the very important point of the sovereignty of States over their natural resources and the right to nationalize, his delegation's position was that reflected in the complete text of the amendment. The fact that, as a result of a procedural incident, his delegation had found itself voting in favour of a set of provisions comprising only paragraphs 1 and 2 of the amendment did not in any way mean that it would have approved, in chapter II of the Charter, an article 2 worded in that way. To be acceptable, article 2 would have had to include the full text of paragraphs 1, 2 and 3 of the amendment. The other sponsors of the amendment had asked him to state that that was also their unanimous interpretation. Secondly, his delegation had abstained from voting on the Western amendment proposing the deletion of article 28. Its abstention had been intended to signify that on an issue of such importance as the price of exports of developing countries a consensus would have been essential, because otherwise markets could not be organized in a satisfactory manner. However, if there had been a separate vote on article 28 itself, his delegation would have voted in favour of the text proposed by the Group of 77.

7. Speaking on behalf of the nine States members of EEC he recalled that those States had submitted amendments to articles 4 and 26 (A/C.2/L.1405) and article 6 (A/C.2/L.1407). The wording of those amendments, which had been drafted with a view to achieving a consensus, wsas not entirely satisfactory and required some explanation. With regard to articles 4 and 26, the members of EEC were quite prepared to extend most-favoured-nation treatment to all States, irrespective of differences in political, economic or social systems, in

accordance with their bilateral or multilateral international commitments. However, they considered, firstly, that that could be done only pursuant to formal bilateral or multilateral agreements providing for reciprocal and equivalent concessions and, secondly, that the benefits deriving in certain cases from regional arrangements could apply only to countries in similar legal and economic circumstances. With regard to article 6, in the view of the members of EEC, its main purpose should be to emphasize the interdependence of all States in the promotion of a regular flow of trade in raw materials. Case-by-case commodity agreements would be a useful method of achieving that objective in appropriate cases. What had prevented most of them from voting in favour of article 6 as it stood in document A/C.2/L.1386 was the fact that, in their view, the wording used seriously distorted the basic idea.

8. The members of EEC expressly reserved their position with regard to the legal consequences of article 29, in view of the work on the law of the sea in progress elsewhere under United Nations auspices.

9. Mr. CAVAGLIERI (Italy) said that his delegation had consistently supported the initiative of the President of Mexico in proposing a Charter of Economic Rights and Duties of States and had actively participated in all negotiations on the draft Charter. In view of the process achieved at each round of the negotiations, and particularly over the past few days, his delegation believed that a gradual approach would have led to unanimous approval of the Charter, and it was for that reason that it had co-sponsored draft resolution A/C.2/L.1419. Unfortunately the Charter had been put to the vote before all the difficulties concerning the text had been resolved. His delegation shared many of those difficulties, as indicated by the amendments it had introduced together with its partners in EEC.

10. His Government considered that the legal or non-legal nature of documents such as the Charter of Economic Rights and Duties should be established from the beginning. It could not regard the Charter as it stood as legally binding, and therefore welcomed the revisions of the preamble introduced by the respresentative of Mexico. The Charter was an important instrument containing a set of general guidelines for the reorganization of international economic relations and, as such, should be kept outside the judicial field.

11. His delegation's position regarding the problems mentioned in article 2 was well known; its wording and in particular that of paragraph 2(c), could not meet with its approval owing to the lack of adequate consideration of the existing rules of international law. His Government's views on the questions dealt with in articles 4, 6, 26 and 29 were reflected in the statement by the representative of France on behalf of the nine members of EEC. With regard to article 19, his delegation could not support a provision relating to so broad and unspecific a subject as "international economic co-operation" or restrictions which would prevent a country from adopting special measures in favour of other countries needing particular assistance owing to very grave circumstances. As for article 28, he could only reiterate his delegation's serious doubts with regard to the possibility of establishing a link between the prices of exports and imports of developing countries. He hoped that the points he had mentioned would be modified positively in the forthcoming reviews of the Charter provided for in article 34.

12. Mr. STURKEY (Australia) said that Australia had served on the UNCTAD Working Group and had participated in negotiations extending over two years on a text which had become a large part of the draft Charter as adoped. It was unfortunate, however, that the Working Group had been unable to present the Second Committee with an agreed text as a whole, capable of commanding general acceptance.

13. His Government's general support for the aspirations of developing countries and its firm intention to do all it could to help to bring about those changes that were necessary and desirable in the existing international economic order were well known. Its support for the draft resolution should be seen in that light. It was a document which set forth principles for the proper conduct of international economic relations and his delegation, while it had not been able to give unqualified endorsement to all the provisions of the document, had recognized its value in recommending patterns of international behaviour which should lead to economic development and advancement for all.

14. The changes in the fourth and thirteenth preambular paragraphs agreed to by the sponsors, and the provision in article 34, for the evolution of "the principles upon which the present charter is based", had enabled his delegation to support the draft resolutions as a whole. The resolution might have a significant part in the development of international economic law; while it could not create law, it might help to determine or influence the *opinion juris* and might influence States in determining what their practice should be in the light of international law.

15. His delegation supported the broad principles towards which article 2 was directed; but, as both a capital-importing and a new capital-exporting nation it attached importance to the need for host countries to ensure that foreign investors were able to operate in an environment which was fair to the interests of all parties concerned. It had supported the first clause of that article because it endorsed the right of States in the exercise of their sovereignty, freely to use and dispose of their natural resources. However, it shared the concern ex-

pressed by the Canadian delegation about the problems of definition posed by "wealth" and "economic activities". It did not regard the provisions of article 2, paragraph 2(a), as in any way prejudicing the right of a State to extend consular protection on behalf of its investors. In respect of paragraph 2(c), his delegation was of the view that any act of nationalization should be accompanied by the payment of just compensation, without undue delay, to be determined where necessary through recourse to internationally agreed procedures for the settlement of disputes.

16. In supporting article 3, Australia reserved its position on the apparent inflexibility in the provision for a system of information and prior consultations on the sharing of natural resources.

17. Although his delegation supported article 5, it was bound to observe that it saw the duty imposed in that article as correlative to the right to associate, both being qualified by the general duty of States, expressed in article 6, to contribute to the development of international trade taking into account the interests of both producers and consumers.

18. His delegation noted the absence in the third sentence of article 14 of any specification or qualification of the measures that States would be obliged to take to promote an expansion in international trade. Australia would, however, continue to do what it could in terms of its trade policies to try to secure additional benefits for developing countries.

19. The Australian Government interpreted its general support for article 17 as not derogating from the right of States to put such conditions on development assistance as might be required by their obligation to account for the expenditure of public funds. Similarly, in supporting article 26, it interpreted its provisions in terms of their feasibility.

20. It was Australia's understanding that article 29 was a reaffirmation of General Assembly resolution 2749 (XXV) and did not go beyond it. His delegation therefore interpreted that article as subject to the same reservation as had been made by Australia concerning that resolution at the time of its adoption. Consequently, its acceptance of article 29 was conditional upon the successful completion of the work of the Third United Nations Conference on the Law of the Sea and the existence of a widely accepted international treaty régime dealing with the international sea-bed area.

21. With regard to article 32, his delegation saw no place for coercion in commerce.

22. If separate votes had been taken on articles 16 and 28, his delegation would have abstained. While it supported the general spirit of article 16, it considered that the definition of responsibility of States in relation to the consequences of colonialism was unclear and could give rise to dispute. As for article 28, Australia supported a thorough examination of the concept of indexation but did not believe that Governments were in a position to consider endorsing such a concept at the present time.

23. Australia reserved its position on all articles on which it had entered reservations or made interpretations. That applied also to article 12, paragraph 1, relating to regional arrangements for economic co-operation.

. . .

28. Mr. WOLTE (Austria) said that his delegation had followed the negotiations on the Charter of Economic Rights and Duties of States with interest and would have wished that it might be adopted by consensus. The negotiations had clarified many points, and significant progress had been made towards achieving an agreed text. His delegation had seen much merit in the propoals contained in draft resolution A/C.2/L.1419; however, the majority of members of the Committee had favoured a vote on the document as submitted by the Group of 77.

29. His delegation had expressed a preference for specific wording in certain chapters, and disapproval and concern in connexion with certain articles. Referring to article 2, paragraph 2(c), he stated that his delegation was not opposed to nationalization provided it was effected in accordance with the relevant rules of international law. With regard to article 5, it did not contest the right of States to associate but considered that such organizations should not be limited to primary commodity producers. While agreeing with the basic provisions of article 16, it considered that more precise wording was required. With regard to article 26, it would have preferred a reference to most-favoured-nation treatment based on bilateral or multilateral arrangements.

30. He hoped that all possible efforts would be made in the future to re-examine the controversial provisions of the Charter with a view to achieving general agreement and stimulating efforts to promote economic development.

. . .

42. Mr. VAN DER TAK (Netherlands) said that the Netherlands endorsed the spirit of the draft Charter and shared the aspirations of its sponsors. It would have preferred a continuation of negotiations and final approval by consensus. While it supported a major portion of the document, it was not in a position to accept some provisions and had therefore abstained from voting on the draft Charter as a whole.

43. He had voted in favour of the entire preamble and all of chapter I with the exception of subparagraph (*f*), on which he had abstained not because the concept was unacceptable, but because it was a political matter and not an economic one. He had abstained on article 4 because, like other members of EEC, he was not clear regarding the meaning of the second sentence. With regard to article 5, he had favoured the deletion of the last sentence and would have voted for the article with that deletion, if it had been put to a separate vote. Similarly, if articles 15 or 28 had been voted on separately, he would have voted for them. Article 16 was out of place in the Charter, which should be limited to rights and duties of an economic nature. For article 19, he would have preferred the text which had emerged from earlier negotiations calling on developed countries to identify further areas of economic co-operation in which generalized preferences and non-disciplinary treatment could be granted to developing countries and to take the necessary measures as appropriate. If article 16 and 19 had been voted on separately, he would have abstained. He had voted against article 2, paragraph 1 because his delegation preferred a text stating that every State had an inalienable right fully and freely to dispose of its natural resources. He had voted against article 2, paragraph 2(*c*), because it failed to specify the basic conditions for nationalization and expropriation, namely, the obligation to pay prompt, adequate and effective compensation and respect for international law in case of disputes. He had voted against article 26 because, while his delegation shared the aspirations of the sponsors stated in that article, it agreed with other EEC countries that most-favoured-nation treatment should be subject to prior negotiation.

. . .

46. Mr. FREELAND (United Kingdom) said his delegation deeply regretted that the considerable effort devoted to the elaboration of the draft Charter of Economic Rights and Duties of States had resulted in a contested vote. Much progress had been made during the long negotiations, and even in recent days: his delegation's participation in those negotiations had been guided by its belief that it was only if the Charter commanded the full support of all Members of the United Nations that its great potential could be realized. It was to preserve that progress, and because of its sincere hope that consensus could be achieved, that his delegation had co-sponsored draft resolution A/C.2/L.1419. With the rejection of that proposal, it had felt obliged to vote against the draft Charter as a whole.

47. It had done so, first because many provisions of the Charter were couched in terms appropriate to a legislative document and were designed to impose far-reaching obligations of a long-term character on developed countries. Secondly, the Charter was a package. While there was much in that package which his delegation was willing to endorse and apply in practice, it had not wished to give the impression, by expressing reservations concerning certain of its provisions and abstaining in the voting, that it had been prepared to acquiesce in the package as a whole. His delegation had taken its action not in any spirit of confrontation or out of opposition to the aspirations of developing countries. It remained willing to co-operate in efforts to achieve a Charter acceptable to all, but it did not wish to be regarded as in any way committed to the text as it stood.

48. With regard to article 2 of the text as it stood, he recalled his delegation's preference for alternative 4, to be found on page 10 of the report of the fourth session of the UNCTAD Working Group (TD/B/AC.12/4). His delegation's willingness to seek compromise in the field in question had been demonstrated by its co-sponsorship of amendment A/C.2/L.1404, in connexion with which he endorsed the remarks made by the representative of France at the current meeting. In the absence of any provision making it clear that States taking the measures referred to in article 2 of the draft Charter were under a duty to fulfill their international obligations in good faith, no part of the article was acceptable to his delegation.

49. His delegation had abstained from voting on even the revised version of the fourth preambular paragraph because it considered, as a matter of principle, that the formulation universally agreed upon in the Working Group should have been maintained. Its vote on the seventh preambular paragraph had been motivated by the view that the concept of collective economic security should have been expressed in a more balanced way, as proposed in amendment A/C.2/L.1400. His delegation had been disappointed at the use in chapter I, subparagraph (*f*), of the term "peaceful coexistence." A more neutral expression would have aided the search for a consensus.

50. He associated himself with the remarks made by the representative of France on behalf of EEC concerning articles 4, 6, 26 and 29. His delegation had opposed article 5 as being unbalanced because it failed to take account of the community of interests which existed between producers and consumers in an interdependent world. With regard to article 15, his delegation accepted that both disarmament and development were desirable aims in themselves, but did not think that a direct link could be drawn between them. Its detestation of *apartheid*, racial discrimination and other injustices referred to in the first sentence of article 16, paragraph I, was well known, but it considered the vague and far-reaching proposals contained in the article to have no real place in a document such as the Charter. Article 19 was unacceptably imprecise, and he could not agree that all preferences in that uncertain field should be non-discriminatory. The present wording of article 28 pre-

judged a matter still under consideration by the United Nations and concerning the practicability of which his delegation had serious doubts. Finally, his delegation had abstained from voting on article 34 because, having regard to the difficulties it saw in the Charter as a whole and to the attitude it had been constrained to adopt in the voting, it had felt unable to endorse the reference in the second sentence of that paragraph to consideration of the implementation of the Charter.

51. The minority in which his delegation had placed itself by its negative vote on the draft Charter as a whole was not without its economic significance. All who had participated in the negotiations on the draft Charter had been aware that the difficulties experienced by that minority were serious and real and that sincere and intensive efforts had been made to overcome them. His delegation had been unable to ignore the potential damage to its national interests which it saw in the draft as it stood, but its vote should not be taken as being indicative of any desire to harm the interests of the developing countries or of abandonment of hope that a universally acceptable text could be evolved.

United Nations, General Assembly, Twenty-ninth Session: 2315th Meeting, Thursday, December 12, 1974.

. . .

The PRESIDENT: . . . I shall now call on those delegations which have asked to explain their vote before the vote.

. . .

Mr. RYDBECK (Sweden): The Swedish delegation voted in favour of the draft resolution on the Charter of Economic Rights and Duties of States in the Second Committee and will be happy to do so in the plenary Assembly today.

We want to pay a tribute to His Excellency President Luis Echeverria of Mexico for his highly important initiative. Through the charter Member States give expression to the general principles that should guide intergovernmental economic relations within the framework of a new international economic order.

We regret that it has not proven possible to reach a consensus, and we should like to express our hope that the efforts to broaden agreement on the text will continue.

I want to make some brief remarks on the position of my Government in regard to some of the articles of the charter. In this connexion I refer also to the more comprehensive statement that my delegation made in its explanation of vote after the vote in the Second Committee, as well as to our votes on the separate articles of the charter.

As to article 2, the Swedish Government fully supports paragraph 1, as well as paragraphs 2(*a*) and 2(*b*). As regards paragraph 2(*c*) my Government, while recognizing the sovereign right of States to nationalize foreign property, still holds the view, which is in conformity with General Assembly resolution 1803 (XVII), that in cases where national means of justice have been exhausted and the result of that process still appears unsatisfactory to a foreign State, there exists a dispute on the international level, a dispute which in the view of the Swedish Government should be settled by an international court.

Both article 5 and article 6 relate to trade and commodities. Sweden has no objection to the principle that primary commodity producers should have the right to associate themselves in our organizations, but, as we have pointed out on previous occasions, we are of the opinion that co-operation among primary commodity producers would be facilitated if it was carried out within the framework of broad international co-operation, taking into account the interests of both the producers and the consumers.

With regard to article 15, the Swedish aim in participating in disarmament negotiations is to further these negotiations through practical and realistic proposals that may lead to tangible results in the not-too-distant future. We do, however, believe that the two objectives, disarmament and development, must be striven for each one in its own right, and development must never be made dependent on progress in disarmament. In accordance with those views, my delegation abstained from voting in the Committee on this article.

. . .

The PRESIDENT: I shall now call on those representatives wishing to explain their vote after the vote.

. . .

Mr. HAYS (Canada): My delegation, at the outset, wishes to pay tribute as we did in the Second Committee, to the bold and statesmanlike initiative of President Echeverria of Mexico in proposing, two years ago, the preparation and adoption of a United Nations Charter on Economic Rights and Duties of States.

The document presented to us deals with a vast range of exceedingly complex issues and it is a tribute to the tireless efforts of those who participated actively in the negotiations on it that agreement was achieved on by far the greater portion of the issues facing them. That agreement was not reached on all issues in the time available is a clear indication of the sensitivity of those issues. In this connexion, I should note that we were among those delegations which favoured some extension of the negotiating time-table of the charter in the hope that this might permit a fully agreed text to emerge.

I wish to underline once again the firm support of the Canadian Government for the basic objective of the charter, namely, the formulation of principles and guidelines to enable the international community to establish and maintain an equitable distribution of the world's wealth and thereby to contribute to an international peace based upon justice. This was the objective which guided us in the negotiations on the charter and which will continue to guide us when the issues to which the charter addresses itself are considered here and in other bodies.

Before commenting on particular provisions of the chapter and on Canada's voting position, I should like to note that my delegation has actively sought some procedure whereby our views on the charter registered in the Second Committee could be fully reflected in the records of the General Assembly without the need to reiterate our remarks in full here in the plenary Assembly. Unfortunately, it appears that it is not possible to proceed in this fashion, and I am therefore constrained to make the following comments.

The Canadian delegation took considered positions on certain of the fundamental issues in the charter. I should like to turn first to chapter II, article 2, on permanent sovereignty and the treatment of foreign investment, and to remind representatives that Canada approaches this article from the viewpoint of a country which, while being the origin of a certain amount of foreign investment abroad, receives as host country a far larger amount of such investment from abroad.

We are a country in whose economy foreign investment plays a major role and we are thus very much aware of both its advantages and its disadvantages. My Government has only recently enacted legislation to ensure that new foreign investment takes a place in a manner which will bring significant economic benefit to Canada.

The text of article 2 presents several difficulties for my delegation. The United Nations has, for a number of years, asserted in various resolutions the permanent sovereignty of States over their natural resources. Paragraph 1 of article 2, however, asserts the permanent sovereignty of every State not only over its natural resources but, in addition, over its wealth and economic activities. The paragraph contains no element restricting the territorial application of these concepts. It is thus clearly open to the interpretation that if a State chooses to transfer a portion of its wealth abroad—for example, by investing in the economies of other countries—it nevertheless retains full permanent sovereignty over that wealth. I rather doubt that many countries would accept investment on such terms. I can certainly give no assurance that my country could do so. Indeed, in this respect the unqualified references to full permanent sovereignty over wealth and economic activities are in direct contradiction to the later provisions of article 2 which assert the primary jurisdiction of the host State in respect of foreign investment.

Paragraph 2(a) asserted in its original version that no State whose nationals invest in a foreign country shall demand privileged treatment for such investors. Our problem here was in determining what, in the view of the sponsors of that text, constituted "privileged treatment". It is not the view of my Government that Canadian investors should occupy a privileged position in the economies of the countries in which they invest. But it is our view that, when a host State takes measures against foreign investment, it should not discriminate against Canadian foreign investment in relation to foreign investment from other sources, and the measures which it applies to all foreign investment should be in accordance with its international obligations. If either of those requirements were not met, my Government would feel it was entitled to raise the matter with the Government of the host State and to rely on any relevant principles of international law. We could not consider this as constituting a demand for preferential treatment, but we are not at all confident that all the sponsors of the text share this view. Our problem was not solved by the amendment made to that text.

I am happy to say that my delegation fully supports the text of paragraph 2(b) of article 2 respecting the regulation of transnational corporations.

As for paragraph 2(c), my delegation does not deny the right of a State to nationalize foreign property, but it does maintain that that right is conditional upon the payment of compensation. The question of what amount of compensation is just or equitable will naturally depend upon the particular circumstances of each individual case. But my delegation is unable to accept a text which seeks to establish the principle that a State may nationalize or expropriate foreign property without compensation—in effect, confiscate such property. This, in the view of my delegation, is the effect of paragraph 2(c) of article 2.

I wish to refer now to an issue which constitutes one of the most important obstacles to my delegation's support of the charter as a whole, namely, the absence of any reference in article 2 to the applicability of international law to the treatment of foreign investment. There is, of course, a very relevant distinction between the body of law to be applied in the event of a dispute and the tribunal which is to apply that law. It is clear that, in the absence of a relevant acceptance of the compulsory jurisdiction of the International Court of Justice—in the case of disputes between States--or some other agreement between the parties respecting settlement of disputes, jurisdiction in respect of a dispute rests with the appropriate tribunal of the host State. That does not, however, alter the fact that the host State's measures must be carried out in conformity with its international legal obligations. There is, of course, disagreement among States over whether such obligations arise only from treaties or from principles of customary international law as well. The amendment to articles 2--which my delegation had the honour of co-sponsoring in the Second Committee--deliberately used, in paragraph 3, the words "international obligations" rather than "international law" in order to allow both groups of States to maintain their respective positions on this issue.

Even among States which, like Canada, hold the view that there are principles of customary international law which are relevant to the treatment of foreign investment, there is disagreement about the precise content of those principles. Where the old law is unjust or ineffective, it must be changed to reflect the present economic interdependence of States and the need for the development of the developing countries, which are the two most important facts of economic life in our generation. It had been the hope of my delegation that this charter would command the consensus necessary to enable it to contribute to the codification and progressive development of law in this area; unhappily, this is not the case.

The third paragraph proposed in the amendment to article 2 prejudged neither the content of international law relating to foreign investment nor the source of such law. It merely sought to establish the principle that in this very important area of international relations the rule of law is to apply among States. We are aware that chapter I refers to the fulfillment in good faith of international obligations, but the application of this principle to article 2 is, in the view of my delegation, seriously impaired by the unqualified reference in paragraph 2(c) to the domestic law of the nationalizing State.

I have already said that the proposed paragraph 3 merely sought recognition that the rule of law would apply among States in respect of foreign investment. The reason my delegation attaches such importance to this point is that, if we are to achieve and maintain the equitable distribution of the world's wealth which this charter is intended to promote, a significant flow of private capital from developed to developing countries in the form of investment will be required. This movement of capital will take place only in conditions which provide at least a certain degree of security--which cannot possibly exist if the rule of law is rejected.

It is therefore the view of my delegation that article 2, as it now appears, far from promoting the development of developing countries, will constitute an obstacle to that development, which the individual countries concerned will have to overcome in seeking to attract the funds required for their development. It is for this reason that my delegation is unable to support this article.

With respect to article 5, Canada understands the desire of nations to achieve stable and remunerative export earnings. However, as a major exporter and importer of many important commodities, it is the Canadian view that, where international action is required to resolve commodity problems, this should be jointly devised and implemented by the exporters and the importers.

Canada has supported the text of article 6 because it feels this text approximately reflects the Canadian position on this issue. We interpret the text to mean that just as exporting nations have a responsibility to promote the flow of commercial goods, so too do importing nations have a corresponding and balancing responsibility to facilitate access of goods, including processed and fabricated products.

With respect to article 15, my delegation was unable to support the text because Canada has long been a strong supporter of disarmament measures. However, we would note that the concept of a link between disarmament and development financing has for some time been the subject of discussion amongst interested States. Canada, for one, would at this stage of these discussions continue to question the validity of the concept that development funds may be automatically generated by disarmament.

The Canadian delegation abstained in the Second Committee on the text of article 16. We are quite in sympathy with the goals of that article. We do, however, have reservations with respect to the obligations which the article would impose on all States to extend assistance to the countries, Territories and peoples mentioned. Additionally, we consider the degree of interpretation which may be attached to subarticle 2 of this article is far too broad to serve the best purposes of the charter as a whole, particularly when the important question of the sovereignty of States which are host countries to foreign investments is considered.

My delegation was constrained to abstain in the vote on article 19 in the Committee for the reason that while generalized preferential, non-reciprocal and non-discriminatory treatment of developing countries may be technically feasible in terms of formulating a mechanism whereby such preferences may be expressed, the extension of preferences in some fields may not be appropriate.

My delegation would have been able to accept the text of article 26 but for the manner in which most-favoured-nation treatment was referred to. Canada recognizes that the exchange of most-favoured-nation treatment may in a great many cases be an appropriate basis for international trade relations. It is Canada's view, however, that the establishment of such a basis is for the States concerned to work out in each instance between themselves, through the negotiation of either bilateral or multilateral arrangements.

Regarding article 28, Canada considers that techniques aimed at protecting the terms of trade of developing countries both merit and require detailed examination. However, we have some strong doubts about the desirability and feasibility of linking the prices of exports of developing countries to the prices of their imports. The question of linkage involves several difficult and complex issues and has not been considered in depth in various forums; therefore, it is the Canadian view that it would be premature to include this concept in the charter.

To sum up, it is a matter of considerable disappointment to my delegation that after two years of effort by the UNCTAD Working Group on the Charter, in which Canadian representatives consistently played a leading role, it was not possible to reach agreement on a charter which engaged the general support of the international community. In view of the manner in which this document has been adopted, I must make clear that in the view of my delegation the document cannot be considered as a basis for the evolution of international law in the controversial areas where the charter did not gain general acceptance.

United Nations, General Assembly, Twenty-ninth Session: 2316th meeting, Thursday, December 12, 1974

The PRESIDENT (interpretation from French): The Assembly will now resume the hearing of explanations of vote on this item in connexion with the voting that took place this morning.
. . .
Mr. ROUGE (France) (interpretation from French): The member States of the European Economic Community, as well as the Community itself, welcomed with enthusiasm the idea, launched in Santiago in the spring of 1972 by His Excellency Mr. Luis Echeverria, President of Mexico, of drafting a Charter of Economic Rights and Duties of States. The member States of the Community and the Community itself have participated with considerable interest in the discussions on this subject that have taken place since then. They therefore regret all the more the abrupt ending of negotiations before complete agreement could be reached on some of the highly important points that still remained unresolved, just when the consultations conducted here in October outside the Assembly had revealed prospects that were not fully explored.

The presence in the text just adopted of provisions which they do not approve explains the votes cast by the nine delegations on whose behalf I have the honour of speaking. On behalf of those delegations, I wish to reaffirm the positions which follow from the amendments they submitted. I would refer also to the votes they cast and the explanations of vote they gave in the Second Committee.

Mr. KANAZAWA (Japan): I wish to take this opportunity to pay the most profound respect of my delegation to the initiative taken by His Excellency President Echeverria of Mexico for the elaboration of a Charter of Economic Rights and Duties of States, and to express its full agreement with the objectives underlying that initiative.

My delegation abstained in the vote on the draft charter as a whole for reasons which have been explained in the Second Committee and which I shall therefore refrain from repeating here in the plenary Assembly. However, I should like to state that if separate votes had been taken on individual articles my delegation would have voted against articles 2, 5, 6, 19 and 28, respectively, as it did in the Second Committee. My delegation's abstention on the draft charter as a whole does not imply any change in its negative position on the articles that I have just mentioned.

Mr. JANKOWITSCH (Austria): My Government has, on a number of occasions and in different contexts, expressed its support for the concept of a Charter of Economic Rights and Duties of States, as proposed by His Excellency Mr. Luis Echeverria, President of Mexico. We have done so in order to underscore our interest in the evolution of economic and social principles corresponding to the requirements of the rapidly developing interdependent world economy.

It was our hope that the new Charter of Economic Rights and Duties could be based on the widest possible degree of agreement and could thus be adopted by consensus. Given the complexity and sensitivity of the issues at stake, it was to be expected, however, that negotiations would be difficult and extensive. Full recognition must be given in this context to the sincerity and diligence of all those who participated in these negotiations.

A special word of tribute is due to the delegation of Mexico, which did everything it could to further the negotiating process in a constructive spirit.

My delegation feels--and I am sure that this feeling is shared by many others--that the negotiations did clarify many points and resulted in significant progress in the formulation of agreed texts for a large section of the document.

My delegation was thus able in the course of the voting to express its agreement on a large number of provisions, whereas on others we gave preference to specific wordings which, in our view, might have widened the basis of agreement and, in the last analysis, of the document itself. On some provisions, however, we felt bound to register concern and disagreement; this is particularly true with reference to the provisions contained in articles 2(c), 4, 5, 16, 26 and 28.

I do not wish at this stage to go into the reasons why we could not agree to the above-mentioned articles, because the Austrian delegation did that extensively in explaining its vote in the Second Committee. But I would not wish to conclude without stating once more that my country regrets the lack of a consensus on the Charter of Economic Rights and Duties of States. At the same time, we do hope that all possibilities regarding the future examination of those provisions which at present are still controversial will be fully explored, in a spirit of understanding and compromise and with the objective of ensuring the widest possible agreement. It should not be overlooked that despite considerable differences of opinion on specific issues, a large measure of agreement has emerged. All this tends to justify our hope that the forward-looking initiative which the charter represents will further stimulate and give momentum to our deliberations and the efforts to promote economic and social development, in the interests of all.

It is in that sense that we warmly welcome and gladly respond to the appeal made from this rostrum this morning by the Minister of Foreign Affairs of Mexico, His Excellency Mr. Emilio Rabasa, to all countries to combine their efforts to create a new, genuine era of global solidarity.

Mr. TEMBOURY (Spain) (interpretation from Spanish): Although the Spanish delegation, at the 1949th meeting of the Second Committee, gave a detailed explanation of its vote on the Charter of Economic Rights and Duties of States—an explanation that I would ask representatives to regard as repeated here—I cannot but restate some views that my Government feels are of interest.

Since the idea of drafting a charter of economic rights and duties of States was launched in Santiago de Chile, the delegation of Spain has actively and willingly co-operated, in that and other international forums, in the effort to bring that idea to fruition.

The work carried out and the road which has been traversed during this period of time of two and a half years are of positive value and of far greater scope than that which could have been envisaged in 1972. Nonetheless, there was still a great distance to go, and that is why we should not have rushed our fences.

Nevertheless, the official text put forward at this session of the Assembly is very different from the one on which we were negotiating and which was the outcome of the meeting in Mexico and subsequent meetings.

The delegation of Spain believes that a Charter of Economic Rights and Duties of States which does not reflect unanimity, or if not unanimity at least the consensus of all delegations, is a document of only relative value. We see now with deep regret that the balance we wished to establish in the charter has been completely altered.

Because of this, and in view of the fact that we have a document which suffers from serious defects, in particular a notable imbalance in a particular direction, the Spanish delegation was not able to support it as a whole, and for that reason it abstained from voting on it. We very sincerely regret that as a result of the decision to press on to a vote many efforts have come to naught, and thus a document which would undoubtedly have had a great impact on the new international order has been deprived of its effectiveness. Its adoption at the forthcoming special session of the General Assembly would have been well timed and would have resulted in the adoption of a better text.

. . .

C. Seventh Special Session of the United Nations General Assembly:

1. Development and International Economic Co-operation

3362 (S-VII). Development and international economic co-operation

The General Assembly,

Determined to eliminate injustice and inequality which afflict vast sections of humanity and to accelerate the development of developing countries,

Recalling the Declaration and the Programme of Action on the Establishment of a New International Economic Order,* as well as the Charter of Economic Rights and Duties of States,** which lay down the foundations of the new international economic order,

Reaffirming the fundamental purposes of the above-mentioned documents and the rights and duties of all States to seek and participate in the solutions of the problems afflicting the world, in particular the imperative need of redressing the economic imbalance between developed and developing countries,

---

*Resolutions 3201 (S-VI) and 3202 (S-VI).

**Resolution 3281 (XXIX).

Recalling further the International Development Strategy for the Second United Nations Development Decade,* which should be reviewed in the light of the Programme of Action on the Establishment of a New International Economic Order, and determined to implement the targets and policy measures contained in the International Development Strategy,

Conscious that the accelerated development of developing countries would be a decisive element for the promotion of world peace and security,

Recognizing that greater co-operation among States in the fields of trade, industry, science and technology as well as in other fields of economic activities, based on the principles of the Declaration and the Programme of Action on the Establishment of a New International Economic Order and of the Charter of Economic Rights and Duties of States, would also contribute to strengthening peace and security in the world,

Believing that the over-all objective of the new international economic order is to increase the capacity of developing countries, individually and collectively, to pursue their development,

Decides, to this end and in the context of the foregoing, to set in motion the following measures as the basis and framework for the work of the competent bodies and organizations of the United Nations system:

I. INTERNATIONAL TRADE

1. Concerted efforts should be made in favour of the developing countries towards expanding and diversifying their trade, improving and diversifying their productive capacity, improving their productivity and increasing their export earnings, with a view to counteracting the adverse effects of inflation—thereby sustaining real incomes—and with a view to improving the terms of trade of the developing countries and in order to eliminate the economic imbalance between developed and developing countries.

2. Concerted action should be taken to accelerate the growth and diversification of the export trade of developing countries in manufactures and semi-manufactures and in processed and semi-processed products in order to increase their share in world industrial output and world trade within the framework of an expanding world economy.

3. An important aim of the fourth session of the United Nations Conference on Trade and Development, in addition to work in progress elsewhere, should be to reach decisions on the improvement of market structures in the field of raw materials and commodities of export interest to the developing countries, including decisions with respect to an integrated programme and the applicability of elements thereof. In this connexion, taking into account the distinctive features of individual raw materials and commodities, the decisions should bear on the following:

(*a*) Appropriate international stocking and other forms of market arrangements for securing stable, remunerative and equitable prices for commodities of export interest to developing countries and promoting equilibrium between supply and demand, including, where possible, long-term multilateral commitments;

(*b*) Adequate international financing facilities for such stocking and market arrangements;

(*c*) Where possible, promotion of long-term and medium-term contracts;

(*d*) Substantial improvement of facilities for compensatory financing of export revenue fluctuations through the widening and enlarging of the existing facilities. Note has been taken of the various proposals regarding a comprehensive scheme for the stabilization of export earnings of developing countries and for a development security facility as well as specific measures for the benefit of the developing countries most in need;

(*e*) Promotion of processing of raw materials in producing developing countries and expansion and diversification of their exports, particularly to developed countries;

(*f*) Effective opportunities to improve the share of developing countries in transport, marketing and distribution of their primary commodities and to encourage measures of world significance for the evolution of the infrastructure and secondary capacity of developing countries from the production of primary commodities to processing, transport and marketing, and to the production of finished manufactured goods, their transport, distribution and exchange, including advanced financial and exchange institutions for the remunerative management of trade transactions.

4. The Secretary-General of the United Nations Conference on Trade and Development should present a report to the Conference at its fourth session on the impact of an integrated programme on the imports of developing countries which are net importers of raw materials and commodities, including those lacking in natural resources, and recommend any remedial measures that may be necessary.

5. A number of options are open to the international community to preserve the purchasing power of developing countries. These need to be further studied on a priority basis. The Secretary-General of the United

*Resolution 2626 (XXV).

Nations Conference on Trade and Development should continue to study direct and indirect indexation schemes and other options with a view to making concrete proposals before the Conference at its fourth session.

6. The Secretary-General of the United Nations Conference on Trade and Development should prepare a preliminary study on the proportion between prices of raw materials and commodities exported by developing countries and the final consumer price, particularly in developed countries, and submit it, if possible, to the Conference at its fourth session.

7. Developed countries should fully implement agreed provisions on the principle of standstill as regards imports from developing countries, and any departure should be subjected to such measures as consultations and multilateral surveillance and compensation, in accordance with internationally agreed criteria and procedures.

8. Developed countries should take effective steps within the framework of multilateral trade negotiations for the reduction or removal, where feasible and appropriate, of non-tariff barriers affecting the products of export interest to developing countries on a differential and more favourable basis for developing countries. The generalized scheme of preferences should not terminate at the end of the period of ten years originally envisaged and should be continuously improved through wider coverage, deeper cuts and other measures, bearing in mind the interests of those developing countries which enjoy special advantages and the need for finding ways and means for protecting their interests.

9. Countervailing duties should be applied only in conformity with internationally agreed obligations. Developed countries should exercise maximum restraint within the framework of international obligations in the imposition of countervailing duties on the imports of products from developing countries. The multilateral trade negotiations under way should take fully into account the particular interests of developing countries with a view to providing them differential and more favourable treatment in appropriate cases.

10. Restrictive business practices adversely affecting international trade, particularly that of developing countries, should be eliminated and efforts should be made at the national and international levels with the objective of negotiating a set of equitable principles and rules.

11. Special measures should be undertaken by developed countries and by developing countries in a position to do so to assist in the structural transformation of the economy of the least developed, land-locked and island developing countries.

12. Emergency measures as spelled out in section X of General Assembly resolution 3202 (S-VI) should be undertaken on a temporary basis to meet the specific problems of the most seriously affected countries as defined in Asembly resolutions 3201 (S-VI) and 3202 (S-VI) of 1 May 1974, without any detriment to the interests of the developing countries as a whole.

13. Further expansion of trade between the socialist countries of Eastern Europe and the developing countries should be intensified as is provided for in resolutions 15 (II) of 25 March 1968* and 53 (III) of 19 May 1972** of the United Nations Conference on Trade and Development. Additional measures and appropriate orientation to achieve this end are necessary.

II. TRANSFER OF REAL RESOURCES FOR FINANCING THE DEVELOPMENT OF DEVELOPING COUNTRIES AND INTERNATIONAL MONETARY REFORMS

1. Concessional financial resources to developing countries need to be increased substantially, their terms and conditions ameliorated and their flow made predictable, continuous and increasingly assured so as to facilitate the implementation by developing countries of long-term programmes for economic and social development. Financial assistance should, as a general rule, be untied.

2. Developed countries confirm their continued commitment in respect of the targets relating to the transfer of resources, in particular the official development assistance target of 0.7 per cent of gross national product, as agreed in the International Development Strategy for the Second United Nations Development Decade, and adopt as their common aim an effective increase in official development assistance with a view to achieving these targets by the end of the decade. Developed countries which have not yet made a commitment in respect of these targets undertake to make their best efforts to reach these targets in the remaining part of this decade.

3. The establishment of a link between the special drawing rights and development assistance should form part of the consideration by the International Monetary Fund of the creation of new special drawing rights as

---

Proceedings of the United Nations Conference on Trade and Development, Second Session, vol. 1 and Corr.1 and 3 and Add.1 and 2. *Report and Annexes* (United Nations publication, Sales No. E.68.II.D.14), p. 32.

**See *Proceedings of the United Nations Conference on Trade and Development, Third Session,* vol. 1, *Report and Annexes* (United Nations publication, Sales No. E.73.II.D.4), annex I.A.

and when they are created according to the needs of international liquidity. Agreement should be reached at an early date on the establishment of a trust fund, to be financed partly through the International Monetary Fund gold sales and partly through voluntary contributions and to be governed by an appropriate body, for the benefit of developing countries. Consideration of other means of transfer of real resources which are predictable, assured and continuous should be expedited in appropriate bodies.

4. Developed countries and international organizations should enhance the real value and volume of assistance to developing countries and ensure that the developing countries obtain the largest possible share in the procurement of equipment, consultants and consultancy services. Such assistance should be on softer terms and, as a general rule, untied.

5. In order to enlarge the pool of resources available for financing development, there is an urgent need to increase substantially the capital of the World Bank Group, in particular the resources of the International Development Association, to enable it to make additional capital available to the poorest countries on highly concessional terms.

6. The resources of the development institutions of the United Nations system, in particular the United Nations Development Programme, should also be increased. The funds at the disposal of the regional development banks should be augmented. These increases should be without prejudice to bilateral development assistance flows.

7. To the extent desirable, the World Bank Group is invited to consider new ways of supplementing its financing with private management, skills, technology and capital and also new approaches to increase financing of development in developing countries, in accordance with their national plans and priorities.

8. The burden of debt on developing countries is increasing to a point where the import capacity as well as reserves have come under serious strain. At its fourth session the United Nations Conference on Trade and Development shall consider the need for, and the possibility of, convening as soon as possible a conference of major donor, creditor and debtor countries to devise ways and means to mitigate this burden, taking into account the development needs of developing countries, with special attention to the plight of the most seriously affected countries as defined in General Assembly resolutions 3201 (S-VI) and 3202 (S-VI).

9. Developing countries should be granted increased access on favourable terms to the capital markets of developed countries. To this end, the joint Development Committee of the International Monetary Fund and the International Bank for Reconstruction and Development should progress as rapidly as possible in its work. Appropriate United Nations bodies and other related intergovernmental agencies should be invited to examine ways and means of increasing the flow of public and private resources to developing countries, including proposals made at the current session to provide investment in private and public enterprises in the developing countries. Consideration should be given to the examination of an international investment trust and to the expansion of the International Finance Corporation capital without prejudice to the increase in resources of other intergovernmental financial and development institutions and bilateral assistance flows.

10. Developed and developing countries should further co-operate through investment of financial resources and supply of technology and equipment to developing countries by developed countries and by developing countries in a position to do so.

11. Developed countries, and developing countries in a position to do so, are urged to make adequate contributions to the United Nations Special Fund with a view to an early implementation of a programme of lending, preferably in 1976.

12. Developed countries should improve terms and conditions of their assistance so as to include a preponderant grant element for the least developed, land-locked and island developing countries.

13. In providing additional resources for assisting the most seriously affected countries in helping them to meet their serious balance-of-payments deficits, all developed countries, and developing countries in a position to do so, and international organizations such as the International Bank for Reconstruction and Development and the International Monetary Fund, should undertake specific measures in their favour, including those provided in General Assembly resolutions 3201 (S-VI) and 3202 (S-VI).

14. Special attention should be given by the international community to the phenomena of natural disasters which frequently afflict many parts of the world, with far-reaching devastating economic, social and structural consequences, particularly in the least developed countries. To this end, the General Assembly at its thirtieth session, in considering this problem, should examine and adopt appropriate measures.

15. The role of national reserve currencies should be reduced and the special drawing rights should become the central reserve asset of the international monetary system in order to provide for greater international control over the creation and equitable distribution of liquidity and in order to limit potential losses as a consequence of exchange rate fluctuations. Arrangements for gold should be consistent with the agreed objective of reducing the role of gold in the system and with equitable distribution of new international liquidity and should in particular take into consideration the needs of developing countries for increased liquidity.

16. The process of decision-making should be fair and responsive to change and should be most specially responsive to the emergence of a new economic influence on the part of developing countries. The participation of developing countries in the decision-making process in the competent organs of international finance and development institutions should be adequately increased and made more effective without adversely affecting the broad geographic representation of developing countries and in accordance with the existing and evolving rules.

17. The compensatory financing facility now available through the International Monetary Fund should be expanded and liberalized. In this connexion, early consideration should be given by the Fund and other appropriate United Nations bodies to various proposals made at the current session—including the examination of a new development security facility—which would mitigate export earnings shortfalls of developing countries, with special regard to the poorest countries, and thus provide greater assistance to their continued economic development. Early consideration should also be given by the International Monetary Fund to proposals to expand and liberalize its coverage of current transactions to include manufactures and services, to ensure that, whenever possible, compensation for export shortfalls takes place at the same time they occur, to take into account, in determining the quantum of compensation, movements in import prices and to lengthen the repayment period.

18. Drawing under the buffer stock financing facility of the International Monetary Fund should be accorded treatment with respect to floating alongside the gold tranche, similar to that under the compensatory financing facility, and the Fund should expedite its study of the possibility of an amendment of the Articles of Agreement, to be presented to the Interim Committee, if possible at its next meeting, that would permit the Fund to provide assistance directly to international buffer stocks of primary products.

III. SCIENCE AND TECHNOLOGY

1. Developed and developing countries should co-operate in the establishment, strengthening and development of the scientific and technological infrastructure of developing countries. Developed countries should also take appropriate measures, such as contribution to the establishment of an industrial technological information bank and consideration of the possibility of regional and sectoral banks, in order to make available a greater flow to developing countries of information permitting the selection of technologies, in particular advanced technologies. Consideration should also be given to the establishment of an international centre for the exchange of technological information for the sharing of research findings relevant to developing countries. For the above purposes institutional arrangements within the United Nations system should be examined by the General Assembly at its thirtieth session.

2. Developed countries should significantly expand their assistance to developing countries for direct support to their science and technology programmes, as well as increase substantially the proportion of their research and development devoted to specific problems of primary interest to developing countries, and in the creation of suitable indigenous technology, in accordance with feasible targets to be agreed upon. The General Assembly invites the Secretary-General to carry out a preliminary study and to report to the Assembly at its thirty-first session on the possibility of establishing, within the framework of the United Nations system, an international energy institute to assist all developing countries in energy resources research and development.

3. All States should co-operate in evolving an international code of conduct for the transfer of technology, corresponding, in particular, to the special needs of the developing countries. Work on such a code should therefore be continued within the United Nations Conference on Trade and Development and concluded in time for decisions to be reached at the fourth session of the Conference, including a decision on the legal character of such a code with the objective of the adoption of a code of conduct prior to the end of 1977. International conventions on patents and trade marks should be reviewed and revised to meet, in particular, the special needs of the developing countries, in order that these conventions may become more satisfactory instruments for aiding developing countries in the transfer and development of technology. National patents systems should, without delay, be brought into line with the international patent system in its revised form.

4. Developed countries should facilitate the access of developing countries on favourable terms and conditions, and on an urgent basis, to *informatique,* to relevant information on advanced and other technologies suited to their specific needs as well as on new uses of existing technology, new developments and possibilities of adapting them to local needs. Inasmuch as in market economies advanced technologies with respect to industrial production are most frequently developed by private institutions, developed countries should facilitate and encourage these institutions in providing effective technologies in support of the priorities of developing countries.

5. Developed countries should give developing countries the freest and fullest possible access to technologies whose transfer is not subject to private decision.

6. Developed countries should improve the transparency of the industrial property market in order to facilitate the technological choices of developing countries. In this respect, relevant organizations of the United Nations system, with the collaboration of developed countries, should undertake projects in the fields of information, consultancy and training for the benefit of developing countries.

7. A United Nations Conference on Science and Technology for Development should be held in 1978 or 1979 with the main objectives of strengthening the technological capacity of developing countries to enable them to apply science and technology to their own development; adopting effective means for the utilization of scientific and technological potentials in the solution of development problems of regional and global significance, especially for the benefit of developing countries; and providing instruments of co-operation to developing countries in the utilization of science and technology for solving socio-economic problems that cannot be solved by individual action, in accordance with national priorities, taking into account the recommendations made by the Intergovernmental Working Group of the Committee on Science and Technology for Development.

8. The United Nations system should play a major role, with appropriate financing, in achieving the above-stated objectives and in developing scientific and technological co-operation between all States in order to ensure the application of science and technology to development. The work of the relevant United Nations bodies, in particular that of the United Nations Conference on Trade and Development, the United Nations Industrial Development Organization, the International Labour Organisation, the United Nations Educational, Scientific and Cultural Organization, the Food and Agriculture Organization of the United Nations, the World Intellecutal Property Organization and the United Nations Development Programme, to facilitate the transfer and diffusion of technology should be given urgent priority. The Secretary-General of the United Nations should take steps to ensure that the technology and experience available within the United Nations system is widely disseminated and readily available to the developing countries in need of it.

9. The World Health Organization and the competent organs of the United Nations system, in particular the United Nations Children's Fund, should intensify the international effort aimed at improving health conditions in developing countries by giving priority to prevention of disease and malnutrition and by providing primary health services to the communities, including maternal and child health and family welfare.

10. Since the outflow of qualified personnel from developing to developed countries seriously hampers the development of the former, there is an urgent need to formulate national and international policies to avoid the "brain drain" and to obviate its adverse effects.

IV. INDUSTRIALIZATION

1. The General Assembly endorses the Lima Declaration and Plan of Action on Industrial Development Co-operation* and requests all Governments to take individually and/or collectively the necessary measures and decisions required to implement effectively their undertakings in terms of the Lima Declaration and Plan of Action.

2. Developed countries should facilitate the development of new policies and strengthen existing policies, including labour market policies, which would encourage the redeployment of their industries which are less competitive internationally to developing countries, thus leading to strutural adjustments in the former and a higher degree of utilization of natural and human resources in the latter. Such policies may take into account the economic structure and the economic, social and security objectives of the developed countries concerned and the need for such industries to move into more viable lines of production or into other sectors of the economy.

3. A system of consultations as provided for by the Lima Plan of Action should be established at the global, regional, interregional and sectoral levels within the United Nations Industrial Development Organization and within other appropriate international bodies, between developed and developing countries and among developing countries themselves, in order to facilitate the achievement of the goals set forth in the field of industrialization, including the redeployment of certain productive capacities existing in developed countries and the creation of new industrial facilities in developing countries. In this context, the United Nations Industrial Development Organization should serve as a forum for negotiation of agreements in the field of industry between developed and developing countries and among developing countries themselves, at the request of the countries concerned.

4. The Executive Director of the United Nations Industrial Development Organization should take immediate action to ensure the readiness of that organization to serve as a forum for consultations and negotiation of agreements in the field of industry. In reporting to the next session of the Industrial Development Board

*See A/10112, chap. IV.

on actions taken in this respect, the Executive Director should also include proposals for the establishment of a system of consultations. The Industrial Development Board is invited to draw up, at an early date, the rules of procedure according to which this system would operate.

5. To promote co-operation between developed and developing countries, both should endeavour to disseminate appropriate information about their priority areas for industrial co-operation and the form they would like such co-operation to take. The efforts undertaken by the United Nations Conference on Trade and Development on tripartite co-operation between countries having different economic and social systems could lead to constructive proposals for the industrialization of developing countries.

6. Developed countries should, whenever possible, encourage their enterprises to participate in investment projects within the framework of the development plans and programmes of the developing countries which so desire; such participation should be carried out in accordance with the laws and regulations of the developing countries concerned.

7. A joint study should be undertaken by all Governments under the auspices of the United Nations Industrial Development Organization, in consultation with the Secretary-General of the United Nations Conference on Trade and Development, making full use of the knowledge, experience and capacity existing in the United Nations system of methods and mechanisms for diversified financial and technical co-operation which are geared to the special and changing requirements of international industrial co-operation, as well as of a general set of guidelines for bilateral industrial co-operation. A progress report on this study should be submitted to the General Assembly at its thirty-first session.

8. Special attention should be given to the particular problems in the industrialization of the least developed, land-locked and island developing countries—in order to put at their disposal those technical and financial resources as well as critical goods which need to be provided to them to enable them to overcome their specific problems and to play their due role in the world economy, warranted by their human and material resources.

9. The General Assembly endorses the recommendation of the Second General Conference of the United Nations Industrial Development Organization to convert that organization into a specialized agency and decides to establish a Committee on the Drafting of a Constitution for the United Nations Industrial Development Organization, which shall be an intergovernmental committee of the whole, including States which participated in the Second General Conference, to meet in Vienna to draw up a constitution for the United Nations Industrial Development Organization as a specialized agency, to be submitted to a conference of plenipotentiaries to be convened by the Secretary-General in the last quarter of 1976.

10. In view of the importance of the forthcoming Tripartite World Conference on Employment, Income Distribution, Social Progress and the International Division of Labour, Governments should undertake adequate preparations and consultations.

V. FOOD AND AGRICULTURE

1. The solution to world food problems lies primarily in rapidly increasing food production in the developing countries. To this end, urgent and necessary changes in the pattern of world food production should be introduced and trade policy measures should be implemented, in order to obtain a notable increase in agricultural production and the export earnings of developing countries.

2. To achieve these objectives, it is essential that developed countries, and developing countries in a position to do so, should substantially increase the volume of assistance to developing countries for agriculture and food production, and that developed countries should effectively facilitate access to their markets for food and agricultural products of export interest to developing countries, both in raw and processed form, and adopt adjustment measures where necesary.

3. Developing countries should accord high priority to agricultural and fisheries development, increase investment accordingly and adopt policies which give adequate incentives to agricultural producers. It is a responsibilitiy of each State concerned, in accordance with its sovereign judgement and development plans and policies, to promote interaction between expansion of food production and socio-economic reforms, with a view to achieving an integrated rural development. The further reduction of post-harvest food losses in developing countries should be undertaken as a matter of priority, with a view to reaching at least a 50 per cent reduction by 1985. All countries and competent international organizations should co-operate financially and technically in the effort to achieve this objective. Particular attention should be given to improvement in the systems of distribution of food-stuffs.

4. The Consultative Group on Food Production and Investment in Developing Countries should quickly identify developing countries having the potential for most rapid and efficient increase of food production, as well as the potential for rapid agricultural expansion in other developing countries, especially the countries with food deficits. Such an assesssment would assist developed countries and the competent international

organizations to concentrate resources for the rapid increase of agricultural production in the developing countries.

5. Developed countries should adopt policies aimed at ensuring a stable supply and sufficient quantity of fertilizers and other production inputs to developing countries at reasonable prices. They should also provide assistance to, and promote investments in, developing countries to improve the efficiency of their fertilizer and other agricultural input industries. Advantage should be taken of the mechanism provided by the International Fertilizer Supply Scheme.

6. In order to make additional resources available on concessional terms for agricultural development in developing countries, developed countries and developing countries in a position to do so should pledge, on a voluntary basis, substantial contributions to the proposed International Fund for Agricultural Development so as to enable it to come into being by the end of 1975, with initial resources of SDR 1,000 million. Thereafter, additional resources should be provided to the Fund on a continuing basis.

7. In view of the significant impact of basic and applied agricultural research on increasing the quantity and quality of food production, developed countries should support the expansion of the work of the existing international agricultural research centres. Through their bilateral programmes they should strengthen their links with these international research centres and with the national agricultural research centres in developing countries. With respect to the improvement of the productivity and competitiveness with synthetics of non-food agricultural and forestry products, research and technological assistance should be co-ordinated and financed through an appropriate mechanism.

8. In view of the importance of food aid as a transitional measure, all countries should accept both the principle of a minimum food aid target and the concept of forward planning of food aid. The target for the 1975–1976 season should be 10 million tons of food grains. They should also accept the principle that food aid should be channelled on the basis of objective assessment of requirements in the recipient countries. In this respect all countries are urged to participate in the Global Information and Early Warning System on Food and Agriculture.

9. Developed countries should increase the grant component of food aid, where food is not at present provided as grants, and should accept multilateral channelling of these resources at an expanding rate. In providing food grants and financing on soft terms to developing countries in need of such assistance, developed countries and the World Food Programme should take due account of the interests of the food-exporting developing countries and should ensure that such assistance includes, wherever possible, purchases of food from the food-exporting developing countries.

10. Developed countries, and developing countries in a position to do so, should provide food grains and financial assistance on most favourable terms to the most seriously affected countries, to enable them to meet their food and agricultural development requirements within the constraints of their balance-of-payments position. Donor countries should also provide aid on soft terms, in cash and in kind, through bilateral and multilateral channels, to enable the most seriously affected countries to obtain their estimated requirements of about 1 million tons of plant nutrients during 1975–1976.

11. Developed countries should carry out both their bilateral and multilateral food aid channelling in accordance with the procedures of the Principles of Surplus Disposal of the Food and Agriculture Organization of the United Nations so as to avoid causing undue fluctuations in market prices or the disruption of commercial markets for exports of interest to exporting developing countries.

12. All countries should subscribe to the International Undertaking on World Food Security. They should build up and maintain world food-grain reserves, to be held nationally or regionally and strategically located in developed and developing, importing and exporting countries, large enough to cover foreseeable major production shortfalls. Intensive work should be continued on a priority basis in the World Food Council and other appropriate forums in order to determine, *inter alia*, the size of the required reserve, taking into account among other things the proposal made at the current session that the components of wheat and rice in the total reserve should be 30 million tons. The World Food Council should report to the General Assembly on this matter at its thirty-first sesssion. Developed countries should assist developing countries in their efforts to build up and maintain their agreed shares of such reserves. Pending the establishment of the world food-grain reserve, developed countries and developing countries in a position to do so should earmark stocks and/or funds to be placed at the disposal of the World Food Programme as an emergency reserve to strengthen the capacity of the Programme to deal with crisis situations in developing countries. The aim should be a target of not less than 500,000 tons.

13. Members of the General Assembly reaffirm their full support for the resolutions of the World Food Conference and call upon the World Food Council to monitor the implementation of the provisions under section V of the present resolution and to report to the General Assembly at its thirty-first session.

VI. CO-OPERATION AMONG DEVELOPING COUNTRIES

1. Developed countries and the United Nations system are urged to provide, as and when requested, support and assistance to developing countries in strengthening and enlarging their mutual co-operation at subregional, regional and interregional levels. In this regard, suitable institutional arrangements within the United Nations development system should be made and, when appropriate, strengthened such as those within the United Nations Conference on Trade and Development, the United Nations Industrial Development Organization and the United Nations Development Programme.

2. The Secretary-General, together with the relevant organizations of the United Nations system, is requested to continue to provide support to ongoing projects and activities, and to commission further studies through institutions in developing countries, which would take into account the material already available within the United Nations system, including in particular the regional commissions and the United Nations Conference on Trade and Development, and in accordance with existing subregional and regional arrangements. These further studies, which should be submitted to the General Assembly at its thirty-first session, should, as a first step, cover:

(*a*) Utilization of know-how, skills, natural resources, technology and funds available within developing countries for promotion of investments in industry, agriculture, transport and communications;

(*b*) Trade liberalization measures including payments and clearing arrangements, covering primary commodities, manufactured goods and services, such as banking, shipping, insurance and reinsurance;

(*c*) Transfer of technology.

3. These studies on co-operation among developing countries, together with other initiatives, would contribute to the evolution towards a system for the economic development of developing countries.

VII. RESTRUCTURING OF THE ECONOMIC AND SOCIAL SECTORS OF THE UNITED NATIONS SYSTEM

1. With a view to initiating the process of restructuring the United Nations system so as to make it more fully capable of dealing with problems of international economic co-operation and development in a comprehensive and effective manner, in pursuance of General Assembly resolutions 3172 (XXVIII) of 17 December 1973 and 3343 (XXIX) of 17 December 1974, and to make it more responsive to the requirements of the provisions of the Declaration and the Programme of Action on the Establishment of a New International Economic Order as well as those of the Charter of Economic Rights and Duties of States, an *Ad Hoc* Committee on the Restructuring of the Economic and Social Sectors of the United Nations System, which shall be a committee of the whole of the General Assembly open to the participation of all States,* is hereby established to prepare detailed action proposals. The *Ad Hoc* Committee should start its work immediately and inform the General Assembly at its thirtieth session on the progress made, and submit its report to the Assembly at its thirty-first session, through the Economic and Social Council at its resumed session. The *Ad Hoc* Committee should take into account in its work, *inter alia*, the relevant proposals and documentation submitted in preparation for the seventh special session of the General Assembly pursuant to Assembly resolution 3343 (XXIX) and other relevant decisions, including the report of the Group of Experts on the Structure of the United Nations System entitled *A New United Nations Structure for Global Economic Co-operation,*** the records of the relevant deliberations of the Economic and Social Council, the Trade and Development Board, the Governing Council of the United Nations Development Programme and the seventh special session of the General Assembly, as well as the results of the forthcoming deliberations on institutional arrangements of the United Nations Conference on Trade and Development at its fourth session and of the Governing Council of the United Nations Environment Programme at its fourth session. All United Nations organs, including the regional commissions, as well as the specialized agencies and the International Atomic Energy Agency, are invited to participate at the executive level in the work of the *Ad Hoc* Committee and to respond to requests that the Committee may make to them for information, data or views.

2. The Economic and Social Council should meanwhile continue the process of rationalization and reform which it has undertaken in accordance with Council resolution 1768 (LIV) of 18 May 1973 and General Assembly resolution 3341 (XXIX) of 17 December 1974, and should take into full consideration those recommendations of the *Ad Hoc* Committee that fall within the scope of these resolutions, at the latest at its resumed sixty-first session.

2349th plenary meeting
16 September 1975

---

*It is the understanding of the General Assembly that the "all States" formula will be applied in accordance with the established practice of the General Assembly.

**E/AC.62/9 (United Nations publication, Sales No. E.75, II.A.7).

2. Reservations
Seventh Special Session of the United Nations General Assembly

[Resolution 3362 (S-VII), adopted by consensus by the Seventh Special Session on September 16, 1975, had been prepared and adopted unanimously by the *Ad Hoc* Committee of the Seventh Special Session. After the adoption of the resolution by the Committee, a number of delegations made statements which were reproduced verbatim as an annex to the report of the Committee on the understanding that they would not be repeated in the plenary meetings of the General Assembly. These statements contain the reservation made by the developed market economies. They are reproduced below.*]

Statements made at the 3rd meeting of the *Ad Hoc* Committee of the Seventh Special Session on 16 September 1975 following the adoption of the draft resolution on development and international economic co-operation.

Mr. MYERSON (United States of America): The United States joins in most of the specific provisions of the resolution adopted by the Committee and we warmly associate ourselves with its larger objectives. The United States cannot and does not accept any implication that the world is now embarked on the establishment of something called the "new international economic order." Further, while we have joined in the consensus on this report—and we are very pleased to have done so—I wish to make it clear that the United States maintains its position on the resolutions of the sixth special session, the Charter of Economic Rights and Duties of States and on the Lima Declaration.

With regard to trade, I should like to make some short comments. We join others in pledging a series of actions of benefit to developing countries—specific actions are left to each country. It is our expectation that these actions will substantially increase the growth of developing countries, thus counteracting inflation and thereby sustaining real incomes, but our purpose is not to set world prices or to manipulate the terms of trade. It was proposed that commodity prizes be indexed, that is, fixed by agreement and augmented as prices for industrial goods rise. We have agreed to join others in the study of such a proposal. However, the United States has to make clear that it does not support such a proposal. The commitments we have made are to assist developing countries' exports within the market rather than by supplanting market mechanisms.

With regard to transfer of resources, the United States recognizes the need of developing countries for a transfer of real resources and it recognizes the importance of a smoothly functioning, stable international monetary system. There are, however, several specific paragraphs in this section with which the United States is unable to concur.

First, the United States fully supports the objective of an effective increase in official development assistance and intends to increase the level of its own assistance. It does not, however, consider the establishment of specific targets as likely to achieve the intended result. The United States does not subscribe to the paragraph dealing with the link between special drawing rights and development assistance. The position of the United States is that it does not support a link between special drawing rights and assistance. This position is unchanged.

The United States differs with the paragraph dealing with the reform of the international monetary system. We share the general objective of placing the special drawing rights in the centre of the international monetary system, but we believe that, in the absence of agreement on all the interrelated components of a fully reformed international monetary system, it is inappropriate to specify selected aims or elements.

Finally, the United States is not fully in accord with the paragraph dealing with decision-making in international financial institutions. We support an evolving role for developing nations. We believe, however, that participation in decision-making in international financial institutions must be equitable for all members and take due account of relative economic positions and contributions of resources to those institutions, as well as of the need for efficient operational decision-making.

With regard to science and technology, just one brief comment for the record: we support work on international guidelines for the transfer of technology, including, most especially, the progress being achieved at the United Nations Conference on Trade and Development. We do not believe that adoption of a legally binding code of conduct is the path to pursue and we do not read the resolution as so indicating.

With regard to the section on industrialization, we believe that redeployment of industry should be a matter of the evolution of economies rather than a question of international policy or negotiation. While government policy can facilitate such an evolutionary approach, we believe it must take into account the economic structures of the countries concerned as well as their economic, social and security goals, including, especially, protection of working men's rights. The United States does not support those paragraphs dealing with the system of consultations of the United Nations Industrial Development Organization.

---

*United Nations, *Official Records of the General Assembly, Seventh Special Session,* Part II, *Annexes,* Document A/10232: "Report of the *Ad Hoc* Committee of the Seventh Special Session," pp. 14–16.

On food and agriculture, one very brief remark: with regard to the statement in the second paragraph about market access and adjustment measures, we understand developing countries' interests, but we cannot concur in the sentence as formulated since it is inconsistent with United States policy.

Mr. VINCI (Italy): Since Italy at present holds the presidency of the Council of the European Economic Community, I have been asked by my partners to speak on behalf of the whole Community. Owing to the business-like character of this night meeting and the respect we owe to you, Sir, and all those who have worked so hard these past days, and in response also to your invitation, I will restrict myself to a few brief remarks.

I take note with satisfaction that the decision has been taken that these remarks will be reproduced *in extenso* in the report of this *Ad Hoc* Committee on the understanding that they will not be reiterated in the plenary tomorrow.

I must specify that it is the Community and the Governments of its member States which have agreed to adopt the conclusions set down in the resolution and other decisions adopted by the Committee. As a matter of fact, in the many activities in which we will be involved, business enterprises will have an important role to play. Although in market economies Governments do not have unlimited power of action, our Governments can and certainly will encourage these activities.

The section on industrialization is a valuable follow-up to the Second UNIDO Conference in Lima, whose Declaration and Plan of Action we have endorsed in the same spirit and understanding which guided us when adopting resolution 45(IX) of the Industrial Development Board.

Regarding the food emergency reserve, EEC and its member States are of the opinion that the choice of procedures for distribution should be made so as to ensure the most effective satisfaction of the emergency needs of affected populations.

I now wish to record a few points on behalf of some individual member States. France considered that the recommendations concerning contributions to new international funds and mechanisms, untying and debt burden must be assessed in the light of the progress which must be made towards the alignment of the various Governments' efforts relating to aid and the over-all increase in financial assistance in accordance with the objectives of the International Development Strategy for the Second United Nations Development Decade.

The Governments of Ireland and Luxembourg regret that they are unable at present to go beyond their existing commitments in respect of aid targets. However, they confirm that it is the intention of both Governments to meet their existing commitments and to improve their performance on official development assistance as quickly as circumstances will allow.

Because of the present economic situation, the Governments of Italy and the United Kingdom cannot give any undertaking as to when they will be able to transfer official development aid amounting to 0.7 per cent of gross national product, and access to the United Kingdom capital market must remain limited.

Mr. SMID (Czechoslovakia): I have been authorized by the delegations of Bulgaria, the Byelorussian SSR, the German Democratic Republic, Hungary, Mongolia, Poland, the Ukrainian SSR, the USSR and Czechoslovakia to express our principled support of the final documents—that is, the resolution and decisions we have just adopted. As is well known, the socialist countries welcomed the convening of this special session. They have made every effort to contribute to the success of its deliberations.

During these deliberations they stated their principles, positive attitudes resulting in concrete proposals submitted by the group of the developing countries, and re-emphasized their basic approach to the problems of development and international co-operation.

We have noted with satisfaction that, during the discussions and also in the final documents, the paramount importance of the Declaration on the Establishment of a New International Economic Order and of the Charter of Economic Rights and Duties of States has been reiterated. The implementation of the principles contained therein undoubtedly should contribute, to a decisive degree, to the betterment of the present economic situation in the world and particularly to the accelerated economic and social advancement of the developing countries. We consider the above-mentioned Declaration, the Charter, and the final document of this special session as inseparably interrelated.

While supporting the developing countries in their just demands, we maintain that there cannot be an equal responsibility of all for the unfavourable economic situation of the developing countries which was inherited from the colonial system and preserved and, in many cases, even made worse by neo-colonial policies. Our non-acceptance of such an untrue placing of responsibility will be relevant as regards some recommendations in the final document.

In conclusion, permit me to assure you that the socialist countries will do their utmost to further develop economic co-operation with all countries, to support the developing countries in their struggle for independence and rapid development of their national economies, and to strive for the strengthening of world peace and international security as the necessary condition of continued and intensified development of international economic co-operation.

Mr. JANKOWITSCH (Austria): I should like to make a brief statement concerning paragraph 2 of section II. In this regard the Austrian delegation wishes to reiterate the statement made on the occasion of the sixth special session of the General Assembly to the effect that Austria, within the limits of its financial and budgetary responsibilities, will continue to make every effort in order to increase assistance to developing countries with a view to achieving the aims set out in paragraph 2 of section II.

Mr. SAITO (Japan): My delegation wishes to express its support of the resolution which has just been adopted by consensus. This is a result of the sincere effort of all the countries represented here for the past several months. I am happy that my delegation has been able to contribute to this common effort for the promotion of development and international economic co-operation.

With respect to the aid target, I appreciate the effort made by the Group of 77 to accommodate the position of my delegation. Although we regret that we cannot commit ourselves to this target at this moment, I can assure you that my country will make its best effort to attain this target.

Mr. TEMBOURY (Spain): My delegation is glad that an agreement has been reached at the last minute which enables us to close this special session.

Just as the views expressed by my country on the problems of science and technology have been taken into account, we should also have liked an opportunity to discuss other matters which we feel are of particular interest, in order to avoid that dichotomy between developed and developing countries which is unduly simplistic. We believe that there are a number of intermediate positions which certainly deserve more detailed consideration.

My delegation hopes that, when problems of the magnitude of those discussed at this special session are considered in the future, better working arrangements will be made so that countries can state their views and contribute to the solution of such important matters.

We should have liked this agreement to have been reached in time to be studied in all its aspects by all the countries represented at this special session. Although that was not possible, we are nevertheless gratified to see that a constructive result has been achieved and we shall submit it to our Government, with appropriate recommendations, so that final approval can be given to the agreement if that is deemed appropriate.

Mr. RAE (Canada): The important resolution which we are adopting tonight represents a significant step forward in our progress towards a new international economic order. Canada supports the direction which this establishes for the future work of the United Nations system. While we are not in complete accord with all of the recommendations, we will work to make them effective as we interpret their intent.

May I add that we interpret the second sentence of paragraph 8 of section I, the section dealing with international trade, as applying in the context of existing national legislation and authorities which established the various generalized preference schemes.

Appendix C—Statistical Annex to Chapter 3

Table 3.1. Share of Developing Countries in World Exports, 1950–1978
(Percentage)

Year	All developing countries[a]	Major petroleum exporters only[b]	Other developing countries
1950	30.8	6.2	24.6
1955	25.5	7.1	18.8
1960	21.5	6.8	14.9
1965	19.6	6.4	13.2
1970	17.8	6.0	11.8
1971	17.8	7.0	10.8
1972	17.9	6.9	10.9
1973	19.2	7.7	11.5
1974	26.9	15.7	11.2
1975	24.2	13.7	10.5
1976	25.9	14.5	11.3
1977	25.7	13.9	11.8
1978	22.9	11.6	11.3

Source: UNCTAD, *Handbook of International Trade and Development Statistics 1979* (New York: United Nations, 1979).

[a]Excluding socialist countries of Asia whose share, since 1965, has been under 1 percent.

[b]Defined as those countries for which petroleum and petroleum products accounted for more than 50 percent of their total exports in 1974. These countries are: Algeria, Angola, Bahrain, Brunei, Ecuador, Gabon, Indonesia, Iran, Iraq, Kuwait, Libyan Arab Jamahiriya, Nigeria, Oman, Qatar, Saudi Arabia, Trinidad and Tobago, United Arab Emirates, and Venezuela.

Table 3.2. Terms of Trade[a] of Developed and Developing Countries, 1954–1978
(1970 = 100)

| Year | Developed market economies | Developing countries | | |
		All	Major petroleum exporters[b]	Other developing countries
1954–56[c]	90	108	97	112
1960	96	100	113	95
1961	97	96	111	91
1962	98	94	111	87

238

Table 3.2. Terms of Trade[a] of Developed and Developing Countries, 1954–1978 (cont.)

		Developing countries		
Year	Developed market economies	All	Major petroleum exporters[b]	Other developing countries
1963	97	94	109	89
1964	97	95	107	91
1965	98	94	103	91
1966	98	97	101	95
1967	99	94	98	92
1968	99	100	103	99
1969	99	102	103	102
1970	100	100	100	100
1971	99	101	116	93
1972	100	100	114	93
1973	99	105	123	96
1974	87	172	335	93
1975	90	164	341	87
1976	89	170	362	88
1977	89	170	361	91
1978[d]	91	151	324	86

Source: Same as Table 3.1.

[a]Unit value index of exports divided by unit value index of imports.

[b]See footnote *b*, Table 3.1.

[c]Average.

[d]Preliminary.

Table 3.3. Volume Indices of the Development of World Exports,
by Major Commodity Groups, 1963–1977
(1963 = 100)

	Commodity group			
Year	All commodities	Agricultural products	Minerals[a]	Manufactures
1963	100	100	100	100
1968	149	121	144	166
1970	178	135	165	204
1971	189	137	164	220
1972	208	149	173	244
1973	231	147	192	280
1974	240	142	190	304
1975	232	150	180	292
1976	259	160	185	327
1977	270	165	190	345

Source: GATT, *International Trade 1977/78* (Geneva: GATT, 1978).

[a]Including fuels and non-ferrous metals.

Table 3.4. Export Dependence of Developing Countries, by Commodity, by Region, 1965 and 1975
(Number of countries)

	Number of countries for which one or two commodities accounted for 30 percent or more of exports		Number of countries for which one or two commodities accounted for 50 percent or more of exports	
	1965	1975	1965	1975
OPEC	12	12	12	12
Other developing countries				
Africa	35	34	27	25
Asia	15	16	7	9
Western hemisphere	22	20	17	13
TOTAL	84	82	63	59

Source: United Nations, *Statistical Yearbook 1977* (New York: United Nations, 1978).

Table 3.5. Price Fluctuations of Primary Products

Index of instability[a]							
0–5		5–10		10–15		Over 15	
Tea	1.3	Coffee	6.5	Sugar	13.9	Copper	5.0
Bananas	1.2	Cotton	4.0	Rubber	3.5	Cocoa	2.6
		Iron Ore	3.6	Phosphate rock	2.6	Zinc	0.7
		Maize	2.3	Rice	1.6	Fishmeal	0.5
		Logs	2.2	Palm oil	1.4	Copra	0.4
		Tobacco	1.9	Beef	0.7	Sisal	0.2
		Tin	1.7	Wool	0.6		
		Oranges	1.4	Coconut oil	0.5		
		Soybean meal	0.8	Groundnut oil	0.4		
		Bauxite	0.7	Lead	0.4		
		Manganese ore	0.6	Lemons	0.2		
		Wheat	0.6				
		Grain sorghum	0.5				
		Groundnuts	0.5				
		Jute	0.2				
TOTAL	2.5		27.5		25.8		9.4

Source: World Bank, *World Development Report, 1978* (Washington: World Bank, 1978).
Note: The figure shown against each commodity indicates its percentage share in total developing country exports of all primary commodities, excluding fuel, in 1975.
[a]The index is based on a five-year moving average of prices for 1955–76. It measures the average percentage deviation of the annual price from the five-year moving average. It does not take account of short-term fluctuations in prices.

Table 3.6. Raw Material Production and Consumption of Nine Major Minerals, by Region, 1950–1980[a]
(Dollars and percent)

Region	Production				Consumption			
	1950	1960	1970	1980 (esti-mated)	1950	1960	1970	1980 (esti-mated)
	(Billions of dollars)							
Developed market economies	3.1	4.4	7.3	10.0	4.6	7.0	11.6	17.9
Developing countries	1.8	3.5	5.3	10.3	0.2	0.5	0.8	2.2
Centrally planned economies	0.8	2.5	4.4	7.0	0.9	2.6	4.6	7.1
TOTAL	5.7	10.4	17.0	27.3	5.7	10.1	17.0	27.2
	(Percentage)							
Developed market economies								
USA and Canada	39	27	25	22	47	29	26	23
Western Europe	11	10	7	4	30	34	27	24
Japan	1	2	1	1	1	5	12	15
Australia and South Africa	3	4	8	10	2	2	3	4
TOTAL, developed market economies	54	43	41	37	80	70	68	66
Developing countries	32	33	33	39	4	5	6	8
Centrally planned economies	14	24	26	25	16	25	26	26
TOTAL	100	100	100	100	100	100	100	100

Source: United Nations, "Problems of Availability and Supply of Natural Resources. Survey of Current Problems in the Fields of Energy and Minerals: The World Mineral Situation. Report of the Secretary-General" (E/C.7/51), Feb. 13, 1975.

[a]Bauxite, copper, iron ore, lead, manganese ore, nickel, phosphorus, tin, and zinc. These nine minerals account for 86 percent of the value of world mineral production.

Table 3.7. Degree of Mineral Processing, by Region, 1950–1970[a]
(Percentage)

Region	Minerals processed as a percentage of total minerals mined in the region (year)[b]		
	1950	1960	1970
Developing countries	30	28	29
Developed countries			
United States and Canada	146	179	179
Western Europe	250	381	1,046
Australia and South Africa	89	72	38
Centrally planned economies	99	102	108
TOTAL	100	100	100

Source: Rex Bosson and Bension Varon, *The Mining Industry and the Developing Countries* (New York: Oxford University Press, 1977).

[a]Included are bauxite and aluminum, copper, iron ore, lead, manganese ore, nickel, phosphate rock, tin, and zinc.

[b]Computed as the value produced by mining and processing operations as a percentage of total value produced, had all ore mined been processed to metal ingot stage, except for iron ore, manganese ore, and phosphate rock for which pelletized or sinterized iron ore, ferromanganese, and superphosphate fertilizers were taken as representing the processed product.

Table 3.8. The Structure of the World Aluminum Industry: Patterns of Location, Distribution of Benefits, Tariffs

Level of production	Value added (Ratio)	Import tariffs		Tonnage ratio	Production of market economies (1971) (Tons and percent)	
		Year, country	Percentages in terms of value			
Bauxite	1			4.5	Total: 55.7 mil. t.	= 100%
		1961:			*DMEs*	38
		Canada	0		France	6
		EC	0		Greece	6
		Japan	0		U.S.A.	4
		U.S.A.	0		Australia	22
		1973:			*DCs*	62
		Canada	0		Jamaica	23
		EC	0		Suriname	11
		Japan	0		Guyana	7
		U.S.A.	0		Guinea	5
					India	3
Alumina	2.5			2	Total: 19.3 mil. t.	= 100%
		1961:			*DMEs*	77
		Canada	0		U.S.A.	38
		EC	11.1		Japan	8
		Japan	0		France	6
		U.S.A.	0		Canada	6
		1973:			Australia	14
		Canada	0		*DCs*	23
		EC	5.6		Jamaica	9
		Japan	0		Suriname	5
		U.S.A.	0		Guinea	3
					India	2
					Guyana	2
Primary aluminum	8			1	Total: 8.6 mil. t.	= 100%
		1961:			*DMEs*	93
		EC	9		U.S.A.	42
		Japan	15		Canada	12
		U.S.A.	5.3		Japan	11
					Norway	6
					F.R.G.	5

Table 3.8. The Structure of the World Aluminum Industry: Patterns of Location, Distribution of Benefits, Tariffs (cont.)

| Level of production | Value added (Ratio) | Import tariffs | | Tonnage ratio | Production of market economies (1971) (tons and percent) |
		Year, country	Percentages in terms of value		
		1973:			*DCs*	7
		Canada	4 approx.		India	2
		EC	7		Ghana	1
		Japan	10.4		Brazil	1
		U.S.A.	4 approx.		Suriname	1
					Cameroon	1
Fabricated aluminum products	17			1	Total: 7.2 mil. t.	= 100%
		1961:			*DMEs*	98
		Canada	15–20		U.S.A.	53
		EC	15–20		Japan	12
		Japan	20		F.R.G.	9
		U.S.A.	15–20		France	5
					U.K.	5
		1973:			*DCs*	2
		Canada	10 approx.			
		EC	10 approx.			
		U.S.A.	10 approx.			

Source: Michael Morris, Farid G. Lavipour, and Karl P. Sauvant, "The Politics of Nationalization: Guyana *vs.* Alcan," in *Controlling Multinational Enterprises: Problems, Strategies, Counterstrategies,* edited by Karl P. Sauvant and Farid G. Lavipour (Boulder, Col.: Westview Press, 1976).

Table 3.9. Share of Developing Countries in the Final Consumer Price
of Selected Commodities Exported by Them[a]
(Percentage)

Commodity	Period				Market
	Average 1955–1960	Average 1961–1966	Average 1967–1972	1973	
Iron ore[b]	15	13	10	9	FRG
	13	15	12	7	Continental producers
	12	10	8	7	US
Copper[c]	61	59	66	64	France
	81	81	77	90	US
Bauxite[d]	3.5	4.7	4.7	5.3	US
	3.3	4.5	4.2	3.8	France
Alumina[e]	15	13	14	14	US
	14	13	12	10	France
Aluminum[f]	45	44	38	42	US
	43	42	34	30	France
Coffee	46	43	43	50	US
	20	17	18	18	FRG
	38	35	34	33	France
Tea	18	16	13	9	FRG[g]
	61	57	53	48	UK
	56	46	38	28	Netherlands
Cocoa	12	8	12	11	FRG
	14	10	14	14	France
	21	14	20	23	UK
Groundnut oil	51	50	48	42	France
	64	58	51	41	FRG
Citrus fruit[h]	34	37	30	26	France
	31	33	29	25	FRG
Bananas	24	23	24	25	US
	25	23	23	19	FRG
	21	20	21	17	UK
	21	20	20	17	France
Sugar[i]	20	22	21	39	Japan
Jute[j]	51	48	40	34	US
	20	22	21	16	France

Source: UNCTAD, "Commodities: Proportion between Export Prices and Consumer Prices of Selected Commodities Exported by Developing Countries: Study by the UNCTAD Secretariat" (TD/184/Supp. 3), Jan. 14, 1976.

[a] Export unit value as percentage of retail price, except for iron ore, copper, bauxite, alumina, aluminum, and jute, for which wholesale prices were taken. Interproduct comparisons of the proportions are difficult to make because a whole host of factors — including cost of transportation, packing and processing (if any), import duties and internal taxes, wholesale and retail margins — play a different role for different products. A number of these factors also distort intercountry comparisons.

[b] Ore-merchant bars.

[c] Refined copper-copper wire.

[d] Bauxite Al content-aluminum sheets.

[e] Alumina Al content-aluminum sheets.

[f] Aluminum ingot-aluminum sheets.

[g] Sri Lanka tea only.

[h] Fresh oranges from Morocco only.

[i] Average Caribbean Gulf only.

[j] Raw jute-jute fabric.

Table 3.10. Selected Natural Resources: Economic Rent as Percent of Final Price, 1972-1976
(Percentage)

Country group and year	Economic rent[a]						
	Bauxite	Copper	Iron ore	Phosphate rock	Tin	Petroleum	
						Shell	OPEC
Economic rent accruing to exporting country[b]							
1972	3	8	10	4	18	16	9
1973		c	9	3	18	19	11
1974	7	c	9	33	21	47	34
1975	7	c	2	28	20	46	33
1976	7	c	4	13	24	43	32
Economic rent accruing to importing country[d]							
1972	5	3	10	23	2	48	55
1973	-7		8	24	5	48	56
1974	1		6	9	13	35	39
1975	3		9	30	2	43	41
1976	7	c	7	37	4	36	41
TOTAL economic rent							
1972	8	11	20	27	20	64	65
1973	-5	c	17	27	23	66	67
1974	8	c	15	42	34	82	73
1975	10	c	11	58	22	89	74
1976	14	c	11	50	28	79	73

Source: Helen Hughes and Shamsher Singh, "Economic Rent: Incident in Selected Metals and Minerals," *Resources Policy* 4 (1978).

[a]Calculated as final consumer price minus costs incurred in the throughput of a product from a given deposit to the final user. The economic rent estimates reported in this table refer to specific (usually very efficient) exporting and specific importing countries and, hence, cannot necessarily be generalized for the particular metal or mineral.

[b]The economic rent accruing to the exporting country is the sum of the royalties, taxes and duties levied on a product, or the difference between f.o.b. export prices and production costs.

[c]Negative.

[d]The economic rent accruing to the importing country is the sum of import duties, levies and other internal taxes, or is computed as the difference between the wholesale price and processing and marketing costs (including normal profits or markups) plus import price.

Table 3.11. Bauxite/Aluminum: Estimates of Economic Rent Elements
for Jamaica-United States, 1972–1976
(Dollars per metric ton of aluminum)

Economic-rent elements	Year				
	1972	1973	1974	1975	1976
(A) Mining, inland transportation costs	25	28	34	38	39
(B) Export price, f.o.b. Kingston	41	41	87	98	106
(C) Economic rent to Jamaica (B - A)	16	13	53	60	67
(D) Ocean freight, insurance, and costs (Jamaica — US)	11	13	13	11	11
(E) Production costs in USA, excluding costs of bauxite	502	535	648	740	792
(F) Production costs in USA, including costs of bauxite (B + D + E)	554	589	748	849	909
(G) Aluminum price	582	551	752	877	977
(H) Economic rent to USA (G - F)	28	-38	4	28	68
(I) TOTAL economic rent (C + H)	44	-25	57	88	135
(J) Percentage share of Jamaica in total economic rent (C ÷ I × 100)	36	—	93	68	50

Source: Same as Table 3.10.

Table 3.12. Share of Activity by Ownership in the Petroleum Industry
in Market Economies,[a] 1963, 1968, 1972, and 1975
(Percentage)

Activity	1963	1968	1972	1975
Crude oil production				
Majors[b]	82	78	73	30
Governments	9	9	12	62
Others	9	13	15	8
Refining				
Majors[b]	65	61	56	47
Governments	14	16	17	24
Others	21	23	27	29
Marketing				
Majors[b]	62	56	54	45
Governments	11	14	15	21
Others	27	31	31	34

Source: G. Chandler, "The Innocence of Oil Companies," *Foreign Policy* 27 (Summer 1977).
[a]Excluding North America.
[b]British Petroleum, Exxon, Gulf, Mobil, Shell, Standard of California, and Texaco.

Table 3.13. Concentration in the Bauxite/Aluminum Industry in Market Economies, 1976
(Percentage)

Company[b]	Country	Percent of total capacity[a]		
		Bauxite	Alumina	Aluminum
Alcoa	USA	22.0	22.4	13.0
Kaiser	USA	13.2	9.6	7.8
Alcan	Canada	6.8	9.9	13.1
Rio Tinto Zinc	UK	6.6	2.0	2.1
Reynolds	USA	6.0	9.6	9.4
SUBTOTAL		54.6	53.5[c]	45.4[d]
Alusuisse	Switzerland	4.9	5.3	5.2
Pechiney	France	4.9	8.6	6.8
Guyana Bauxite Co.	Guyana	4.2	. . .	—
Ergoinvest	Yugoslavia	3.7	2.0	. . .
PT Timah	Indonesia	1.4	—	—
TOTAL		73.7	69.4[e]	57.4[f]

Source: Metal Bulletin, *World Aluminium Survey* (London: Metal Bulletin, 1977).

[a] Including proportionate share of capacity in joint venture projects.
[b] Enterprises are ranked in terms of their share in bauxite capacity.
[c] The 5 enterprises with the largest alumina capacity account for 60.1 percent of the total.
[d] The 5 enterprises with the largest aluminum capacity account for 50.1 percent of the total.
[e] The 10 enterprises with the largest alumina capacity account for 77.3 percent of the total.
[f] The 10 enterprises with the largest aluminum capacity account for 67.6 percent of the total.

Table 3.14. Concentration in the Copper Industry of Market Economies, 1977
(Percentage)

Company[a]	Country	Percent of total capacity		
		Mining	Smelting	Refining
Codelco	Chile	11.1	7.9	5.4
NCCM-RCM	Zambia	10.7	9.9	8.3
Gecamines	Zaire	8.5	6.3	2.6
Asarco	USA	7.3	9.9	7.8
Kennecott	USA	5.5	5.5	5.9
SUBTOTAL		43.1	39.5[b]	30.0[c]
Rio Tinto Zinc	UK	5.5	2.8	2.6
Phelps Dodge	USA	3.9	5.1	5.4
Anaconda	USA	2.9	3.5	2.6
Newmont	USA	2.7	2.7	. . .
Inco	Canada	2.2	. . .	. . .
TOTAL		60.3	53.6[d]	40.6[e]

Source: UNIDO, "Joint Study on International Industrial Co-operation," forthcoming.

[a] In order of mining capacity
[b] These are also the enterprises with the largest smelting capacity.
[c] The 5 enterprises with the largest refining capacity account for 38.8 percent of the total.
[d] The 10 enterprises with the largest smelting capacity account for 59.9 percent of the total.
[e] The 10 enterprises with the largest refining capacity account for 52.4 percent of the total.

Table 3.15. Concentration in the Iron Ore Industry of Market Economies, 1976
(Percentage)

Company	Country	Percent of total	Cumulative share
Cia. Vale do Rio Doce	Brazil	12.0	12.0
Broken Hill Pty. Ltd.	Australia	8.7	20.7
Hamersley Iron (RTZ)	UK	8.5	29.2
Hanna Mining Co.	USA	8.1	37.3
US Steel	USA	7.7	45.0
Cleveland Cliffs	USA	7.1	52.1
LKAB	Sweden	5.2	57.3
Pickands-Mather	USA	4.8	62.1
CVG Ferrominera Orinoco	Venezuela	4.1	66.2
Mineracoes Brasileiras Reunidas	Brazil	3.2	64.4

Source: Same as Table 3.14.

Table 3.16. Concentration in the Steel Industry of Market Economies, 1976
(Percentage)

Company	Country	Percent of total	Cumulative share
Nippon Steel	Japan	7.5	7.5
US Steel	USA	5.7	13.2
British Steel	UK	4.2	17.4
Bethlehem Steel	USA	3.8	21.2
NKK	Japan	3.5	24.7
Finsider	Italy	2.9	27.6
Sumitomo	Japan	2.9	30.6
Kawasaki	Japan	2.9	33.4
ATH	FRG	2.8	36.2
Estel (Hoesch/Hoogovens)	FRG/NL	2.3	38.5

Source: Same as Table 3.14.

Table 3.17. Concentration in the Primary Lead Refining Industry
in Market Economies, 1977
(Percentage)

Company	Country	Percent of total	Cumulative share
Asarco-Mt. Isa	USA	7.7	7.7
Peñarroya	France	7.0	14.7
Broken Hill	Australia	6.9	21.6
Amax	USA	6.1	27.7
St. Joe Minerals	USA	6.0	33.7
Penolas	Mexico	5.3	39.0
Industria Minera	Mexico	4.7	43.7
Cominco	Canada	4.5	48.2
Rio Tinto Zinc (RTZ)	UK	4.4	52.6
Metallgesellschaft	FRG	4.1	56.7

Source: Same as Table 3.14.

Table 3.18. Concentration in the Zinc Mining Industry in Market Economies, 1977
(Percentage)

Company	Country	Percent of total	Cumulative share
Asarco/Mt. Isa	USA	6.8	6.8
Noranda	Canada	6.1	12.9
Texasgulf	USA	5.3	18.2
Centromin Peru	Peru	4.9	23.1
Cominco	Canada	4.4	27.5
RTZ/CRA	UK	3.8	31.3
Amax	USA	3.2	34.5
Societé Generale	Belgium	3.0	37.5
St. Joe Minerals	USA	2.8	40.3
Cyprus Mines	USA	2.6	42.9

Source: Same as Table 3.14.

Table 3.19. Concentration in the Zinc Reduction Industry in Market Economies, 1977
(Percentage)

Company	Country	Percent of total	Cumulative share
Societé Generale	Belgium	12.2	12.2
Mitsui	Japan	5.5	17.7
Cominco	Canada	4.8	22.5
RTZ/CRA	UK	4.7	27.2
Asarco/Mt. Isa	USA	4.5	31.7
St. Joe Minerals	USA	4.3	36.0
Imetal-Peñarroya	France	3.8	39.8
Metallgesellschaft	FRG	3.7	43.5
Noranda	Canada	3.6	47.1
EZ	Australia	3.5	50.6

Source: Same as Table 3.14.

Table 3.20. Concentration in the Tin Smelting Industry in Market Economies, 1977
(Percentage)

Company	Country	Percent of total	Cumulative share
Patino NV	Netherlands	29.6	29.6
Overseas Chinese Banking Group	Malaysia	17.1	46.7
Shell Billiton	UK/NL	10.7	57.4
PT Timah	Indonesia	11.1	68.5
Rio Tinto Zinc-Capper Pass	UK	8.5	77.0
COMIBOL	Bolivia	6.0	83.0
Gulf Chemicals	USA	3.8	86.8
Metallurgie Hoboken-Overpelt	Belgium	2.1	88.9

Source: Same as Table 3.14.

Table 3.21. Concentration in the Nickel Industry in Market Economies, 1977
(Percentage)

Company	Country	Percent of total	Cumulative share
Inco	Canada	36.8	36.8
Falconbridge	Canada	15.3	51.6
Japanese Cos. [a]	Japan	14.1	65.7
SLN-Peñarroya	France	6.6	72.3
Western Mining	Australia	5.5	77.8
Amax	USA	5.0	82.8
Cubaniquel	Cuba	4.9	87.7
Freeport Minerals	USA	3.4	91.1
Marinduque	Philippines	3.1	94.2
Sherritt-Gordon Mines	Canada	2.5	96.7

Source: Same as Table 3.14.

[a] Japanese group includes Nippon Nickel, Tokyo Nickel, Taiheiyo, Sumitomo, Shimura, Nippon Mining, and Nippon Yakin.

Table 3.22. Concentration in the Tungsten Industry in Market Economies, 1975
(Percentage)

Company	Country	Percent of total	Cumulative share
Korea Tungsten Mining Co. Ltd.	Rep. of Korea	12.2	12.2
International Mining Co.	Bolivia	8.9	21.1
Union Carbide Corporation	USA	8.3	29.4
Beralt Tin and Wolfram	Portugal	7.3	36.7
Amax	USA	7.1	43.8
Peko Wallsend Ltd	Australia	6.9	50.7
Soc. Minière d'Anglade	France	2.8	53.5
Minis de Borralha	Spain	1.7	55.2

Source: United Nations, *Transnational Corporations in World Development: A Re-examination* (New York: United Nations, 1978).

Table 3.23. The Tariff Structure: Average Tariff Levels,
by Developed Market Economy and Product Group, 1973
(Percentage)

Country	Product group		
	Raw materials	Semi-finished manufactures	Finished manufactures
European Community	0.5	8.1	9.3
United States	2.7	7.6	7.9
Japan	5.9	8.6	11.2
Canada	0.3	8.4	10.2
Australia	0.9	11.1	21.0
Sweden	0.0	4.5	6.6
Austria	5.9	8.4	16.0
Switzerland	0.3	4.4	3.6
Finland	0.0	4.1	8.0
Norway	0.1	4.8	7.4
New Zealand	0.6	8.5	32.6
Combined average	2.0	8.0	9.8

Source: GATT, *Basic Documentation for the Tariff Strategy: Summary by Industrial Product Categories, Tariff 1973, Import 1970/71* (Geneva: GATT, 1974).

Table 3.24. Present Trade Barriers in Developed Market Economies,
by Product Group

Product group	Average nominal tariffs	Nontariff barriers
Industrial raw materials (ores, fibers, etc.)	Very low (about 2%); majority enter duty free	Rarely exist, except in fuels
Relatively unprocessed food products	Very low to low (3–8%) not counting variable levies	Very common, often high
Processed food products	Generally low to intermediate (6–13%); high in tobacco, liquor	Very common, often high
Most industrial products	Low (7–10%)	Very few
Textiles and clothing	Relatively high (fabrics 18%, clothing 25%)	Numerous, serious, and increasing
Other developing country manufactured specialities	Intermediate (generally 11–17%)	Increasingly frequent

Source: Helen Hughes et al., "Prospects for Developing Countries, 1978–1985" (Washington: World Bank, 1977).

Table 3.25. Major Developed Market Economies: Selected Measures Specifically Directed Against Developing Countries' Exports, 1970–1977[a]

Date	Country adopting measure	Partner countries affected	Commodity affected	Measure
Late 1960s–Dec. 1973	Japan, other Asian suppliers	EC, US	Cotton textiles	"Voluntary" export restraint agreements to replace import quotas[b]
March 1970	France	Algeria, Morocco, Tunisia	Wine	Quota established
Oct. 1971	Japan, other major suppliers	US	Man-made and woolen textiles	"Voluntary" export restraint agreements
Jan. 1972	United Kingdom	Commonwealth preference area	Cotton textiles	Duties of 6.5–17 percent imposed
Jan. 1974	France	All	Crude petroleum	Tax of F6 per ton imposed on imports
Jan. 1974	Fed. Rep. of Germany	Asia	Textiles	Quota on imports decreased
June 1974	Bangladesh	EC	Jute	Bilateral agreement limiting jute exports from Bangladesh in exchange for EC tariff reductions
Aug. 1974–May 1975; Feb. 1976	Japan	Mainly China, Republic of Korea	Raw silk	Government designated sole importer
Sept. 1974	France	All	Crude petroleum and products	Monetary limit of F51 billion placed on 1975 imports
Sept., Oct. 1974	US	Brazil, Spain	Specified footwear	Countervailing duties on imports imposed
Late 1974	12 supplying countries	US	Beef, veal	Bilateral agreements for "voluntary" export restraints in 1975
Feb. 1975–1 Jan. 1976	US	All	Crude petroleum and petroleum products	Special fee of $1/barrel imposed on imports, later raised to $2/barrel
April, July, Sept., Nov. 1975	India, Pakistan, Hong Kong, Singapore, Macao, Malaysia, Rep. of Korea	EC	Textiles	"Voluntary" restraint agreements to limit anual growth of textile exports to EC[b]

253

Table 3.25. Major Developed Market Economies: Selected Measures Specifically Directed Against Developing Countries' Exports, 1970–1977[a] (cont.)

Date	Country adopting measure	Partner countries affected	Commodity affected	Measure
1976	EC	Specified producing countries	Textiles, clothing	Continuation of import restrictions taken previously under safeguard clause of Multi-Fiber Agreement
1976	EC	Specified developing countries	Footwear	Continuation of an earlier "voluntary" export restraint agreement
1 Jan. 1976–31 Dec. 1976	Ireland	All	Footwear	Import licensing and duties
1 Jan. 1976–31 Dec. 1977	US	Major exporters	Meat	Import quotas imposed
15 Feb. 1976–15 May 1976	France	Non-EC countries	Specified footwear	Requirement for administrative visa
15 Feb. 1976–15 May 1976	France	Mauritius	Specified clothing	Requirement for administrative visa
1 March 1976	Australia	All	Electrical appliances; opthalmic items	Tariffs, import quotas
1 April 1976–31 March 1977	New Zealand	All	Certain polyester fabrics	Import restrictions extended for 12 months
April 1976	United Kingdom	Brazil	Men's fashion footwear	Countervailing duty imposed
May 1976	Australia	All	Footwear	Import quotas extended to cover additional items
June 1976	Australia	All except New Zealand	Textiles, clothing	Tariff quotas extended to cover additional clothing items
1 July 1976–30 June 1977	Australia	All	Textiles, clothing and footwear	Current import quotas extended; government to allot fixed share of home markets to domestic producers
July 1976	Australia	All	Hosiery	Import duties of 30% imposed
1 July 1976–30 June 1977	France	All	Specified leather footwear	Requirement for administrative visa
1 July 1976–30 June 1979	Canada	All	Work gloves	Three-year global import quota introduced

254

Date	Country	Coverage	Product	Measure
July 1976	Canada	All	Specified yarns	Temporary surtax on imports imposed
Sept. 1976	US	All except beneficiaries of US GSP scheme	Raw sugar	Import duty trebled
1 Oct. 1976–31 Dec. 1977	United Kingdom	Taiwan	Portable monochrome TV	Import quotas extended
Oct. 1976	Canada	China, Hong Kong, Republic of Korea, Philippines	Specified clothing	"Voluntary" export restraints (the agreements supersede the suspension of imports from these countries in July 1976)
Oct. 1976	Canada	All	Specified textiles	Temporary import quotas introduced
1977	United Kingdom	China	Certain synthetic garments	Import quotas imposed
1977	United Kingdom	Thailand	Specified clothing	Import quotas imposed
1 July 1977–31 Dec. 1977	EC	Nine, mainly Mediterranean, producing countries	Four specified "sensitive" textile products	Import quotas limited to 1976 levels
August 1977	United Kingdom	Taiwan	Non-leather shoes	Import quotas imposed
1 Jan. 1978–31 Dec. 1983	EC	31 "low-cost" producing countries, including the five major suppliers: Hong Kong, India, Rep. of Korea, Taiwan, Brazil	133 textile and clothing items	"Voluntary" export restriction agreements negotiated bilaterally; to be incorporated into the New Multifiber Agreement
1 Jan. 1978	Canada	All	Footwear	1978 imports will be reduced by 25% from 1977 levels. Agreement renewable for up to 3 years
1 Jan. 1978–31 Dec. 1983	US	Hong Kong	Textiles	5-year export restraint agreement renegotiated to allow overall growth of 1.5% in Hong Kong exports to United States in 1978; thereafter 6%.

Source: United Nations, *World Economic Survey, 1975: Fluctuations and Development in the World Economy* (New York: UN, 1976), table 47; IMF, *28th Annual Report on Exchange Restrictions* (Washington, D.C.: IMF, 1977); GATT, *Activities in 1976* (Geneva: GATT, April 1977), and various other sources.

[a] During the same period, a number of trade-restriction measures directed against a wider group of countries have also been taken; cases in which developing countries were among those particularly affected have also been included (e.g., quota imposed on textile imports from all countries).

[b] Under the auspices of GATT's Long-Term Arrangement regarding International Trade in Cotton Textiles or the Multifiber Agreement that replaced it in January 1974.

Table 3.26. Export Dependence of Developing Countries,
by Major Trading Partner, 1965 and 1975[a]
(Percentage)

Exporting country	Percentage of country's total exports		Partner country	Percentage of partner's total imports	
	1965	1975		1965	1975
OPEC					
Ecuador	56.8	47.2	USA	0.4	0.4
Indonesia	15.8	44.1	Japan	1.4	5.4
Venezuela	34.7	39.4	USA	4.7	3.7
Other DCs					
Africa					
Angola	23.0	38.3[b]	USA	0.2	0.5[b]
Burundi	76.6	45.5	USA	0.0	0.0
Cent. African Empire	37.7	42.0	France	0.1	0.0
Egypt	21.7	43.2	USSR	1.6	1.6
Gabon	48.4	38.8	France	0.3	0.7
Gambia	49.7	38.7	U.K.	0.0	0.0
Madagascar	44.7	35.3[b]	France	0.4	0.2[b]
Malawi	44.6	39.6	U.K.	0.1	0.1
Mauritius	77.9	77.9	U.K.	0.3	0.4
Niger	56.2	63.7	France	0.1	0.1
Réunion	87.5	94.0	France	0.3	0.1
Senegal	80.7	31.5	France	1.0	0.4
Sierra Leone	75.5	63.1[b]	U.K.	0.4	0.2[b]
Somalia	—	57.0[c]	Saudi Arabia	—	1.6[c]
Togo	43.3	39.3	France	0.1	0.1
Upper Volta	52.3	48.1	Ivory Coast	3.1	1.9
Asia					
Afghanistan	25.0	38.7	USSR	0.3	0.2
Brunei	0.0	78.0	Japan	0.0	1.4
Cyprus	31.0	35.0	U.K.	0.1	0.1
Korea, Rep. of	35.2	30.3	USA	0.3	1.6
Lao, P.D.R.	27.8	72.8[b]	Thailand	0.0	0.3[b]
Papua-New Guinea	3.7	32.2	Japan	0.0	0.3
Philippines	28.3	37.9	Japan	2.7	1.5
Western hemisphere					
Bahamas	71.5[d]	79.0	USA	0.2[d]	2.0
Barbados	10.7	30.2	USA	0.0	0.0
Belize	35.0	78.9[b]	USA	0.0	0.0[b]
Bolivia	42.7	31.3	USA	0.3	0.2
Colombia	46.7	32.0	USA	1.2	0.5
Costa Rica	50.4	41.9	USA	0.3	0.2
Cuba	47.0	36.5	USSR	4.0	3.9
Dominican Rep.	80.6	66.6	USA	0.5	0.6
Ecuador	56.8	47.2	USA	0.4	0.4
Fiji	44.8	59.6	U.K.	0.1	0.2
Guadeloupe	80.1	72.7	France	0.3	0.1
Haiti	60.0[d]	74.2	USA	0.1[d]	0.1
Honduras	58.9	51.9	USA	0.3	0.2
Jamaica	38.0	38.4	USA	0.4	0.3
Martinique	88.3	69.0	France	0.3	0.1
Mexico	62.2	58.3	USA	3.0	1.7
Neth. Antilles	42.6	62.1	USA	1.2	1.5
New Hebrides	52.6	43.4	France	0.0	0.0

Table 3.26. Export Dependence of Developing Countries (cont.)

Panama	66.8	59.5	USA	0.1	0.2
Trinidad and Tobago	33.7	68.3	USA	0.6	1.2

Source: United Nations, *Statistical Yearbook 1977.*
[a]Countries shown are those for which one trading partner accounted for 50 percent or more of the country's exports in 1975.
[b]Figures refer to 1974.
[c]Figures refer to 1973.
[d]Figures refer to 1970.

Table 3.27. Export Dependence of Developing Countries, by Region,
1965 and 1975
(Number)

Region	Number of countries for which one trading partner absorbed 30 percent or more of exports	
	1965	1975
OPEC	5	3
Other DCs		
Africa	27	16
Asia	7	7
Western hemisphere	26	20
TOTAL	65	46

Source: United Nations, *Statistical Yearbook 1977.*

Table 3.28. The 18 Commodities of the Integrated Programme for Commodities:
Shares in World Exports and Imports, by Region
(Percentage, 1970–1975 averages)

Commodity	World exports			World imports		
	Develop-ing countries	Devel-oped market economies	Socialist countries	Develop-ing countries	Devel-oped market economies	Socialist countries
Ten "core" commodities						
Cocoa	99.3	0.7	—	4.2	74.9	20.9
Coffee	96.6	3.3	—	5.3	90.0	4.7
Copper	54.3	39.1	6.6	6.0	85.7	8.3
Cotton	52.2	30.7	17.3	17.1	51.4	31.5
Jute	98.6	1.2	—	27.7	56.4	15.9
Rubber	97.0	2.3	—	10.6	65.4	24.0
Sisal	98.7	—	—	8.2	81.9	9.9
Sugar	71.3	21.8	6.9	21.2	59.2	19.6
Tea	78.9	11.9	9.2	29.6	60.3	10.1
Tin	79.5	16.1	4.4	12.5	77.6	9.9
TOTAL 10	72.4	21.2	6.4	12.7	71.5	15.8
Eight other commodities						
Bananas	92.8	1.4	5.8	7.5	90.4	2.1
Bauxite	82.3	16.1	1.6	2.1	90.3	7.6
Beef	25.2	69.1	5.7	4.5	88.4	7.1
Iron Ore	39.7	47.5	12.8	—	87.9	11.2
Manganese	51.0	38.9	10.1	3.6	88.1	8.3
Phosphates	60.3	20.3	19.4	12.6	66.2	21.2
Tropical timber	79.0	16.4	4.6	11.8	80.7	7.5
Vegetable oil and oil seeds	34.3	60.1	5.6	12.6	76.2	11.2
TOTAL 18	59.2	33.9	6.9	10.7	76.2	13.1

Source: UNCTAD, "Statistics of International Trade in Commodities Covered by the Integrated Programme for Commodities, 1970–1975" (TD/IPC/CF/CONF/MISC. 5), Oct. 27, 1977.

Table 3.29. The 18 Commodities of the Integrated Programme for Commodities: Importance in Imports and Exports, by Region and Income Group of Countries, Average 1970–1975

(Dollar and percentage)

Region and income category	Imports				Exports			
	10 core commodities (1)	18 commodities (2)	As % of total imports (1)	As % of total imports (2)	10 core commodities (3)	18 commodities (4)	As % of total imports (3)	As % of total imports (4)
Developed countries	17,913	39,613	4.4	9.7	4,737	17,075	1.2	4.4
Above $4,000 1973 per capita	10,520	21,413	4.1	8.3	2,985	11,998	1.1	4.6
Below $4,000 1973 per capita	7,393	18,200	4.9	12.0	1,752	5,077	1.4	4.1
Developing countries	2,973	4,947	3.0	5.1	17,521	24,953	16.2	23.1
Major petroleum exporters	655	1,022	2.8	4.3	1,404	2,095	2.7	4.0
Fast-growing exporters of manufactures	565	1,246	2.9	6.4	424	662	3.2	5.1
Other countries with per capita income in 1973 above $400	767	1,249	2.5	4.1	9,277	13,231	37.0	52.8
Countries with per capita income in 1973 between $200 and $400	413	608	3.5	5.1	3,158	4,962	34.3	53.9
Countries with per capita income in 1973 below $200 (excluding "hard core" least developed countries)	328	514	4.1	6.5	2,124	2,580	34.7	42.2
"Hard core" least developed countries	245	308	6.0	7.5	1,134	1,423	44.3	55.7
TOTAL	20,886	44,560	4.1	8.8	22,258	42,028	4.5	8.5

Source: Commonwealth Technical Group, *The Common Fund* (London: Commonwealth Secretariat, 1977).

259

Table 3.30. Balance-of-Payments Developments, 1971–1977
(Billions of dollars)

Region and subgroup	Year						
	1971	1972	1973	1974	1975	1976	1977
All developing countries							
Trade balance[a]	1.9	4.4	13.4	61.0	25.9	50.7	50.7
Current account balance[b]	-11.6	-7.8	-4.3	34.7	-5.1	12.0	5.5
Major petroleum exporters[c]							
Trade balance[a]	10.5	10.8	19.0	84.3	56.9	68.2	67.3
Current account balance[b]	2.4	3.2	7.0	66.9	36.1	40.3	33.4
Other developing countries							
Trade balance[a]	-8.7	-6.4	-5.6	-23.3	-31.0	-17.5	-16.5
Current account balance[b]	-14.0	-11.0	-11.3	-32.2	-41.2	-28.4	-27.8
of which:							
Fast growing exporters of manufactures[d]							
Trade balance[a]	-3.2	-2.5	-2.0	-10.8	-11.1	- 5.3	-0.7
Current account balance[b]	-5.2	-4.4	-4.8	-14.8	-16.1	-11.6	-7.5
Least developed countries[e]							
Trade balance[a]	-0.4	-0.4	-0.9	-2.0	-2.9	-1.5	-2.2
Current account balance[b]	-0.8	-0.7	-1.2	-2.5	-3.4	-1.6	-2.1

Source: UNCTAD, *Handbook of International Trade and Development Statistics, 1979.*

[a] Exports, f.o.b., minus imports f.o.b.

[b] Trade balance plus balance of services and private transfers.

[c] Algeria, Angola, Bahrain, Brunei, Ecuador, Gabon, Indonesia, Iran, Iraq, Kuwait, Libyan Arab Jamahiriya, Nigeria, Oman, Qatar, Saudi Arabia, Trinidad and Tobago, United Arab Emirates, Venezuela.

[d] Argentina, Brazil, Hong Kong, Republic of Korea, Mexico, Singapore.

[e] Countries with less than $200 per capita in 1974 at 1973 prices are the following: Afghanistan, Bangladesh, Benin, Bhutan, Botswana, Burundi, Cape Verde, Central African Empire, Chad, Comoros, Ethiopia, Gambia, Guinea, Haiti, Lao People's Democratic Republic, Lesotho, Malawi, Maldives, Mali, Nepal, Niger, Rwanda, Samoa, Somalia, Sudan, Uganda, United Republic of Tanzania, Upper Volta, Yemen, and Democratic Yemen.

Table 3.31. External Financing Requirements of Developing Countries, 1970-1985[a]
(Billion current dollars)

Item	Year		
	1970	1976	1985
Net imports	8	26	94
(Imports of goods and nonfactor services)	(62)	(301)	(979)
Less: (Exports of goods and nonfactor services)	(55)	(275)	(885)
Interest on medium and long-term loans	3	10	44
Amortization	6	20	122
Increase in Reserves	−1	8	23
TOTAL to be financed	17	64	283
Net factor income, excluding interest on medium and long-term loans	−4	5	21
Transfers[b]	3	18	49
Direct investment and other (net)	3	−6	25
Medium and long-term loans (gross)	15	49	188
TOTAL sources of finance	17	64	283

Source: World Bank, *World Development Report, 1978* and *World Development Report, 1979* (Washington: World Bank, 1979).

[a]The assumed annual rate of inflation between 1975 and 1985 is about 7 percent. Not included are the capital-surplus oil exporters Kuwait, Libya, Oman, Qatar, Saudi Arabia, and United Arab Emirates. Included are, however, Greece, Portugal, Spain, and Turkey.

[b]Official grants and concessional loans (gross) and private transfers (net).

Table 3.32. Total Net Financial Disbursements to Developing Countries,[a] by Type of Disbursement and Origin, 1970, 1973–1977

(Billion dollar and percent)

Type of disbursement and origin	1970		1973		1974		1975		1976		1977	
	$ bn	%	$ bn	%	$ bn	%	$ bn	%	$ bn	%	$ bn	%
Concessional development assistance												
DAC[bc]	6.8	40.2	10.7	29.6	12.5	29.1	14.9	25.2	15.0	23.7	16.2	21.5
OPEC	0.4	2.4	1.3	3.6	3.4	7.9	5.5	9.3	5.6	8.8	5.7[d]	7.5
Centrally planned economies[e]	0.8	0.5	1.3	3.6	1.1	2.6	0.9	1.5	0.8	1.3	0.7[d]	0.9
SUBTOTAL	8.0	47.3	13.3	36.7	17.0	39.6	21.3	36.0	21.4	33.8	22.6	29.9
Nonconcessional flows												
DAC[cf]	8.0	47.3	13.9	38.4	15.4	35.9	25.5	43.1	25.7	40.5	33.3	44.1
OPEC[g]	0.2	1.2	0.4	1.1	2.4	5.6	2.7	4.6	2.5	3.9	1.8[d]	2.4
Centrally planned economies[e]	0.1	0.6	0.1	0.3	0.09	0.2	0.09	0.2	0.08	0.1	0.03[d]	—
International bank lending[h]	0.6	3.6	8.5	23.5	8.0	18.6	9.5	16.1	13.7	21.6	17.8	23.6
SUBTOTAL	8.9	52.7	22.9	63.3	25.9	60.4	37.8	64.0	42.0	66.2	52.9	70.0
TOTAL net disbursement	16.9	100	36.2	100	42.9	100	59.1	100	63.4	100	75.5	100

Source: OECD, *Development Co-operation* (Paris: OECD, various years).

[a] Including Gibraltar, Greece, Israel, Portugal, Spain, Turkey, and Yugoslavia.

[b] Official development assistance (bilateral and multilateral) plus grants by private voluntary agencies.

[c] Figures prior to 1975 exclude Finland and New Zealand.

[d] Provisional.

[e] China, Eastern Europe, USSR and including aid to Cuba, Kampuchea, Korea PDR, and Viet Nam.

[f] Other official flows (bilateral and multilateral) plus private flows at market terms (direct investment plus bilateral portfolio investment plus multilateral portfolio investment plus private export credits).

[g] Official flows only.

[h] From banks in DAC countries and their affiliates in financial centers.

262

Table 3.33. Members of the Development Assistance Committee: Composition of Net Financial Flows to Developing Countries and to Multilateral Agencies, 1961–1976 (Percentages)

Type of flow	Year								
	1961	1965	1970	1971	1972	1973	1974	1975	1976
1. Official	65.4	61.1	55.6	51.1	46.7	38.2	39.6	33.0	27.2
a. Bilateral official development assistance (ODA)	56.5	56.5	40.3	36.6	30.9	23.1	25.8	21.2	16.4
b. Bilateral other official flows			5.0	4.9	4.7	6.2	4.1	3.4	3.1
c. Multilateral official development assistance (ODA)	8.9	4.6	8.3	8.0	9.3	7.5	9.7	8.3	7.5
d. Multilateral other official flows	...	...	2.0	1.6	1.8	1.3	-0.1	0.2	0.2
TOTAL ODA	...	...	48.5	44.7	40.2	30.6	35.5	29.5	23.9
2. Private	28.7	33.1	29.9	28.4	31.5	31.8	30.8	35.0	35.3
a. Bilateral	27.6	30.6	27.4	23.8	28.2	31.0	31.0	30.1	29.8
of which: Direct investment[a]	20.5	23.0	23.6	20.3	19.8	20.4	19.9	21.0	13.4
b. Multilateral[b]	1.1	2.5	2.5	4.6	3.2	0.9	-0.2	5.0	5.5
3. Net private export credits[c]	5.9	5.8	14.5	14.6	6.8	3.5	6.2	7.9	7.3
4. Eurocurrency credits[d]	...	...	...	5.9	15.0	26.5	23.4	24.0	30.2
TOTAL (1 + 2 + 3 + 4) Percentage	100	100	100	100	100	100	100	100	100
Millions of dollars	8,350	9,785	13,718	16,797	20,594	30,044	31,568	45,834	56,707

Source: UNCTAD, *Handbook of International Trade and Development Statistics: Supplement 1977* (New York: United Nations, 1978).

[a] Including reinvested earnings, sometimes on the basis of estimates.

[b] Represents mainly bond flotation by multilateral institutions in the private capital market of DAC countries.

[c] Net change in guaranteed private export credits reported by the OECD until 1964; from 1965 onwards the figures include also estimates of the nonguaranteed part of export credits guaranteed by a government agency.

[d] Gross commitments as announced.

Table 3.34. Members of the Development Assistance Committee: Net Official Development Assistance
to Developing Countries and Multilateral Agencies as Percentage of GNP, by Country, 1961–1977
(Percentages)

DAC country[a]	Year										
	1961	1965	1970	1971	1972	1973	1974	1975	1976	1977
Sweden	0.06	0.19	0.38	0.44	0.48	0.56	0.72	0.82	0.82	0.99
Netherlands	0.45	0.36	0.61	0.58	0.67	0.54	0.63	0.75	0.82	0.85
Norway	0.14	0.16	0.32	0.33	0.43	0.43	0.57	0.66	0.70	0.82
France	1.35	0.76	0.66	0.66	0.67	0.57	0.59	0.62	0.62	0.60
Denmark	0.12	0.13	0.38	0.43	0.45	0.48	0.55	0.58	0.56	0.60
Canada	0.16	0.19	0.42	0.42	0.47	0.43	0.48	0.55	0.46	0.51
Belgium	0.76	0.60	0.46	0.50	0.55	0.51	0.51	0.59	0.51	0.46
United Kingdom	0.59	0.47	0.36	0.40	0.38	0.34	0.37	0.37	0.38	0.37
Australia	0.44	0.53	0.59	0.53	0.59	0.44	0.55	0.60	0.42	0.45
New Zealand[b]			0.23	0.23	0.25	0.27	0.31	0.52	0.41	0.39
TOTAL DAC countries	0.53	0.44	0.34	0.35	0.33	0.30	0.33	0.35	0.33	0.31
Germany, Fed. Rep. of	0.44	0.40	0.32	0.34	0.31	0.32	0.37	0.40	0.31	0.27
Austria	0.04	0.11	0.07	0.07	0.09	0.15	0.18	0.17	0.12	0.24
United States	0.56	0.49	0.31	0.32	0.29	0.23	0.24	0.26	0.25	0.22
Japan	0.20	0.27	0.23	0.23	0.21	0.25	0.25	0.23	0.20	0.21
Switzerland	0.08	0.09	0.15	0.12	0.21	0.16	0.14	0.19	0.19	0.19
Finland[b]			0.07	0.12	0.15	0.16	0.17	0.18	0.18	0.17
Italy	0.15	0.10	0.16	0.18	0.09	0.14	0.14	0.11	0.13	0.10
For reference:										
TOTAL ODA (million $)	5,197	5,895	6,807	7,691	8,538	9,351	11,304	13,588	13,666	14,759
TOTAL GNP of DAC countries (billion $)		1,334	2,020	2,214	2,553	3,099	3,445	3,830	4,167	4,716

Source: OECD, Development Co-operation (Paris: OECD, various issues).
[a] In descending order of 1977 performance. Included is ODA for Greece, Israel, Portugal, Spain, Turkey, and Yugoslavia; the sums involved are, however, not high.
[b] Not a member of DAC for years for which no data are shown.

Table 3.35. Members of the Development Assistance Committee:
Share of Tied Aid in Total Gross Disbursements of Official
Development Assistance, by Country, 1977[a]
(Millions of dollars and percentages)

DAC country	Total ODA (Million $)	of which (percentage)		
		Untied	Partially tied	Tied
Australia	429.5	79	—	21
Austria	118.6	79	—	21
Belgium	372.7	28	20	52
Canada	995.2	52	—	48
Denmark	263.3	53	10	37
Finland	49.9	45	7	48
France	2,793.1	41	17	42
Germany, Fed. Rep. of	1,732.9	76	4	20
Italy	254.8	81	—	19
Japan	1,591.8	44	21	35
Netherlands	954.2	48	18	34
New Zealand	52.6	70	—	30
Norway	295.3	80	—	20
Sweden	781.9	81	2	17
Switzerland	182.3	76	5	19
United Kingdom	1,015.3	47	21	32
United States	4,778.0	27	19	54
TOTAL DAC countries	16,661.4	47	14	39

Source: OECD, *Development Co-operation: 1978 Review* (Paris: OECD, 1978).

[a]Included is ODA for Greece, Israel, Portugal, Spain, Turkey, and Yugoslavia; the sums involved are, however, not substantial.

Table 3.36. Distribution of Export Credits, Foreign Direct Investment, and International Bank Lending to Non-Oil-Exporting Developing Countries,[a] by Income Group Country, Selected Years (Millions of dollars and percentages)

Income group of countries	Export credit		Foreign direct investment		International bank lending
	1969/71	1975/76	1969/71	1975/76	1977[b]
Low-income[c]					
Million dollars	198	1075	259	1324	498
Percent	9	22	14	21	1
Least-developed countries[d]					
Million dollars	32	179	14	56	4
Percent	2	4	0	1	0
Lower middle-income[e]					
Million dollars	671	1727	416	1088	3572
Percent	30	36	23	17	26
Upper middle-income[f]					
Million dollars	959	1477	904	2378	5570
Percent	43	30	49	38	41
Higher-income[g]					
Million dollars	384	587	256	1458	3982
Percent	18	12	14	24	29
TOTAL					
Million dollars	2213	4865	1836	6248	13622
Percent	100	100	100	100	100
For reference:					
OPEC countries except Indonesia and Nigeria (million dollars)	660	1384	301	114	4153

Source: OECD, *Development Co-operation: 1978 Review.*

[a] Including Indonesia and Nigeria and the European developing countries.
[b] Over 1-year lending by DAC banks and their foreign affiliates to DCs other than offshore financial centers.
[c] Countries with an average per capita income in 1976 of up to $400.
[d] An internationally recognized list of 31 countries (at the end of 1977).
[e] Countries with an average per capita income in 1976 of between $400 and $1000.
[f] Countries with an average per capita income in 1976 of between $1000 and $2500.
[g] All other DCs.

Table 3.37. Total External Debt (Disbursed) and Debt Service of Developing Countries,[a] by Income Group of Countries, 1967–1977 (Billions of dollars and percentages)

Income group	Year 1967 $bn	1967 %	1970 $bn	1970 %	1971 $bn	1971 %	1972 $bn	1972 %	1973 $bn	1973 %	1974 $bn	1974 %	1975 $bn	1975 %	1976 $bn	1976 %	1977[b] $bn	1977[b] %
Non-oil-exporting DCs																		
Poor countries[c]																		
Debt	10.7	22.1	15.1	20.4	16.8	19.9	18.7	19.6	21.3	18.6	23.9	17.1	27.9	15.9	33.3	15.7	38.9	15.9
Debt service	0.8	12.9	1.0	11.0	1.1	10.4	1.3	10.1	1.4	8.8	1.7	8.4	2.0	7.9	2.0	6.4	2.2	6.0
Other non-oil																		
Debt	30.9	63.8	47.3	63.8	53.3	63.0	59.8	67.8	70.7	61.8	91.6	65.5	118.4	67.5	144.0	67.9	166.2	68.1
Debt service	5.0	80.6	7.0	76.9	8.0	75.5	9.3	72.1	11.6	72.5	14.5	71.4	18.0	71.4	22.6	72.2	26.4	72.1
TOTAL non-oil DCs																		
Debt	41.6	85.9	62.4	84.2	70.1	82.9	78.5	82.5	92.0	80.4	115.5	82.6	146.3	83.5	177.3	83.6	205.1	84.1
Debt service	5.8	93.5	8.0	87.9	9.1	85.9	10.6	82.2	13.0	81.3	16.2	79.8	20.0	79.3	24.6	78.6	28.6	78.1
OPEC																		
Debt	6.8	14.1	11.7	15.8	14.5	17.1	16.7	17.5	22.4	19.6	24.4	17.4	29.0	16.5	35.0	16.4	38.9	15.9
Debt service	0.4	6.5	1.0	12.1	1.5	14.1	2.3	17.8	3.0	18.7	4.1	20.2	5.2	20.7	6.7	21.4	8.0	21.9
TOTAL DCs																		
Debt	48.4	100	74.1	100	84.6	100	95.2	100	114.4	100	139.9	100	175.3	100	212.2	100	244.0	100
Debt service	6.2	100	9.1	100	10.6	100	12.9	100	16.0	100	20.3	100	25.2	100	31.3	100	36.6	100

Source: OECD, *Development Co-operation: 1978 Review.*

[a] Including intra-DC and Greece, Israel, Portugal, Spain, Turkey, and Yugoslavia.

[b] Provisional.

[c] Countries with per capita GNP of $265 or less in 1975.

Table 3.38. The Ten Largest Debtor Countries, end-1976,
and Their Debt Service Payments, 1977[a]
(Billions of dollars and percentages)

Country	Debt (1976)		Debt-service payments (1977)	
	$bn	% of total	$bn	% of total
Brazil	26.0	12.3	6.22	17.1
Mexico	21.7	10.2	5.20	14.3
India	13.6	6.4	0.91	2.5
Indonesia	10.2	4.8	1.41	3.9
Algeria	7.4	3.5	1.69	4.6
Spain	7.3	3.4	1.75	4.9
Korea	7.1	3.3	1.40	3.8
Yugoslavia	6.9	3.3	1.62	4.4
Pakistan	6.0	2.8	0.32[b]	0.9[b]
Argentina	5.5	2.6	1.59	4.3
Subtotal	111.7	52.6	22.11	60.4
TOTAL DCs	212.2	100	36.6	100

Source: OECD, *Development Co-operation: 1978 Review.*
[a]Provisional.
[b]1976.

Table 3.39. Debt Service Ratios[a] of Individual Developing Countries by Region, 1977 (Percentages)

Region	Less than 5 percent	5–9.9 percent	10–14.9 percent	15–19.9 percent	20–24.9 percent	25 percent and over
Africa, south of the Sahara	Botswana (2) Burundi (3) Gambia (1) Ghana (4) Lesotho (3) Madagascar (3) Mali (4) Mauritius (2) Niger (4) Nigeria (1) Rwanda (1) Swaziland (1) Uganda (4) Upper Volta (4)	Benin (6) Cameroon (7) Central African Empire (5) Chad (9) Comores (7) Ethiopia (6) Kenya (5) Liberia (5) Malawi (5) Senegal (8) Sudan (9) Tanzania (7)	Congo(10) Gabon (10) Ivory Coast (12) Sierra Leone (10) Somalia (11) Togo (12) Zaire (10)	Zambia (19)	Mauritania (23)	Guinea (44)
SUBTOTAL	14	12	7	1	1	1
Asia	Fiji (2) Nepal (1) Papua New Guinea (4) Singapore (1) Taiwan (4) Thailand (3)	Afghanistan (8) Korea (9) Malaysia (7) Philippines (6)	Bangladesh (12) Burma (13) India (11) Indonesia (12) Pakistan (14)	Sri Lanka (15)		
SUBTOTAL	6	4	5	1		
Developing western hemisphere	Barbados (3) Guatemala (1) Trinidad and Tobago (1)	Colombia (9) Costa Rica (9) Dominican Republic (7) Ecuador (8) El Salvador (6) Haiti (7) Honduras (7)	Nicaragua (14) Panama (12)	Argentina (15) Brazil (19) Guyana (16) Jamaica (15)	Bolivia (21)	Chile (32) Mexico (48) Peru (30) Uruguay (28)

Table 3.39. Debt Service Ratios[a] of Individual Developing Countries by Region, 1977 (cont.)

Region	Less than 5 percent	5–9.9 percent	10–14.9 percent	15–19.9 percent	20–24.9 percent	25 percent and over
		Paraguay (6) Venezuela (8)				
SUBTOTAL	3	9	2	4	1	4
North Africa and Middle East	Bahrain (0) Iran (3) Iraq (1) Jordan (3) Lebanon (1) Oman (4) Yemen Arab Republic (0) Yemen People's Democratic Republic (0)	Syria (7) Tunisia (9)	Morocco (11)	Algeria (6)	Egypt (23)	
SUBTOTAL	8	2	1	1	1	
TOTAL	31	27	15	7	3	5

Source: World Bank, *1979 Annual Report* (Washington: World Bank, 1979).
[a]Service payments on external public debt as percentage of exports of goods and services.

Table 3.40. Public Debt Service Ratios of Developing Countries,
by Income Group, 1970–1985[a]
(Percentages)

Country-group	Debt service payments as percentage of exports of goods and nonfactor services			Debt service payments as percentage of GNP		
	1970	1975	1985	1970	1975	1985
Low-income Asia[b]	16.8	12.6	12.6	1.0	1.3	1.4
Low-income Africa[c]	4.8	6.7	9.6	1.2	1.5	2.5
Middle-income countries[d]	15.6	11.8	22.0	2.4	2.7	4.8
TOTAL DCs	15.2	11.8	21.0	2.1	2.4	4.3

Source: World Bank, *World Development Report, 1978.*

[a] Debt service on public and publicly guaranteed medium and long-term loans only. Not included are the capital-surplus oil exporters; see footnote a) in Table 3.31.

[b] Asian countries with a 1976 per capita income of $250 or below: Afghanistan, Bangladesh, Bhutan, Burma, Cambodia, India, Indonesia, Lao PDR, Nepal, Pakistan, Sri Lanka, Viet Nam, and Yemen.

[c] African countries with a 1976 per capita income of $250 or below: Benin, Burundi, Central African Empire, Chad, Ethiopia, Guinea, Kenya, Lesotho, Malawi, Madagascar, Mali, Mozambique, Niger, Rwanda, Somalia, Sierra Leone, Tanzania, Uganda, Upper Volta, Zaire.

[d] All other non-OPEC developing countries plus Haiti.

Table 3.41. Quotas in the IMF and Subscriptions to the World Bank, by Region
(Billion SDRs and percentages)

Region	IMF quotas (1980)[a]		World Bank subscriptions (1978)	
	Amount (Billion SDRs)	Percent of total	Amount (Billion SDRs)	Percent of total
Developed market economies	38.9	66.5	19.5	73.0
European Community	15.9	27.1	7.8	29.1
North America	14.6	25.0	7.9	29.6
Other	8.4	14.4	3.8	14.2
Developing countries	18.9	32.3	6.9	26.0
OPEC	6.2	10.5	1.2	4.3
Non-OPEC	12.8	21.8	5.8	21.7
Africa and Middle East	3.3	5.7	1.1	4.0
Asia	4.8	8.3	3.0	11.3
Western hemisphere	4.6	7.8	1.7	6.3
Socialist countries of Europe	0.8	1.3	0.3	1.1
TOTAL	58.6	100.0	26.7	100.0

Source: IMF Survey 7 (Dec. 13, 1978); and World Bank, *Annual Report 1978* (Washington: World Bank, 1978).

[a] Assuming adoption of maximum quotas proposed under the Seventh General Review of Quotas.

Table 3.42. Distribution of Reserves, by Region, 1950, 1960, 1970–1977[a]
(Billion SDRs and percentages)

Region	Year									
	1950	1960	1970	1971	1972	1973	1974	1975	1976	1977
Developed countries										
FRG	0.2	7.0	13.6	17.2	21.9	27.5	26.5	26.5	30.0	32.7
Japan	0.6	1.9	4.8	14.1	16.9	10.2	11.0	10.9	14.3	19.1
UK	4.8	5.1	2.8	8.1	5.2	5.4	5.7	4.7	3.6	17.3
US	24.3	19.4	14.5	12.1	12.1	11.9	13.1	13.6	15.8	16.0
Other[b]										
SUBTOTAL										
SDRs	40.3	52.1	74.3	100.9	116.9	115.9	115.2	119.4	129.3	155.3
Percent	80.3	85.1	79.7	81.9	79.6	76.0	63.9	61.4	66.5	59.1
Major oil-exporting countries[c]										
SDRs	1.3	2.3	5.0	7.8	10.0	12.0	38.4	48.3	56.1	62.1
Percent	2.6	3.8	5.4	6.3	6.8	7.9	21.3	24.8	25.2	23.6
Other developing countries										
Western hemisphere	2.4	2.2	4.5	4.5	7.5	10.0	9.7	8.6	13.1	16.7
Asia[d]	4.8	3.4	7.4	8.3	10.5	12.4	14.4	15.7	21.3	25.6
Africa	0.5	0.9	2.0	1.7	1.9	2.2	2.4	2.4	2.6	3.0
SUBTOTAL[e]										
SDRs	8.6	6.7	13.9	14.5	19.9	24.6	26.5	26.7	37.0	45.4
Percent	17.1	10.9	14.9	11.8	13.6	16.1	14.7	13.7	16.6	17.3
TOTAL										
SDRs	50.2	61.2	93.2	123.2	146.8	152.6	180.2	194.5	222.4	262.8
Percent	100	100	100	100	100	100	100	100	100	100

Source: IMF, *Annual Report 1978* (Washington: IMF, 1978).

[a]Reserves of Fund members, except Romania, plus the Netherlands Antilles and Switzerland. Gold is valued at SDR 35 per ounce.
[b]Including Yugoslavia.
[c]Algeria, Indonesia, Iran, Iraq, Kuwait, Libyia, Nigeria, Saudi Arabia, Venezuela, and beginning in 1970, Oman and Qatar, and, in 1973, the United Arab Emirates.
[d]Including Egypt and Israel.
[e]Includes residual.

Table 3.43. Percentage Holdings of IMF Quotas, by Region, 1950–1981
(Percentage)

Region	Year					
	1950	1961	1971	1975	1978	1980[a]
Developed market economies						
Europe	34.4	35.0	35.4	34.5	32.0	31.9
North America	38.5	31.1	27.1	26.7	25.0	25.0
Oceania and Japan	2.5	6.8	7.1	7.1	6.9	6.9
Other	3.1	2.8	2.9	2.7	2.7	2.7
SUBTOTAL	78.5	76.1	72.7	71.0	66.6	66.5
Developing countries						
Africa and Middle East	1.1	2.0	8.0	9.0	12.5	13.1
Asia	12.8	14.6	10.0	10.3	10.0	9.5
Western hemisphere	6.0	7.3	8.6	8.6	9.7	9.7
SUBTOTAL	19.9	23.9	27.2	27.9	32.2	32.3
TOTAL						
Percent[b]	100	100	100	100	100	100
Billion SDRs[c]	7.9	9.2	28.5	29.2	39.0	58.6
TOTAL numerical IMF membership	47	74	118	126	134	137[d]
Memoranda items						
United States share	34.7	29.8	23.3	22.9	21.6	21.5
OPEC share	0.8	3.5	4.8	4.5	9.9	10.5
Indonesia	[e]	1.1	0.9	0.9	1.2	1.2
Iran	0.4	0.5	0.7	0.7	1.7	1.8
Saudi Arabia	[e]	0.4	0.5	0.5	1.5	1.8
Venezuela	0.2	1.0	1.1	1.1	1.7	1.7

Source: IMF, *Annual Report* (Washington: IMF, various years); IMF, *International Financial Statistics,* and *IMF Survey* 7 (Dec. 1978).

[a] Assuming that all members accept (before November 1980) their individual increases as proposed in December 1978 under the Seventh General Review of Quotas.

[b] Including share of some centrally planned economies.

[c] Quotas valued in US dollars before 1970.

[d] As of December 31, 1978.

[e] Country was not a member of the IMF.

Table 3.44. World R & D Expenditures: Total Amounts, per Economic
Active Person and as Percent of GNP, by Area, 1973

Area	Total amount		Per economic active person (Dollars)	As percent of GNP
	Million dollars	Percent of total		
Developing countries	2,770	2.9	3.0	0.35
Africa	298	0.31	2.8	0.34
Asia	1,571	1.63	2.1	0.34
Western hemisphere	902	0.94	9.0	0.37
Developed countries	64,139	66.5	182.1[a]	2.29[a]
Europe	21,418	22.2	135.1	1.55
North America	33,716	35.0	331.1	2.39
Other	9,005	9.3	129.8	1.76
Socialist countries of Eastern Europe[b]	29,509	30.6	160.0	3.82
World	96,418	100.0	66.4	1.97

Source: Jan Annerstedt, "Technological Dependence: A Permanent Phenomenon of World Inequality?"
in *The New International Division of Labour, Technology and Underdevelopment: Consequences for the Third World,* (Frankfurt: Campus, 1980), ed. Dieter Ernst.
[a] Including socialist countries of Eastern Europe.
[b] Including USSR.

Table 3.45. R & D Scientists and Engineers:
Total Numbers and per Economic Active Person, by Area, 1973

Area	Total		Per million economic active persons
	Number (Thousands)	Percent of total	
Developing countries	288	12.6	307
Africa	28	1.2	271
Asia	214	9.4	292
Western Hemisphere	46	2.0	461
Developed countries	1,260	55.4	3,871[a]
Europe	387	17.0	2,441
North America	548	24.1	5,386
Other	325	14.3	4,687
Socialist countries of Eastern Europe[b]	730	32.0	3,958
World	2,279	100.0	1,570

Source: Same as Table 3.44.
[a] Including socialist countries of Eastern Europe.
[b] Including USSR.

Table 3.46. Third-level[a] Student Enrollment and Teaching Staff, 1960–1974
(Numbers and index numbers, 1960 = 100)

Region	Year				Annual average rate of growth (percentage)	
	1960	1965	1970	1974	1960–1965	1965–1974
Developing countries[b]						
Student enrollment						
Number (thousands)	2,112	3,489	5,728	8,453	10.6	9.3
Index numbers	100	165	271	400		
Teaching staff						
Number (thousands)	144	245	377	561	11.2	8.6
Index numbers	100	170	262	390		
Developed countries						
Student enrollment						
Number (thousands)	9,544	14,828	21,006	24,831	9.2	5.3
Index numbers	100	155	220	260		
Teaching staff						
Number (thousands)	699	1,063	1,533	1,791	8.7	5.4
Index numbers	100	152	219	256		
World[bc]						
Student enrollment						
Number (thousands)	11,656	18,317	26,734	33,284	9.5	6.2
Index numbers	100	157	229	286		
Teaching staff						
Number (thousands)	843	1,308	1,910	2,352	9.2	6.0
Index numbers	100	155	227	279		

Source: UNESCO, *Statistical Yearbook 1976* (Paris: UNESCO, 1977).
[a]Universities and other institutions of higher education.
[b]Not including China, Democratic People's Republic of Korea, and Viet Nam.
[c]Including an allowance for teachers in the USSR.

Table 3.47. The Brain Drain: Share of Developing Countries in Total Skilled
Immigration into the United States, Canada,
and the United Kingdom, Total 1961–1975/76
(Number and percentage)

Occupation and country of destination	Skilled migrants[a] from (number)		DCs as percent of all countries (percent)
	Developing countries	All countries	
United States of America[b]	118,816	190,813	62
Physicians and surgeons	40,876	56,447	72
Engineers and scientists	77,279	133,478	58
All others	661	888	74
Canada[c]	81,613	297,211	27
Physicians, surgeons, and dentists	4,850	13,023	37
Engineers and scientists	13,601	42,711	32
All others	63,162	241,477	26

Table 3.47. The Brain Drain: Share of Developing Countries in Total Skilled
Immigration into the United States, Canada,
and the United Kingdom (cont.)

Occupation and country of destination	Skilled migrants[a] from (number)		DCs as percent of all countries
	Developing countries	All countries	
United Kingdom[d]	84,040	380,751	22
Physicians, surgeons, and dentists	15,655	32,065	49
Engineers and scientists	9,225	54,705	17
All others	59,160	293,981	20
Total	284,469	868,775	33
Physicians, surgeons, and dentists	61,381	101,535	60
Engineers and scientists	100,105	230,894	43
All others	122,983	536,346	23

Source: UNCTAD, "Technology: Development Aspects of the Reserve Transfer of Technology. Study by the UNCTAD Secretariat" (TD/239), January 29, 1979.
[a]The concept of skilled migrants used is wider for Canada and the United Kingdom than for the United States.
[b]For years 1961–1975.
[c]For years 1963–1976.
[d]For years 1964–1972.

Table 3.48. Industrial R & D Expenditures of United States Transnational Enterprises
and Their Foreign Affiliates, 1966–1975[a]
(Millions of dollars and percentage)

Performer of R & D	Year				
	1966	1971	1972	1973	1975
R & D expenditures (millions of dollars)					
Total federal and company- funded industrial R & D	15,548	18,314	19,521[b]	20,450[c]	. . .
Transnational enterprises, domestic and foreign	12,134	15,415	16,606	17,009[d]	18,579[e]
Foreign affiliates only	537	1,063	1,212	1,240[d]	1,331[e]
R & D of foreign affiliates as percentage of					
Total transnational enterprise R & D	4.4	6.9	7.3	7.3	7.2
Total industrial R & D	3.4	5.8	6.2	6.1	. . .

Source: Daniel Creamer, Anthony D. Apostolides, and Selina L. Wang, *Overseas Research and Development by United States Multinationls, 1966–1975: Estimates of Expenditures and a Statistical Profile* (New York: The Conference Board, 1976).
[a]Based on a survey conducted by The Conference Board.
[b]Preliminary.
[c]NSF estimates.
[d]Based on budgeted R & D expenditures reported in Conference Board survey.
[e]Based on projected R & D expenditures in 1972 prices reported in Conference Board survey.

Table 3.49. United Kingdom Receipts and Payments of Royalties and Fees from and to Affiliate and Nonaffiliate Enterprises, 1971–1977
(Millions of dollars)

	1971	1972	1973	1974	1975	1976	1977
Affiliate firms[a]							
Receipts	94.4	112.0	134.8	164.9	181.8	187.8	226.9
(from United States)	(21.1)	(27.1)	(27.7)	(31.2)	(35.1)	(33.4)	
Payments	-149.3	-184.4	-216.3	-266.6	-286.7	-273.1	-349.1
(to United States)	(-123.9)	(-154.5)	(-181.0)	(-220.7)	(-240.4)	(-230.0)	
Balance	-54.9	-72.4	-81.5	-101.7	-104.9	-85.3	-122.2
	(-102.8)	(-127.4)	(-153.3)	(-189.5)	(-205.3)	(-196.6)	
Nonaffiliate firms[a]							
Receipts	138.6	172.0	206.6	233.2	246.7	292.4	523.7
(from United States)	(43.4)	(51.1)	(60.8)	(65.3)	(71.6)	(78.3)	
Payments	-90.9	-101.5	-110.2	-125.1	-132.6	-142.7	-226.0
(to United States)	(-41.8)	(-53.1)	(-57.4)	(-69.4)	(-66.7)	(-64.7)	
Balance	47.9	70.5	96.4	108.1	114.1	149.7	296.8
	(1.6)	(-2.0)	(3.4)	(-4.1)	(4.9)	(13.6)	
Total[a]							
Receipts	357.9	415.8	494.1	573.8	609.7	699.0	750.6
Payments	-299.9	-344.7	-391.9	-465.0	-529.5	-534.6	-576.0
Balance	58.0	71.1	102.2	108.8	80.2	164.4	174.6

Source: United Kingdom, *Trade and Industry*, various years; and *Balance of Payments 1967–1977* (London: Government Statistical Service, 1978).
[a] For the years 1971–1976, the data for affiliate and nonaffiliate firms do not add up to the totals since the former are for a sample of firms only while the totals of the latter are estimates for all firms. By the same token, the affiliate and nonaffiliate data of 1977 are not strictly comparable to those of the earlier years.

Table 3.50. United States Receipts and Payments of Royalties and Fees from and to Affiliate and Nonaffiliate Firms, 1971–1978
(Millions of dollars)

Item	1971	1973	1974	1975	1976	1977	1978
				Affiliate firms			
Receipts	1,927	2,513	3,070	3,543	3,531	3,793	4,806
Payments	-118	-209	-160	-287	-293	-243	-396
Balance	1,809	2,304	2,910	3,256	3,238	3,550	4,410
				Nonaffiliate firms			
Receipts	618	712	751	757	822	920	1,065
Payments	-123	-176	-186	-186	-189	-191	-214
Balance	495	536	565	571	633	729	851
				Total			
Receipts	2,545	3,225	3,821	4,300	4,353	4,713	5,871
Payments	-241	-385	-346	-473	-482	-434	-610
Balance	2,304	2,840	3,475	3,827	3,871	4,279	5,261

Source: United States Department of Commerce, *Survey of Current Business*, various years.

Table 3.51. Payments of Royalties and Fees by Selected Developing Countries
(Millions of dollars and percentage)

Country	Year	Payments	
		Millions of dollars	Percentage of exports
Argentina	1974	101	2.56
Brazil	1976	272	2.68
Chile	1972	17	1.98
Colombia	1975	17	1.16
Mexico	1971	167	11.11
Trinidad and Tobago	1975	18	1.02
India[a]	1973	24	0.81

Source: United Nations, *Transnational Corporations in World Development: A Re-examination* (New York: United Nations, 1978).

[a]Fiscal year ending March 31.

Table 3.52. Patent Holdings, by Region, Ownership, and Use, 1972
(Number and percentage)

Item	Number of patents held (Thousands)	Percentage distribution
World distribution		
Developed countries	3,300	94
Developing countries	200	6
TOTAL	3,500	100
Distribution in developing countries:		
Held by nationals	30	16
Held by foreigners	170	84
of which:		
used	10–20	5–10
not used	150–160	90–95

Source: United Nations, *The Role of the Patent System in the Transfer of Technology to Developing Countries* (New York: United Nations, 1975).

Note: Estimates of patent holdings, in view of their approximate nature, are rounded to the nearest ten thousand. The figures for distribution by use are even less precise and should be treated as a broad order of magnitude only.

Table 3.53. United States Patent Activity, 1890–1976[a]

Country	Year								
	1890	1910	1950	1960	1970	1973	1974	1975	1976
Total patent grants (number)	26,194	35,769	47,847	49,828	67,697	78,304	80,838	76,426	74,976
Total grants to foreign residents									
Number	2,105	3,719	4,408	7,698	17,872	23,344	26,514	26,271	27,134
Percent	8.0	10.4	9.2	15.5	26.4	29.8	32.8	34.4	36.2
Of which (number):									
Developed countries[b]									
Japan	2	8	2	232	2,720	5,157	6,116	6,574	6,780
F.R.G.[c]	452	1,083	25	2,186	4,496	5,661	6,243	6,171	6,320
U.K.	761	961	1,587	1,867	3,063	2,931	3,273	3,158	3,098
France	178	315	685	835	1,771	2,189	2,626	2,436	2,519
Switzerland	56	77	429	547	1,124	1,351	1,484	1,473	1,500
Canada	371	534	492	625	1,151	1,447	1,415	1,409	1,303
Sweden	32	124	294	352	650	793	984	995	1,111
Italy	6	47	38	253	596	791	870	784	788
Netherlands	6	18	357	375	553	707	754	629	771
USSR	12	47	1	—	218	383	493	407	429
TOTAL ten countries	1,876	3,214	3,910	7,272	16,342	21,410	24,258	24,036	24,619
Percent of total patent grants	7.2	9.0	8.2	14.6	24.1	27.3	30.0	31.5	32.8
Percent of foreign	89.1	86.4	88.7	94.5	91.4	91.7	91.5	91.5	90.7
Developing countries[b]									
Mexico	14	31	14	33	44	42	58	76	88
Hong Kong	—	—	—	4	17	22	20	20	48
Argentina	3	8	25	30	24	30	24	29	24
Brazil	2	3	7	5	19	19	22	20	22
Congo	—	—	—	—	3	—	5	—	22
India	1	3	3	2	16	21	17	13	18
Br. West Indies	—	2	2	—	1	10	—	14	9
Philippines	—	—	5	1	4	14	6	9	9
Peru	—	1	2	5	6	3	1	7	8

Korea	—	—	—	—	3	5	8	12	7
TOTAL ten countries	20	48	58	80	137	166	161	200	255
Percent of total patent grants	0.1	0.1	0.1	0.2	0.2	0.2	0.2	0.3	0.3
Percent of foreign	1.0	1.3	1.3	1.0	0.8	0.7	0.6	0.8	0.9

Source: United States, Department of Commerce, Patent and Trademark Office, *Technology Assessment and Forecast: Seventh Report* (Washington: Department of Commerce, 1979).

[a]Including design and plant patents.
[b]The ten most active countries in 1976.
[c]Germany before 1945.

Table 3.54. Share of Developing Regions in World
Manufacturing Value Added, 1960–1975
(Percentage)

Year	All developing countries[a]	Region			
		Africa	Latin America	South and East Asia	West Asia[b]
1960	6.9	0.7	4.1	1.9	0.3
1963	6.9	0.7	3.9	2.0	0.3
1966	6.8	0.7	3.9	1.9	0.4
1969	7.0	0.7	4.0	2.0	0.4
1972	7.7	0.7	4.4	2.1	0.4
1975	8.6	0.8	4.8	2.5	0.5
Target 2000	at least 25	2	13.5	10	

Source: UNIDO, *World Industry since 1960: Progress and Prospects. Special Issue of the Industrial Development Survey for the Third General Conference of UNIDO* (New York: United Nations, 1979).

[a]85 developing market economies.

[b]Cyprus, Iraq, Jordan, Saudi Arabia, Syria, and Turkey.

Table 3.55. Change in Industrial Production and its Share in GDP, by Country Group and Region, 1966-1975[a]
(Percentage)

| Country group and region | Average annual rate of increase at constant market prices (percentage) | | Ratio to GDP (percentage) | | |
| | | | Average annual change in ratio | | |
	1966-1970	1971-1975	1966-1970	1971-1975	Ratio 1975
A. *Country group*					
Lower-income countries[b]					
All industry	6.7	5.3	0.5	0.3	23.6
Manufacturing	5.0	4.7	0.1	0.1	12.7
Middle-income countries[c]					
All industry	6.5	9.4	0.1	0.7	31.0
Manufacturing	10.1	10.5	0.5	0.5	16.7
Higher-income countries[d]					
All industry	8.5	7.3	0.6	-0.1	37.7
Manufacturing	7.8	8.1	0.2	0.1	23.1
B. *Region*					
Africa					
All industry	11.7	2.3	1.2	-0.4	26.9
Manufacturing	8.3	4.1	0.1	—	5.3
Asia					
All industry	8.1	9.1	0.7	0.6	30.3
Manufacturing	7.2	9.2	0.3	0.3	16.0
Western hemisphere					
All industry	6.9	6.9	0.3	0.2	36.0
Manufacturing	7.4	7.1	0.3	0.1	24.7
TOTAL DCs					
All industry	7.8	7.1	0.6	0.2	32.4
Manufacturing	7.4	7.7	0.3	0.2	19.0

Source: United Nations, Centre for Development Planning, Projections and Policies, "Development Trends since 1960 and Their Implications for a New International Development Strategy," *Journal of Development Planning*, 13 (1978).

[a]Based on value-added data. All industry comprises manufacturing, mining and quarrying, electricity, gas and water, and construction.
[b]Counries with per capita GDP in 1970 of less than $200. See Table 1.3 for countries.
[c]Countries with per capita GDP in 1970 of $200 or more but less than $400. See Table 1.3 for countries.
[d]Countries with per capita GDP in 1970 of $400 or more. See Table 1.3 for countries.

Table 3.56. Average Annual Growth Rates of Manufacturing Output in Developed and Developing Countries, by Light and Heavy Manufacturing, 1960–1972[a]
(Percentage)

Industry	ISIC	Developing countries				Developed market economies	Centrally planned economies
		Total	Asia	Latin America			
Total manufacturing	3	6.7	6.5	6.7		5.5	8.5
Light manufacturing	31–33, 342, 355 and 356, 39	5.0	4.6	5.0		4.3	4.6
Heavy manufacturing	341, 351–354, 36–38	8.8	9.5	8.6		6.1	10.5

Source: UNCTAD, *Restructuring of World Industry: New Dimensions for Trade Co-operation* (New York: United Nations, 1978).
[a]Based on production index numbers.

Table 3.57. Structure of Manufacturing Output in Developed and Developing Countries in 1972, and Projected Output Pattern for Developing Countries in 2000 (Percentage)

Industry	Socialist countries of Eastern Europe, 1972	Developed market-economy countries 1972	Developing countries		
			1972	2000	Implied growth rates
Food processing	13.3	10.8	21.8	12.4	7.4
Textiles	4.4	4.6	11.8	7.8	8.0
Clothing, leather, footwear	4.3	4.0	6.3	5.4	9.0
Wood products, furniture	3.4	4.2	3.3	3.6	9.9
Printing	1.2	4.4	3.1	3.8	10.4
Rubber and plastic products	1.9	3.1	3.2	3.0	9.4
Miscellaneous light industry	2.7	2.1	1.6	2.0	10.5
TOTAL light industry	31.2	33.2	51.1	38.0	8.4
Paper	1.2	3.4	1.8	2.4	10.7
Chemicals	7.2	9.8	·9.4	10.2	9.9
Petroleum products	1.8	1.7	7.2	4.1	7.4
Non-metallic minerals	6.4	4.1	5.2	4.9	9.4
Basic metals	7.7	8.0	6.2	8.8	11.0
Machinery	23.9	21.0	8.9	16.1	11.9
Electrical equipment	9.9	8.7	4.2	7.0	11.6
Transport equipment	10.7	10.1	6.0	8.5	11.0
TOTAL heavy industry	68.8	66.8	48.9	62.0	10.5
TOTAL manufactures	100.0	100.0	100.0	100.0	9.6

Source: Same as Table 3.56.

Table 3.58. Share of Developing and Developed Countries in the World Production (or Industrial Consumption) of Selected Products, 1972 (quantities and percentage)

Product	World total[a]		Percentage share of:		
	Unit	Quantity	DC[b]	DMEC[b]	SEE[b]
Sugar	million tons	72.8	48.8	32.7	18.5
Cigarettes	1,000 million units	2,905	23.3	56.1	20.6
Beer	million hectol.	676	12.1	71.2	16.7
Cotton (mill consumption)	1,000 tons	10,451	35.7	40.2	24.1
Wool (mill consumption)	1,000 tons	1,663	14.6	58.5	26.9
Rayon (mill consumption)	1,000 tons	3,561	15.1	55.7	29.2
Synthetic fibers (mill consumption)	1,000 tons	6,304	11.8	79.7	8.5
Sawn wood, coniferous	million m^3	323	4.2	58.7	37.1
Sawn wood, broad-leaved	,,	89	30.0	46.6	23.4
Veneer sheets	1,000 m^3	3,608	35.2	39.6	25.2
Plywood	million m^3	38.9	10.8	81.6	7.6
Particle board	,,	27.2	4.7	77.1	18.2

Table 3.58. Share of Developing and Developed Countries in the World Production (or Industrial Consumption) of Selected Products, 1972 (cont.)

Product	World total[a]		Percentage share of:		
	Unit	Quantity	DC[b]	DMEC[b]	SEE[b]
Rubber tires	million units	584	6.7	85.8	7.5
Mechanical woodpulp	million tons	27.0	2.8	88.4	8.8
Chemical woodpulp	,,	70.0	3.2	88.3	8.5
Other fiber pulp	,,	4.0	36.4	41.5	22.1
Fiberboard	,,	16.5	5.1	78.1	16.8
Newsprint	,,	21.1	2.7	90.1	7.2
Other paper and paper-board	,,	84.6	6.0	83.5	10.4
Sulphuric acid	,,	93.0	7.1	70.5	22.4
Nitrogenous fertilizers	,,	35.6	11.2	59.8	28.9
Plastic materials	,,	34.2	2.2	87.3	10.5
Synthetic rubber	1,000 tons	5,740	3.6	87.7	8.7
Artifical textile fibers	,,	3,528	10.0	64.5	25.5
Synthetic textile fibers	,,	6,545	6.2	86.5	7.3
Energy production (coal equivalent)	million tons	7,089	31.3	44.0	24.7
Energy consumption (coal equivalent)	,,	6,929	9.8	66.1	24.1
Petroleum (refining capacity)	,,	2,927	20.0	64.1	15.9
Petroleum (crude output)	,,	2,495	60.1	23.1	16.8
Cement	,,	616	17.9	57.4	24.7
Iron ore (Fe content)	,,	403	29.5	41.4	29.0
Pig iron	,,	431	4.8	67.6	27.6
Crude steel	,,	601	4.3	67.3	28.4
Bauxite (actual weight)	,,	68.3	53.9	32.8	13.3
Aluminium	1,000 tons	11,313	6.5	74.6	18.9
Copper ore (Cu content)	,,	6,894	38.8	42.7	18.5
Copper smelter output	,,	6,961	31.9	49.7	18.4
Copper refinery output	,,	7,822	20.3	60.4	19.3
Lead ore (Pb content)	,,	3,272	24.2	53.9	21.9
Lead metal	,,	3,821	14.0	64.8	21.2
Zinc ore (Zn content)	,,	5,226	23.0	58.1	18.9
Zinc metal	,,	5,119	8.3	71.8	20.0
Tin ore (Sn content)	,,	209	83.7	10.0	6.2
Tin metal	,,	210	69.1	24.8	6.2
Steel, industrial consumption	million tons	596	8.4	63.7	27.9
Aluminium, industrial consumption	1,000 tons	11,303	5.8	76.8	17.4
Copper, industrial consumption	,,	7,623	5.6	75.7	18.8
Lead, industrial consumption	,,	3,920	8.8	68.7	22.5
Zinc, industrial consumption	,,	5,247	8.7	73.6	17.7
Tin, industrial consumption	,,	216	8.3	76.9	14.8
Nickel, industrial consumption	,,	576	2.3	71.7	26.0
Passenger cars	million units	27.9	4.4[c]	91.5	4.1
Commercial vehicles	,,	7.7	6.0[c]	83.2	10.7

Source: Same as Table 3.56.

[a]World totals exclude the socialist countries of Asia.

[b]DC = the developing countries; DMEC = the developed market economy countries; SEE = the Socialist countries of Eastern Europe.

[c]Including assembly.

Table 3.59. Share of Developing and Developed Countries in the World[a]
Production of Metal and Engineering Products, 1955, 1960, 1965 and 1970
(Percentage)

Region	Year			
	1955	1960	1965	1970
Developing countries				
Africa	0.2	0.1	0.2	0.2
Asia	0.5	0.7	1.0	0.9
Western hemisphere	1.4	1.9	1.8	2.0
SUBTOTAL	2.1	2.7	3.0	3.1
Developed market economies				
Europe	27.2	26.6	23.2	21.2
Japan[b]	1.2	3.2	4.1	8.3
North America	49.5	39.3	37.5	29.8
Other	1.2	1.3	1.3	1.0
SUBTOTAL	79.1	70.4	66.1	60.3
Socialist countries of Europe	18.8	26.9	30.9	36.6
TOTAL	100.0	100.0	100.0	100.0

Source: Economic Commission for Europe, *Role and Place of Engineering Industries in National and World Economies* (New York: United Nations, 1974), vol. 1.

[a]Excluding Albania, China, Democratic People's Republic of Korea, Mongolia, and Democratic Republic of Viet Nam.

[b]And Israel.

Table 3.60. Stock of Direct Investment Abroad of Developed Market Economies, by Major Country of Origin, 1967, 1973, 1978 (Billions of dollars and percentage share)

Country of origin	1967		1973		1978	
	Amount	Share	Amount	Share	Amount	Share
North America	60.3	52.8	109.1	51.2	181.7	49.2
United States	56.6	49.5	101.3	47.5	168.1	45.5
Canada	3.7	3.3	7.8	3.7	13.6	3.7
Western Europe	50.1	43.8	90.9	42.7	155.6	42.1
Belgium-Luxemburg	2.0	1.7	2.9	1.4	5.4	1.5
France	6.0	5.3	8.8	4.1	14.9	4.0
Germany, Federal Rep. of	3.0	2.7	11.9	5.6	31.8	8.6
Italy	2.1	1.8	3.2	1.5	3.3	1.0
Netherlands	11.0	9.6	15.4	7.2	23.7	6.4
Sweden	1.7	1.5	3.0	1.4	6.0	1.6
Switzerland	4.9	4.3	15.6	7.3	24.6	6.7
United Kingdom	17.5	15.3	26.9	12.6	41.1	11.1
Other[a]	2.0	1.7	3.4	1.6	4.8	1.2
Japan	1.5	1.3	10.3	4.8	26.8	7.3
Southern hemisphere[b]	2.4	2.1	2.7	1.3	5.2	1.4
Australia	0.4	0.4	0.5	0.2	1.1	0.3
South Africa	1.9	1.7	2.1	1.0	3.8	1.0
TOTAL	114.3	100.0	213.1	100.0	369.3	100.0

Source: United Nations, Transactional Corporation in World Development and national sources.
[a] Other Europe includes Austria, Denmark, Finland, Norway, Portugal, and Spain.
[b] Also includes New Zealand.

Table 3.61. Concentration of International Direct Investment by Parent Enterprises

Home country[a]	Stock of foreign direct investment, 1971 (Million dollars)	Number of transnational enterprises	Concentration		
			Year	Percentage of foreign direct investment accounted for	Amount of 1971 stock of foreign investment accounted for by specified number of enterprises (Million dollars)
United States	86,000	50	1966	55	47,300
United Kingdom	24,000	52	1962[b]	71	17,100
Federal Republic of Germany	7,300	24	1964	52	3,900
Switzerland	6,800	7	1965	65	4,400
Canada	5,900	13	1963	70	4,200
Japan	4,500	20	1972[b,c]	28	1,300
Sweden	3,500	5	1965[d]	50	1,700
TOTAL	138,000	171		58	79,900
World	165,000	over 10,000	1969–1970	100	165,000

Source: Karl P. Sauvant, "The Potential of Multinational Enterprises as Vehicles for the Transmission of Business Culture," in Sauvant and Lavipour, Controlling Multinational Enterprises.

Note: The figures for the number of enterprises and the percentage of foreign direct investment for which they account are for the years in column 3. In applying the respective percentage ratios to 1971 foreign direct investment book values, it has been assumed that the degree of national concentration in foreign direct investment has not changed significantly in recent years. This assumption appears to be supported by data for the United States: in 1966, 50 enterprises accounted for 55 percent of that country's foreign direct investment; in 1957, 45 enterprises accounted for 58 percent. See United States, Department of Commerce, U.S. Business Investment in Foreign Countries (Washington: Government Printing Office, 1960).

[a] Arranged in descending order of stock of foreign direct investment.

[b] Mining and manufacturing.

[c] In the case of Japan, another observation has to be made: many foreign direct investment projects are joint undertakings of several Japanese firms. Frequently, one of the partners is one of the ten largest trading companies. If these joint undertakings, or a number of them, were allocated to the trading companies, the concentration ratio of Japanese foreign direct investment would be considerably higher.

[d] Percentage of foreign direct investment accounted for refers to sales of foreign affiliates.

Table 3.62. Foreign Content of the 50 Largest Industrial Corporations, end 1976

Rank[a]	Company	Nationality	Major industry	Government ownership (Percentage)	Total consolidated sales (Millions of dollars)	Exports from home country — As percentage of total consolidated sales	Sales of overseas affiliates to third parties — As percentage of total consolidated sales	Foreign assets as percentage of total assets	Foreign earnings as percentage of total earnings	Foreign employment as percentage of total employment
1	Exxon	United States	Petroleum	—	48,631		72	54	...	...
2	General Motors	United States	Motor vehicles and parts	—	47,181		24	12	18	...
3	Royal Dutch/Shell Group	Netherlands-United Kingdom	Petroleum	—	36,087		62^b	50^b	64^b	49^b
4	Ford Motor	United States	Motor vehicles and parts	—	28,840		31	40	45	51
5	Texaco	United States	Petroleum	—	26,452	...	...	54	45	...
6	Mobil	United States	Petroleum	—	26,063	...	...	49	38	...
7	National Iranian Oil	Iran	Petroleum	100	19,671	...	...	...	...	...
8	Standard Oil of California	United States	Petroleum	—	19,434		59		48	...
9	British Petroleum	United Kingdom	Petroleum	68	19,103	5	78	43	...	52
10	Gulf Oil	United States	Petroleum	—	16,451	...	55	43	46	...
11	IBM	United States	Office equipment	—	16,304	...	50	36	55	...
12	Unilever	United Kingdom-Netherlands	Food	—	15,762	8^c	40^c	36^c	51^c	44^c
13	General Electric	United States	Electrical	—	15,697	12	26	27	37	30
14	Chrysler	United States	Motor vehicles and parts	—	15,538		28	33	22	47
15	ITT	United States	Electrical	—	11,764		49	36	39	...
16	Standard Oil (Indiana)	United States	Petroleum	—	11,532		25	34	22	13^d
17	Philips	Netherlands	Electrical	—	11,522		37^b	26^b	...	78
18	ENI	Italy	Petroleum	100	9,983		...	65^f	...	17^c
19	Française des Pétroles	France	Petroleum	35	9,925	...	54	...	...	...
20	Renault	France	Motor vehicles and parts	100	9,353		45	...	...	...
21	Hoechst	Germany, Federal Republic of	Chemicals	—	9,333	35	32	...	...	43
22	BASF	Germany, Federal Republic of	Chemicals	—	9,203	25^f	20^f	...	41^f	21
23	Petróleos de Venezuela	Venezuela	Petroleum	100	9,084	96		...	...	...
24	Daimler-Benz	Germany, Federal Republic of	Motor vehicles and parts	14^g	8,938	39	21	...	...	17^f
25	United States Steel	United States	Metal refining	—	8,604	3	—	—	...	...

Rank	Corporation	Country	Industry		Sales					
26	Volkswagenwerk	Germany, Federal Republic of	Motor vehicles and parts	40	8,513	62	...	...	...	32
27	Atlantic Richfield	United States	Petroleum	—	8,463	17		6	7	7
28	E. I. Du Pont	United States	Chemicals	—	8,361	11	16	17		21
29	Bayer	Germany, Federal Republic of	Chemicals	—	8,298	27	48	44[f]	28[f]	62
30	Nippon Steel	Japan	Metal refining	—	8,090	31	1	4	...	1[f]
31	Siemens	Germany, Federal Republic of	Electrical	—	8,060	50		...	...	33
32	Continental Oil	United States	Petroleum	—	7,958	41		35	22	16
33	August Thyssen-Hütte	Germany, Federal Republic of	Metal refining	—	7,948	29	...	...	...	...
34	Toyota Motor	Japan	Motor vehicles and parts	—	7,696	35	...	2	2	15[f]
35	Nestlé	Switzerland	Food	—	7,628	97		...	...	95
36	ELF-Aquitaine	France	Petroleum	100	7,536	...		...	...	16[f]
37	Imperial Chemical Industries	United Kingdom	Chemicals	—	7,465	20	41	...	20	35
38	Peugeot-Citröen	France	Motor vehicles and parts	—	7,347	19	28	...	...	16
39	Petrobrás	Brazil	Petroleum	100	7,252	3	—	—	...	—
40	Hitachi	Japan	Electrical	—	6,680	17	4	2	...	11
41	BAT industries	United Kingdom	Tobacco	—	6,669	2	86	83	90	79
42	Nissan Motor	Japan	Motor vehicles and parts	—	6,584	41	25	6	...	15
43	Procter and Gamble	United States	Soaps and cosmetics	—	6,513	25		19	18	33
44	Tenneco	United States	Petroleum	—	6,389	14		19	7	...
45	Union Carbide	United States	Chemicals	—	6,346	9	33	36	25	45
46	Westinghouse Electric	United States	Electrical	—	6,145	13	18	18	11	24
47	Mitsubishi Heavy Industries	Japan	Non-electrical	—	6,137	33	1	11	...	6
48	Saint-Gobain-Pont-à-Mousson	France	Building materials	—	5,979	10	48	46	...	53
49	Montedison	Italy	Chemicals	16	5,826	28	13	...	...	6
50	Goodyear Tire and Rubber	United States	Rubber	—	5,791	38		44	9	46

Source: United Nations, *Transnational Corporations in World Development.*

[a] Ranked in descending order of total consolidated sales.
[b] Foreign excludes Europe.
[c] Foreign excludes European Community.
[d] Foreign excludes North America.
[e] 1975 data.
[f] Estimated.
[g] Kuwait interest.

Table 3.63. Foreign Content[a] of the World's 422 Largest Industrial Corporations by Country of Origin, 1976
(Number of firms)

Foreign content (percentage)	United States	Japan	United Kingdom	Germany, Federal Republic of	Other developed countries	Developing countries	Total
More than 75	—	—	6	—	14	1	21
51–75	12	1	9	—	9	—	31
26–50	70	4	14	4	9	—	101
5–25	97	21	10	14	14	—	156
Less than 5[b]	21	16	1	1	6	2	47
Nil	13	—	1	3	4	4	25
Unknown	10	7	—	5	16	3	41
Total	223	49	41	27	72	10	422

Source: Same as Table 3.62.

[a] Measure used for foreign content is sales of overseas (foreign) affiliates to third parties as percentage of total consolidated sales or, in the absence of sales data of overseas affiliates, foreign (net) assets as percentage of total assets or foreign employment as percentage of total employment have been used.
[b] Corporations with no foreign activity are excluded.

Table 3.64. Stock of Direct Investment Abroad of Developed Market Economies, by Host Area and Selected Host Countries, 1967–1975

Host country and host area	1967	1971	1975
Total value of stock (billions of dollars)	105	158	259
Distribution of stock (percentage)			
Developed market economies	69	72	74
of which:			
Canada	18	17	15
United States	9	9	11
United Kingdom	8	9	9
Germany, Federal Republic of	3	5	6
Other	30	32	33
Developing countries	31	28	26
of which:			
OPEC countries	9	7	6
Tax havens[a]	2	3	3
Other	20	17	17
TOTAL	100	100	100

Source: Same as Table 3.62.

[a] Bahamas, Barbados, Bermuda, Cayman Islands, Netherland Antilles, and Panama

Table 3.65. Direct Investment Stock in Developing Countries, by Host Area and Major Country, 1967–1975
(Billions of dollars and percentage)

Host country, territory and group	1967		1971		1975	
	Billions of dollars	Percentage	Billions of dollars	Percentage	Billions of dollars	Percentage
Total stock	32.8	100.0	43.3	100.0	68.2	100.0
OPEC countries	9.1	27.7	11.6	26.8	15.6	22.9
of which:						
Venezuela	3.5	10.6	3.7	8.5	4.0	5.9
Indonesia	0.2	0.6	1.0	2.3	3.5	5.1
Nigeria	1.1	3.3	1.7	3.9	2.9	4.3
Iran	0.7	2.1	0.9	2.1	1.2	1.8
Tax havens[a]	2.3	7.0	3.9	9.0	8.9	13.0
All other developing countries and territories	21.4	65.3	27.8	64.2	43.7	64.1
of which:						
Brazil	3.7	11.3	5.1	11.8	9.1	13.3
Mexico	1.8	5.5	2.4	5.5	4.8	7.0
India	1.3	4.0	1.6	3.7	2.4	3.5
Malaysia	0.7	2.1	0.9	2.1	2.3	3.4
Argentina	1.8	5.5	2.2	5.1	2.0	2.9
Singapore	0.2	0.6	0.4	0.9	1.7	2.5
Peru	0.8	2.4	0.9	2.1	1.7	2.5
Hong Kong	0.3	0.9	0.6	1.4	1.3	1.9
Philippines	0.7	2.1	0.9	2.1	1.2	1.8
Trinidad and Tobago	0.7	2.1	1.0	2.3	1.2	1.8
Total above ten countries	12.0	36.5	16.0	37.0	27.7	40.6

Source: Same as Table 3.62.
[a]Bahamas, Barbados, Bermuda, Cayman Islands, Netherlands Antilles, and Panama.

Table 3.66. Distribution of Foreign Direct Investment Stock by Income Group of
Developing Countries and Its Share in GNP, 1975
(Billions of dollars and percentage)

Country and country group	Gross national product (Billion dollars)	Foreign direct investment stock end-1975 Billion dollars	Foreign direct investment stock end-1975 Percentage	Foreign direct investment stock as percentage of gross national product (Percentage)
Countries with *per capita* income in 1975 of:				
$1,000 or more[a]	235.4	22.3	45.4	9.5
$500 to $999	107.3	10.4	21.2	9.7
$200 to $499	85.6	5.8	11.8	6.8
under $200	197.0	6.5	13.2	3.3
Others	(112.1)	(4.1)	(8.4)	(3.7)

Source: Same as Table 3.62.
[a]Excluding OPEC countries and tax-havens.

295

Table 3.67. Sectoral Distribution of Foreign Direct Investment
of Major Home Countries in Developing Countries
(Millions of dollars and percentage)

| Country and year | Total | Sector | | |
		Extractive	Manufac-turing	Service
United States				
1973				
Millions of dollars	22,904	8,339[a]	7,820	6,745
Percent	100.0	36.4	34.1	29.5
1976				
Millions of dollars	29,050	5,191[a]	11,362	12,497
Percent	100.0	17.9	39.1	43.0
United Kingdom				
1971				
Millions of dollars	4,511	1,159[b]	1,828[b]	1,524
Percent	100.0	25.7	40.5	33.8
1974				
Millions of dollars	5,059	989[b]	2,409[b]	1,661
Percent	100.0	19.6	47.6	32.8
FRG[c]				
1971				
Millions of dollars	2,044	92	1,605	347
Percent	100.0	4.5	78.5	17.0
1977[d]				
Millions of dollars[c]	8,034	673[e]	5,168[f]	2,193
Percent	100.0	8.4	64.3	27.3
Japan				
1974				
Millions of dollars	5,678	1,362[g]	2,887	1,429
Percent	100.0	24.0	50.8	25.2

Source: United Nations, *Transnational Corporations;* and Federal Republic of Germany, Bundesministerium für Wirtschaft, "Runderlaß Aussenwirtschaft."

[a] Refers to mining and smelting and petroleum.
[b] Refers to agriculture and petroleum only; mining and quarrying are included in manufacturing.
[c] Including developing countries of Europe.
[d] Figures are for end-June 1978.
[e] Extractive includes agriculture.
[f] Manufacturing includes private households and other.
[g] Refers to mining, agriculture, and fishing.

Table 3.68. Estimated Shares of Manufacturing Held by Foreign Enterprises,
Selected Countries and Territories, Latest Available Year
(Percentage)

Country or territory	Year	Percentage foreign share of:			
		Sales	Employ-ment	Assets	Value added
Nigeria	1968	. . .	. . .	70[a]	. . .
Malaysia	1971	. . .	. . .	50[b]	. . .
Ghana	1974	50[c]	. . .	. . .	. . .
Brazil	1974	49[d]	. . .	29[e]	37[e]
Peru	1969	46	. . .	. . .	. . .
Central American Common Market	1971	31	. . .	. . .	. . .
Argentina	1972	31	. . .	. . .	. . .
Singapore	1968	. . .	30	. . .	. . .
Mexico	1972	27	. . .	. . .	23
India	1973	13[f]	. . .	. . .	. . .
Korea, Rep. of	1974	11	. . .	. . .	. . .
Hong Kong	1971	. . .	11	. . .	. . .
Thailand	1970	. . .	9	. . .	. . .

Source: Same as Table 3.62.

[a] Based on the 625 largest manufacturing enterprises.

[b] Based on all commercial enterprises. Foreign share of assets based on all limited companies was 62 percent in 1971.

[c] Based on total industry.

[d] Based on the 1,000 largest enterprises.

[e] Based on the 5,113 largest nonfinancial enterprises.

[f] 50 percent and more foreign ownership only.

Table 3.69. Indicators of Foreign Participation in Selected Industries in Developing Countries, Selected Years (Percentage)

ISIC No.	Chemicals (351-352)	Rubber (355)	Iron and steel basic industry (371)	Estimated percentage of foreign share of: Nonelectrical machinery (382)	Electrical machinery (383)	Motor vehicles (384)	Year
Argentina	37(O)	75(O)	...	82(O)	33(O)	84(O)	1969
Brazil	51(O)	44(O)	61(O)[a]	55(A)[a]	33(A)[a]	100(A)	1976
India	27(O)	52(O)	41(O)	25(O)	33(O)	10(O)	1973
Korea, Rep. of	22(E)	...	37(O)	19(O)	...	...	1970
Mexico	67(O)	84(O)	37(O)	31(O)	63(O)	...	1973
Peru	67(S)	88(S)	...	25(S)	62(S)	...	1969
Philippines	...	73(O)	...	...	...	43(A)	1973
Singapore	46(E)	76(E)	21(E)	...	...	...	1968

Source: Same as Table 3.62.

Note: A = assets, E = employment, O = output, S = sales.

[a] Based on the 5,113 largest nonfinancial enterprises.

Table 3.70. Estimated Foreign-Controlled Shares of the Pharmaceutical Industry,
Selected Developing Countries, 1975
(Percentage)

Country or country group	Share of sales (Percentage)
Saudi Arabia	100
Nigeria	97
Colombia	90
Venezuela	88
Brazil	85
Indonesia	85
Mexico	82
Central American Common Market (1970)	80
India	75
Iran	75
Argentina	70
Egypt (1971)	19

Source: Same as Table 3.62.

Table 3.71. Estimated Foreign-Controlled Shares of Selected Industries
in Brazil, Turkey, and India, 1974
(Percentage)

	Shares of:		
	Assets		Output
Industry	Brazil[a]	Turkey	India[b]
Manufacturing (total)	29	41	13
of which:			
Textiles	. . .	74	. . .
Food	31	} 58	. . .
Tobacco	99		. . .
Paper	. . .	56	. . .
Chemicals	. . .	. . .	33
Rubber	61	59	52
Electrical machinery	61	54	. . .
Nonelectrical machinery	. . .	43	25
Transport equipment	} 68	. . .	} 10
Motor vehicles		38	
Ferrous and nonferrous products	. . .	. . .	41
Metal goods	. . .	23	. . .
Nonmetallic products	35	. . .	. . .
Mining	12	. . .	8

Source: Same as Table 3.62.
[a]Based on 5,113 nonfinancial enterprises.
[b]Data for 1973.

Table 3.72. Foreign Representation in the Insurance Sector as Percentage of Total Number of Insurance Entities, Selected Developing Countries and Territories, 1975
(Percentage)

Under 10	10 to under 20	20 to under 40	40 to under 60	60 to under 80	80 to 100
Brazil	Argentina	Bolivia	Honduras	Cameroon	Chad
Mexico	Chile	Ecuador	Nicaragua	El Salvador	Cyprus
Morocco	Colombia	Nigeria	Pakistan	Dominican Republic	Gabon
Peru	Indonesia	Paraguay	Panama	Hong Kong	Guam
Sudan	Iran	Sierra Leone		Jordan	Kenya
Venezuela	Korea, Rep. of	Uganda		Lebanon	Liberia
	Philippines			Mauritius	Malawi
	Thailand			Singapore	Malaysia
				Tunisia	Senegal
					Uruguay

Source: Same as Table 3.62.

Table 3.73. Foreign Ownership in Advertising, by Country, Placement of Agency, Country of Origin, Parent Agency, and Degree of Control, 1977

Country	Placement of agency[a]				
	Largest	Second	Third	Fourth	Fifth largest
Developed countries					
Australia	US(8)	US(1)	D(xUS6)	US(22)	US(7)
Austria	US/UK(9)	US(1)	US(3)	CH	US(5)
Belgium	US(1)	US/UK(9)	US(15)	US(5)	US(4)
Britain	US(3)	US(1)	US(12)	US(5)	US(4)
Canada	US(3)	D	D	D	D
Denmark	D	US(8)	US(12)	D	US/UK(9)
Finland	D	US(1)	D	D	D
France	D	D	US(1)	D	US(4)
Greece	D	D	D	D	US/UK(9)
Ireland	D	UK	D	D	D
Israel	D	D	D	D	. . .
Italy	US(1)	US(3)	US(4)	D	D
Japan	D	D	D	D(xUS18)	D
Netherlands	US(6)	US(1)	US/UK(9)	D	US(3)
New Zealand	D	D(xUS6)	US(1)	US(5)	D
Norway	US(8)	D	US(15)	US(4)	US/UK(9)
Portugal	US(23)	US(1)	US/UK(9)	F(19)	D
South Africa	US(1)	F(20)	US(6)	US(3)	D(xUS5)
Spain	US(3)	US(15)	F(20)	US(1)	US/UK(9)
Sweden	US(5)	D	D	D(xUS1)	D(xxUS18)
Switzerland	D(xxUS6)	F(19)	D	D	D
United States	D(1)	D(3)	D(4)	D(5)	D(6)
West Germany	US(1)	US/UK(9)	US(6)	US(3)	US(10)
Developing countries					
Argentina	US(3)	US(10)	D	US(21)	D(xUS5)
Barbados	D(xxUS18)	D	. . .	. . .	. . .
Bermuda	D(xxUS18)	. . .	. . .	. . .	. . .
Brazil	US(1)	US(3)	US(21)	D	D
Chile	US(3)	D(xUS10)	. . .	. . .	. . .
Colombia	US(7)	US(1)	D	D	D(xUS6)
Costa Rica	D	US(1)	D	. . .	. . .
Dominican Republic	US(4)	. . .	. . .	. . .	. . .
Ecuador	US(1)	. . .	. . .	. . .	. . .
Egypt	D	US(21)	. . .	. . .	. . .
El Salvador	US(1)	. . .	. . .	. . .	. . .
Ghana	US/UK(9)	. . .	. . .	. . .	. . .
Guatemala	US(3)	US(1)	. . .	. . .	. . .
Honduras	US(1)	D	. . .	. . .	. . .
Hong Kong	US(7)	US(1)	D	US(21)	US(8)
India	D(xxUS3)	US/UK(9)	US(5)	D	D
Indonesia	US/UK(9)	. . .	. . .	. . .	. . .
Iran	D	D(xxUS1)	D	. . .	. . .
Jamaica	US(1)	D(xxUS18)	US(23)	US(21)	. . .
Kenya	US(1)	D	US(5)	. . .	. . .
Kuwait	D	. . .	. . .	. . .	. . .
Lebanon	F(20)	US(4)	US(21)	D	D
Malaysia	US(7)	US(5)	US/UK(9)	US(8)	US(3)
Malta	D	. . .	. . .	. . .	. . .
Mexico	D	US(1)	D(xxUS18)	US(12)	US(4)
Morocco	F(20)	. . .	. . .	. . .	. . .
Nicaragua	US(1)	D	. . .	. . .	. . .

Table 3.73. (cont.)

Country	Placement of agency[a]				
	Largest	Second	Third	Fourth	Fifth largest
Nigeria	US/UK(9)	US(1)	. . .	. . .	. . .
Pakistan	US/UK(9)	D	D	D	. . .
Panama	US(1)	D	D	. . .	. . .
Peru	US(1)	US(3)	. . .	. . .	. . .
Paraguay	D	. . .	. . .	. . .	. . .
Philippines	US(18)	US(3)	D	US(1)	D
Sierra Leone	US/UK(9)	. . .	. . .	. . .	. . .
Singapore	US(5)	US(7)	US(21)	US/UK(9)	US(1)
South Korea	D	D	D	. . .	. . .
Sri Lanka	US(21)	. . .	. . .	. . .	. . .
Taiwan	D	D	US(21)	. . .	. . .
Thailand	US/UK(9)	US(5)	US(8)	D	US(1)
Trinidad and Tobago	US(1)	D(xxUS18)	US(23)	. . .	. . .
Turkey	D	D	D	US(1)	. . .
Uruguay	D	US(3)	US(1)	. . .	. . .
Venezuela	D(xxUS5)	US(4)	US(3)	US(7)	US(10)
Yugoslavia	D	. . .	. . .	. . .	. . .

Source: Compiled from *Advertising Age,* various issues; *Werben und Verkaufen,* various issues; and various newspaper and magazine reports.

[a]In terms of 1977 billings.

Note: For each rank placement, the following information is provided:

1. D: domestic agency;
2. The country of origin (CH = Switzerland, F = France, UK = United Kingdom, US = United States) is indicated if the agency is 50 percent or more owned by an agency outside the respective country;
3. x: minority interest held by a foreign agency in a domestic agency;
4. xx: substantial minority held by a foreign agency in a domestic agency;
5. The numbers, which correspond to the rank of the advertising agencies among the world's 25 largest agencies (1977 billings) represent the following agencies: (1) Interpublic Group and Co., (3) J. W. Thompson, (4) Young and Rubicam, (5) Ogilvy and Mather, (6) BBDO, (7) Leo Burnett, (8) Ted Bates, (9) SSC and B-Lintas (this agency was acquired, in 1979, by the Interpublic Group and Co.), (10) Grey Adv., (12) D'Arcy-McManus and Masius, (15) Doyle Dane Bernbach (18) Compton Adv., (19) Publicis-Intermarco-Farner, (20) Univas Network, (21) Kenyon and Eckhardt, (22) Needham, Harper and Steer, (23) Norman, Craig and Kummel.

Table 3.74. The World's 25 Largest Banks and Their Foreign Affiliate Networks, end 1976[a]

Rank	Bank[b]	Home country	Assets[c] (Millions of dollars)	Foreign network[d] (Number of affiliates)		
				Developed market economies	Developing countries	Socialist countries
1.	Bankamerica Corporation	United States	72,219	92	151	1
2.	Citicorp	United States	63,139	73	176	1
3.	Caisse Nationale de Crédit Agricole	France	52,744	—	—	—
4.	Chase Manhattan Corp.	United States	44,995	76	139	1
5.	Deutsche Bank	Germany, Fed. Rep. of	44,382	33	30	1
6.	Crédit Lyonnais	France	40,601	29	33	1
7.	Groupe BNP	France	40,559	46	52	2
8.	Banco do Brazil	Brazil	38,816	24	18	—
9.	Dai-Ichi Kangyo Bank	Japan	36,926	16	18	—
10.	Société Générale	France	36,514	22	18	2
11.	Dresdner Bank	Germany, Fed. Rep. of	35,911	33	28	1
12.	Barclays Bank	United Kingdom	32,969	73	103	—
13.	Banca Nazionale del Lavoro	Italy	32,661	32	29	—
14.	Fuji Bank	Japan	32,435	15	20	—
15.	Sumitomo Bank	Japan	32,432	16	12	—
16.	Westdeutsche Landesbank Girozentrale	Germany Fed. Rep. of	30,902	18	5	—
17.	Mitsubishi Bank	Japan	30,700	13	21	—
18.	Manufacturers Hanover Corp.	United States	30,438	24	25	1
19.	Sanwa Bank	Japan	30,128	17	19	—
20.	National Westminster Bank	United Kingdom	29,080	7	1	—
21.	Royal Bank of Canada	Canada	28,581	23	50	—
22.	J. P. Morgan and Co.	United States	27,867	31	23	—
23.	Commerzbank	Germany, Fed. Rep. of	26,831	34	26	1
24.	Chemical New York Corp.	United States	26,614	18	23	—
25.	Canadian Imperial Bank of Commerce	Canada	25,986	25	23	—

Source: Same as Table 3.62.

[a] Japanese bank figures reflect the status as of September 30; Canadian bank figures are for October 31.

[b] Consolidated bank group. Banks are listed in descending order of their total assets.

[c] Excluding contra accounts. Currencies have been converted at the rates of exchange which were current at the time the accounts were made.

[d] Includes subsidiaries, affiliates, foreign branches, and representative offices.

Table 3.75. Entry and Ownership Strategies of United States Transnational
Manufacturing Enterprises
(Number and percentage)

Strategy	Time period				Total
	Pre-1951	1951–1960	1961–1965	1966–1971	
Number of new entries[a]	2,196	2,946	3,225	5,290	13,657
Entry strategy[b]					
Percentage acquisitions	21	32	41	50	39
Ownership strategy[c]					
Percentage wholly owned	70	68	61	72	68
Percentage majority owned	13	17	21	17	17
Percentage minority owned	7	9	10	8	9

Source: Joan P. Curhan, William H. Davidson, and Rajan Suri, *Tracing the Multinationals: A Sourcebook on U.S.-Based Enterprises* (Cambridge: Ballinger, 1977).

[a]Based on 180 enterprises which account for approximately three-fourths of United States' foreign direct investment.

[b]The totals include a number of affiliates whose method of entry is unknown; for the time before 1950, these represent approximately one-fourth of all affiliates, for later years this share decreases to below 10 percent. Hence, the actual share of acquisitions is likely to be higher.

[c]The totals include affiliates whose ownership position at entry data was unknown. Data do not, therefore, add to 100 percent.

Table 3.76. Agricultural Population and Labor Force, by Region, 1960, 1975, 2000
(Millions and percentage)

Region	Total population (Millions)			Agricultural labor force (Millions)			Agricultural labor force as percentage of total labor force		
	1960	1975	2000	1960	1975	2000	1960	1975	2000
Developed countries									
Developed market economies	130	80	38	56	34	16	20	10	4
Europe	78	47	19	33	19	8	24	13	5
North America	14	7	3	6	3	2	7	3	1
Oceania	2	1	1	1	1	—	12	8	3
Other	36	24	15	17	11	6	33	17	7
Socialist countries of Europe	132	86	41	68	44	21	42	24	10
SUBTOTAL	262	166	80	124	79	37	28	15	6
Developing countries									
Developing market economies	920	1,174	1,569	369	437	574	71	62	44
Africa	174	225	343	76	91	126	81	72	54
Latin America	104	122	137	34	38	45	48	37	22
Near East	88	111	150	31	36	47	70	58	39
Far East	552	713	934	227	270	354	74	65	48
Other	3	3	5	1	2	2	81	74	61
Socialist countries of Asia	526	583	525	256	272	249	75	64	41
SUBTOTAL	1,446	1,757	2,094	625	709	823	73	63	43
World	1,708	1,923	2,173	748	788	860	58	48	34

Source: Food and Agriculture Organization, *The Fourth World Food Survey* (Rome: FAO, 1977).

Table 3.77. Average Annual Rates of Growth of Agricultural Production in Relation to Population and Agricultural Workers, by Region, 1961/65 to 1970 and 1970-1976

(Percentage)

| Region | Total population | | Agricultural production | | | | | |
| | 1961/65 to 1970 | 1970-1976 | Total | | Per caput | | Per agricultural worker | |
			1961/65 to 1970	1970-1976	1961/65 to 1970	1970-1976	1961/65 to 1970	1970-1976
Developed countries								
Developed market economies	1.0	0.9	1.9	2.2	0.9	1.3	5.5	5.3
Europe	0.7	0.6	2.2	1.6	1.5	1.0	6.3	4.7
North America	1.2	0.9	1.4	2.8	0.2	1.9	5.4	6.6
Oceania	1.8	1.7	2.8	1.3	1.0	-0.4	3.5	2.4
Other	1.4	1.6	3.1	2.0	1.7	0.4	5.7	4.9
Socialist countries of Europe	1.0	0.9	2.8	2.0	1.8	1.1	6.2	4.3
SUBTOTAL	1.0	0.9	2.2	2.1	1.2	1.2	5.7	4.8
Developing countries								
Developing market economies	2.6	2.6	3.1	2.6	0.5	0.0	2.0	1.4
Africa	2.5	2.7	2.7	1.1	0.2	-1.5	1.4	-0.2
Latin America	2.7	2.8	2.9	2.9	0.2	0.1	2.2	2.0
Near East	2.7	2.8	3.1	3.9	0.4	1.1	2.2	2.9
Far East	2.5	2.5	3.3	2.6	0.8	0.1	2.1	1.4
Other	2.5	2.5	2.3	1.6	-0.2	-0.8	0.9	0.0
MSA countries	2.4	2.5	3.1	1.9	0.6	-0.5		
Non-MSA countries	2.7	2.7	3.1	3.1	0.4	0.4		
Socialist countries of Asia	1.8	1.7	2.8	2.5	1.0	0.7	2.3	2.1
SUBTOTAL	2.3	2.3	3.0	2.6	0.7	0.2	2.1	1.7
World	1.9	1.9	2.5	2.3	0.6	0.4	2.2	1.8

Source: Same as Table 3.76.

306

Table 3.78. Agricultural Output per Agricultural Worker,
by Region, 1964/66 and 1974/76

Region	Agricultural output per agricultural worker	
	1964–66	1974–76
Developed countries		
Developed market economies	2.93	5.00
Europe	2.02	3.56
North America	14.33	25.72
Oceania	14.14	19.28
Other	0.54	0.96
Socialist countries of Europe	1.12	1.96
Subtotal	1.94	3.30
Developing countries		
Developing market economies	0.23	0.26
Africa	0.18	0.19
Latin America	0.67	0.82
Near East	0.35	0.44
Far East	0.16	0.19
Other	0.42	0.44
Socialist countries of Asia	0.16	0.22
Subtotal	0.21	0.25
World	0.46	0.55

Source: Same as Table 3.76.

Note: The agricultural production estimates, on which the above indicators are based, are expressed in terms of wheat-price equivalents.

Table 3.79. Gross Fixed Capital Formation in Agriculture, Selected Countries,
Annual Average, 1970/75
(Millions of dollars, percentage, and numbers)

Country	Total (Millions of Dollars)	Per hectare[a,b] (Dollars)	Per agricul- tural worker[b] (Dollars)	Per caput GNP[b] (Dollars)	As propor- tion of agri- cultural GDP
Developing countries					
Costa Rica[c]	28	55	113	960	10
Cyprus	14	32	133	1,240	12
Egypt[c]	127	44	23	260	5
El Salvador[d]	7	10	10	460	2
Ethiopia[d]	24	—	3	100	3
India[c]	1,984	12	12	140	7
Iraq[c]	103	19	85	1,250	14
Kenya	5	3	1	220	7
Korea, Rep. of	364	150	64	560	9
Jamaica[c]	17	65	102	1,110	13
Mauritius	10	90	102	610	9
Pakistan[c]	198	10	18	160	7
Papua New Guinea[d]	7	21	6	470	3
Syrian Arab Republic	94	17	100	720	17
Thailand	207	12	14	350	7
Tunisia	55	13	89	730	11
Developed countries					
Australia[d]	605	13	1,501	5,700	22
Belgium	232	264	1,514	6,270	17
Canada	1,605	37	2,605	6,930	33
Denmark	300	112	1,421	6,810	19
Finland	319	121	859	5,420	18
France	2,550	136	1,045	5,950	20
Greece	364	94	234	2,340	14
Italy	1,888	153	632	2,810	17
Israel	127	294	1,253	3,790	23
Japan	5,778	1,037	681	4,450	32
Netherlands	515	612	1,513	5,750	28
Norway	297	375	2,048	6,760	31
Portugal[c]	85	23	84	1,570	6
Sweden	448	149	1,883	8,150	24
South Africa	429	30	157	1,270	21
United Kingdom	987	142	1,491	3,780	25
United States	8,156	39	3,133	7,120	20

Source: UNCTAD, "The Agricultural Commodity Outlook and Development/Investment Needs: Paper Prepared by the FAO Secretariat" (TD/B/C.1/208), April 17, 1979.

[a] Arable land and permanent crops.

[b] Area, labor force and per caput GNP are based on 1975 data.

[c] 1970/74.

[d] 1970/72.

Table 3.80. Tractors in Use and Consumption of Fertilizers, by Region, 1961/65 and 1975
(Numbers and grams)

Item	Developed countries	Developing countries					
		Total	Africa	Latin America	Near East	Far East	Socialist countries of Asia
A. Tractors in use							
Total (number in 1000s)							
1961/65	9,711	703	88	446	97	69	93
1975	11,990	1,706	187	818	361	336	229
Per 1000 hectares of arable land							
1961/65	26.6	1.3	0.6	4.8	1.4	0.3	0.8
1975	30.0	2.8	1.0	7.2	5.9	1.4	1.6
B. Consumption of fertilizers per hectare of arable land and permanent crops (in 100 grams)							
Nitrogen							
1961/65	240	33	7	51	48	38	88
1975	460	113	24	144	160	144	358
Phosphate							
1961/65	240	15	6	34	17	12	36
1975	293	55	20	107	83	42	105
Potash							
1961/65	189	8	4	21	2	6	10
1975	251	28	11	67	4	26	34
TOTAL							
1961/65	669	57	17	106	66	57	134
1975	1,004	196	56	319	247	212	497

Source: Food and Agriculture Organization, *Review and Analysis of Agrarian Reform and Rural Development in the Developing Countries since the Mid-1960s* (Rome: FAO, 1979).

Table 3.81. Average Annual Rates of Growth of Food Production in Relation
to Population, by Region, 1961/65 to 1970 and 1970–1976
(Percentage)

Region	Total		Per caput	
	1961/65–1970	1970–1976	1961/65–1970	1970–1976
Developed countries				
Developed market economies	2.2	2.4	1.2	1.5
Europe	2.3	1.6	1.6	1.0
North America	1.9	3.1	0.7	2.1
Oceania	2.9	3.1	1.1	1.3
Other	3.3	2.1	1.8	0.6
Socialist countries of Europe	2.9	1.9	1.9	1.0
SUBTOTAL	2.4	2.3	1.4	1.4
Developing countries				
Developing market economies	3.3	2.8	0.7	0.2
MSA countries	3.1	2.1	0.7	−0.4
Non-MSA countries	3.3	3.4	0.6	0.7
Africa	2.7	1.2	0.1	−1.4
Latin America	3.5	3.3	0.8	0.5
Near East	3.0	4.2	0.3	1.4
Far East	3.5	2.8	0.9	0.2
Other	2.1	1.5	−0.4	−1.0
Socialist countries of Asia	2.7	2.4	0.9	0.6
SUBTOTAL	3.1	2.7	0.7	0.3
World	2.7	2.4	0.8	0.5

Source: Same as Table 3.76.

Table 3.82. Per Caput Daily Food Supply, Absolute and
as Percentage of Requirements
(Kilocalories and percentage)

Region	Calorie supply (Kilocalories per caput)		Supply as percentage of requirements	
	1961/63	1972/74	1961/63	1972/74
Developed countries				
Developed market economies	3,130	3,340	123	131
Europe	3,200	3,390	125	132
North America	3,320	3,530	126	134
Oceania	3,300	3,370	124	127
Other	2,570	2,850	109	121
Socialist countries of Europe	3,240	3,460	126	135
SUBTOTAL	3,170	3,380	124	132
Developing countries				
Developing market economies	2,110	2,180	92	95
MSA countries	2,040	2,030	91	90
Non-MSA countries	2,210	2,360	95	101
Africa	2,070	2,110	89	91
Latin America	2,400	2,540	101	107
Near East	2,290	2,440	93	100
Far East	2,010	2,040	91	92
Other	2,130	2,340	93	103
Socialist countries of Asia	1,960	2,290	83	97
SUBTOTAL	2,060	2,210	89	96
World	2,410	2,550	101	107

Source: Same as Table 3.76.

Table 3.83. Food Trade Developments of 90 Developing Countries,[a] by Commodity, 1961/65 and 1974/76
(Million tons and percentage)

Commodity	Total trade 1974/76 (Million tons)		Net balance[b] (Million tons)		Growth rates 1961/65 to 1974/76	
	Exports	Imports	1961/65	1974/76	Imports	Exports
Total cereals	18.2	50.7	-10.27	-32.50	5.4	0.8
Wheat	2.6	34.4	-14.34	-31.79	5.4	-3.6
Rice, milled	3.3	5.6	0.07	-2.24	1.2	-3.1
Coarse grains	12.3	10.8	3.92	1.54	11.8	5.1
Total meat	1.2	0.9	0.75	0.37	4.3	-0.3
Beef and veal	1.1	0.5	0.79	0.58	2.1	-0.8
Mutton and lamb	0.1	0.2	0.02	-0.08	8.3	1.6
Milk and milk products[c]	0.5	8.8	-4.86	-8.31	4.8	d
Roots and tubers	7.8	1.0	2.06	6.86	2.6	9.0
Pulses	0.9	0.6	0.36	0.28	3.1	1.0
Oilseeds and vegetable oils[e]	5.6	2.4	2.70	3.14	6.7	3.2
Sugar, raw	15.1	4.6	7.66	10.47	2.6	2.6
Bananas	5.8	0.4	3.21	5.35	3.1	4.2
Citrus	2.1	0.6	1.06	1.57	13.4	5.0
Other fruit	3.6	1.4	1.38	2.28	4.1	4.2
Vegetables	1.8	0.8	0.54	1.05	2.4	4.1
Cocoa	1.2	—	1.01	1.14	0.8	1.0
Coffee	3.4	0.2	2.63	3.26	1.9	1.8
Tea	0.7	0.3	0.40	0.43	2.1	1.2
Tobacco, unmanuf.	0.7	0.2	0.36	0.52	4.4	3.5
Cotton[f]	5.7	2.0	4.95	3.66	3.8	-0.8
Other fibers	1.2	0.3	1.65	0.90	3.3	-3.6
Rubber, natural	3.1	0.4	1.96	2.73	4.6	3.0

Source: Food and Agriculture Organization, *Agriculture: Toward 2000* (Rome: FAO, 1979).
[a]These countries account for 98 percent of total developing country population, excluding China.
[b]Total exports less total imports.
[c]Fresh milk equivalent.
[d]Insignificant exports.
[e]Vegetable oil equivalent.
[f]Seed cotton equivalent.

Table 3.84. Net Trade in Cereals, by Region, 1934/38 to 1976/78
(Annual averages in millions of tons)

Region	Year							
	1934/38	1948/52	1952/56	1956/60	1961/65	1966/70	1971/75	1976/77
Developed countries								
Developed market economies								
Western Europe	-23.1	-21.9	-21.9	-23.3	-26.2	-23.0	-21.5	-25.2
Japan	-1.9	-2.7	-4.1	-4.2	-7.2	-12.6	-17.2	-21.2
North America	5.3	22.4	24.2	31.0	49.2	52.0	78.7	94.8
Oceania	2.8	3.4	3.1	3.1	6.7	7.0	9.7	11.2
Socialist countries of Europe								
Eastern Europe	2.7	0.5	-1.4	-5.4	-6.5	-4.4	-7.1	-11.7
USSR	1.3	1.7	2.0	5.3	2.1	2.9	-7.1	-13.1
Developing countries								
Africa	0.6	-0.3	0.1	-0.9	-2.4	-3.9	-6.3	-8.3
Asia	0.3	-3.4	-2.1	-7.5	-14.9	-19.7	-24.8	-26.1
Latin America	9.0	0.9	1.2	1.6	2.1	3.3	-1.2	1.6
SUBTOTAL, developing countries	9.9	-2.8	-0.8	-6.8	-15.2	-20.3	-32.3	-32.8

Source: United Nations, World Food Council, "World Food Security for the 1980s: Report by the Executive Director" (WFC/1979/5), April 26, 1979.

Index

315

Index

About the Contributors

Odette Jankowitsch is currently Programme Specialist in UNESCO. She has previously been consultant in the United Nations Centre on Transnational Corporations and has been associated with the Institute de Développement Economique Africain, Dakar; the Vienna Institute for Development; the United Nations Industrial Development Organization; and the Center for International Studies of the New York University. Current address: UNESCO, 7 place de Fontenoy, 75700 Paris.

Donald O. Mills is currently Permanent Representative and Ambassador extraordinary and plenipotentiary of Jamaica to the United Nations where he was President of the Economic and Social Council for the year 1978 and, during January 1979, the President of the Security Council. During 1977/78 he was the chairperson of the Group of 77. He has previously been Alternate Executive Director of the International Monetary Fund; Secretary in charge of Development and Planning in Barbados; Director of Jamaica's Central Planning Unit; and Deputy Director of Jamaica's Bureau of Statistics. Current address: Permanent Mission of Jamaica to the United Nations, 866 Second Ave., New York, N.Y. 10017.

Karl P. Sauvant is currently Transnational Corporations Affairs Officer, Centre on Transnational Corporations, United Nations. He has previously been with the United Nations Department of Economic and Social Affairs; the Multinational Enterprise Unit, the Wharton School, University of Pennsylvania; and the Foreign Policy Research Institute. Current address: Rm. BR-1008, Centre on Transnational Corporations, United Nations, c/o Box 20, Grand Central P.O., New York, N.Y. 10017.

Baron Rüdiger von Wechmar is currently Permanent Representative and Ambassador extraordinary and plenipotentiary of the Federal Republic of Germany to the United Nations where he was the President of the 35th General Assembly and the Vice President of the 29th General Assembly and, during September 1977 and December 1978, the President of the Security Council. He has previously been the Spokesperson for the Government of the Federal Republic of Germany and the Head of its Press and Information Office; the Director of the New York German Information Center; and Chief Eastern European Correspondent for West German Television. Current address: Permanent Mission of the Federal Republic of Germany to the United Nations, 600 Third Ave., New York, N.Y. 10016.